Henry Cabot Lodge and the Search for an American Foreign Policy

WILLIAM C. WIDENOR

Henry Cabot Lodge and the Search for an American Foreign Policy

University of California Press

BERKELEY   LOS ANGELES   LONDON

Library of Congress Cataloging in Publication Data

Widenor, William C
  Henry Cabot Lodge and the search for an American
foreign policy.

    1.   Lodge, Henry Cabot, 1850–1924.   2.   United
States—Foreign relations—1865–1921.   I.   Title.
E664.L7W45   327.73   78–62863
ISBN 0–520–03778–2

University of California Press
Berkeley and Los Angeles, California

University of California Press, Ltd.
London, England

© 1980 by
The Regents of the University of California

Printed in the United States of America

1   2   3   4   5   6   7   8   9

For My Mother and Father

Contents

Preface

My purpose in this book is to provide an account of the development of Henry Cabot Lodge's thought on questions of foreign policy. It is intellectual biography, but intellectual biography limited to a particular aspect of his thinking. The approach may seem somewhat limited in an era when so many historical figures are being subjected to psychohistorical treatment. Lodge might even be a good candidate for psychoanalysis, and I would welcome such a study. But since his political positions have long been explained in terms of his personality, I would demonstrate that they can also be understood in terms of ideas.

I found Lodge both more interesting and more perceptive than I expected. While his doings and undoings have not been neglected by historians, his thinking has. Many of his ideas are indefensible, and his thinking was always conditioned by Lodge the political man. Nevertheless, he held and acted on a fairly consistent set of beliefs about the way the foreign policy of the United States ought to be conducted. Moreover, he was sensitive to some of the enduring problems of American foreign policy formulation, especially the conduct of foreign policy in a democracy, and the relationship between force and peace. However, my concern is not to restore Lodge's reputation. Just as Lodge understood that he could never make Hamilton a lovable figure, I recognize the obstacles to Lodge's rehabilitation. Rather my interest flows from the fact that because Lodge both wrote about and helped make American foreign policy, he proves a good vehicle for exploring the relationship between foreign policy and domestic political structure, and the role of ideology in international relations.

I freely acknowledge that the following account is interpretative in character. My hope is that it sheds new light on Lodge's foreign policy stands and on the intellectual history of American foreign policy formulation in general. I have attempted to explicate the causes of Lodge's jingoistic nationalism and the nature of his attraction to imperialism. In the process, I have discovered that his historical thinking and his Federalist sympathies had more to do with his foreign policy views than has generally been recognized. Moreover, he helped to formulate, and was very attracted, both emotionally and intellectually, to what I have come to call "the Rooseveltian solution" to the conduct of foreign policy under American and democratic conditions. This did much to color his view of the Wilsonian approach to foreign policy. Finally, I believe that the traditional distinction between the "idealistic" Wilson and the "realistic" Lodge has outgrown its usefulness. In many respects Lodge was just as idealistic as Wilson. I emphasize the depth of Lodge's commitment to the Allied cause prior to American entry into World War I, the rival idealisms of Lodge and Wilson, and their conflicting visions of an effective and lasting postwar settlement.

. . .

Without the assistance of many individuals and institutions this study could not have been completed. My greatest debt is to Samuel Haber, who supervised this project in the dissertation stage, gave unstintingly of his time, and, when I thought I had Lodge figured out, would invariably ask questions and suggest relationships which I had not yet even considered. I also owe a great deal to Richard Abrams, who saved me from a number of embarrassing mistakes, and to Paul Seabury, who helped push my dissertation toward conceptualization. A number of my colleagues at the University of Illinois (Urbana) have read the manuscript and improved it greatly by their helpful comments both on style and substance: J. Leonard Bates, Frederic Jaher, Thomas Krueger, Robert McColley, Nancy Jo Padgett, and Winton Solberg. I would also like to extend special thanks to Arthur S. Link and to William H. Harbaugh for their careful reading of the manuscript and their suggestions for its improvement, and to John Thompson of St. Catharine's College, Cambridge, not only for offering helpful criticism, but also for providing a useful perspective from which to view Lodge.

I would also like to thank Charles Gillispie, who many years ago first sparked my interest in history; Norman Graebner, whose endeavors in the explication of the relationship between ideas and diplomacy have long been an encouragement; and Gerald Stourzh, whose *Benjamin Franklin and American Foreign Policy* served as a model study. Without John Garraty's thorough and reliable biography of Lodge, a study such as this one could not have been written. I would also like to acknowledge the suggestion of John A. S. Grenville and George Berkeley Young that a general reinterpretation of Lodge's ideas might be attempted.

In the category of institutions my greatest debt is to the staff of the Massachusetts Historical Society for the service and consideration I received at a difficult time when the building that houses the society was undergoing extensive renovation: I would like to extend my gratitude to Stephen Riley, Director; to John Cushing, Librarian; and to Winifred Collins, Assistant Librarian. I would also like to thank the staffs of the Library of Congress and of the libraries of the University of California (Berkeley), Harvard University, the University of Illinois (Urbana), and Yale University. The Research Board of the University of Illinois (Urbana) funded the typing of the manuscript, and for that I am especially grateful. This general listing conceals scores of debts to individuals who did much to facilitate and expedite my research.

Thanks are due to the Massachusetts Historical Society for permission to quote from the manuscript collections in their possession, and to the Yale University Library for permission to quote from the Henry L. Stimson Papers. My editors at the University of California Press, William McClung, Marilyn Schwartz, and Stanley Scott have been exceptionally helpful and have made the editing process an altogether pleasurable experience. I would also like to express my appreciation to Kim Howard for her expert typing and for the care she lavished on the manuscript. Finally, I would thank Mary Helen Barrett Widenor for her help and encouragement, Caroline Buckler and George M. Cushing, for supplying photocopies of the illustrations, and Thomas Schwartz for his assistance in proofing and indexing the manuscript.

Urbana, Illinois   William C. Widenor

Chapter One

The Attractions and Uses of History

In 1876, the year of the national centennial, Henry Cabot Lodge was one of three young men to receive from Harvard the first Ph.D.'s in history ever granted in the United States. There is no indication that he appreciated the symbolism at the time, but in later years he came to regard a widespread interest in history as "proof of national consciousness and of the abiding sense that a nation has come to its place in the world."[1] And if it was fitting that the first American doctorates in history should have been granted in 1876, it was perhaps more than coincidence that they were bestowed in Massachusetts and that a Cabot Lodge, scion of one of Boston's first families and student of an Adams, grandson and great-grandson of presidents of the United States, was one of the recipients. In a nation so intoxicated with the present that it appeared on the verge of a prejudice against memory, and in a city beset by immigrants who seemed to understand so little of the origin and nurture of American institutions, upper-class Boston took exceptional pride in its antecedents and considered history its special preserve.

Years later, in explanation of what prompted the writing of his semiautobiographical *Early Memories*, Lodge was to claim that "the waves of democracy have submerged the old and narrow lines within which the few sat apart, and definition of a man's birth and ancestry

1. Henry Cabot Lodge, *A Frontier Town and Other Essays* (New York, 1906), p. 220.

[1]

has become more necessary."[2] Not less important, which was democracy's verdict, but rather "more necessary." Lodge's Boston still believed in itself, and a Brahmin's pride in his city, his class, and his ancestors nourished the belief that ancestry determined character. This was true in the personal, biological sense to be sure, but also in the larger civic and political sense. Both paths led inexorably to an interest in history. It was almost inevitable that young Lodge's first book would be a justificatory biography of his most illustrious ancestor, his great-grandfather, George Cabot. But if the Brahmin tended to exalt his own ancestry, he was also proud of the society that had evolved in parts of New England. It was not difficult for a young Bostonian in the year 1876, after eight years of "Grantism," to think that Massachusetts had something of a monopoly on culture and virtue. From there it was but a short step to an interest in history, to an investigation of the sources of New England's special character and distinction. History was still uniquely visible and tangible in Boston.[3] It would serve as the nation's memory and recall it to the path from which it had so obviously strayed.[4]

Lodge brought to his history the interest of a class reeling before the assaults of the magnates of the new industrialism and of an immigration which appeared to recognize neither the same God nor the same values. He also brought the viewpoint of a region which had long since assumed the role of the nation's conscience, but which was becoming aware that its voice no longer carried its former weight. New England's political power was on the wane and its achievements seemed to matter only to itself. It was some years yet before Barrett Wendell was to declare that the days of the Yankee folk were numbered, that "we are vanishing into provincial obscurity; America has swept from our grasp; the future is beyond us."[5] But in the "brown era," in the atmosphere of sapped idealism that followed in the wake

2. *Early Memories* (New York, 1913), p. 3.

3. Van Wyck Brooks, *New England: Indian Summer, 1865–1915* (New York, 1940), p. 4.

4. See Ernest Samuels, *The Young Henry Adams* (Cambridge, Mass., 1949), p. 140, for an interesting discussion of the influence of Tocqueville on Adams in this regard. If the New England element was, as Tocqueville maintained, the true source of democracy in America, then its rescue would have to be effected by that same element.

5. Brooks, *New England: Indian Summer*, p. 409.

of the Civil War, there was among Boston's Brahmins both concern lest Boston become "a New England hill town" and a determination not to let that happen.[6]

In later years Lodge was to cultivate the image of a rabid nationalist and to become adept at wrapping himself in the flag. Yet his was always an American nationalism in the service of New England ideals and interests. For as Henry Adams remarked, Lodge was ever "Boston incarnate—the child of his local parentage; and while his ambition led him to be more, the intent, though virtuous, was—as Adams admitted in his own case—restless."[7] Or consider the equally trenchant observation of Owen Wister, who wrote:

Copley, and only Copley, is the right man to have painted Henry Cabot Lodge. . . . it is unmitigated Boston that you see recorded; the eye of a robust, stiff-necked race of seventeenth and eighteenth century dissenters, with its plain living, high thinking, dauntless intolerance, bleak bad manners, suppression of feeling, tenacity in its stern beliefs, and its cantankerousness, stares down at you with cold disapprobation. . . . Cabot Lodge remained unmitigated Boston to the end. Nothing outside of it ever really got into him deep.[8]

Boston knew that it was superior and that it was right. Cabot Lodge suffered from the same consciousness of superior culture and righteousness. No amount of instruction by Henry Adams in the virtues of scientific history could erase from his mind the special attractions which history held for his class, his race, and his region. It proved both their worth and their distinction.

As a result Lodge's historical writing was defensive. His was a history written in justification of men and manners not recalled in the rest of the nation with any particular favor and, hence, by definition, a history written with a strong partisan flavor. Adams saw this tendency in Lodge's approach to history and early warned him against it:

Your danger is a very simple one. . . . It is that of adopting the view of one side of a question. . . . Unless you can find some basis of faith in general principles, some theory of the progress of civilization which is outside and above all temporary questions of policy, you must infallibly think and act under the

6. Geoffrey T. Blodgett, "The Mind of the Boston Mugwump," *Mississippi Valley Historical Review* 48 (March 1962): 615.

7. *The Education of Henry Adams* (New York, 1931), p. 419.

8. *Roosevelt: The Story of a Friendship, 1880–1919* (New York, 1930), p. 153.

control of the man or men whose thought, in the times you deal with, coincides most nearly with your prejudices. This is the fault with almost every English historian.[9]

For a variety of reasons, personal and generational, Lodge, like Henry's brother Brooks, never attained what to Henry was the requisite detachment. Lodge was too much of an Anglo-Saxon particularist to be able to believe in general principles or theories of civilization (except for those that would lead one to believe that New England was chosen). Moreover, he came to have some legitimate doubts about Henry's own detachment and objectivity.[10] But if his approach to history was partisan, it was essentially a function of his feeling that there was an urgent message to be conveyed. Brooks Adams was, if anything, even more wont to organize historical facts around predetermined values, and it was probably Brooks rather than Henry who first put the study of American history into Lodge's head.[11]

Lodge accepted the new historical methodology that Henry had brought back from Germany and sought to inculcate in his students. He saw the relevance of science to historical method and developed a lifelong reverence for historical fact. In his early works both his research and documentation were painstaking and thorough, and far superior to the standards of the day. The scientist in him was so strong that he came to regard an unwillingness to look facts in the face as evidence of weakness of character. But his methodology was ever the servant of his purpose and science was never a purpose in itself. To his credit he usually admitted as much. In the introduction to his *George Cabot* he put it this way: "I have not sought in treating New England Federalism to write a judicial and impartial history of the country; my object was to present one side and that the Federalist, in the strongest and clearest light." His immediate purpose was to rescue the reputation of his great-grandfather, but he was also setting up as a model "the mode of thought and manner of life which bred up a class of clear-headed, strong-willed, sensible men," men who "never fell

9. Worthington C. Ford, ed., *Letters of Henry Adams* (Boston, 1930), I, p. 305.

10. However subtly he may have masked it, Adams's own work had a distinctly apologetic aspect and Lodge caught him "omitting the most personal passage relating to Mr. Otis" from the correspondence of the Adamses in his *Documents of New England Federalism*. See Lodge's "New England Federalism," *The Nation* 26 (Jan. 3, 1878): 11–12.

11. Brooks Adams to Lodge, July [?] 1876, Henry Cabot Lodge Papers, Massachusetts Historical Society, Boston, Mass. (hereafter cited as Lodge MSS).

into the mistake of abandoning practice in favor of theory," and men the likes of which were now so sorely needed at the nation's helm.[12]

If one has a message, one needs an audience. Even in 1876 while still in Henry Adams's camp and venting his caustic pen on the tastes of the American reading public, Lodge knew where that audience lay. In a review of one of the historical potboilers occasioned by the centennial year he acknowledged:

The general public does not care to have such pretty stories as that of Pocahontas exploded in a popular work [which is just what Adams had done in an article], prefers to have the Revolution given in great detail because it is the only picturesque period, and are gratified by eulogistic sketches of the 'fathers,' who are represented as striving together harmoniously against an indefinite evil character (not named) in order to found a nation.[13]

In a sarcastic vein he then added: "There are no theories good or bad in the book, and no useless searching for cause and effect"; "beyond increasing the national tendency to self-complacency" it can have "no permanent value."[14] He chafed under them but recognized conditions for what they were.

Given the impetus which drove him to history in the first place, it should not be surprising that he soon made his accommodation with those conditions. Years later in self-justification he was to have harsh words for scientific history and the concept of an impartial approach to history; he warned against the tendency to "give way too much to the nineteenth-century contention about scientific history," and called the dogma that history be judicial "a bit of cant."[15] Barrett Wendell, a close friend and political admirer, thereupon wrote to Lodge questioning his position on impartiality and historical understanding:

If impartiality in historians means inhuman lifelessness you are right. If, on the other hand, it means sympathy with all phases of earnest emotion,—each in itself too intense to understand the other, in the heat of conflict,—I think you are mistaken. Neither Puritans nor Cavaliers were all in the right; . . .

12. *The Life and Letters of George Cabot* (Boston, 1877), pp. vi, 10.
13. Lodge's review of Jacob H. Patton's *Concise History of the American People* in *The Nation* 23 (Aug. 31, 1876): 140.
14. *Ibid.*
15. Lodge, *Frontier Town*, pp. 87, 97. Perhaps thinking unconsciously of his own dissertation, "Anglo-Saxon Land Law," written under Adams's close supervision, he went on to declare that "a scientific history, crammed with facts, well arranged, but unreadable . . . [is] as sad a monument of misspent labor as human vanity can show."

[5]

nor patriots or Tories in the Revolution; nor Unionists or Secessionists in the Civil War.[16]

Lodge stood, of course, squarely on the side of the Puritans, the patriots, and the Unionists and had anticipated Wendell's criticism when he wrote that "the history of man is in large measure governed . . . by passion, sentiment, and emotion, and cannot be gauged, or understood, without the sympathy and the perception which only imagination and the dramatic instinct can give."[17] If he had been a little more candid he might well have added—and of which only the actively engaged and committed are really capable. Wendell was being deferential but also perceptive when he observed: "The difference between you and me I take to be that between a man who has known the stress of life, and thus has to be partisan in conviction, and one who has only admired it, and thus can thrill conscientiously with pretty various impulse. It is the difference, I fear, between real experience and quasi-histrionic admiration thereof."[18]

Lodge's active engagement in politics had a profound effect on his history. As he noted in his journal in 1890: "Some days ago Theodore said to me 'we must write our side; they think that history will be written by them or their successors who will take their—i.e., the mugwump view of us.' "[19] But it is also true that Lodge brought his political prejudices and the interests of his class and region to his history long before he became an office-seeker. To speak of Lodge having first pursued a career in history and then having abandoned it for one in politics is misleading, for actually he was active in politics, under Adams's tutelage, as a Liberal Republican organizer before he saw a word of his own historical writing in print. His interest in politics and his interest in history developed in tandem, and it probably never occurred to him to attempt to separate the one from the other.

If Lodge's politics colored his history and gave it a defensive and partisan aspect, he also sought to learn from history. He agreed with his friend George Otto Trevelyan that history was philosophy teaching by example and that one of its prime functions was to teach the

16. M. A. DeWolfe Howe, *Barrett Wendell and His Letters* (Boston, 1924), p. 179.

17. Lodge, *Frontier Town*, p. 106.

18. Howe, *Barrett Wendell*, pp. 179–80.

19. Lodge Journal, entry for Dec. 20, 1890, Lodge MSS.

lessons of political wisdom.[20] Consequently, his history had a didactic and utilitarian quality. History was a substitute for philosophy. It was the one true guide and its lessons ought to be respected. All his life he preached its value, and what he said in 1921 as president of the Massachusetts Historical Society was often in his mind, namely that "there never was a time when reverence for and knowledge of the past were more necessary than at this moment to deal with the great problems of the present and to encourage hopes and stimulate preparation for the future."[21] It was in essence a modern-day and Lodgian version of the traditional New England Jeremiad, a call to respect and be guided by past virtue. Lodge never once faltered in his Brahmin belief that "no other people ever displayed political talents of so high an order as that derived from the Anglo-Saxon stock." And if, writing in 1879, he found those talents at low ebb and was willing to concede that "we are not, as a people, so well able to make a democracy succeed as we were when the government was founded," that only increased his inclination to "look into the past, and see whether we cannot find suggestions that will help us in our difficulties." The pages of the history of "our own race" were always relevant; there was no better guide than the lessons which were there set down.[22]

For an American living in a period of profound change, Lodge had an exceptionally strong sense of historical continuity and always felt (if sometimes wishfully) that there was little new under the sun. But it was more than a case of the wish being father to the thought. In the words of Langdon Mitchell, Lodge had a "white-heat, concentrated, moral and intellectual passion of a belief in historical continuity, in American historical continuity; in the Constitution; in our hitherto policies with regard to Europe."[23] For Lodge the past *was* relevant to the present, and Americans more than any other people needed to remember "that however conditions change, the great underlying qualities which make and save men and nations do not alter."[24] The didacticism of his style was deliberate and arose not only out of prejudice but also out of deep-seated conviction. "It reflected not only his de-

20. Lodge, *Frontier Town*, pp. 93–94.
21. *Proceedings of the Massachusetts Historical Society* 55 (Oct. 1921): 31–32.
22. [Lodge], "Limited Sovereignty in the United States," *Atlantic Monthly* 53 (Feb. 1879): 185–87.
23. Langdon Mitchell to Lodge, March 14, 1919, Lodge MSS.
24. Lodge, *Frontier Town*, p. 27.

[7]

termination to extract knowledge from the past but, having assembled it, to wield it against the problems of the present."[25]

Another characteristic of his history was its patriotic and nationalistic quality. This too was partly defensive in origin. Lodge believed with Henry Adams in interpreting American history as the growth and advance of the national principle, which was comforting so long as the ideals of Boston and those of the nation were synonymous and one could show that it was the civilization of New England and "the democracy of Plymouth" which were destined to prevail.[26] And the more he doubted the greater was his need to establish that it was in fact so. Boston had always sought to imbue American nationalism with its own ideals and to cover its own interests with the flag, and in its estrangement in the Gilded Age it tried even harder. For to surrender the mantle of nationalism then would have been tantamount to giving up hope of ever converting the heathen.

Lodge never underestimated the historical importance of ideals. He was convinced that "men cannot live on negations. . . . If the Church was a fraud, and religion a superstition, salvation must be found in the worship of humanity."[27] And, by extension, if unbridled humanity did not measure up to expectations and history demonstrated the need for its restraint, where could a conservatively-minded man turn but to the state. He was particularly sensitive to the fact that he was living in an age that was having an erosive effect on traditional values. He liked to remind his listeners that they were living at a time "when adoration of money is an ever present peril" and to admonish them to "beware . . . how you destroy patriotism, one of the few great ideals left to men, for it is by faith and ideals alone that man has been able to rise to higher things."[28]

If, as Lodge believed, the study and knowledge of American history was the best means of fostering the development of that patriotic

25. "Henry Cabot Lodge: American Statesman and Scholar," *North American Review* 220 (Dec. 1924): 197.

26. Henry Adams and Lodge, "Critical Review of Von Holst's *Constitutional and Political History of the United States*," *North American Review* 123 (Oct., 1876): 360–61; Lodge, "Von Holst's *History of the United States*," *International Review* 7 (Oct. 1879): 438; Lodge, *A Short History of the English Colonies in America* (New York, 1881), pp. 342, 521.

27. Lodge, *The Story of the Revolution* (New York, 1903), p. 276.

28. Lodge, *Frontier Town*, p. 246.

sentiment, then history had a special purpose and needed to be approached in a special way. For if the American political experiment was unique, then foreign experience was of little value. "We must study the past, and learn from it, and advance from what has been already tried and found good. . . . But we cannot enter upon that . . . road until we are truly national and independent intellectually, and ready to think for ourselves, and not look to foreigners in order to find out what they think."[29] The object was to have every man in sympathy with his country, and this could only be achieved by approaching the country's history in an "American" way.[30] Lodge's *Hero Tales from American History*, written in collaboration with Roosevelt, is a classic example of history in that genre.

In using his history to inculcate "American" ideals, he clearly reduced its value as scholarship. Objectivity was the inevitable casualty of his need to inspire Americans to a sympathy with their past and to induce them to be guided by traditional ideals. Even someone as basically sympathetic to Lodge's purposes as Roosevelt could not resist the temptation to chide him about the marked contrast between his description of Virginian society in his *Short History of the Colonies* (1881), when it served as little more than a foil to the superior civilization of New England, and the description of that same society in his biography of Washington (1889), when he was engaged in showing how a truly great man was produced.[31] The interesting thing is that Lodge shrugged off such criticism lightly. Purpose was ever so much more important than consistency.

Moreover, that purpose had a consistency of its own; it was ever profoundly conservative and concerned with the preservation of manners, values, and institutions thought to be threatened with extinction. Lodge was not a great or an original thinker. In fact, he mistrusted philosophy. Both by training and inclination he was a historian and it was a historian's knowledge that he brought to bear on all problems. As Clinton Rossiter has written: "The Conservative considers history his special

29. Lodge, *Studies in History* (Boston, 1884), pp. 364–65.
30. Lodge, "True Americanism," *Harvard Graduates' Magazine* 3 (Sept. 1894): 17.
31. Roosevelt to Lodge, July 1, 1889, in Lodge, ed., *Selections from the Correspondence of Theodore Roosevelt and Henry Cabot Lodge, 1884–1918* (New York, 1925), I, p. 81.

preserve." It is "the creator of all . . . [he] holds dear" as well as "man's most reliable teacher."[32] Lodge came to history with a conservative purpose; it was, indeed, the creator of all he held dear and would preserve. "He betrayed," in the succinct words of Henry Adams, "the consciousness that he and his people had a past, if they dared but avow it."[33] And from his history he took a knowledge which was conservative almost by definition. The lesson was ever the same, that of the recurrent folly of those who would undo history. History was tantamount to being Lodge's God; it could not be undone.[34] There was no reality outside the historical process. History simply was, and while man could learn from it he could only do so if he revered it and allowed it to show him the limits of human possibility.

II

Lodge was considerably influenced by three other historians—Henry Adams, Francis Parkman, and Thomas Babington Macaulay. Macaulay, of course, he knew only from his work, and with Parkman he was never really intimate. Of the three only his mentor, Adams, ever exercised direct influence over his historical writing. Adams was a hard taskmaster, and Lodge stood in awe of his intellect.[35] He also became a close personal friend. As Lodge wrote to Worthington Ford shortly after Adams's death:

For forty-seven years he has been my most intimate friend; to whom I have not only been indebted for help, wise counsel and unfailing sympathy . . . , but whose affection was one of my most cherished possessions. . . . He had the most remarkable mind which I have ever known, in its range of knowl-

32. *Conservatism in America* (New York, 1956), pp. 45–46.
33. *The Education*, p. 420.
34. Lodge never had much to say about religion in public. He may, like his great-grandfather, have admired Christianity as a moral system, and yet have had doubts about its supernatural origins (*George Cabot*, p. 578). Margaret Chanler (*Roman Spring* [Boston, 1934], pp. 193–94) claims that "his was the complete irreligiousity of his generation. As it was said of someone else, 'born in Boston and educated at Harvard, what should he know of religion?' He never missed an opportunity to snarl and gibe at it. The Catholic Church was his favorite 'straw man' and he demolished it to his own satisfaction several times a week." If this be an accurate description of his views, then his reticence was politic.
35. Lodge was, for example, forced to rewrite many times his first contributions to the *North American Review*, of which Adams was the editor.

edge, in its grasp of the meaning and causes of events and in its wholly original and independent action.[36]

It should not be assumed that this expression of Lodge's regard for Adams was tailored to the occasion. One can search Lodge's papers in vain for a word of criticism of Adams; he is always mentioned with a respect bordering on reverence.[37]

In 1872 when Lodge was troubled by the choice of a career, Adams wrote advising that he pursue a "historico-literary" career in the tradition of such illustrious Bostonians as Bancroft, Motley, and Parkman, adding that "anyone who has the ability can enthrone himself here as a species of literary lion with ease." One needed only to work hard and master the German historical method.[38] Adams later claimed that he had intended to make Lodge a professor of history at Harvard, but Lodge himself had little thought of pursuing an academic career and never devoted himself exclusively to scholarship.[39] He had prodigious energy and while working on his Ph.D. he also acquired a law degree from Harvard, served as Adams's assistant editor on *The North American Review*, and was so involved in politics that Adams was exaggerating only slightly when he acknowledged that Lodge had played the principal role "in forming that rope of sand, the Independent party."[40]

In *The Education* Adams confessed to imposing Germany on his scholars with a heavy hand,[41] and the fragmentary notes on his reading that survive in Lodge's journal indicate that he read widely in the German historians. One of Lodge's first contributions to *The North American Review* even prescribed "a course of German reading in order to learn method" as a remedy for one French historian's shortcomings.[42] Adams's influence is also discernible in such early Lodgian pronouncements as "good theorizing is the essence of good history" and "nothing can be more certain than that these great social and political forces . . .

36. *Proceedings of the Massachusetts Historical Society* 51 (April 1918): 317–18.
37. In contrast, Adams's correspondence is dotted with sharp and even harsh comments on Lodge.
38. Ford, ed., *Letters of Henry Adams*, I, p. 228.
39. *Ibid.*, II, p. 77.
40. *Ibid.*, I, p. 299.
41. *The Education*, p. 304.
42. "*Découverte de l'Amérique par les Normands au Xe Siècle* par Gabriel Gravier," *North American Review* 119 (July 1874): 182.

are what alone raise history from the level of annals to the rank of the sciences."[43] The fact that these views did not survive the development of Lodge's own rationale for history does not mean that Adams had no lasting impact. Two particularly important aspects of Lodge's approach to history—his regard for the lessons of even the distant past and his stress on the special significance of international relations—are ultimately traceable to Adams.[44] Adams's views on the relationship between history and international relations are best expressed in *The Education*: "For history international relations are the only sure standards of movement, the only foundation of a map. For this reason, Adams had always insisted that international relations was the only sure base for a chart of history."[45] Adams's conviction on this score reflected his experiences in London with his ambassador father during the Civil War when changes in the Union's military prospects were quickly mirrored in the tone of Anglo-American relations. From that perspective Adams, his brother Brooks, and Lodge all came to attach a special significance to international relations and to see reflected therein forebodings of the very rise and fall of civilizations.

However, as one of Lodge's eulogists noted, he and Adams were really "diametrically opposite types," and the fact that their views began to diverge should not be surprising. "Adams was somewhat of a mystic, frankly sceptical and in method distinctly Socratic; Lodge, on the other hand, tempered his intellectual curiosity with the shrewd common sense of a sire who knew an able seaman when he saw one, and his empirical mind forbade him to plumb for what no man had yet succeeded in fathoming."[46] Moreover, though only twelve years separated them in age, they were of essentially different generations. They differed especially in their ability and in their inclination to accept the conditions that were coming to prevail in modern America. As another contemporary observer, Clinton W. Gilbert, acutely remarked in one of his daily Washington "Mirrors":

43. "Rudolph Baxmann's *Die Politik der Paepste von Gregor I bis Gregor VII*," *North American Review* 118 (April 1874): 400; "Lecky's England," *The Literary World* 9 (June 1878): 3.
44. Ford, ed., *Letters of Henry Adams*, I, p. 237. Here, however, Lodge's interest in the classics was at war with his Anglo-Saxon particularism. And in fact he restricted his own historical investigations to England and the United States.
45. *The Education*, p. 422.
46. "Henry Cabot Lodge: American Statesman and Scholar," p. 196.

Had he been born a little earlier he might, like Henry James, have gone abroad to seek the culture which he acknowledged at its source, or he might, like Henry Adams, have stayed at home and regarded the world about him with dismay. Had he been born a little later he might have accepted the United States boisterously as Theodore Roosevelt did. It is a confirming fact that two of his closest friends were precisely those two, Henry Adams and Theodore Roosevelt. Emotionally he belonged to the America of Henry Adams. By an act of will he accepted the America of Theodore Roosevelt.[47]

The role of observer, such as Adams eventually chose for himself, had little appeal for Lodge, and almost perforce the activist and the passive observer took different views of the individual's ability to affect the course of history. Lodge's sympathetic reading of Carlyle may have led him to emphasize the role of the great man in history, but such a view was also a corollary of his own political activism. Once he even wrote that "the personal qualities and individual abilities of public men . . . make the history and determine the fate of nations."[48] But more often he acknowledged that "the romantic, the picturesque or the personally tragic incidents of history, while they touch our imagination most keenly, are not as a rule those which have had . . . real influence."[49] At every turn he was confronted with the determinism of the Adamses, either the economic determinism of Brooks or the cultural determinism of Henry. Neither accorded much of a role to the individual hero. Henry's influence was still apparent as late as 1913 when Lodge wrote to John Jay Chapman emphasizing the fact that after the passing of the "Fathers" American history could claim only a few great men (e.g., Webster and Lincoln) and acknowledging that "the really dramatic subjects in our history . . . [as] they must in any great democracy, lie in the movements of great bodies of people, like the conquest of the continent, the anti-slavery agitation and the uprising of the Civil War."[50]

Yet Lodge never wrote that kind of history. The attraction of the role of the great man was always too strong. Still he was forced into certain interesting and revealing compromises with determinism. He

47. Quoted in *The Literary Digest* 83 (Nov. 29, 1924): 42.
48. Lodge, *Frontier Town*, p. 54.
49. Lodge, ed., *Major Andre's Journal* (Tarrytown, N.Y., 1930), p. 16.
50. Lodge to John Jay Chapman, May 23, 1913, Houghton Library, Harvard University.

accepted the fact that the hero's role was limited, but he felt that the world owed a lot to the right kind of hero worship, that it was necessary to develop character and inspire men. An escape from determinism was seen in the contention that men were governed largely by impressions and sentiment, which truly able leaders like Washington would always know how to harness.[51] Lodge wanted to believe that moral force or "sentiment" rather than economic force moved the world.[52] Brooks Adams fueled his doubts but never entirely converted him. Yet their resolution of the problem was much the same. For Brooks man's only power lay in understanding economic forces and accommodating himself to a greater determinism. Victory could come only through surrender to the inevitable.[53] Irresistible forces were not to be fought but ridden. Webster had erred in his Seventh of March speech, in Lodge's opinion, "in attempting to arrest . . . [that] which all modern history showed was irresistible." Webster understood the force of American national sentiment but not that of the antislavery movement. Lincoln understood both, and this enabled him to embody the great moral forces which moved the world.[54] Only in this Comtean manner was free will to be reconciled with determinism and idealism with practicality. And just here, in understanding how to position oneself within the field of greater determinisms, would a historian's knowledge be of special value to the statesman.

As Van Wyck Brooks has written, Francis Parkman was "the climax and the crown of the Boston historical school." "The last romantic historian, in a world that was turning scientific, . . . Parkman was a lonely man who stood outside his epoch, an aristocrat, a stoic and an artist."[55] His stoicism and courage were an inspiration to Lodge's generation. John T. Morse, Lodge's cousin and fellow historian, noted that Lodge was "especially attracted by Parkman" and "inclined to look upon . . . [him] as an example and model."[56] Lodge himself described Parkman's

51. Lodge, *George Washington* (Boston, 1890), II, pp. 73, 75.
52. Lodge, *Speeches and Addresses, 1884–1909* (Boston, 1909), p. 29.
53. Charles Vevier, "Brooks Adams and the Ambivalence of American Foreign Policy," *World Affairs Quarterly* 30 (April 1959): 5.
54. Lodge, *Daniel Webster* (Boston, 1884), pp. 331, 360.
55. Brooks, *New England: Indian Summer,* p. 17.
56. John T. Morse, Jr., "Tribute to Henry Cabot Lodge," *Proceedings of the Massachusetts Historical Society* 58 (Nov. 1924): 101. Further evidence of Lodge's respect for Parkman can be seen in the dedication of his *Historical and Political Essays* (1892), in his tribute to Parkman's heroic spirit in *Hero Tales from American History* (1895), and in the paper on Parkman he read before the Massachusetts

history as "the one achievement of an American historian which belongs to that small number of histories which never become obsolete and are never superseded."[57]

Parkman was a symbol of hope to Lodge's generation of Brahmins, living proof that an aristocracy still had a role to play and that there survived among some of its members those strong, manly, aggressive, and courageous qualities which had given meaning and personality to the Boston of the 1850s and which Lodge's generation so yearned to resuscitate.[58] Parkman's attacks on the effeteness of Boston society and upon her "pallid and emasculate scholarship" were always among Lodge's favorites.[59] Parkman was for him a symbol of tough-mindedness, of opposition to everything that savored of sentimentality and overrefinement. He represented all that was virile, natural, clear-thinking, and strong—attributes that could be derived from what Roosevelt was later to call "the strenuous life." He had attempted to show the American aristocracy a means of redeeming itself and had staked out history as that aristocracy's special preserve. If Adams gave Lodge some indispensable intellectual tools, Parkman stimulated his prejudices and supplied him with a cause in the belief that the new "economic" men who were coming to dominate the American scene knew little of their nation's past and cared even less. These men were supposedly without insight into the forces of history, incapable of dealing with large political questions, and ever in need of guidance from such aristocratic "scholars in politics" as Lodge and Roosevelt.[60]

Lodge drank deeply of the ideas and biases of the Romantic historians. Basic to these was the conception of history as moral drama, as a movement from the artificial to the natural, and as a conflict between the progressive forces of Protestantism, republicanism, and nationalism and their Catholic, monarchical, and universalist opposites.[61] Lodge's *The War with Spain* (1899), for example, reads as if that con-

---

Historical Society in 1923. For the latter see "Francis Parkman," *Proceedings of the Massachusetts Historical Society* 56 (June 1923): 319–35.

57. Lodge, *Early Memories*, p. 322.

58. *Ibid.*, p. 19.

59. Theodore Roosevelt and Lodge, *Hero Tales from American History* (Philadelphia, 1903), p. 140.

60. Lodge, *Early Memories*, pp. 208–09; Matthew Josephson, *The President Makers* (New York, 1964), pp. 23–24; Lodge, ed., *Correspondence of Roosevelt and Lodge*, I, p. 542.

61. David Levin, *History as Romantic Art: Bancroft, Prescott, Motley and Parkman* (New York, 1963), pp. 32, 41.

flict had taken place in the seventeenth or eighteenth century and was being interpreted by Motley or Parkman. Lodge readily adopted their belief in the causative power of principles and for him, as for all the Romantic historians, this led to an emphasis on the role of character (both individual and national) in historical progress.[62] For Parkman national character was no temporary matter. He believed, as did Ranke, that every state possessed an individuality and that national institutions reflected the particular stage of development that national character had attained. Nor were the characteristics of a people easily eradicated. Not even the American wilderness had altered the Old World impulses.[63] The character or soul of a race was unique, the product of its history, of centuries of struggle and strife.

The racial implications of Darwinian theory were for Lodge but a gloss upon the insights of the Romantic historians. Race had a historical as well as a biological dimension, and change in either national character or in its institutional manifestations could only come about gradually. It was an organic process with which men tampered at their peril. It was historically and scientifically unsound to attempt to graft portions of even the English system of government onto ours (as Woodrow Wilson once proposed); "like all stable and successful political systems, that of the United States has grown gradually, and in conformity with the conditions and the desires of the people."[64] Race and history were the great determinants; national differences could not readily be effaced. Jefferson never understood this: "He was utterly at fault in supposing that there were in the United States the same elements and the same forces as in France. Both race and history made their existence impossible."[65] "The well-ordered liberty of the English-speaking race was something unknown and inconceivable to the French."[66] Lodge never changed these particularist views, and he came rather easily to the conviction that his adversaries shared Jefferson's failings.

Though Henry Adams was inclined to characterize Thomas Babington Macaulay as an "unfair historian," Lodge, in college, had conceived an "intense admiration" for him and had been especially attracted by

62. *Ibid.*, p. 49.
63. Edward N. Saveth, *American Historians and European Immigrants, 1875–1925* (New York, 1965), pp. 103–06.
64. Lodge, *Historical and Political Essays* (Boston, 1892), pp. 188–89.
65. Lodge, *Alexander Hamilton* (Boston, 1895), p. 270.
66. Lodge, *George Washington*, II, p. 137.

"his force" and "his sure confidence in his own judgment." He found the combination of literature and politics effected by Macaulay "the most enviable that could be imagined," and clearly aspired to follow in his footsteps.[67] Both he and Roosevelt were strongly attracted by Macaulay's historical style, but Roosevelt may have revealed the essence of Macaulay's appeal when he chose him as "the man whose writings will most help a man of action" and as the man who had achieved a perfect mix of common sense and high idealism.[68]

Macaulay's inordinate popularity, which has always distressed his critics, was, of course, exactly what made him so attractive to Lodge. For history which was not read was "wholly useless for the highest purpose of its being."[69] Lodge felt that Matthew Arnold's chief objection to Macaulay—"that his opinions are those of the great body of English-speaking people"—ought to be his highest praise. "The general judgment of mankind is right, in the long run," Lodge observed, "and it is because Macaulay represents it, that he appeals so strongly to all who read him."[70]

As a result Lodge and Roosevelt made Macaulay's shortcomings their very own. They never regarded the partisan nature of his history, his combativeness, or his complacency and satisfaction with the outlook of his own time as anything other than strong points. Macaulay, after all, represented the conservative and "practical" element in British liberalism; there was nothing wishy-washy about him. He forthrightly upheld the right and necessary revolutions and strongly condemned the wrong and unnecessary ones. He did not, like Arnold, become enmeshed in the moral thicket which traps and immobilizes those who see too clearly the evil of both sides of historical controversies and who set up ideals which are beyond the reach of those who have to deal with the world as it is and not as it ought to be.[71] In short, the intellectual affinity between Lodge and Macaulay was so great that G. P. Gooch's incisive critique of Macaulay is also of interest here:

67. Henry Adams to Lodge, July 31, 1876, Lodge MSS; Lodge, *Early Memories*, p. 234; an interview granted by Lodge to James B. Morrow and reported in the Boston *Globe* of March 31, 1907; John T. Morse, Jr., "Henry Cabot Lodge," *Harvard Graduates' Magazine* 33 (March 1925): 441.

68. Lodge, "Francis Parkman," p. 331; Joseph B. Bishop, *Theodore Roosevelt and His Time* (New York, 1920), II, pp. 173, 177.

69. Lodge, "Francis Parkman," p. 324.

70. Lodge, "Matthew Arnold's Mixed Essays," *International Review* 6 (June 1879): 698.

71. *Ibid.*, pp. 698–99.

He is the greatest of party writers, not the greatest of historians. . . . There is no affectation of neutrality or indifference. He honestly believed that Whig principles represented the alpha and omega of political wisdom. . . . Another imperfection of the "essays" is their sledge-hammer brutality. The most kind-hearted of men was a truculent controversialist. . . . Like a giant rejoicing in his strength, he dealt staggering blows at his opponents. . . . The notes on his keyboard were few, the range of his emotional experience curiously limited. He had no sympathy with the passionate discontent of the disinherited or the yearnings of the mystic, and he frankly despised the speculations of philosophers from Plato downwards. He was neither a thinker nor a prophet, but a humane and cultured Philistine.[72]

III

No discussion of Lodge's intellectual development would be complete without reference to the impact of the Civil War. This was a history that he lived. Though he was only ten years old when the war began, it was an "overshadowing experience," whose major events "sank deep into the mind even of a boy" and "left an ineffaceable impression." Fifty years later he still wrote of the war as "a great educational force" and confessed that it had left him "with profound convictions which nothing can ever shake."[73]

Lodge's first political recollection was having "hollered for Frémont" in 1856 at the age of six. He was then only reflecting his family's views, but he never departed from them. Lodge was ever confident that his family had pursued the only proper course in the emerging sectional conflict. He was especially proud that both his father and his grandfather had left the Whig party to become Free-Soilers after Webster's Seventh of March speech and that when "respectable and conservative Boston" turned against Charles Sumner and his antislavery agitation, his father's house (where Sumner was a frequent guest) and that of Charles Francis Adams were the only ones to remain open to him.[74]

Not surprisingly the Lodges also came to share much of the disapprobation with which both Sumner and the Adamses had long looked on Boston's State Street. Most of the boys of Lodge's acquaintance were for Bell and Everett in 1860, and he always regretted respectable Bos-

72. G. P. Gooch, *History and Historians in the Nineteenth Century* (London, 1913), pp. 299–300.

73. Lodge, *Early Memories*, pp. 112, 123, 126.

74. *Ibid.*, pp. 113, 276–77.

ton's propensity for being "out of step at the moment of crisis."[75] He had only harsh words for the leaders of the Cotton Whigs; they were

the men whose duty it was to control and guide the anti-slavery movement, yet all they did was to try to put it aside and forget it and pretend that it had no right to exist. They were eternally crying 'peace, peace,' when there was no peace. With a blindness that must have been wilful, and was certainly unpardonable, they would not admit that the movement against slavery was inevitable.[76]

It was probably also from these events that Lodge drew his lifelong prejudice against a policy of drift and came to place such a premium on decisive action. Compromise was not the way to peace; the only manner in which the Civil War could have been avoided would have been to have crushed all opposition to national authority as quickly as it arose.[77]

But Lodge had no use for the Abolitionists. If some issues were ultimately not subject to compromise, compromise was nevertheless a necessary and useful tactic. "The heroes of the household were men like Sumner, Burlingame and Lincoln, and never the Abolitionists," and Lodge always sought to minimize the historical role of the Abolitionists. He objected strenuously to the "commanding influence" which John Jay Chapman attributed to Garrison:

The alarm bell is essential but there must be some one whom the aroused sleeper will follow or else . . . the alarm will be in vain. Perhaps my life has made me care more for results than methods. The great result to be achieved was the abolition of slavery. To that end it was necessary to have men who could make a practical fight advancing from one point to another. The men who through compromises, reticences, reserves, hesitations gradually gathered the people behind them were the men who got rid of slavery because they were able to carry the forces needed for the work with them.[78]

Such historical judgments provide considerable insight into Lodge's personal political philosophy—a philosophy which was otherwise seldom made explicit—and we should not be surprised to find him, in some of the major crises of his own political life, having recourse to the same tactics he found so admirable in the "practical" leaders of the Civil War era.

75. *Ibid.*, p. 114.
76. Lodge, "A Whig Orator," *The Nation* 27 (Nov. 7, 1878): 287.
77. Lodge, *Daniel Webster*, pp. 223, 308–09.
78. Lodge to John Jay Chapman, May 17, 1913, Houghton Library, Harvard University.

Some wartime impressions proved indelible. "The war fever was burning fiercely," he later wrote, "and reached even the youngest"; young Cabot himself wanted to enlist as a drummer. He saw Robert Shaw ride out at the head of his black troops and attended the funeral of his seventeen-year-old schoolmate Huntington Wolcott. A military company was organized in his school, and he and his classmates were thoroughly drilled, "as if it had now become a part of every American's regular education, so that when the time came he might be able to do his duty in a perpetual war."[79] Lodge himself always recognized that the struggle had profoundly affected his outlook on life:

But the feeling about the country of those to whom the Civil War is not mere history, but a living memory, is . . . a little different from that of any others. . . . they have a more tender sentiment about their country, they are more easily moved by all that appeals to their sense of patriotism, and they are less dispassionate no doubt in judging America and the American people than others, just as they are more intolerant of those Americans who live abroad, ape foreign ways, and sneer at their own land and its people, for they know, they who remember, what it all cost and what a price the people once paid to save the country from those who sought to tear it asunder.[80]

The War's most obvious effect, then, was to give a special flavor and intensity to the patriotism of those who had lived through the ordeal.

The fact that the conflict had, from Boston's point of view, an eminently satisfactory conclusion also had important ramifications. It made Lodge, by his own confession, an optimist as far as the United States was concerned. Even as late as 1913 it gave him faith that "the people who were capable of the Civil War will be able to meet any problems the future may have in store."[81] Nor was his just the traditional optimism of American political oratory. Behind it lay the settled conviction that under constitutional government the party of the center constituted a majority, and that majority would always respond when appealed to in nationalistic terms, or as he preferred to put it, when appealed to by "a leader who seems to consult . . . [the] interest and dignity of the country."[82] The Civil War experience was an object lesson both in how a nation might be held together and in how it might be moved.

79. Lodge, *Early Memories*, pp. 50, 118, 123–25.
80. *Ibid.*, pp. 125–26.
81. *Ibid.*, p. 126.
82. Lodge, *George Cabot*, pp. 192–93.

The outcome of the war also reinforced certain tendencies which had long been endemic to New England thought. It renewed New England's faith in moral progress, in the triumph of the "natural principles" of nationalism, republicanism, and free thought so frequently extolled by the Romantic historians, and it gave its citizens new confidence in their long-cherished ability to make moral judgments in history. As with the Puritans' wars with the Indians, the Civil War became "a struggle where the onward march of civilization was at stake."[83] Lodge never wavered in the belief that "there was a right and a wrong in the Civil War," and he held no brief with those who pretended that both sides were right. That was "not only impossible but false"; "it was the right which triumphed at Appomattox."[84] So viewed, the war became a cleansing agent and an instrument of righteousness and moral progress. It is only against this background, for example, that one can possibly understand the facility with which Lodge and so many of his fellow New Englanders came to convert the First World War into a "Second Holy War."

The Civil War also implanted two prejudices which he tempered over the years but never completely overcame. Lodge wrote about the passing of "the bitter hostility to the South and to Southerners which the mass of Northern people felt during the war," but he believed so strongly in the righteousness of the Northern cause that he long found it difficult to look on Southerners as his moral equals.[85] During the debate on his Federal Election Bill in 1891, Lodge, in reply to a vicious personal attack by Democratic Congressman William Stone of Missouri, made much of the contrast between "the civilization of the public school" (New England) and "the civilization of the shotgun" (the South).[86] He made the same point, if not so acidly, in his article "The Distribution of Ability in the United States," in which the South's contributions to American civilization were contrasted unfavorably with those of New England.[87] However much these antipathies were

83. Roosevelt and Lodge, *Hero Tales from American History*, p. 224; Lodge, *Early Memories*, p. 132.
84. Lodge, *Early Memories*, pp. 133–34.
85. *Ibid.*, p. 127.
86. *Congressional Record*, 51st Cong., 2nd sess., 1891, pp. 1265–66. Stone called him, *inter alia*, "the Oscar Wilde of American statesmanship." The reference is obscure but this was the same William Stone who later, when Wilson was President, became Chairman of the Senate Foreign Relations Committee.
87. Lodge, *Historical and Political Essays*, p. 162.

diluted in the tide of nationalism which Lodge did so much to raise, it is doubtful whether he ever outgrew his feeling that Southerners were morally tainted.

He considered England's treatment of the United States during the Civil War to have been "inexcusable," and though in 1913 he declared that his anger had "long since been swallowed up in sheer marvel at the stupidity of the English Government and of the English governing classes," he admitted to having been taught a lesson in those days by the attitude of England and France, which he "could not unlearn if he would." He seemed to be referring to the disproportionate weight of interest as opposed to sentiment in the formulation of foreign policy, and to the importance of meeting hostile acts with firmness and resolution.[88] The diplomatic history of the Civil War held many lessons for Americans, but few of them understood that aspect of the struggle. Those who did were easily convinced of their special wisdom and of the necessity of their attaining to positions where they might implement those lessons.

In other areas the effect of the Civil War was surely as great, but in regard to these Lodge's political instinct dictated circumspection. As George Fredrickson has written, the war "provided an occasion for the open expression of a form of conservative thinking that had been underground since the victory of Jefferson in 1800."[89] Successful prosecution of the war had demanded and shown the necessity for the cultivation of aspects of the American character unattended since Federalist days. The message of the Civil War was that a democratic form of government was not sufficient to guarantee the country's safety and survival. It was the character and determination of its people that had seen the North through to victory. The lesson, as Lodge drew it, was remarkably ethnocentric: "it is on the moral qualities of the English-speaking race that our history, our victories, and all our future rest; . . . more precious even than forms of government are the mental and moral qualities which make what we call our race."[90]

Lodge was determined that the heroic virtues (which in the dark days after Bull Run and Fredericksburg had seemed to be so wanting

88. Lodge, *Early Memories*, pp. 131–32.
89. *The Inner Civil War: Northern Intellectuals and the Crisis of the Union* (New York, 1965), p. 78.
90. Lodge, *Speeches and Addresses*, pp. 264–66.

in the North) become a permanent national possession, that the American character thereafter give evidence of the fact that it too had been forged in a crucible of blood and iron. When he spoke of "the mental and moral qualities of the English-speaking race" and stressed the importance of "character" (as he frequently did), he was invariably talking about those virtues or qualities which he considered crucial to the success and safety of the nation. As we have seen, he shared with the Romantic historians the belief that character was a nation's most important possession and that both the type and the success of government were but functions of that character.[91] Moreover, national character could not be distinguished from individual character; the requirements were in each case the same and the one was clearly dependent on the other.[92] Nations and individuals were subject to the same moral judgments. As a fellow Brahmin, William Lawrence, noted, Lodge thought that the essentials of a nation, as of an individual, were character, integrity, unity, and self-respect and that the intelligence and character of the people were the foundations of national life.[93] The prescription for success was to make sure that society always produced a sufficient proportion of Robert Gould Shaws and Charles Russell Lowells.[94]

Since "character" had proven such an important resource, Northern intellectuals were inclined to preoccupation with the historical conditions of its development. The many contrasts Lodge drew between life in New England and life in the South in his *Short History of the English Colonies* can easily be read as an essay on the reasons the North won the war. He was also led back to the frontier, where he discovered anew the principles which had enabled his people "to strive and conquer." The qualities that marked the Anglo-Saxon—"a character of force, fitted for conquest, government and freedom"—were historically unique.[95] Those qualities gave Lodge faith in the future of his country;

91. Clipping from the New York *Advertiser*, Nov. 28, 1895, Scrapbooks, Lodge MSS. Lodge, *The Democracy of the Constitution and Other Addresses and Essays* (New York, 1915), p. 23.
92. This was tantamount to orthodoxy among Lodge's generation. Woodrow Wilson also believed that character could be expressed on a national scale. See Arnold Wolfers and Laurence W. Martin, eds., *The Anglo-American Tradition in Foreign Affairs* (New Haven, 1956), pp. 264–68.
93. *Henry Cabot Lodge: A Biographical Sketch* (Boston, 1925), pp. 57–58.
94. See Lodge's essay on Lowell in *Hero Tales from American History*.
95. Lodge, *Frontier Town*, p. 28; Lodge, *Studies in History*, p. 113.

he sought throughout his life to do all he could to preserve them and to pass them on intact to the next generation.

Lodge and his friend Theodore Roosevelt endeavored to lead their own lives in accordance with their preachings. Lodge rode because "for the development of nerve, energy and courage, so useful in all the affairs of life and so pre-eminently valuable to a people called to arms . . . no outdoor sport can equal riding on horseback."[96] They believed not only in the need, but also in the possibility, of conditioning themselves so as to be able to assume the role of "the strong man who uses his strength disinterestedly for the public good."[97] Both the frequency and the intensity of Lodge's denunciations of "decrepit dilettantism" suggest that more was involved here than an attempt to preserve the social utility of his class; he was also trying to overcome his own tendencies in that direction.[98]

The Civil War gave new life to the conservative idea of American nationality and patriotism. The rationalist and universalist conception of these qualities, an inheritance of the Enlightenment, did not evoke the responses demanded by the stresses of war, and recourse was therefore had to the Hamiltonian conception with its emphasis on the necessity for judging the United States by the traditional standards of national power and for cultivating an instinctive patriotism.[99] To Lodge and many of his generation this was dogma; "true Americanism" inevitably meant patriotism. "The first duty of an American university," he told the Phi Beta Kappa Society at Harvard in 1894, "should be to make its students good Americans."[100]

The heroic ideal cultivated by Lodge and Roosevelt came naturally to members of their class, the descendants of America's colonial and preindustrial aristocracy. It justified their existence and rationalized their antirelativist and anticommercial prejudices. The Civil War, in demonstrating the need for leadership and example, and for loyalty and steadfastness, lent it new respectability. In the search for national cohesion the preoccupations of a small class with the maintenance of a

96. Lodge, "Horses and Riders," *Cosmopolitán* 9 (Oct. 1890): 701.

97. Roosevelt to Lodge, July 19, 1908, Elting Morison, ed., *The Letters of Theodore Roosevelt* (Cambridge, Mass., 1951–53), VI, pp. 1135–36.

98. Lodge's review of *Every Man His Own Poet*, in *International Review* 7 (August 1879): 217.

99. Fredrickson, *The Inner Civil War*, pp. 141–44.

100. Lodge, *Certain Accepted Heroes* (New York, 1897), p. 166.

role in American society were converted into a national concern for the preservation of the beliefs that had seen the nation through its crises. The situation was tailor-made for the historian as propagandist.

Both Lodge and Roosevelt stepped easily into that role. Nor did they lack a ready and appreciative audience. Both class prejudice and respect for "frontier" qualities inclined many Americans to listen with sympathy to their excoriations of the effete. For Lodge and for Roosevelt, personal belief and good politics often pointed in the same direction, to attacks on the conduct and attitudes of the nation's "leisure class."[101] The university president who warned his students against the tendency to magnify the savage virtues was one of Lodge's favorite targets. "These primary or 'savage' virtues make states and nations possible," Lodge rejoined, "and in their very nature are the foundations out of which other virtues have arisen. If they decay, the whole fabric they support will totter and fall."[102]

Lodge was worried about the growth of the critical spirit and the relativity in values which seemed to accompany liberalism. The "true American" was not a mere critic but a man who had the faith and enthusiasm necessary to enable him "to do battle with sword or pen." And should the "true American" not prevail and the critical, indifferent spirit reign, Lodge was convinced that it would mean sure and continued defeats. It would sap the very roots of action and success.[103] Devotion to a cause, intense conviction, and even prejudice acquired at Lodge's hand a new *raison d'être*. The following quotation from an essay in which he discovered hidden virtues in the character of Timothy Pickering typifies his feeling about the qualities necessary for leadership:

The majority of successful men are the men of intense prejudices and intense convictions. They may not be of so high a type as the broad and liberal-minded men, but they attain the greatest measure of immediate and practical success. They appeal most strongly to the sympathies and passions of their fellow-men; for to the mass of humanity liberality is apt to look like indifferentism, and independence like unreliable eccentricity.[104]

Later generations would draw different conclusions from even more terrible wars, but for Lodge and many of his generation the lessons

101. Lodge, *Studies in History*, p. 358.
102. Lodge, *A Fighting Frigate* (New York, 1902), p. 21.
103. Lodge, *Certain Accepted Heroes*, pp. 181–82.
104. Lodge, *Studies in History*, pp. 217–18.

of the Civil War era were the essence of political and social wisdom. Their concern was the transmission of that wisdom to the generations with no experience of the war. Lodge often voiced the fear "that the insidious gentleness of peace and prosperity had relaxed . . . the practice of some of the virtues called out by war."[105] An obvious solution was to extend the war crisis mentality, and many a New England speech of the last quarter of the nineteenth century was a secular Jeremiad to that end.[106] Lodge worked hard at the theme that although "we live in a time of profound peace and great prosperity, we too have our dangers to be met and overcome, just as the men of 1789 and 1861 had theirs."[107] But as time passed it became increasingly apparent that justification could be found only in new crises, and much that follows, from Lodge's flirtation with imperialism to Roosevelt's style in the White House, can be explained in terms of a desire to simulate conditions which would once again call forth "the best" in the American people.

IV

Accompanying the belief in heroic virtue was a renewed interest in other forms of conservatism. In his first major public speech Lodge declared that "the great secret of the political success of our race lies in its conservatism, in its ability to reform and not destroy in order to create anew." He admonished his audience to "revert to the traditions of our race, and practice a little more wholesome conservatism."[108] The new history would nurture tradition and old modes of thought, that the nation built upon them might survive in a new and different age.

105. Lodge, "Address Before the Citizens of Nahant, Memorial Day, 1882," Massachusetts Historical Society.

106. Some of the more famous were Henry Lee Higginson's "Soldiers' Field Address," June 10, 1890, which impressed Lodge so much he sent it to Roosevelt (Bliss Perry, *Life and Letters of Henry Lee Higginson* [Boston, 1921], pp. 337, 534–36); and the Memorial Day injunction given by Oliver Wendell Holmes, Jr., to the Harvard graduating class of 1895, that war was a teacher "of the kind we all need" (Edward Burns, *The American Idea of Mission* [New Brunswick, N. J., 1957], pp. 240–41). More than a year after the event, Lodge was still talking about Holmes's "noble and beautiful address" (Lodge to John T. Morse, Jr., July 4, 1896, John T. Morse, Jr., Papers, Massachusetts Historical Society).

107. "Problems of the Nation," an oration delivered at Lowell on July 4, 1889, Scrapbooks, Lodge MSS.

108. "Oration," Boston City Council, July 4, 1879, p. 37, Massachusetts Historical Society.

Hope lay in the conservatism of habit, in his conviction that "habits of thought slowly formed through long periods of time, and based on physical, climatic, and geographical peculiarities, are more indestructible than the pyramids themselves,"[109] and in the prospect of rewriting American history to point up the necessity for the preservation of those traditions and habits of thought which had permitted the United States to survive and prosper. To that end old battles would have to be refought and new heroes enthroned.

The first group to benefit from Lodge's reinterpretation was the Puritans. Lodge celebrated not the religious but rather the political virtues of the Puritans. Here was the source of "the ingrained conservatism and the reverence for law and order which New England [had] always cherished," and here too was a civilization which had produced men "fit for leadership and command."[110] In the Puritan character was also to be found the conservative apotheosis, the perfect union of the ideal and the practical.[111]

Lodge tended to dwell, as have few other writers, on the Puritans' martial qualities. For him "the English Puritan was essentially a fighting man, and excelled in the art of war." Little sentimentality marked his accounts of the Puritans' struggles with the Indians; he even approved of the "true Puritan fashion" in which the Pequod tribe had been exterminated.[112] The Civil War had shown that "the fighting spirit of the Puritans lived on in their children," and now the object was to prevent those old qualities from being "refined and cultivated to nothingness."[113]

Lodge found the public spirit of the Puritans a perfect contrast to the "ignorant and vicious vote" of the great American cities. This public spirit he attributed not solely to membership in a state where religion was the test of citizenship and every religious man sensed his debt to the Commonwealth, but rather to "pride of race, and to the lingering faith in the declared belief of the early Puritans that they were a chosen people." It was the New Englanders' "intense belief in themselves, their race, and their traditions" that had made their municipal

---

109. Lodge, *Speeches and Addresses*, p. 346.
110. Lodge, *Fighting Frigate*, pp. 179–80.
111. Lodge, "A Personal Tribute to Senator Hoar," *Harvard Graduates' Magazine* 13 (Dec. 1904): 216.
112. Lodge, *Short History*, pp. 349, 421.
113. Lodge, *Boston* (New York, 1891), p. 224; Lodge, *Fighting Frigate*, p. 180.

and state governments "such conspicuous examples of successful popular government."[114] Puritan society was also seen to have rested on grounds other than racial homogeneity: "Community of race was strengthened, and its effects increased, by community of class."[115] Here his conservatism led him back to liberalism. Only the Puritan leaven could save American society from domination by mere wealth, from the "danger that the growth of wealth here may end by producing a class grounded on mere money [in contrast to an aristocracy of service], and thence class feeling, a thing noxious, deadly, and utterly wrong in this country."[116]

But the Puritans were only of passing interest; the Federalists had first claim on Lodge's sympathies.[117] The Civil War had evoked a new interest in Federalism, and Lodge's interest in the "restoration" was the greater for the fact of his own distinguished Federalist lineage. He was well aware of the direction in which the historiographical tide was running. Whereas before the war the early history of the United States had been neglected, after the war "the American people . . . awoke to a full realization of the greatness of the work in which they had been engaged and of the meaning and power of the nation they had built up." As Lodge also observed, "no one . . . profited by these changed conditions more than Hamilton." Lodge the historian rode the crest of that tide, and the opinions and ideas about government and politics which he formulated in the 1870s and 1880s while studying the Federalists became a permanent part of his outlook. If anything his admiration for Hamilton grew with time. In 1904 he claimed that events had more and more justified Hamilton's conception of the government of the United States.[118] Hamilton "was the greatest constructive mind in all our history," he told James Beck in 1923, "and I should come pretty near saying, or in the history of modern statesmen in any country."[119]

He thought the Federalists had possessed "a greater amount of ability than was ever displayed by all other political parties in America,"

114. Lodge, *Boston*, pp. 204–05.
115. Lodge, *Short History*, pp. 407–08.
116. Lodge, *Speeches and Addresses*, pp. 6–7.
117. The clerical strain was conspicuously absent from his ancestral pedigree, a condition unusual in a Bostonian of his station (*Early Memories*, p. 13).
118. Lodge, ed., *The Works of Alexander Hamilton* (2d ed.: New York, 1904), I, pp. iv–vii.
119. Lodge to James M. Beck, July 17, 1923, Lodge MSS.

but he knew that their political theory had been unpopular.[120] Unre-furbished, the Federalists were no longer marketable. Precisely because he perceived the danger so clearly, Lodge was determined to become neither a relic nor a reactionary. He would take from the past only what was of value to the present. He feared and dreaded, but also appreciated, the profound changes which were affecting the life of the country.[121] He was strongly attracted to Federalist theory as well as to Federalist policy and methods, but the problems attendant to writing a conservative and aristocratic history in a liberal and democratic country were well nigh insurmountable. Lodge did the best he could under the circumstances. Even as a historian he was a politician.

His grave reservations about democracy were restricted to such anonymously published articles as "Limited Sovereignty in the United States" and to private correspondence.[122] "Limited Sovereignty" was only a faintly veiled attempt to restrict the popular will and to reserve decision in important matters to "the wise and the good."[123] Lodge was "not ready to admit that the principles of which he [Jefferson] was the apostle and which he did more than anyone else to stamp upon our nation were sound." They were still on trial and their prospect of success at best uncertain.[124] The Federalist feeling that the American political fabric was frail and that democracy must soon produce a crisis was still strong, but Lodge in his political ambition had no alternative but to accept and accommodate himself to American democracy. He probably believed with his great-grandfather that the election of Jefferson had assured the ascendancy of pure democratic theories, and was convinced "that this evil was radical, and not to be overcome by resistance; it must be left to work out its destiny with such modifications as were possible."[125]

As a result his public writings are devoid of open assault on the principles of democracy. He even made frequent public declaration

120. Lodge, *George Cabot*, p. 264.
121. See, for example, his *Early Memories*, p. 16, where he asserts that "there was a wider difference between the men who fought at Waterloo and those who fought at Gettysburg or Sedan or Mukden than there were between the followers of Leonidas and the soldiers of Napoleon."
122. *Atlantic Monthly* 43 (Feb. 1879): 184–92.
123. At the time he (and most of "respectable" Massachusetts with him) was genuinely frightened by the specter of "Butlerism," by what he considered to be Ben Butler's demagogic attempts to exploit class feeling for political benefit.
124. Lodge to George Bancroft, May 28, 1878, Lodge MSS.
125. Lodge, *George Cabot*, p. 575.

of his faith, but it was usually in the democracy that had survived the crisis of the war, in that amalgam of Hamiltonian nationalism and Jeffersonian democracy forged by Lincoln. He knew that the theory upon which the American political system rested was Jeffersonian, but that events, especially those of 1800–1815 and more recently those of the Civil War, had forced the Jeffersonians to rule "in the manner and after the methods prescribed by Hamilton."[126] His concern was to cement that amalgam and to prevent another Jeffersonian or Jacksonian outbreak. To that end it was necessary to disavow a portion of his Federalist heritage, to soft-pedal the aristocratic nature of his Federalist heroes and to recast them in the role of American nationalists. But doing so would allow him to demonstrate that Hamiltonian leadership and methods would always be indispensable.

A definite filio-pietistic tone pervades his works, but none of them is as antidemocratic as writers like Karl Schriftgiesser and Matthew Josephson contend.[127] Though his Washington may have been a paragon of virtue, his acceptance of Hamilton was never uncritical. Contrary to Josephson, he did not condone his hero's willingness to "accomplish a great right by doing a little wrong" in the case of Hamilton's letter to John Jay urging irregular means in securing the vote of New York in the 1800 presidential election. While Josephson, quoting Lodge out of context, claims that Lodge associated himself with "the champions of order, the saviours of society, the 'strong men' and the imperialists of this world," Lodge was only saying that arguments for the use of irregular means are never wanting. He did not approve of Hamilton's

126. Lodge, "Notice of George Shea's *Alexander Hamilton*," *The Nation* 24 (May 10, 1877): 283; see also Lodge, *Alexander Hamilton*, p. 283.

127. Schriftgiesser, for example, has only praise for those works—his *George Cabot* and his *Short History of the Colonies*—which were written while Adams's influence was paramount. According to Schriftgiesser both are notable for their objectivity and originality, while his biography of Hamilton, written after he had sold his soul to the Republican Party, was "the first of his many books in which prejudice supplanted scholarship and his strong anti-democratic leanings found full expression." (*The Gentleman from Massachusetts* [Boston, 1944], pp. 41–43, 94). The case is much overdrawn. Lodge's early work was, indeed, better researched and documented and marked by a style less propagandistic than his later efforts. It is also true, as John Garraty notes (*Henry Cabot Lodge: A Biography* [New York, 1953], p. 58n), that his criticisms of Hamilton became progressively milder. But to draw any sharp distinction between his earlier and later work is to miss the point that all his history reflects an underlying body of thought which is consistent and cohesive.

action. On the contrary he contended that Hamilton was motivated by a dread of the success of the other side and that his letter to Jay was "a most melancholy example of the power and the danger of such sentiments which are wholly foreign to free constitutional systems."[128]

As John Garraty claims, sections of Lodge's later histories came to resemble Republican campaign tracts; his "reverence for the old Puritan virtues and for the contribution made by the Federalist Party in the early days of the Republic distorted . . . [his] historical judgment." But it was not history written from an identifiably aristocratic or anti-democratic point of view. True, it was anti-Jeffersonian, and Lodge could easily have remarked: "Let the Jeffersonians and the Jacksonians beware! I will poison the popular mind!"[129] But was he doing any more than writing history for his own age and pandering to its special needs and prejudices? Entirely too much can be made of Henry Adams's proposal that Lodge teach a course in American history parallel to Adams's, but from the federalist and conservative as opposed to Adams's supposedly democratic and radical point of view.[130] A careful reading of Adams's own history will reveal that the matters on which he and Lodge took Jeffersonian democracy to task were remarkably similar. Both tended to dwell on the Jeffersonians' inability to devise a workable foreign policy and on their incapacity for national leadership.[131] There is even a grain of truth in Lodge's remark that "nothing that has been written goes farther in showing that the Federalists, from 1789 to 1801, were the ablest political party this country has ever seen than . . . [Adams's] Life of Albert Gallatin."[132] Both Lodge and Adams wrote in and for a generation which encompassed the Civil War within its immediate experience and knew something of

128. Contrast Josephson's quotations in *The President Makers*, p. 68, where even the question at issue is obscured, with what Lodge actually wrote in *Alexander Hamilton*, pp. 228–29.

129. Garraty, *Lodge*, pp. 57, 59–60. The remark was actually made by his cousin and close friend, John T. Morse, Jr.

130. Harold D. Cater, ed., *Henry Adams and His Friends* (Boston, 1947), p. 81.

131. A good example of Adams's view is a letter to Samuel Jones Tilden dated Jan. 24, 1883, and published in Cater, ed., *Adams and His Friends*, pp. 125–26: "I cannot say as much for his [Gallatin's] friends Jefferson, Madison and Monroe. . . . In regard to them I am incessantly forced to devise excuses and apologies or to admit that no excuse will avail. . . . There is no possibility of reconciling their theories with their acts, or their extraordinary foreign policy with dignity."

132. Lodge, *Studies in History*, pp. 290–91.

the weak spots in the armor of American democracy. The difference between Adams and Lodge lay more in the uses to which they were prepared to put their historical knowledge. Whereas Adams, the observer, was usually content simply to point up democracy's dilemmas, Lodge, the activist, often had a more immediate and partisan purpose.

The type and style of leadership produced by Jeffersonian democracy and its utopian approach to foreign policy drew Lodge's primary fire. Here New England had a special grievance and here Jefferson appeared most vulnerable to those in whom the Civil War experience had instilled a belief in the need for a policy of national strength. Interestingly, all Lodge's lines of attack were related and bore upon the question of what role the United States ought to play in the world at large and how that role might best be implemented and sustained. Lodge paid correspondingly little attention to Jeffersonian domestic policy and may well have made a conscious decision to leave that ground unturned.[133] Accordingly, most of the antipathy which a Brahmin might naturally have been expected to feel for the levelers (Jeffersonian, Jacksonian, or Butlerian) of American history was channeled into one area of public policy, the conduct of foreign affairs. This is why Lodge always attached so much importance to foreign policy and defense matters. Democracy's greatest difficulty was ever the conservatives' most likely opportunity.

V

If after the Civil War the Republicans were guilty of waving "the bloody shirt," the tactics were but similar to those employed by the Democrats in the period of Jacksonian ascendancy when the Hartford Convention of 1814 (of which Lodge's great-grandfather was one of the moving spirits) became a byword for the antinational and antidemocratic treason of New England's Federalist aristocracy. When New England could once again lay claim to being the stronghold of the sentiments of Union and nationality, it was but natural that there

---

133. Still he probably agreed with Gouverneur Morris's *bon mot* on Jefferson: "He believes, for instance, in the perfectability of man, the wisdom of mobs, and the moderation of Jacobins. He believes in payment of debts by diminution of revenue, in defense of territory by reduction of armies, and in vindication of rights by the appointment of ambassadors" (Lodge, *Historical and Political Essays*, p. 110).

should be an attempt to rehabilitate New England Federalism. Lodge's sympathetic, and sometimes vindicatory, biography of his great-grandfather, George Cabot, was an important contribution to that end. On the national level, however, the historical reputation of Federalism was intimately bound up with that of Hamilton, and Lodge turned quickly and eagerly to his rehabilitation, publishing a biography in 1882 and an edition of his *Works* in 1885.

When he made Hamilton the exemplar and the architect of American nationalism, Lodge was using the word *nationalist* in a peculiarly American way that carried definite implications for governmental organization. Lodge was concerned to wed the emotive spirit of American nationalism, brought to fever pitch by the war, to Hamilton's belief in strong national government and faith in the powers of such a government to advance the national interest. He would wean the democracy of its historic suspicion of strong national government and capitalize on the fact that the war had temporarily made Jefferson's state-rights theory more suspect than Hamilton's aristocratic notions of government. Gone was the notion that Hamilton's purpose had been to provide a means and scope for aristocratic government. Instead, the creation of an enduring national sentiment and a powerful national government were seen as the dominant purposes of Hamilton's life.[134] Democracy was no longer an issue. Only two schools of political thought had existed in the United States, nationalism and state rights, and "Hamilton's creed of nationality and union" had "triumphed in the court of last resort" and was "now supreme."[135] Hamilton had made mistakes, but Lodge hoped he would be remembered for his services to the cause of nationality and for "the masterly policies which have done so much to make the nation and guide her along the pathway to her mighty destiny."[136]

Lodge might make Hamilton respectable, but he knew that he could not make him lovable; "his genius and achievements were not of the kind which appeal to the hearts and imagination of the people."[137] He also had difficulty with certain aspects of Hamilton's record. The

134. Lodge, ed., *The Works of Alexander Hamilton* (1st ed.: New York, 1885), I, pp. v–vi; Lodge, *Alexander Hamilton*, p. 106.

135. Lodge, ed., *Works of Hamilton*, 1st ed., I, p. v; Lodge, "Alexander Hamilton," *McClure's* 8 (April 1897): 506.

136. Lodge, "Alexander Hamilton," *McClure's* 8 (April 1897): 507.

137. Lodge, *Alexander Hamilton*, p. 24.

fact that Hamilton "never believed in the Constitution" was a serious obstacle to his rehabilitation, and the best Lodge could do by way of effacement was to add a qualifier and present Hamilton as a man who "never believed thoroughly in the Constitution."[138] Hamilton's marked partiality for England was another problem. Lodge's effort to establish the Federalists as the true champions of American nationality and to blame the Jeffersonians for the "un-American" practice of introducing foreign influence into American politics foundered on the rock of Hamilton's English prejudices and his relations with the British Minister.[139] The best Lodge could do was to insist that the Jeffersonians were initially at fault, that the Federalists' worship of England was only an inevitable reaction to the Jeffersonians' adoration of France, and to condemn both as "a curse upon our politics."[140]

If the Federalists could sometimes be defended only with difficulty, it was, as Henry Adams told Lodge, "always safe to abuse Jefferson."[141] Offense was the best defense. Hamilton's cardinal doctrine in politics and government, "strength and order," was one of which Americans had reason to be suspicious, but Americans also had an instinctive distaste for weakness and disorder.[142] The Jeffersonians already had a strike against them because of their belief in state rights and weak government. Lodge sought to build on that foundation.

Today Lodge's pronouncements on Jefferson seem intemperate and unduly harsh, but such strictures were not unusual among his generation. Roosevelt, for example, held that Jefferson was "the most incompetent chief executive we ever had," and Herbert Croly, who demanded national political responsibility in place of the Jeffersonian assumption of the automatic harmony of the individual and the public interest, found Hamilton much more attractive.[143] Personal attacks on Jefferson crop up frequently in Lodge's history and presage his later treatment of Wilson. They were a means of dramatizing and popu-

---

138. Lodge, "*The Life of Alexander Hamilton* by John T. Morse, Jr.," *North American Review* 123 (July 1876): 141; Lodge, *Studies in History*, p. 174.

139. Lodge, *George Washington*, II, pp. 154, 268–69; Lodge, *George Cabot*, p. 62; Lodge, *Historical and Political Essays*, p. 62.

140. Lodge, *George Cabot*, p. 62.

141. Henry Adams to Lodge, June 7, 1876, Lodge MSS.

142. Lodge, *Alexander Hamilton*, p. 90.

143. Morison, ed., *Letters of Theodore Roosevelt*, V, p. 803; Herbert Croly, *The Promise of American Life* (New York, 1964), pp. v, 152, 154.

larizing the differences between Federalists and Jeffersonians. For example, Lodge once wrote:

Jefferson was a sentimentalist; a great man no doubt, but still a sentimentalist pure and simple. His colleague and opponent was the very reverse. Hamilton reasoned on everything, and addressed himself to the reason of mankind for his support. . . . Hamilton was consistent, strong, masculine, and logical. Jefferson was inconsistent, supple, feminine, and illogical to the last degree.[144]

Lodge was asking his reader to choose between different styles of leadership, and given the manner of presentation, the choice was really no choice at all. In the Lodgian version of American history the Federalists were ever the realists. They looked facts squarely in the face and never succumbed to the Jeffersonian propensity for abandoning practice to theory, a tendency which precluded the possibility of statesmanship.[145] Lodge's Washington always acted quickly and decisively; he steadfastly refused to pursue a "lingering" policy.[146] In fact Washington and Jefferson were so radically different in temperament that they could never have been sympathetic. Similarly, there was "nothing vague or misty" about Hamilton; he was neither an agitator nor "a sentimentalist of muddy morals and high purposes."[147] This pattern was, in fact, so pervasive a feature of Lodge's writing that often he did not even need to instruct his readers as to who *was* possessed of those characteristics.

In Lodge's moral universe "bad" character inevitably meant "bad" policy and "bad" government, and the adjectives that served to contrast the personal traits of Federalists and Jeffersonians were easily carried over into discussions of their respective policies. Lodge's technique can be seen in such a statement as "the President . . . fell back on his *preposterous* theories of commercial warfare, well suited to his *timidity* and love of *shuffling*," or in the assertion that "for a *vigorous* neutrality, ever on the *alert* and *ready* for war, was substituted a *timid*, *exasperating* policy of peace protected by commercial warfare."[148]

144. Lodge, *Studies in History*, p. 148.
145. Lodge, *George Cabot*, pp. 10, 474.
146. Lodge, *George Washington*, II, p. 89.
147. Lodge, ed., *The Works of Alexander Hamilton*, 2d ed., I, p. xiii; Lodge, *Alexander Hamilton*, p. 64.
148. Italics mine. Lodge, "The Last Forty Years of Town Government," in Justin Winsor, ed., *The Memorial History of Boston* (Boston, 1881), III, p. 208; Lodge, *Alexander Hamilton*, p. 163.

[35]

A particularly good example of this tactic, because it shows how early he came to the opinions which were to last a lifetime, is the following assessment of Jeffersonian policy:

In the one case, it was Washington, wise, dignified and calm; in the other, it was Madison, prudent, sagacious, and badly frightened; in the third, it was Jefferson, crafty, selfish, and a French *doctrinaire*. Washington and Madison ratified their treaties, Jefferson rejected his. Without a word to the Senate, or to anyone but Madison, the treaty of 1806 was thrown aside; and the war of 1812 . . . made inevitable. The history of the time presents no single valid reason for Jefferson's secret rejection of the treaty. To the character and principles of the man, we must alone look for explanation. It was the old story: a hatred of England and a love of France, a policy of covertly injuring one and aiding the other, and a firm belief that a constantly manifested detestation of England was the best way to popular support.[149]

If in Lodge's view the Federalists had been partially successful in their efforts to render democracy both acceptable and workable, he also knew they had been blest with little time and had left much undone:

They had initiated the policy of strong and real neutrality, protected by an efficient navy; but they had not habituated the people to it, nor had the glories of Truxtun's victories been sufficient to make men realize that the sea was the field on which our power could be best maintained and asserted. The foreign policy and the navy were, therefore, the two points on which Jefferson's attacks could and did succeed.[150]

Jefferson extended the application of Washington's dictum against permanent alliances, but he rapidly abandoned the Federalist corollary that "our policy of neutrality, found all its strength in the gradual construction and preservation of an efficient navy." Jefferson thought only of his theories and, convinced that interest could rule the world pacifically, began at once to implement his "Chinese policy." The marine corps was disbanded and all naval preparations abruptly halted.[151] Lodge never doubted that Jefferson was sincere in his desire for "peace at all risks," but like his mentor, Adams, he balked at legislating "as though eternal peace were at hand," when in fact they lived "in a world torn by wars and convulsions and drowned in blood."[152]

149. Lodge, *George Cabot*, pp. 467–68.
150. *Ibid.*, pp. 418–19.
151. *Ibid.*, pp. 428–29.
152. *Ibid.*, p. 461; Henry Adams, *History of the United States of America* (New York, 1889), I, p. 146.

Lodge was particularly concerned to establish the fact that the wisdom of the Federalists, the knowledge that only a policy of strong neutrality could protect America, had finally been perceived and incorporated in the Monroe Doctrine. He regarded that doctrine as no more than a natural extension of Washington's policy and tried to put a Federalist gloss on "traditional" American foreign policy in general.[153] He knew how strong the Jeffersonian influence had been, how easily Americans had succumbed to the beliefs that a desire for peace was sufficient to prevent war and that meddling in the affairs of other nations and playing favorites among them did not necessarily entail unpleasant consequences. The Jeffersonian theory was to keep the peace at all costs and to avoid foreign entanglements. The Jeffersonian reality, as Lodge saw it, was a country vacillating in its leadership and militarily vulnerable, and yet a country engaged in a studied attempt to aid France and injure England. Consequently, Jefferson made war "the only possible result."[154]

The intensity of Lodge's feelings about Jeffersonian foreign policy can be explained in terms of the fact that for him these were still live issues. He feared a repetition of the mistakes of Jefferson almost as much as a later generation of American foreign policy "experts" were to fear a repetition of the mistakes of Munich. Jeffersonian foreign policy had a definite appeal and reflected, both Lodge and Adams thought, strong elements in the American psyche. True, it had been a grand delusion. In the post–Civil War world practically everyone could agree to that. But the Jeffersonians, if errant in their foreign-relations theory, also proved that a policy of peace coupled with "a constantly manifested detestation of England was the best way to popular support."[155] Lodge, fearing that horse might be ridden again, sensed that its riders would most likely spring from the other side of the political fence.

Lodge's own attitude toward England requires clarification. He gained a reputation, particularly among Mugwump opponents, as such a violent Anglophobe that writers representing that point of view have difficulty explaining how he came to play such a prominent role in the rapprochement between the two countries or in the move-

153. Lodge, *George Cabot*, p. 460; Lodge, *Alexander Hamilton*, p. 214; Lodge, *Studies in History*, p. 176.
154. Lodge, *George Cabot*, pp. 460, 462.
155. *Ibid.*, pp. 467–68.

ment to enlist America on the Allied side in World War I. One explanation may be that he never thought it politic to concede such a fertile field to his opponents. Hence the occasion for Henry Adams's description of Lodge as a cheap actor who "talks pure rot to order."[156] The advocacy of a policy of "standing up" to England was an effective means of appealing to Irish-American voters, and Lodge used it to that end. But he was also engaged in a rather sophisticated effort to control and channel the Anglophobia which made such a policy popular. He never indulged in the kind of attacks on British institutions and manners which were a standard feature of Jeffersonian rhetoric and in Lodge's day still an earmark of Midwestern politics. Culturally Lodge was an Anglophile. Once he had made the mandatory continental tour, his foreign travel was largely given over to England.[157] By his own account the society of which he was a part "was, aside from politics, in its standards and fashions essentially English."[158] This may help to explain his admiration for British imperialism and his great interest in rapprochement when, after 1898, it became a political possibility. Even as early as 1881 he had labeled the possibility of an Anglo-American alliance "no very extravagant hypothesis."[159]

But he was also a historian who knew a great deal about past British transgressions. His hostility to England was "traditional," a means of defining his America, and his historical writing provides good ammunition for those who would picture him a violent Anglophobe. John Morse was forever trying to get him to soften the polemics on British policy which marked his contributions to the *American Statesmen* series. Lodge believed that British policy with respect to the United States had long been stupid and unjust, but in truth he may very well have resented American vulnerability more than he resented British high-handedness. He felt, for example, that "the best way to meet her was to use against her those weapons which she herself considered to be so effective."[160] Knowing how to deal with the British was the *sine qua non* of a successful American foreign policy. Washington "had

156. Ford, ed., *Letters of Henry Adams*, II, pp. 267, 313.
157. Morse, "Henry Cabot Lodge," p. 453.
158. Lodge, *Early Memories*, p. 203.
159. Lodge, *Studies in History*, p. 88.
160. Morse, "Henry Cabot Lodge," p. 454; William Lawrence, *Henry Cabot Lodge*, pp. 13–14; Morse to Lodge, May 3, 1889, Lodge MSS.

grasped instinctively the general truth that Englishmen are prone to mistake civility for servility, and become offensive, whereas if they are treated with indifference, rebuke, or even rudeness, they are apt to be respectful and polite."[161] Webster had put an end to impressment by telling Lord Ashburton that "if you take sailors out of our vessels, we shall fight," and Seward had "convinced foreign powers of our readiness to fight, which . . . enabled us better than anything else to keep clear of actual hostilities."[162] There was nothing intrinsically wrong with the weapons of British foreign policy; the fault was to be vulnerable, to be unable or unwilling to stand up to them.

From this same source sprang his lifelong devotion to the cause of American independence. Independence was the equivalent of Americanism. It meant invulnerability and immunity from foreign influence. It meant the possibility of being "American in word, in thought, in deed, in policies" and of putting "Yankee notions and American thought" in the place of foreign ideas.[163] It was a concept somewhat defensive in character, a concept for a nation not yet so conscious of its power that independence meant only unilateralism and for a man who still feared America's inability to conduct a successful foreign policy. Lodge was often more inclined to look backward with the fears and insights of the historian rather than forward to a period of American world dominance. The lesson of the Puritan experience had been that isolation meant independence and most of American history bespoke the same message.[164] Moreover, Lodge doubted whether American power could ever be more than ephemeral. His cultivation and worship of the image of power betrayed a suspicion and fear that power could not be sustained, that Americans would not prove strong enough, either militarily or psychologically, to conduct an effective and independent (hence "American") foreign policy.

161. Lodge, *George Washington*, I, pp. 144–45.
162. Lodge, *Daniel Webster*, pp. 255–56; Lodge, *Historical and Political Essays*, p. 43.
163. Unidentified clipping giving the text of Lodge's remarks to a Republican "Ratification Meeting" in Boston, July 24(?), 1888, Scrapbooks, Lodge MSS. He was in all this but echoing the concerns of his Federalist heroes. See his *Alexander Hamilton*, pp. 258–59, where Hamilton is quoted as saying: "We are laboring hard to establish in this country principles more and more national and free from all foreign ingredients so that we may be neither Greeks nor Trojans, but truly Americans."
164. Lodge, *Boston*, pp. 101–02.

The Federalists and the Jeffersonians differed not only in their conduct of foreign policy but on basic assumptions about the behavior of nations. A favorite Jeffersonian concept was that of the basic equality of all nations. Lodge found it particularly objectionable because it explained so little about the actual workings of international relations. Long before Darwin, the Federalists had seen that the various powers were ranked according to their strength, leadership, and reputation. As Washington put it: "There is a rank due to the United States among nations, which will be withheld, if not absolutely lost, by a reputation of weakness." That rank was important, for it meant dignity, self-respect, the success of the neutrality policy, and a reduced likelihood of war.[165] Whereas for the Jeffersonians power meant little and issues between nations were matters of abstract justice, their Federalist counterparts took a more practical view and were prepared to settle for what they could get under prevailing circumstances. George Cabot had been one of the most uncompromising defenders of the Jay Treaty, taking "the ground that, defective as it was, we could rationally expect nothing more, in view of our strength as compared with that of England."[166] The belief that nations were equal and all subject to the same justice encouraged irrational and dangerous thinking about foreign policy, impeded the accommodation of differences, and made war more likely.

The other utopian and dangerous Jeffersonian postulate was the assumption that each nation in pursuit of self-interest would see the folly of war and be prepared to make its economic contribution to the betterment of all. Interest would govern actions, but interest was narrowed by definition so as to make all foreign policy moral. It had, so Lodge thought, little to do with the conceptions of interest which prevailed in the capitals of Europe and which had determined whether aid was to be extended to the rebellious American colonists.[167] Interest in the broader sense of what would serve to advance the prestige and wealth of a particular nation actually determined policy, and to mask that operation was to invite the force of Lodge's sarcasm. For a false assumption led invariably to a false, and therefore dangerous, policy. The theory of the embargo as propounded by Jefferson was

. 165. Lodge, *George Cabot*, p. 65.
166. *Ibid.*, p. 70.
167. Lodge, *Alexander Hamilton*, pp. 50–51.

wholly false, for it assumed that a great and powerful nation, mistress of the oceans, flushed with the triumphs of Nelson, struggling as she believed for her very existence, would, by a partial injury to material interests and to a fraction of her mercantile population, be constrained to make concessions to an unarmed republic acting apparently in the interests of her most deadly enemy. . . . Almost any one but Jefferson would have appreciated the hard facts of the case, and would have yielded to them; but preconceived and rooted theories are fatal to statesmanship as well as to the dictates of reason.[168]

Lodge often had recourse to Washington's dictum that "if we desire peace . . . it must be known that we are at all times ready for war."[169] Nor was preparedness always sufficient; sometimes it was even necessary to fight. It had been necessary to fight for "a national existence worth having"; in fact "all the peace that any nation, which is neither subject nor trivial, can ever have, is by readiness to fight if attacked."[170] He spoke with the voice of a militarist, but as has been recently written with reference to Henry Adams, "his seeming militarism . . . was far from simple; it grew from studious reflection on the nature and possibility of peace."[171] The same might be said for Lodge, who shared many of Adams's views. Both men repeatedly criticized Jefferson's sanguine and liberal assumptions about international relations, and Lodge could only have applauded Adams's judgment that, Jeffersonian theory notwithstanding,

in the actual state of mankind, safety and civilization could still be secured only through the power of self-defence. Desperate physical courage was the common quality on which all great races had founded their greatness; and the people of the United States, in discarding military qualities, without devoting themselves to science, were trying an experiment which could succeed only in a world of their own.[172]

Theirs was a generation who had seen the value of militarism at first hand and who had been forced, with Lincoln, to acknowledge that it was upon the progress of our arms that all else depended.[173] Far from being either a militarist or a warmonger, Lodge thought that he

---

168. Lodge, *George Cabot*, p. 474.
169. First used in 1877 in his *George Cabot*, p. 65.
170. Lodge, *One Hundred Years of Peace* (New York, 1913), p. 22; Lodge, *Fighting Frigate*, pp. 19–20.
171. J. C. Levenson, *The Mind and Art of Henry Adams* (Stanford, 1968), p. 174.
172. Adams, *History of the United States*, IV, p. 136.
173. Roosevelt and Lodge, *Hero Tales from American History*, p. 288.

had a prescription for peace, a prescription based on careful study of the behavior of nations and of past American mistakes. "Weakness, fear, and defencelessness mean war and dishonor. Readiness, preparation, and courage mean honor and peace." Those who cried peace when there was no peace and never could be perfect peace were the greatest enemies of peace and Lodge's *bête noire*. Relating the story of how John Quincy Adams, whom he greatly admired, had once warned Stratford Canning that America was now capable of going to war with England more quickly than before, Lodge judged Adams to have been

entirely right in his attitude toward England, and in reality the best friend and maintainer of peace. Jefferson and Madison were hesitating and timid. They swallowed insult in the interests of peace and landed us in war. . . . John Quincy Adams and Andrew Jackson after him took a strong and self-respecting tone with all the world and kept an unbroken peace.[174]

It all went back to the Federalist formula for commanding respect. If a nation forfeited that respect by neglecting its preparations and pursuing a servile policy, it invited depredations. War was then the only means of regaining respect and international stature. The War of 1812 had been necessary to establish and secure respect for American nationality, but that was only because "the crazy policy" of Jefferson had brought the country to such a pass.[175]

In the words of his Democratic colleague, Senator David Walsh, Lodge was a statesman because he knew "the rocks on which nations have been shattered, and he steered his course far away."[176] But he was also susceptible to falling under the spell of history, to meriting the charge that "he lived in the past, when the impulse of the age was towards the future."[177] For a man living in a rapidly changing world and seeking personal identity and meaning in history that danger was particularly manifest. Rapid change made the preservation of the ideals and traditions which bound the United States together and protected it seem especially important. But the difficulty was in knowing what needed to be preserved and what might be given up in an effort to

174. Lodge, *Fighting Frigate*, pp. 18, 20.
175. Lodge, *George Cabot*, p. 316; Lodge, *Fighting Frigate*, p. 4.
176. Massachusetts Executive Department, *A Memorial to Henry Cabot Lodge* (Boston, 1932), p. 38.
177. This was William Ellery Channing's judgment of George Cabot (Lodge, *Early Memories*, p. 12).

meet new conditions. Lodge was never possessed of more than half the necessary equation, but was inclined to feel that he had it all within his command. The lessons of history can seem so obvious and appear so imperative as to render all other knowledge superfluous.

Chapter Two

A Place to Stand

Henry Cabot Lodge became one of "the most perfervid" exponents of militant American nationalism and also one of the most adamant partisans ever to grace the halls of Congress.[1] In neither case was the posture necessarily a natural one for a Brahmin like Lodge who tended to measure the rest of the nation by the standards of Boston and find it wanting and who was never really at home with either the Yahoo spirit of American nationalism or with the businessmen who played such a prominent role in national Republican politics.[2] Neither his Americanism nor his Republicanism were of that naive variety so common to his contemporaries. Rather they were the product of conscious commitment—the means of resolving a personal dilemma—and the more unshakeable for their being so.

Lodge was a man whose nature and upbringing disposed him to be out of step with his times. He cherished values and standards which were passing into desuetude if not being openly challenged. As John Morse put it: "The trouble with Lodge was that he was a gentleman and could not conceal the fact."[3] He never understood the new type of American being bred in the West and in the great Northern cities; Boston remained the Hub of the Universe and New England the

1. Josephson, *The President Makers*, p. 71.
2. Lodge, *Certain Accepted Heroes*, p. 96.
3. "Henry Cabot Lodge," p. 452. H. L. Mencken made much the same observation. See Alistair Cooke, ed., *The Vintage Mencken* (New York, 1961), pp. 80–83.

apex of American civilization and the cradle of American nationality.[4]

Whereas the social and political power of the Brahmin aristocracy had once been taken for granted, in the Gilded Age Massachusetts society was in a state of flux and no one's position was any longer secure. Lodge's class and race stood in apparent danger of displacement. Where he thought there had once been unity and a homogeneous society, there was now only chaos.[5] As Henry Adams later explained: "nowhere in America was society so complex or change so rapid" as in Massachusetts. Industrialization and immigration brought new values and interests, and as a result New England standards had become "scarcely reconcilable with each other, and constantly multiplying in number, until balance between them threatened to become impossible."[6] As a young man just out of Harvard College Lodge was already worried about social cohesion and apprehensive about "the conflict with Rome [the Catholic Church] which must come in America."[7]

Massachusetts had become so diverse that "no one could represent it faithfully as a whole" any longer and no one had a mandate to try. Lodge's standing, once he entered political life, was by Adams's reckoning always "highly insecure."[8] This personal insecurity was but a facet of the insecurity of Lodge's Boston in its national relations and of his class and race within its confines. Everywhere he looked things were no longer ordered as they once had been. He wanted to turn the clock back to the emotional security of his childhood, to the time when the preeminent position of his kind of people had been readily acknowledged and when the virtues of Protestantism, republicanism, nationalism, and the Anglo-Saxon way of doing things were taken for granted. "Society," as he first remembered it, "was based on the old families," defined by Doctor Holmes in the "Autocrat" as "the families which held high position in the colony, the province, and during the Revolution and the early decades of the United States." He lived to see many people of this sort "pushed out of sight, if not actually driven against the conventional wall" and regretted it deeply.[9] The Boston of

4. Paraphrase of an excerpt from the London *Outlook* in *The Living Age* 323 (Dec. 20, 1924): 633.

5. Lodge, *Short History*, pp. 407–08.

6. *The Education*, p. 419.

7. Lodge to his father-in-law, Admiral Davis, March 24, 1872, Lodge MSS.

8. *The Education*, p. 419.

9. Lodge, *Early Memories*, pp. 208–09.

his youth was the only Boston he could describe movingly. He wanted to preserve as much of that society as possible and to that end was willing to make his accommodation with change and yet never quite sure how to proceed. His determination to live the life of his time, to breathe in "the spirit which puts . . . [men] in sympathy with their country and their time," betrayed the fact that he often found it difficult to do so.[10] He was ill at ease, a man looking for a place to stand, and yet a man intelligent enough to see that the footing was everywhere treacherous. Adams, perceptive as ever, caught this side of Lodge as has no one else:

> . . . he could never feel perfectly at ease whatever leg he stood on, but shifted, sometimes with painful strain of temper, from one sensitive muscle to another, uncertain whether to pose as an uncompromising Yankee; or a pure American; or a patriot in the still purer atmosphere of Irish, Germans, or Jews; or a scholar and historian of Harvard College. . . . standing first on the social, then on the political foot; now worshipping, now banning; shocked by the wanton display of immorality, but practising the license of political usage; sometimes bitter, often genial, always intelligent—Lodge had the singular merit of interesting.[11]

Politics would help determine how much of Henry Cabot Lodge's world could be preserved. If, as has been alleged, Lodge "carried into his national politics the remnants of a political belief that America had passed irrevocably away from him," he entered politics in the first place for the same reasons he had turned to history, as a means of arresting that passing and preserving the standards of his culture and class.[12] He never had an easy time of it. In the "rough and tumble" of late nineteenth century American politics his background was not the asset it once had been and later again became.[13] The Brahmin with his high-

10. Lodge, *Certain Accepted Heroes*, p. 185. Lodge was addicted to this phrase. It was an important landmark on the path which led him from the alienation and pessimism of Henry Adams to at least partial acceptance of the new America which his friend Roosevelt embraced so avidly. Living the life of their time was the "supreme test" to "all men who are real" (*Frontier Town*, p. 11).

11. *The Education*, p. 420.

12. Arthur Fell Low, "Living American Statesmen: Henry Cabot Lodge," *The Forum* 65 (March 1921): 270.

13. John Garraty once observed (*Lodge*, p. 61) that "it would be difficult to conceive of anyone seeking political office under greater disadvantages than did Henry Cabot Lodge in 1879," and the standard interpretation has long been that it was in those days no easy matter to pass from Harvard College to the United States Senate. Actually "gentlemen" have never been entirely out of fashion in the United States, and an old and widely recognized family name has usually been

pitched, nasal intonation and aristocratic bearing ('Lah-de-dah' Lodge, the 'silver spoon young man' who 'parted his hair and his name in the middle') found little initial rapport with the shoe factory operatives of Lynn.[14] He was very uncomfortable at first, but that only made him the more determined to establish his mastery of the situation.

Much could be accomplished by means of organization, and Lodge devoted himself to the mechanics of politics as have few politicians of his station.[15] The Irish could sometimes be won over by "twisting the British lion's tail." Senator George Frisbie Hoar had early warned Lodge to look to the Canadians and Irish: "Unless we can break this compact foreign vote, we are gone, and the grand chapter of the old Massachusetts history is closed."[16] Lodge took the admonition to heart; "the old Massachusetts history" was his very life. He was fascinated with the theater and in time became a consummate political actor (Henry Adams thought the French adjective "cabotin" particularly appropriate), learning to appear at ease in roles often distasteful to him.[17] But this produced only tactical advantage. The problem remained that of effecting a reintegration of Massachusetts society and securing a place in American life for the standards of Lodge's class, of giving Lodge a place where he might confidently stand. Even in the formulation of the problem there appeared to be a considerable degree of identity between the needs of the country and what for Lodge would be the solution to a personal problem.

Lodge needed to break little new ground. The intellectual tools for forging a solution to his, and what he considered the nation's, identity crisis were ready at hand. The atomistic, libertarian ideas which had dominated the prewar era were now generally held in opprobrium.

---

an asset in American politics. Least of all were the gentry displaced in Massachusetts. As Stow Persons has pointed out (*The Decline of American Gentility* [New York, 1973], p. 134), of Massachusetts' thirty-one governors in the nineteenth century all but two were identified with the gentry. Twenty-four were college graduates and fourteen Harvard alumni. In the last two decades of the century, every Massachusetts governor was a college graduate and all but one attended Harvard. Moreover, all but four of Massachusetts' twenty-seven nineteenth-century U.S. Senators were college graduates.

14. Garraty, *Lodge*, p. 61.

15. Anyone who doubts that he was a skilled and thorough political organizer need only read the vast correspondence by means of which he organized all of the campaigns in which he was involved.

16. Hoar to Lodge, March 18, 1883, Lodge MSS.

17. Garraty, *Lodge*, pp. 11–12; Ford, ed., *Letters of Henry Adams*, II, p. 267.

To say that Lodge came to give his deepest loyalty to his party and to the institutions of government rather than to ideas is but to trace the impact of the war experience on the thinking of New England.[18] The war brought home the singular importance of the growth and cultivation of national sentiment that had characterized the period 1815–1860. Webster's shortcomings shrank, as did Hamilton's, before the fact that he stood as "the preeminent champion and exponent of nationality." Nothing had ever mattered more. "When the hour came, it was love for the Union and the sentiment of nationality which nerved the arm of the North and sustained her courage."[19] The defense of institutions was the essence of the Northern cause, and even someone like Emerson, whose prewar thinking was primarily transcendental, developed a new respect for the practical man and began to look to the state as the source and guardian of the blessings of civilization.[20] Civilization was no longer an individual quest but a collective enterprise whose fortune was now closely allied with government and politics. The period of Lodge's education was coterminous with this profound shift in the intellectual climate of New England. Lodge embraced this new wisdom and tied his hopes for the future to the "doctrine of institutions." In the atmosphere in which he grew to maturity only the contrary would have been noteworthy. When during the electoral crisis of 1876 he told Carl Schurz that he cared "very little for either candidate and a great deal for my country and its institutions," he spoke with the voice of a whole generation.[21]

It is easy to account for the general trend of his thinking, but it is more difficult to account for the intensity of his nationalism and Republicanism. Lodge took the intellectual inheritance of his generation and carried it to extremes. Why? The answer, which probably lies in that area of human motivation where intellectual conviction, personal need, and political opportunity converge and point to the same solution, is difficult to plumb. Lodge had a profound sense of dispossession, and felt that the country was being lost to those of his class and outlook

18. Claude M. Fuess, "Carl Schurz, Henry Cabot Lodge and the Campaign of 1884: A Study in Temperament and Political Philosophy," *New England Quarterly* 5 (July 1932): 478.

19. Lodge, *Daniel Webster*, pp. 361–62.

20. Fredrickson, *The Inner Civil War*, pp. 176–77.

21. Fuess, "Carl Schurz, Henry Cabot Lodge and the Campaign of 1884," p. 461.

who had played such a prominent role in its creation and had only recently come to its rescue. The country was adrift and seemed to disdain what had once been its anchor and strength. As a result Lodge was also adrift. He needed a place where he could stand with assurance and confidence. He envied the British aristocracy, men who had a country and had the satisfaction of knowing that the country was theirs.[22] As Ferdinand Mount has argued: "the association between nationalism and dispossession has always been close"; "nationalism is always in one way or another a search for home."[23] Lodge felt that America was turning away from him and his class. He sensed the danger of becoming an exile in his own country and determined to fight for what he considered rightfully his. The nation might still be saved (both in fact and for Lodge's people) if it could be induced to value the traditions and standards which had made it great. One means to this end was the rewriting of American history, but the crucial arena was the political one.[24]

Lodge entered politics laboring under the disadvantages of an aristocratic image and a reputation (acquired under Adams's tutelage) as a fickle independent. He worked hard at shedding both, and one way of viewing his intense nationalism and Republicanism is as a case of overcompensation. His nationalism was a means of divesting himself of his aristocratic image. It worked for Lodge in real life just as it had worked in his historical rehabilitation of Hamilton. As Robert Grant perceived, Lodge's personal political success was largely due to his nationalist and patriotic image; it enabled him to bridge the social gap and arouse the enthusiasm of the rank and file on the stump.[25] And just as his reputa-

22. Lodge's assessment of Charles Eliot Norton was: "Poor soul; he thinks he is a cosmopolitan and a cultivated person and after all he is only an educated colonist standing in pathetic wonder at men who have a country" (Lodge to Roosevelt, Oct. 27, 1897, Theodore Roosevelt Papers, Library of Congress [hereafter cited as Roosevelt MSS]).

23. "The Sense of Dispossession," *Encounter* (Dec. 1972): 11.

24. Wallace Evans Davies describes how on the national scale these growing social and economic tensions tended to foster a cult of the Constitution and a type of patriotism that placed great emphasis on the country's history; as traditional norms and values disintegrated and cohesive symbols became ever fewer, many turned to patriotism "as a sort of secular religion to unite the American republic" (*Patriotism on Parade* [Cambridge, Mass., 1955], pp. 215–16). Davies sees this spirit of "organic nationalism" beginning to grow in the wake of the Civil War, and I would suggest that the feelings which swept the nation in the 1890s may have been nurtured in Boston a little earlier.

25. Robert Grant, "Lodge," A Commemorative Tribute Prepared for the American Academy of Arts and Letters, 1926, pp. 42–43.

tion as an uncompromising nationalist increased his own political capital so too did his reputation as a party man. He did not shrink from the mechanics of politics and served effectively as Republican state chairman before running for higher office. He winced under the scorn with which Midwestern regulars treated Eastern reformers at both the 1880 and 1884 Republican National Conventions.[26] Independence was a luxury for someone who had to work so hard to belong, and his decision to support Blaine in 1884 may not even have been particularly difficult. In order for a Cabot Lodge to make his way in the American politics of the 1880s certain postures were a necessity.

But Lodge did more than make a virtue of necessity. He entered politics with a purpose—that of reclaiming America, of effecting a reintegration of American society in such a manner that there would continue to be a role for an aristocracy of service. And if his perfervid nationalism and partisanship were a means of personal advancement, he also regarded them as a way of restoring national cohesion. The great institutions of American public life, the national government and the majority party, were, if only they could be made to realize it, the repositories of that tradition of which Lodge needed to feel a part. He thought he knew his America—knew what had made it a success— and would infuse its institutions with the proper spirit.

For Lodge the wisdom of the Federalists was so manifest that it was to be expected that he would attempt to portray the party of his choice and upbringing, the Republican, as the legatee of the Federalists. The fact that many of his Republican colleagues were oblivious to this part of their heritage only enhanced the attractiveness of an attempt to draw Federalism, Whiggery, and Republicanism together within the framework of a single and continuing intellectual tradition. This synthesis offered both a means of reminding the Republican party of what it was and of moving it in the direction in which Lodge wanted it to go. The proposition was the more compelling because his familial political heritage led him in the same direction. Party affiliation was a matter of inheritance in the Lodge family, as Lodge's grandson and namesake has attested.[27] When Lodge entered politics for the second time he determined to act "with the party to which I and my people had always

---

26. Joseph B. Foraker, *Notes of a Busy Life* (Cincinnati, 1916), I, pp. 161, 167.
27. Henry Cabot Lodge, *The Storm Has Many Eyes: A Personal Narrative* (New York, 1973), p. 27.

belonged," and "from the foundation of the government" his people had been Federalists and Whigs.[28] Successive generations of his own family were friends and followers of Hamilton and Webster and Sumner, and he had been "brought up in the doctrines and beliefs of the great Federalist, the great Whig, and the great Republican."[29]

It was not just that he regarded the Republicans as the successors of the Federalists and the Whigs. He went far beyond that in believing that "the party which at different times has borne these three names has been . . . in its essential characteristics and qualities, the same party."[30] There was, he felt, "a great persistence of inherited traits in political parties as well as in men."[31] He decried the theory that political parties in the United States could be started from scratch on wholly new lines; there were "few things more permanent than party division under representative government." To his way of thinking there was an almost natural division of human society into parties; party divisions were more than temporary divisions based on economic interest. They rested in the final analysis on differences which were "inherent in human nature."[32]

The task he set for himself was no small order. Even he recognized that the Republican party in which he rose to prominence was no longer the Republican party of "human rights statesmen like Sumner and Hoar."[33] The complexity of history was against him. In an age of great social change, Lodge sought continuity in an unlikely place, in the principles and postures of America's two great political parties. The effort alone is revealing. It throws considerable light on his own attachment to party, an attachment so great that he, like his great-grandfather Cabot, probably feared party division and disruption above all else.[34] A "practi-

28. A notation in Lodge's hand (definitely added later) on the back of a copy of "The Independents in the Coming Canvas," a letter from Lodge published in *The Nation* of Sept. 25, 1879, Lodge MSS.

29. Lodge, *The Democracy of the Constitution*, p. 160.

30. Lodge, "The Opportunity of the Republican Party," *Harper's Weekly* 38 (Feb. 17, 1894): 150.

31. Boston *Herald*, August 20, 1916.

32. Lodge, "Outlook and Duty of the Republican Party," *The Forum* 15 (April 1893): 250; Lodge, *Historical and Political Essays*, pp. 26–27.

33. Lodge, *Frontier Town*, p. 188.

34. Lodge, *George Cabot*, p. 212. Many historians have accepted the Mugwump view that Lodge betrayed his principles in 1884 when he supported Blaine and accepted the regular Republican nomination for Congress. However, his Mugwump friends were scarcely justified in their expression of surprise at his actions. There are a considerable number of favorable references to party, to the value

cal and sensible party" was a tender plant in America and, as Lodge well knew, all previous attempts to establish such a party on a permanent basis had failed. History's lesson was that the current Republican and Democratic parties were not free agents. They were bound (happily so in Lodge's opinion) by their constituencies and traditions. His own partisanship throve on this identification of his immediate political opponents with those whom he regarded as the villains and pariahs of American history. It made his own position the more comfortable and righteous.

Personally he needed to believe in this continuity, and so believing, strove to impress its logic on others. Constituency was especially important and in Lodge's view had changed little since the days of Jefferson and Jackson.

It is too often forgotten that the composition of parties is quite as important as their principles. The main strength of the Democratic party is in the South, and in the lower wards of our great Northern cities. Out of that combination we may get reaction but we cannot get sound legislation and good administration, even if the compound is sugar-coated with a small number of very estimable and well-educated people in the North, who feel that they have a monopoly of the virtue and intelligence of the country.[35]

A second distinction between the parties, and the one with which Lodge had perhaps the least success, derived from their relationship to progress. The Democratic party was at times reactionary, at times radical, but never truly liberal and progressive in Lodge's Whiggish sense of the word.[36] Only out of the Republican party, as out of its antecedents, could you get constructive legislation and progress.[37] It understood the nature of man and knew how to effect a union of the practical

---

of party unity, and to the need for the individual to sometimes subject himself to his party in both Lodge's *George Cabot* and *Alexander Hamilton*. But certainly no one who read his article on William Seward (published before the Republican National Convention in *The Atlantic Monthly* of May, 1884) could have had any real doubts as to his course of action. It was one long encomium to party regularity and clearly befitted his position as Republican State Chairman.

35. Lodge, "The Opportunity of the Republican Party," p. 150; see also Lodge, "The Results of Democratic Victory," *North American Review* 159 (Sept. 1894): 268. He said essentially the same thing to Carl Schurz in a letter of July 14, 1884 (Lodge MSS): "Despite the nomination of Blaine I firmly believe that to the masses of the Republican party we must look for progress and reform in public affairs."

36. See, for example, his speech to the Boston Young Men's Republican Club, Nov. 1, 1889, unidentified clipping, Scrapbooks, Lodge MSS.

37. Lodge to Edward Whiting, August 1, 1923, Lodge MSS.

and the ideal. The American equivalent of the English Liberals, it was "the party of freedom, of human rights, of reform and progress."[38] It alone had "always stood for all the measures making for the progress and upbuilding of the nation." The Federalist party had been the party of progress, and

> it was the party of progress that fought slavery standing across the pathway of modern civilization, just as it had formed the Constitution, while the party of conservatism clung to slavery as in the earlier days it had clung to the ideas and habits of the old Confederation.[39]

The "outlook" of the Republican party was especially good because its opposition was so obviously burdened by its unprogressive constituency and its "un-American" past. But to win, and here Lodge was wielding a two-edged sword, it had to perform its "duty"—which was but another way of saying that it had to be true to its traditions.

In the McKinley years it became more difficult to sustain the party's progressive image, but Lodge never entirely surrendered it to the Democrats. It was not until the 1920s that Lodge freely applied the term "conservative" to the Republican party and even then he did not concede that the opposition was "liberal," but insisted that it was "radical."[40] During the Roosevelt years there was again some basis in fact for this progressive association. Even though Lodge was uncomfortable with the self-styled progressives of that era and with liberal reformers in general, he supported most of TR's measures. He regarded Roosevelt's program, as did Roosevelt himself, as essentially a Hamiltonian or Bismarckian one, the institution of social and economic change to make the nation stronger. That was tangible progress in the best "American" and "Republican" tradition.

A third characteristic of the major parties was foreshadowed in Lodge's view of progress. It involved the degree of their respective devotion to the cause of American nationalism and was the distinction to which he had most frequent resort. More was involved here than simple flag waving. Behind Lodge's attempt to appropriate the adjectives "national" and "American" for the exclusive use of the Republican party lay a well-conceived plan to affect the public attitude on a whole range of issues which Lodge had at heart. He often dealt only in gen-

38. Schriftgiesser, *The Gentleman from Massachusetts*, p. 69.
39. Lodge, "Outlook and Duty of the Republican Party," pp. 251–52, 258.
40. Lodge to Edward Whiting, August 1, 1923, Lodge MSS.

eralities and liked to speak of the Republican party's "fidelity to American policies," and of its opportunity to give to the country once more "a foreign policy which shall be both dignified and American."[41] He also went to considerable lengths to establish the fact that the Federalists were "the first American party," and to tar the Democrats with the disloyalty of secession and the introduction of foreign influence into American politics.[42] In Lynn during the fateful campaign of 1884 he put it all together. In public confession of his political faith he claimed that

the policy of the Republican party is a national and American one, and as I would have been a federalist or a whig, so am I now a republican, because I find running through all the history of the party the thread of protection to national and American interests.[43]

Concealed under the rubric of devotion to national and American interests were considered opinions on a whole range of crucial questions of domestic and foreign policy which, taken together, constitute a Lodgian version and update of Henry Clay's American System or of Daniel Webster's "National Conservatism." Encompassed therein were views on the distribution of power between the state and federal governments, on defense and foreign policy, and on matters as seemingly disparate as the tariff and immigration restriction. These were tied together by a philosophy of government and politics that was distinctly Hamiltonian and neither inherently reactionary nor inherently progressive.

The touchstone was in every case a regard for what Lodge believed would advance the national interest. His conception of the national interest, however, was considerably broader than that now normally employed by international relations specialists, who use it primarily to refer to the advancement of the interests of the United States *vis-à-vis* those of other nations. Lodge never attempted to define the term; he used it naturally and unselfconsciously. His notion seems to have

41. Lodge, "Outlook and Duty of the Republican Party," p. 258; Lodge, "The Opportunity of the Republican Party," p. 151.

42. Lodge, *Historical and Political Essays*, p. 62; Lodge, *George Cabot*, p. 62; Lodge, *George Washington*, II, pp. 268–69.

43. Boston *Advertiser*, Oct. 24, 1884, p. 8. The two, "Americanism and Republicanism," were seen as so complementary that there was nothing the least selfconscious about Roosevelt's expression of delight to Lodge at finding that his sister Bamie was "just as strongly American and Republican as ever" (*Correspondence of Roosevelt and Lodge*, I, p. 135).

been most closely akin to the traditional concept of the public interest. His conception was inclusive and, being firmly rooted in the American historical experience, did not require the rejection of moral standards.

Lodge liked to claim that the "consolidation" of the United States was the most important event of the nineteenth century.[44] To achieve consolidation it had been necessary to take a strong stand against several nations who wished to prevent it. Consolidation had been effected only by an effort to strengthen the national government at the expense of the states and by the pursuit of policies designed to promote a sense of American nationality. Domestic cohesion was as important as a strong foreign policy and, indeed, the latter could not possibly succeed in the absence of the former. It was impossible to draw any distinct line between domestic and foreign policy. Webster's celebrated Huelsemann letter had a twofold purpose: "One was to awaken the people of Europe to a sense of the greatness of this country, the other to touch the national pride at home."[45] Unity and cohesion at home could sometimes be strengthened by a foreign policy initiative and that cohesion could in turn give additional force to the initiative. Though Lodge shied away from open admission that Webster's "National Conservatism" had been dependent on foreign policy successes, he was certainly aware that foreign policy issues could serve to foster both American nationalism and the political fortunes of domestic conservatism.[46] So viewed, the relationship between domestic and foreign policy was one of considerable complexity, and it should not be surprising that Lodge looked with some suspicion upon the "trained" diplomatist, the foreign policy expert of his day.[47] It was obvious that the historian and the politician also needed to be consulted in matters of national interest.

44. Lodge, *Frontier Town*, p. 179; Lodge to James Ford Rhodes, Dec. 20, 1904, James Ford Rhodes Papers, Massachusetts Historical Society; "A Record of the Dedication of the Monument on Dorchester Heights" (1902), p. 51, Massachusetts Historical Society.

45. Lodge, *Daniel Webster*, p. 334.

46. Webster, however, had to strike a delicate balance, and this Lodge may also have appreciated. He interfered in European affairs on those issues likely to solidify support at home, but proclaimed a policy of noninterference and in practice avoided interference when he thought it likely to have dangerous repercussions. The formula was noninterference except through influence on world opinion in cases where it was "the national destiny" of the United States to lead that opinion (Lodge, *Daniel Webster*, pp. 133–34). Translated into practice, that meant retaining moral leadership but affronting only those European powers who were not naval powers and could not harm the United States.

47. Lodge, *Early Memories*, p. 34.

Webster had always preached "the grandeur of American nationality" and "fidelity to the Constitution" as a bulwark of that nationality.[48] Lodge never saw reason to vary the theme. If, like Webster, he was subject to the charge of being a little too flexible politically, he had his own rudder always clearly in view. He cared as little for "the issues" as had Webster, and when he spoke of Webster it was often as if he were speaking of himself. While dedicating a statue to Webster in 1900 he offered the following insight:

Belief in the Union and the Constitution, because they meant national greatness and national life, was the great dominant conviction of Webster's life. . . . So he admired great states and empires, and had little faith in small ones, or in the happiness or worth of a nation which has no history and which fears its fate too much to put its fortunes to the touch when the accepted time has come.[49]

All that supported "national greatness and national life" could be assured of Lodge's adherence and backing; any policy which might denigrate that "greatness or life" would meet with his implacable opposition. It was the attitude of a Hamilton or a Bismarck. Neither the promotion of industrialism nor the institution of social programs was an end in itself. This was what set Lodge apart from both conservative businessmen and liberal reformers.

Lodge thought of himself as a custodian of the national interest. This attitude came readily to the descendants of America's colonial aristocracy and to those of families whose fortunes were preindustrial in origin. Like his friend Theodore, Lodge believed that his position in the American social and economic structure and his knowledge of American history gave him a unique ability to transcend class and personal interests and to perceive and act upon the interest of the nation as a whole. One can be skeptical about their ability to do so, without necessarily disparaging the effort. Still the very idea was conducive to a preemptive and self-righteous belief in one's own virtue and vision. As a reviewer of Lodge's *Certain Accepted Heroes* noted: "He evidently in his own mind personifies his country as himself; . . . Whenever he wished to tell us what America thinks, he tells us what he

48. Lodge, *Daniel Webster*, p. 22.
49. Lodge, *Fighting Frigate*, p. 132.

thinks himself; the 'true American' is really no other than the author; . . . [And] if he is right, the future of the western half of the world is bound up in his own."[50] There were times when Lodge thought that it was. It was easy to believe that he stood for what was best in and for America—even that he embodied the "true American" spirit.

Lodge had the racial and economic prejudices of his class, and there is truth in Edward Saveth's assertion that "Lodge the politician must have made Lodge the historian squirm."[51] According to Saveth, "the price of a political career for Henry Cabot Lodge was . . . a two-fold compromise: with the industrial capitalists and with the rapidly growing Irish element."[52] But Saveth overstates the case; more than political opportunism was involved. Both industrialism and Irish immigration were facts of American life and Lodge was disposed to accept what he could not change. But perhaps more important in each case was his conception of himself as a custodian of the "national interest" and his concern to promote national strength and cohesion. Too optimistic to be a reactionary (America *was* after all growing stronger), and too national to cut himself off from the mainstream of American developments, Lodge came to his compromises intellectually as well as politically. The year 1884 may stand as a symbol of seduction, of the corruption of the scholar by politics, but it was scarcely a case of rape. Lodge the scholar was not converted into a politician overnight, and one may legitimately doubt whether it was a "high-level intellectual tragedy."[53] Lodge the politician was scarcely more nationalistic than Lodge the historian. Politics and the Whiggish nature of his nationalism both dictated compromise and accommodation. And politics, far from being a corrupting influence, may even have moderated his views on some subjects. If for political reasons he was forced to swallow the high tariff, the same considerations "liberalized" his views on race and saved him from the intellectual eccentricities of the Adamses.

His views on the tariff and immigration restriction are not intelligible apart from his conception of the "national interest." To Lodge immigration restriction was an integral part of any intelligent protec-

50. *The Nation* 65 (Nov. 4, 1897): 360.
51. *American Historians and European Immigrants*, p. 58.
52. *Ibid.*, p. 54.
53. John P. Mallan, review of John Garraty's *Henry Cabot Lodge*, in *New England Quarterly* 26 (Dec. 1953): 553.

tive policy, and protection transcended the interests of individual manufacturers and had a national purpose.[54] The measure of a policy was whether it served to strengthen the United States, whether it facilitated the fulfillment of its historical mission.

To the Mugwumps his greatest apostasy, next to supporting Blaine, was the abandonment of the free-trade convictions of his youth. When he graduated from college he was a free-trader.[55] But he never endowed free trade with the moral qualities his Mugwump friends attributed to it. In 1876 he thought the question "still an open one" and probably sympathized with his great-grandfather, who was "convinced of the soundness of free-trade doctrines, and assented to but a very moderate use of protection."[56] But by the fateful year of 1884 he was willing to excuse Webster's inconsistency on protection and see his reversal of opinion in response to changed conditions as proof of his wisdom. He also came down heavily in favor of Disraeli's declaration that free trade was 'a mere question of expediency.'[57] Interestingly, the free-traders' favorite argument, the idea that it would be conducive to peace, never had the slightest effect on Lodge; he already knew where the path to peace was to be found.

What changed his mind on the tariff? Certainly his embarking on a political career within the Republican party had a lot to do with it. But Lodge's own explanation also deserves consideration. He always claimed that his conversion to protection dated from his study of Hamilton's Report on Manufactures.[58] Hamilton's principal argument was that it was necessary to nurture the manufacturing interest in order to uphold national independence and cease dependency on Europe. This identification of protection with the cause of American nationalism undoubtedly had a great appeal for Lodge, and he may (like Webster before him) have found in Hamiltonianism a means of reconciling himself to industrial capitalism. Industrial capitalism was not originally an end in itself; it was at first only a means of promoting

54. Lodge to William Warland Clapp, Dec. 4, 1890, Houghton Library, Harvard University.
55. Lodge to the Rev. Henry Blanchard, Nov. 24, 1886, Lodge MSS.
56. Lodge, *George Cabot*, p. 564.
57. Lodge, *Daniel Webster*, pp. 168–69.
58. Lodge to the Rev. Henry Blanchard, Nov. 24, 1886, Lodge MSS; Lodge to the Boston *Advertiser*, Oct. 18, [1888?], Scrapbooks, Lodge MSS.

American power and became an end only gradually as it became inseparable from the national historical experience. Lodge's own argument for the tariff was always Hamiltonian. Protection kept up wages and therefore promoted domestic cohesion. It also served to make the United States independent of other countries and hence acted as a bulwark to the American way of life. Above all it was an important feature of the whole Federalist approach to the organization of society and government.

Protection and free trade . . . [were] merely expressions in one direction of the differing theories of society and government which have been struggling for recognition and acceptance during this century . . . the theory that state interference is always and necessarily a wholly bad thing . . . [and the theory that] it is possible to use the united power of the community expressed in the state for the benefit of mankind and the protection of civilization.[59]

He also came to advocate immigration restriction out of concern for the political and social cohesion of the American nation. As an advocate of civil rights for Negroes and cosponsor of the "Force Bill" of 1890–91, he was in a position to stress that "we have now before us race problems which are sufficient to tax to the utmost the fortunate conditions with which nature has blessed us and the highest wisdom of which our public men are capable."[60] He wanted America to be strong, and yet he saw social disorder where he thought there had once been stability.[61] Like many Americans he projected his fears for social stability onto the immigrant.[62] A believer in the importance of race, he viewed American institutions as but a function of the characteristics of the English-speaking people. Good government did not just happen; Irishmen were not Englishmen.

Legislation may ameliorate or injure a nation very greatly. War, conquest, and religious strife may leave lasting traces, but none of them singly, nor all together, have thus far succeeded in obliterating or creating great national

59. Lodge, *Speeches and Addresses*, pp. 87, 96, 111–12, *et passim*.
60. *Cong. Record*, 51st Cong., 2nd sess., p. 2956.
61. See especially the loud paeans to the community of race and class which supposedly existed in colonial New England in Lodge's *Short History*, pp. 407–08, 475.
62. John Higham, "Origins of Immigration Restriction, 1882–1897: A Social Analysis," *Mississippi Valley Historical Review* 39 (June 1952): 85.

characteristics. There are some qualities which are inherent in races from the time when they emerge into the light of history.[63]

The men of each race possess an indestructible stock of ideas, traditions, sentiments, modes of thought, an unconscious inheritance from their ancestors, upon which argument has no effect. What makes a race are their mental and, above all, their moral characteristics, the slow growth and accumulation of centuries of toil and conflict. These are the qualities which determine their social efficiency as a people, which make one race rise and another fall. . . . it is on the moral qualities of the English-speaking race that our history, our victories, and all our future rest.[64]

Lodge also thought that a homogeneous people like those of the United Colonies were "peculiarly fitted to make any system of free institutions work well"[65] (like many New Englanders he was prone to ignore the racial mixture of the Middle Colonies). But if he thought it took both homogeneity and the characteristics of the English-speaking people to produce American institutions and to permit them to function, Lodge should have been a total exclusionist rather than a restrictionist. He was, however, practical rather than theoretical, a politician rather than an ideologue. The very term "English-speaking race" was an anomaly. There was no such thing. It was a convenient means of including the Irish, and political considerations dictated their inclusion. But there was more to it. His Whiggish theory of nationality was far removed from the ethnic and exclusionary nationalism which flourished on the European Continent. He was, for example, a racist who believed that Negroes should be allowed to vote and that they could be successfully incorporated within at least the political fabric of American nationalism. His theory was not so much that humanity ought to be divided into ethnically pure national states, as that people who are alike and adhere to the same basic values—who form a community of stock, language, and law—stand a better chance of making a success of representative government.[66] Unlike his Continental counterparts, he was not troubled by the territorial prerogatives of conflicting nationalisms. He was moved to action only when he thought there was "the possibility of a great and perilous change in the very fabric of

63. Lodge, "Lecky's England," p. 3.
64. Lodge, *Speeches and Addresses*, pp. 262–64.
65. Lodge, *Democracy of the Constitution*, p. 51.
66. Elie Kedourie, *Nationalism* (London, 1960), p. 132.

our race,"[67] or in other words when he believed that English cultural dominance was threatened. The fact that in 1896 he could still speak of "our race" is revealing. He was not oblivious to what had been happening; he was simply not a purist on race. Both the English language and the English race had shown themselves "capable of assimilating new elements without degeneration."[68] He believed in the possibility of assimilation and Americanization.[69] Not just politics but a concern for the strength and cohesion of the Union dictated accommodation just as they also dictated some restriction. Once a group had been sufficiently Americanized its incorporation into the American national fabric was imperative. Lodge was alternately optimistic and pessimistic about the prospects for assimilation. When the nation appeared externally strong and internally cohesive, then all was possible. His views on immigration restriction reflected like so much else his concern for, and assessment of, the health and viability of the American national experiment.

It was impossible for Lodge to accept reform for reform's sake. The national interest which an efficient government might advance and promote could at different times require what others would designate as either "reactionary" or "progressive" programs. Lodge himself never really thought in those terms. True, he was inclined to judge other governments by their "progressivity" and always hoped, for example, to live to see the "reactionary" Turkish Empire disintegrate.[70] But his "progressivity" was that of the Romantic historians who regarded the movement toward the modern national state as intrinsically one of progress. Nationalism, so viewed, was inherently progressive and like republican government an end in itself. The lesson of the American historical experience was that nationalism and progress went hand in hand. Lincoln understood this and was therefore the "true con-

67. Lodge, *Speeches and Addresses*, pp. 259–60.

68. Lodge, *Certain Accepted Heroes*, p. 97.

69. He was, for example, particularly optimistic about the bonds created by a common language. When newcomers learn the language "they inevitably absorb . . . the traditions and beliefs, the aspirations and the modes of thought, the ideals and the attitude toward life, which that language alone enshrines" (*Democracy of the Constitution*, p. 68).

70. Lodge, review of F. V. Greene's *Sketches of Army Life in Russia*, in *International Review* 9 (Dec. 1880): 720; Lodge to Moreton Frewen, May 10, 1897, Moreton Frewen Papers, Library of Congress.

servative," the best representative of conservatism in the American context.[71] The Republican party understood this and was therefore the special guardian of both.

As a result Lodge's nationalism and Republicanism both possessed an idealistic quality, and apart from this Lodge and his political philosophy are incomprehensible. The present Henry Cabot Lodge attests to having inherited his party affiliation from his grandfather and claims that in becoming a Republican he thought he "was joining something affirmative, evolutionary, and idealistic."[72] What may be problematic in the case of the grandson is more credible in the case of the grandfather. Lodge, as Adams said, was "the child of his local parentage" and he clearly bespoke his New England heritage when in his biography of Washington he reminded the nation that true national greatness was moral and intellectual and not to be found in material things.[73] Nationalism meant freedom for a people to give full expression to their character and to their abilities; it was a synonym for moral and intellectual achievement. There was no better answer to the question of what it is to be an American than Washington's. As Lodge asked rhetorically in his biography of the first President:

Is it not to have an abiding and moving faith in the future and in the destiny of America? . . . Is it not to be national and not sectional, independent and not colonial? Is it not to have a high conception of what this great new country should be, and to follow out that ideal with loyalty and truth?[74]

The protection afforded by the state made such national development possible. The state protected the national experiment in two ways. It provided a means of organizing a defense against envious powers. But it was also an agency for superintending domestic arrangements and ensuring that the interests of the community as a whole were taken into account. In both cases it was possible to imbue strong national government with idealism. Strong national government was but the institutional manifestation of practical idealism, but the means of giving effect to the large ideals and unseen goals and standards to which Americans had always given their allegiance. In the American historical context nationalism and idealism were inseparable. But as Henry May

71. Lodge, *Speeches and Addresses*, p. 448.
72. *The Storm Has Many Eyes*, p. 27.
73. Lodge, *George Washington*, II, p. 322.
74. *Ibid.*, p. 314.

has observed: "within the large, vague limits of practical idealism it was possible to be mostly practical or mostly idealistic as long as one maintained some touch with both qualities."[75] And, of course, it was easier to maintain some semblance of a balance between the two, if one could endow the state with idealistic properties, as did Lodge, and then devote oneself to its "practical" advancement.

The cultivation and preservation of the national sentiment upon which Lodge thought all else depended might require the invocation of conservative values, but his conservatism, the claims of his critics notwithstanding, was never quite that of the standpatters. Their conservatism was essentially a function of economic interest and was an aberration insofar as its advocates denied strong government. If Lodge, and most of Massachusetts with him, did not play a prominent role in the Progressives' search for social justice, it was in part because they had less to search for.[76] In Massachusetts the Puritan and Federalist tradition of strong government in the community interest had withstood the onslaughts of laissez faire democracy and was still potent enough to permit some harnessing of the radical tendencies of American capitalism.

But if nationalism in the form of strong government was a means of securing domestic cohesion and well-being, it was also a means of protecting the United States against its enemies and of securing an isolation sufficient to prevent the corruption of the American experiment by external forces. If the experiment was now a governmental rather than a religious one, the defensive psychology attendant to the Puritan conception of a City on a Hill lived on. But that same psychology was also possessed of a missionary potential if the City could acquire sufficient strength. Lodge found that strength in American nationalism as manifested in the Union. It alone made all things possible—"lasting peace," "freedom in every sense," and "wealth and prosperity" for all Americans. It also provided a means whereby America could fulfill her mission in history:

before American competition and American principles of government, the great standing armies and privileged classes must be given up or the countries of Europe will go to bankruptcy and ruin. . . . we are destroying by the gentle

---

75. *The End of American Innocence* (Chicago, 1964), p. 14.
76. Richard M. Abrams, *Conservatism in a Progressive Era: Massachusetts Politics, 1900–1912* (Cambridge, Mass., 1964), p. 14.

hand of peace and prosperity the military systems of Europe. That beneficent power comes from the Union; and think of the good which it means to humanity! . . . we have a great mission and a great work as a nation.[77]

Lodge was by temperament a traditionalist, but he was traditional about a culture which gloried in its antitraditionalism. He was a conservative forced to take refuge in a state whose historical identity derived from the Revolution and the Civil War, and was therefore "liberal" almost by definition. As a result his nationalism had a schizophrenic quality; it harbored both conservative and idealistic elements. The balance was an uneasy one and had to be adjusted periodically to fit his varying estimates of the nation's strength and capabilities. His particularistic nationalism and his missionary Americanism were, similarly, often in conflict. The dilemma, however, was hardly a new one. It was part of his New England intellectual inheritance and implicit in the very concept of a City on a Hill. The Puritans had somehow managed to combine a conservative view of man—one which emphasized his shortcomings and cast doubt on the possibility of even their own success—with a belief in an ongoing Reformation. Lodge shared all of his great-grandfather's "wisdom of experience," but could still fault him for wanting the "wisdom of hope."[78]

Lodge's hopes, however, were tied to the fortunes of the party that looked to national and American interests and which alone seemed capable of supplying truly national leadership. And just as his domestic horizons were limited by his Republicanism so were his international horizons limited by his Americanism. Given the determinations of race and history, he was seldom able to place his hopes anywhere but in the United States. He seems to have shared Washington's view that the United States was "the last great experiment for promoting human happiness by a reasonable compact in civil society."[79] Like most of his countrymen, he was subject to attacks of national euphoria, and under those conditions he thought America capable of influencing the course of world history.[80] But as a general rule he was unable to believe in

77. Lodge, "Address Before the Citizens of Nahant," Memorial Day, 1882, Massachusetts Historical Society.

78. Lodge to Roosevelt, Sept. 2, 1907, Roosevelt MSS. Lodge was reflecting the criticism of William Ellery Channing in his essay "The Union," a copy of which Lodge also sent to TR. See also Lodge's *Early Memories*, p. 12.

79. Lodge, *George Washington*, II, p. 49.

80. In *The Story of the Revolution*, for example, which was published just after

progress except in and for America and occasionally he even had his doubts about that.

Huxley said in one of his lectures, 'The world is very ignorant and very wretched, and the man who in his little corner makes less that ignorance and wretchedness does the highest work that it is given to man to do.' We may apply the same rule to nations. . . . It is our duty to maintain and advance the welfare of our own people, and by so doing we shall best serve mankind. We are concerned with the happiness and prosperity of the United States, and that is enough for us to attend to. It will be well for us if we can even secure that.[81]

Lodge found some refuge in the strength of the new America. He was quite capable of adjusting his view of its historic mission to fit its new talents and abilities. But it was never completely satisfactory to him; he could never embrace it as avidly as did Roosevelt. In truth he was able to embrace it to about the same extent that it was able to embrace him. But neither could he reject it and view it as pessimistically as did Henry Adams. After all what was the alternative? He had succeeded in wrapping his own identity and purpose in life up with the fortunes of the American experiment. He was almost "possessed with the idea of her separate and special individuality."[82] Somehow it had to be made to work. Otherwise American history had no meaning and Lodge no place to stand.

---

the Spanish-American War, he was almost carried away by a vision of the United States as the leader of a worldwide democratic movement (pp. 556–59).

81. Unidentified clipping giving an account of Lodge's speech at the Harvard Meeting in Tremont Temple, Boston, Nov. 2, 1888, Scrapbooks, Lodge MSS.

82. The London *Times* quoted in *The Living Age* 323 (Dec. 20, 1924): 633.

Chapter Three

That Cautious Firebrand

Probably no other aspect of the American experience has generated a history quite like that of American imperialism, in which preconceived notions have so often and so rigorously been imposed on a complex historical landscape. The perspective of British historians, who have reason to know something about imperialism, has at least been chastening. In his comprehensive *The Colonial Empires* (1966) D. K. Fieldhouse devotes only seven pages to American imperialism and concludes that the United States did not need colonies to shore up its economy and did not "exploit" them.[1] And A. E. Campbell considers American imperialism to have been both "hesitant and relatively insignificant."[2]

In the same vein, John A. S. Grenville and George Berkeley Young have provided a provocative interpretation of Lodge's imperialism or, more accurately, of his lack of same. They contend that Lodge was slow to grasp the importance of foreign relations and that he took a middle, pragmatic course in the debate on America's role in world affairs.[3] They do not deny that Lodge became an ardent imperialist, but insist that he did not emerge on the national scene with a full-blown imperialist philosophy. They go too far, however, when they deny what

1. *The Colonial Empires: A Comparative Survey* (London, 1966), p. 346.
2. *America Comes of Age* (New York, 1971), p. 96.
3. In this instance Karl Schriftgiesser was also quite perceptive, and I have chosen his appellation, "that cautious firebrand" (*The Gentleman from Massachusetts*, p. 152), as the title of this chapter.

Lodge's biographers have ably demonstrated, namely that his passionate concern for America's foreign relations developed gradually from childhood.[4] Lodge had distinct views on the conduct of foreign policy and had integrated them into his Hamiltonian philosophy of government long before the 1890s.

Still, as Grenville and Young contend, those views did not necessarily fit an "imperialist" mold; Lodge did not think colonies were an essential requisite of sea power, and before 1895 did not believe in the necessity of foreign markets. Grenville and Young believe "his pre–'98 views fit in much better with the definition of an isolationist."[5] There is some truth to that, but if Lodge was an imperialist in only a "special and limited sense," he was an isolationist in the same manner. His first belief was in a "vigorous" foreign policy, and his ultimate admiration was for "the strong, bold and successful."[6] His nationalism embraced the concept of an American mission, and his continentalism may have contained the seeds of his overseas imperialism.

The road from isolationism to imperialism is a long one and Lodge never needed to travel its full length. Whether one stresses his imperialism or the anti-imperialism implicit in his isolationism, it remains but part of the story. Lodge's isolationism was never more than occasional, and the American imperialism of his era was a somewhat tangential affair, especially when compared with its European counterparts. Lodge's imperialism was but a gloss on his conception of the nature of international relations and of how foreign policy ought to be conducted. There was something in his outlook which, if it predisposed him to favor an imperialist role for the United States, antedated his advocacy of that role and remained with him long after he discovered that imperialism could not be sold to the American public as a long-term policy. Imperialism was not central to his conception of a proper

4. Grenville and Young, *Politics, Strategy and American Diplomacy* (New Haven, 1966), pp. 202, 208–10, 237.

5. *Ibid.*, p. 224.

6. Boston *Transcript*, Sept. 20, 1884; *Certain Accepted Heroes*, p. 251. Lodge confirmed that foreign policy was his special milieu when he wrote with reference to his work on the subcommittee on Cuba that he had never before "been engaged in public work which interested me like this" and when he confessed that the Chairmanship of the Foreign Relations Committee was "the one place in the Senate I desire to have" (Lodge to Anna Cabot Lodge, Jan. 19, 1896, and to E. B. Hayes, Dec. 3, 1900, Lodge MSS).

foreign policy. In fact, some of the considerations which made him receptive to a policy of imperialism pointed the road back, once imperialism became a liability to his point of view.

Of Lodge's early pronouncements on foreign policy, the only one which has received much attention is the description of America's isolation in his 1889 biography of Washington:

> Our relations with foreign nations today fill but a slight place in American politics, and excite generally only a languid interest. We have separated ourselves so completely from the affairs of other people that it is difficult to realize how large a place they occupied when the government was founded.[7]

Lodge gloried in America's invulnerability to European influence and accurately depicted the prevailing state of affairs.[8] This period, which Thomas Bailey once dubbed "the nadir of diplomacy," caused Lodge himself to distinguish between foreign relations (which the United States had always had) and foreign policy (which in this period was so simple that people seemed to forget about it).[9] If there appeared to be little need for a foreign policy, there was no defense establishment worthy of the name and not even the vestiges of a military or strategic policy. Military expenditures in the 1880s were never more than four-tenths of one percent of gross national product.[10]

It is important to understand which of these conditions Lodge celebrated and which troubled him. If he reveled in America's invulnerability, that is no reason to conclude that he approved of the prevailing indifference to foreign policy. His isolationism was limited; he was a Bostonian, not a Midwesterner. He knew too much history to be indifferent to considerations of foreign policy or sanguine about military unpreparedness. If one looks carefully at his *Washington*, it becomes apparent that there was an assertive quality to his conception of America's role. This lent a special character to his isolationism. His

7. Lodge, *George Washington*, II, pp. 129–30.
8. He rejoiced in the perception that a revolution much greater than the actual French Revolution "might take place in Europe today without producing here anything at all resembling the excitement of 1790" (*Studies in History*, p. 337) and he admitted to his pleasure in thinking "how impossible it now would be to couple the United States . . . [as had Jefferson] with any foreign nation" (*Historical and Political Essays*, p. 66).
9. Thomas A. Bailey, *Diplomatic History of the American People* (New York, 1944), p. 426; Lodge, "Our Foreign Policy," *Youth's Companion*, March 1, 1906, p. 103.
10. C. Vann Woodward, "The Age of Reinterpretation," *American Historical Review* 66 (Oct. 1960): 5.

position was essentially the one Washington stated to Sir Edward Newenham:

I hope the United States of America will be able to keep disengaged from the labyrinth of European politics and wars; and that before long they will, by the adoption of a good national government, have become respectable in the eyes of the world, so that none of the maritime powers . . . shall presume to treat them with insult or contempt. . . . And it is not in the power of the proudest and most polite people on earth to prevent us from becoming a great, a respectable, and a commercial nation if we shall continue united and faithful to ourselves.[11]

It was not Lodge's intention to preach the gospel of isolationism. As he told John Morse: "I think that Washington's work in lifting the country up from 'Colonialism' to Americanism and Nationality was one of the greatest things he did, and . . . that the most useful sermon to be preached at the present day is one which would proceed with his example as a text."[12] Isolationism was but a means to a further end, the assertion of American power and the domination of a continent. Insofar as it was necessary to withdraw from European affairs to accomplish that end, well and good. But Lodge was not happy, as his Federalist heroes would not have been, with isolationism's intellectual traveling companions. Isolationism was a means of permitting the United States to realize its world role without opposition, not an end in itself. And the indifference to foreign policy and national defense which came in its wake were especially to be deplored.

In his first major public speech Lodge announced that:

We are in the very prime of life as a nation. . . . we are vigorous, powerful, rich and masters of a continent. . . .

. . . We have undertaken a gigantic task. We are making the greatest experiment in government ever attempted. We have built up an empire so great that, whether for evil or good, it is a chief factor in the affairs of civilized mankind and of the world.[13]

A well-conceived policy and attention to the nation's defenses had enabled the United States to conquer a continent and attain this position of influence. Lodge would not be responsible for their neglect. He had scarcely arrived upon the political scene when he announced in

11. Lodge, *George Washington*, II, p. 131.
12. Lodge to John T. Morse, Jr., May 6, 1889, Morse MSS.
13. Lodge, "Oration" (Boston City Council, July 4, 1879), pp. 19, 35, Massachusetts Historical Society.

favor of a larger navy and a vigorous foreign policy.[14] In the same year that he finished his *Washington* he was complaining that the public was not paying sufficient attention to the conduct of foreign affairs, and berating the Administration (Cleveland's first) for conducting a feeble, undignified, and "un-American" foreign policy.[15]

When Alfred Mahan wrote to Lodge enclosing a copy of *The Influence of Sea Power upon History,* he expressed the hope that he could "make the experience of the past influence the opinions and shape the policy of the future."[16] The argument from history was the one most likely to influence Lodge. His very approach to history established a framework for his thinking on foreign policy. Inherent in his Whiggism and historicism was a tendency to glorify the struggles which had led to present conditions and something which came close to an affirmation of might makes right. He was saved from the latter conclusion only by his conception of history as moral drama. Confident as to where the angels stood and knowing that history was struggle, he considered military power in the right hands the first requisite for peace and progress. But that did not make him a philosophical "realist" as that term is generally employed in discussions of foreign policy. His realism was anchored in his conception of the American historical experience, and hence not incompatible with a heady infusion of moralism. Was America not proof that the two might successfully be combined!

Given his racial assumptions and his conviction that the spread of republican government and of individual freedom were hallmarks of progress, it was natural that Lodge would celebrate the spread of the English-speaking race. As the English-speaking race extended over the world it carried successful government in its train.[17] And from the view that the American people had "carried civilization to the highest point it had ever touched," it was but a short step to the belief that American expansion was good for civilization.[18] As a result, it was possible for Lodge to speak in one and the same breath of the race's character "for

14. Boston *Transcript*, Sept. 20, 1884, p. 2.
15. *Cong. Record*, 50th Cong., 1st sess., 1888, p. 481; clipping dated May 9, 1888 from an unidentified Philadelphia paper, Scrapbooks, Lodge MSS.
16. Alfred Thayer Mahan to Lodge, May 19, 1890, Lodge MSS.
17. Lodge, *George Washington*, II, p. 50.
18. Lodge, "True Americanism," p. 22.

conquest, government and freedom."[19] Such attributes were reconcilable because the English-speaking race had a special "talent . . . for founding new states and governing distant provinces."[20] As a historian Lodge was already an imperialist.

Lodge's Federalist interpretation of American history also disposed him to favor a policy of national expansion and assertion. As a historian he was well aware of the Federalist leaders' visions of national greatness. He wrote of Washington repeatedly referring to the United States as "an infant empire" and of the grasp which he shared only with Hamilton of "the imperial future which stretched before the United States."[21] Gouverneur Morris's prediction that "the proudest empire in Europe is but a bauble compared to what America will be" delighted him.[22] And he was such a continentalist that he thought that Canada must inevitably become a part of the United States; it was so obviously "a case of manifest destiny."[23] These were views that he expressed in the 1880s. Consequently, it is doubtful that any "astonishing transformation" in his thinking was necessary before he embarked on a career of full-fledged imperialism.[24]

From Lodge's New England point of view, there was an even better historical argument for an assertive foreign policy and a strong national defense. Both were integral parts of his Hamiltonian conception of strong and efficient national government. Throughout his political career Lodge had two soft spots in his heart, the United States Navy and New England's fishing industry. He had barely entered the political arena when he began complaining about the abandonment of "our old and successful naval policy of always maintaining a small but highly efficient fleet, which led the world in naval architecture, in ordnance, and in equipment."[25] His first full-scale attack on the manner in which American foreign policy was being conducted was in response to what he saw as the Adminis-

19. Lodge, *Studies in History*, p. 113.
20. Lodge, *Short History*, p. 159.
21. Lodge, *George Washington*, II, p. 7.
22. Lodge, *Historical and Political Essays*, p. 113.
23. Lodge, "The Fisheries Question," *North American Review* 146 (Feb. 1888): 130.
24. Grenville and Young, *Politics, Strategy and American Diplomacy*, p. 208.
25. Lodge, "Naval Courts-Martial and the Pardoning Power," *Atlantic Monthly* 50 (July 1882): 44.

tration's failure to stand up for the rights of New England's fishermen.[26] These matters had also been of special concern to the Federalists. As Lodge explained in his biography of his great-grandfather:

. . . Mr. Cabot's bill for the encouragement of the fisheries . . . [was] a part of Hamilton's general scheme. The pecuniary value of the fisheries was enhanced by their importance as a nursery for seamen, an object appealing strongly to the Federalists, whose policy included, among its objects of first necessity, the establishment of a navy.[27]

Lodge was interested in a revival of Hamiltonianism per se. Support for the new Navy in 1890 was an important step for the United States, but nothing could have come more naturally to Lodge. Certainly he did not "yet think of American foreign policy in any but the most traditional terms."[28] He didn't have to. He pitched his argument at home to New England's historic support for an effective navy and in Washington to the national naval policy which emerged from the War of 1812.[29] Moreover, he had pronounced views on what constituted "traditional American foreign policy," and they differed greatly from those held in many quarters.[30] The attitudes of those who had historically "resisted the creation of any navy whatever" and who proposed "to meet the encroachments of a foreign power by a diplomat on a ferry-boat"[31] he dismissed with scorn. And while he disavowed all interest in an "offensive navy," he also reminded Congress of the relationship between diplomacy and force and of the disadvantage under which American diplomatists labored due to the vulnerability of the country's coastal cities.

The "traditional" Federalist conception of American security and nationality dominated his outlook. He sensed democracy's indifference

26. Lodge, "The Fisheries Question," pp. 121–30; *Cong. Record*, 50th Cong., 1st sess., 1888, p. 5011, and Appendix, p. 481.

27. Lodge, *George Cabot*, pp. 41–42.

28. Grenville and Young, *Politics, Strategy and American Diplomacy*, p. 210.

29. Undated clipping from the Boston *Transcript* of a letter from Lodge to the editor dated April 11, 1890, Scrapbooks, Lodge MSS; *Cong. Record*, 51st Cong., 1st sess., 1890, p. 3169.

30. See, for example, the essay "Our Foreign Policy" in his *Certain Accepted Heroes*, pp. 241, 260, 262, 264. The dispute, as one reviewer pointed out, was not, however, whether the United States had a distinct historical foreign policy, but whether Lodge's description of that policy was an accurate one (*The Nation*, 65 [Nov. 4, 1897]: 360).

31. Lodge, *Studies in History*, p. 278; *Cong. Record*, 51st Cong., 1st sess, 1890, pp. 3169–70.

to foreign policy and sought in tradition a means of protecting the United States against that tendency. Lodge wanted to believe that "we have always had and that we have now a foreign policy which is of great importance to our national well-being."[32] That policy was based on Washington's doctrine of strong neutrality and its Monrovian corollary, but it had also been possessed of a style whose absence from contemporary American diplomacy Lodge greatly lamented.[33] He described it in various terms, most frequently as "firm," "strong," "vigorous," and "dignified."[34] If the words themselves are vague and subject to many interpretations, Lodge's object in employing them is more apparent. It is even possible that he was more interested in recapturing the style and *élan* which he thought had once characterized American foreign policy than he was in imperialism per se. It was an interest that both preceded and survived his imperialism.

One of the special attractions of an assertive foreign policy was that it would supposedly make for peace. If strong enough, the United States could command peace, even in the face of the hostility of all the powers of Europe.[35] On the contrary, as Roosevelt put it in his famous letter to the Harvard *Crimson*: "Nothing will more certainly in the end produce war than to invite European aggressions on American states by abject surrender of our principles."[36] Moreover, an assertive foreign policy was but the functional derivative of American nationalism. Once it had been necessary to protect and foster a sense of American nationality. Now the success of that policy could be gauged by whether the United States actually stood for something in world affairs. Lodge never contended that a state owed it to itself to achieve maximum relative power.[37] But he was concerned that Americans recognize that they had attained to a position of power and influence, and agree to pursue a foreign policy which would allow that influence and power to be exerted. He was particularly anxious lest Americans "fail to see our true

32. Lodge, "Our Blundering Foreign Policy," *The Forum* 19 (March 1895): 15.
33. Lodge, *Speeches and Addresses*, pp. 198–99, 204.
34. The Republican party platform of 1896 (and the language may well be Lodge's) stated that "our foreign policy should be at all times firm, vigorous and dignified."
35. *Cong. Record*, 54th Cong., 1st sess., 1896, pp. 6048–49.
36. Morison, ed., *Letters of Theodore Roosevelt*, I, p. 506. Lodge saw and approved the letter *before* it was sent. See the reference thereto in a letter of Lodge to Roosevelt, Jan. 11, 1896, Roosevelt MSS.
37. Ernest May, *American Imperialism: A Speculative Essay* (New York, 1968), p. 184.

place in the scale of nations," and wanted them educated to a "just knowledge of our place in history" so that they might understand the present and be prepared to act in it.[38]

His thinking reflected the Federalist preoccupation with securing a proper rank among the nations.[39] Standing, however, was not just a function of power, but also of character and reputation. While he acknowledged the importance of trade, business, and currency, he thought there were "things more important than any of them both to nations and to men." Among those was "the maintenance of our place among nations."[40] A nation should try to put its ideals into practice and maintain itself in a position to do so. Lodge in his historically conditioned naiveté never doubted that America would play a moral role if only it could be persuaded to play the part on the world's stage to which its power entitled it.[41] A great nation had its duties and responsibilities and could not be great without them. The danger was that the American people would fail to recognize their power and the responsibility that went with it. Force was not only a legitimate means to a moral end, but occasionally the only means. The fruits of peace were sometimes, as in Armenia and Cuba, more awful than war itself.[42] He frowned upon the expenditure of moral energy involved in the protests against the atrocities in Armenia in 1895, for that was something the United States could do little about.[43] But when the U.S. could influence events, as in Cuba, then failure to act was an admission that the country's vaunted morality was only pretense.[44] He wanted instead a foreign policy which would bring American power and American morality into a closer relationship, a foreign policy equivalent of the practical idealism which he considered the essence of the American approach to politics.

The combination of jingoistic nationalism with an idealistic and re-

38. Lodge, "True Americanism," pp. 15–16.
39. Lodge, *Speeches and Addresses*, p. 198.
40. Lodge to George (Lyman?), Dec. 21, 1895, Lodge MSS.
41. *New York Times*, Nov. 25, 1900, p. 1. The formula was not a new one. The Republican platform of 1896 (and again the language may well be Lodge's) had called for the possession by the United States of a "naval power commensurate with its position and responsibilities."
42. Lodge to John (Morse, Jr.?), Feb. 25, 1898, Lodge MSS.
43. *Cong. Record*, 54th Cong., 1st sess., 1896, p. 1972. Initially, however, he, and the whole Massachusetts Republican party with him, had made much of the Cleveland Administration's "immoral" unconcern.
44. Lodge, *Speeches and Addresses*, p. 298.

sponsible internationalism such as Lodge tried to effect seems an unlikely one. It is difficult to sympathize with an idealism which put so little restraint upon national egotism, and our impulse is to regard his idealism and internationalism as little more than a front for his nationalism.[45] Yet such an attitude was common in his day.[46] Lodge and Roosevelt thought an assertive nationalism was a prerequisite for the exercise of *any* international influence, and under the conditions created by the free security which the United States enjoyed in the nineteenth century they may have been right. Nationalism might be a counter to isolationism. Nationalism brought with it the sense of power which made a larger world role possible. As Roosevelt once put it:

The useful member of the brotherhood of nations is that nation which is most thoroughly saturated with the national idea, and which realizes most fully its rights as a nation and its duties to its own citizens. . . .

As yet no nation can hold its place in the world or can do any work really worth doing unless it stands ready to guard its rights with an armed hand.[47]

In this manner great power status, a strong defense establishment, and an assertive foreign policy became goals in and of themselves.

Lodge and Roosevelt were to suffer many reverses in their efforts to get the American people to accept their version of America's future. There was always the question whether a people who had "an inborn and a carefully cultivated dread of standing armies and military power" could attain that "social efficiency in war, peace and government without which all else is vain."[48] A nation's foreign policy was a reflection of that efficiency. It mirrored not only domestic conditions but also the character of a people, even the state of a nation's soul.

His doubts about his success in a matter to which he attached so much importance explain his extreme sensitivity. A concomitant of

45. Robert E. Osgood, *Ideals and Self-Interest in America's Foreign Relations* (Chicago, 1964), p. 45.

46. It was, for example, almost universal among the patriotic and hereditary societies. See Davies, *Patriotism on Parade*, p. 310.

47. *American Ideals and Other Essays, Social and Political* (New York, 1907), pp. 225–26, 242. First published in 1897, the book was dedicated to Lodge, who in TR's opinion was the very embodiment of those ideals (*Correspondence of Roosevelt and Lodge*, I, pp. 288–89). Lodge had previously written Roosevelt that he thought *American Ideals* represented "our meaning" in life (Lodge to Roosevelt, Oct. 26, 1897, Roosevelt MSS).

48. Lodge, *George Washington*, I, p. 324; Lodge, *Fighting Frigate*, p. 261. His concerns on this score were identical with those of Henry Adams, as expressed in his *History of the United States*, IX, p. 227.

his assertive nationalism was an exaggerated fear of insult to American power (which could only be evidence that others doubted, as he sometimes did himself, the United States' ability to apply its power with any purpose). The result was jingoism and a propensity for seeing all foreign policy issues as questions of national honor and dignity. This tendency in Lodge's thinking was evidenced early.[49] He was ever fearful that a feeble foreign policy would encourage others to "insult us with impunity." Even in victory he worried lest the European powers interfere and the United States be put on a level with China and Japan.[50]

The Samoan crisis with Germany in the winter of 1888–89 may have "first aroused American opinion to the possibility that the United States might be a loser in failing to participate in the scramble for colonial spoils." But Lodge was more concerned about "a disposition on the part of other nations to treat us slightingly."[51] Similarly it was not British imperialism as such, but rather "the wise aggressiveness" which characterized British policy, that he wanted the United States to emulate.[52] He could not stand to see the United States in a subservient role, and what really impressed him during an 1895 visit to England was the recognition which the British were now according to American power.[53] He wanted to establish the fact that "we are a great nation and intend to take a nation's part in the family of nations."[54] Great-power status was the primary goal. Imperialism was attractive, but only insofar as it contributed to that end.

Lodge enjoyed political combat and was a fierce adversary. He was happiest when he could find someone or something to oppose, and in this case he did not have to look very far. There were always those who, in his opinion, sought to denigrate patriotism at home and render the achievement of great power status even more problematic, those

49. See, for example, his interpretation of the fisheries question, *Cong. Record*, 50th Cong., 1st sess., 1888, pp. 4993–94.

50. Lodge to Henry (Higginson?), Jan. 19, 1892, and to Judge Day, July 9, 1898, Lodge MSS.

51. Julius W. Pratt, "The 'Large Policy' of 1898," *Mississippi Valley Historical Review* 19 (Sept. 1932): 224; Lodge to his mother, Anna Cabot Lodge, Feb. 3, 1889, Lodge MSS.

52. Lodge, *Speeches and Addresses*, pp. 160, 167.

53. Unidentified clipping giving the text of Lodge's remarks to a Republican Ratification Meeting in Boston on July 24, 1888, Scrapbooks, Lodge MSS; *Correspondence of Roosevelt and Lodge*, I, p. 155.

54. Lodge, *Speeches and Addresses*, pp. 287, 294.

"opposed to our having any foreign policy at all."[55] The scorn that Lodge felt for "those people" knew few bounds. Despite his satisfaction with the results of the Spanish-American War, the utterances of certain men and newspapers made Lodge "sick to think that there are such creatures crawling between Heaven and Earth in America."[56]

Robert Osgood once observed that much in the imperialist rationale bore no logical relation to a realistic view of world politics and described a "struggle between groups of broadly divergent attitudes toward international politics competing for control of the symbolic spigots of a vast reservoir of popular idealism."[57] He erred primarily in categorization, in labeling Lodge, Roosevelt and Co. as "egoistic Realists" and their Mugwump and Anti-Imperialist opponents as "idealistic utopians." True, there were "irreconcilable temperamental antipathies" between the two groups, and those antipathies were often of overriding importance and capable of taking on a life of their own. For Lodge an assertive foreign policy became the more important because of the identity and characteristics of those who opposed it. The argument from the nature of one's opponents was an important ingredient in the attitudes of both Lodge and Roosevelt. In their view the same people who took an impractical approach to domestic politics were also utopian and softheaded about foreign policy. But that did not make them "Realists." Osgood failed to make sufficient allowance for their own idealism and for their efforts to reconcile realism with idealism. They not only competed for control of the spigots of idealism; they were, in fact, idealists themselves. William James saw this clearly. He too recognized the basic antipathy, and how desperately hard it was to bring the peace party and the war party together. Pacifist though he was, James appreciated the idealism inherent in the militarist imagination. The fact that it was a struggle between conflicting idealisms made reconciliation difficult. "In the whole discussion both sides . . . were on imaginative and sentimental ground. It . . . was but one Utopia against another."[58]

Lodge's idealism and his antipathy toward the "peace-party" had an

55. Lodge, *Certain Accepted Heroes*, p. 233; *Cong. Record*, 54th Cong., 1st sess., 1896, p. 4713.
56. *Correspondence of Roosevelt and Lodge*, I, p. 400.
57. *Ideals and Self-Interest*, pp. 19, 47, 87.
58. "The Moral Equivalent of War," *McClure's* 35 (Aug. 1910): 464.

important historical dimension. They were ancillary to a bitter and internecine political struggle. For his decision to support Blaine and accept the Republican nomination for Congress in 1884 Lodge was vilified unmercifully by the Mugwumps. "They pursued him relentlessly as long as he lived."[59] They even engineered his defeat when he stood for reelection as an Overseer of Harvard College.[60] Moorfield Storey snubbed Lodge whenever they met, and thereafter he and Lodge were to be found on opposite sides of nearly every public issue.[61] E. L. Godkin, who once offered Lodge the editorship of *The Nation*, developed such an enmity that he sometimes violated his own convictions in order that he might attack Lodge's stand.[62] Both in terms of the politics and of the social code of the day Lodge could not allow these opponents to assume a position more moral than his own. The result was twofold: he responded in kind (making a political virtue out of the enemies he had made), and, not to be outdone, he pitched his own arguments on an even higher moral and idealistic level.[63] Lodge thereafter took special pains to collect derogatory information on Godkin; he was, one might say, Lodge's first Wilson.[64]

The question is, of course, how a quarrel which had its origins in domestic politics could affect the attitude of Lodge on foreign policy issues. It is not my intention to argue that there was a perfect identity between the Mugwumps of 1884 and the Anti-Imperialists of 1898–1900. But there was considerable affinity. The Mugwumps and their businessmen allies had an overriding interest in government economy and would have opposed Lodge's foreign policy if only because of the increased military expenditures it envisaged.[65]

59. Garraty, *Lodge*, p. 84.
60. Robert Grant, *Fourscore: An Autobiography* (Boston, 1934), pp. 188–89.
61. M. A. DeWolfe Howe, *Portrait of an Independent* (Boston, 1932), p. 156.
62. William Armstrong, *E. L. Godkin and American Foreign Policy, 1865–1900* (New York, 1957), pp. 150–51.
63. Boston *Evening Record*, Oct. 31, 1888. A great deal of the satisfaction Lodge derived from the Federal Election Bill he and Hoar sponsored in 1890–91 probably came from the fact that it served to expose the moral hypocrisy of the Mugwumps. They squirmed in the embrace of their Southern Democratic allies but could not entirely escape.
64. John G. Sproat, *The Best Men: Liberal Reformers in the Gilded Age* (New York, 1968), p. 136. "Godkin is the one man of my thirty years' experience about whom I mean to make a record. . . . to expose that particular fraud who in his lifetime did a good deal of harm among the class of men who, above all others, did not require to have their patriotism turned down, or their love of country weakened" (Lodge to Barrett Wendell, Dec. 31, 1908, Lodge MSS).
65. Abrams, *Conservatism in a Progressive Era*, p. 34.

The political constellation which was to take definite form only in the Anti-Imperialist movement made its appearance as soon as Lodge and Roosevelt started to push for an assertive foreign policy. During the Chilean crisis Lodge was already decrying the howl emanating from "the moneyed interests in New York and Boston" and fulminating against those "peace at any price" people.[66] Because such opposition was predictable he could never consider it on its merits. Each new foreign policy crisis only served to confirm the pattern of opposition and increase his sense of outrage. In his obsession with checking this "State St.-Mugwump opposition" he came to identify his own cause ever more closely with that of the nation.[67] But Roosevelt, as usual, was the more outspoken. Mugwump opposition drove him to extremity. It was not so much that he really wanted to go to war with England over Venezuela. Rather, the clamor of the peace faction convinced him that the country needed a war.[68] Lodge never shared Roosevelt's enthusiasm for war,[69] but he too wanted to stand in opposition to "the stock-jobbing timidity, the Baboo kind of statesmanship, which is clamored for . . . by the men who put monetary gain before national honor . . . [and] thereby invite war."[70] In return, they were attacked by President Eliot as "degenerated sons of Harvard" and that really set Roosevelt off:

It is a fine alliance, that between the anglo-maniac mugwumps, the socialist working men, and corrupt politicians like Gorman, to prevent the increase of our Navy and coast defenses. The moneyed and semi-cultured classes, espe-

66. Lodge to Brooks Adams, Jan. 24 and 28, 1892, Lodge MSS.
67. Lodge to Anna Cabot Lodge, Jan. 1, 1896, Lodge MSS.
68. *Correspondence of Roosevelt and Lodge*, I, pp. 205–06.
69. Karl Schriftgiesser indiscriminately accepts Mugwump accusations and claims that Lodge was "spoiling for a fight with England" (*The Gentleman from Massachusetts*, pp. 137–38, 147). There is no evidence to support such a conclusion. Lodge went to England in 1895, for the first time in nearly 25 years, to apprise the English of American opinion on Venezuela. He did not fear the ultimate result of war (Canada would pass from British control), but he had "no desire for war" and did "not believe that if we are firm . . . any war will come" (Lodge to Frank L. Sanford, Dec. 20, 1895, Lodge MSS). See also his letter of Jan. 10, 1896, to Henry White, White Papers, Library of Congress. He was, in fact, already laying the groundwork for an Anglo-American rapprochement. See his letter of Feb. 1, 1896, to Arthur J. Balfour, Lodge MSS.
70. Morison, ed., *Letters of Theodore Roosevelt*, I, p. 506. The phrase is from Roosevelt's famous letter to the Harvard *Crimson* of Jan. 2, 1896, his effort to save Harvard "for Patriotism and Americanism." Lodge saw and approved it before it was sent and the "Baboo" terminology in this context is his (*Correspondence of Roosevelt and Lodge*, I, p. 204; Lodge to Roosevelt, Jan. 11, 1896, Roosevelt MSS).

cially of the Northeast, are doing their best to bring this country down to the Chinese level. If we ever come to nothing as a nation it will be because the teaching of Carl Schurz, President Eliot, the Evening Post and the futile sentimentalists of the international arbitration type, bears its legitimate fruit in producing a flabby, timid type of character, which eats away the great fighting features of our race.[71]

Lodge's own rogues gallery never differed substantially. But in the context of the depression-ridden 90s, his opponents took on a new guise. Lodge complained of the "indifference of the money power to the claims of humanity and patriotism," and contrasted the vigorous attitude of the old merchant class of New England (from which he was descended) with the fear and trembling of the financial community.[72] This went beyond personal indulgence to affect his attitudes on important matters of state. Lodge warned President-elect McKinley against selecting a Secretary of State from a large Eastern city where "many of the local influences would press a man . . . towards a yielding policy." On the eve of the Spanish-American War he told McKinley that "in a great, broad question like this, where right and wrong are involved, I believe profoundly in the popular instinct. . . . At such times the vast, utterly selfish money interests represented by a few men are perilous guides."[73] The lessons of history, personal prejudice, and good politics seemed so often to point in the same direction.

True, Lodge took a more realistic view of international politics than did many of his American contemporaries. But his realism was derivative rather than experiential; it was a matter of temperament, of historical interpretation, and of domestic politics. His and Roosevelt's efforts to get the United States to pursue a more vigorous foreign policy were firmly rooted in domestic political and social configurations. As Roosevelt later confessed, it was "the Anglomania of our social leaders and indeed of most of our educated men" that made him "feel that we should be extremely careful to teach England her proper position."[74] They gave lip service to the primacy of foreign policy, but their views on foreign policy were shaped on the anvil of domestic politics. Ironically, those foremost in urging the acceptance of international responsi-

71. *Correspondence of Roosevelt and Lodge*, I, p. 218.
72. Lodge to William (Bigelow?), Dec. 22, 1896; to R. W. Hughes, Jan. 6, 1896; and to Col. Higginson, March 25, 1896; Lodge MSS.
73. Lodge to McKinley, Nov. 9, 1896, Lodge MSS; Lodge to McKinley, March 21, 1898, McKinley Papers, Library of Congress.
74. Morison, ed., *Letters of Theodore Roosevelt*, II, p. 52.

bilities were themselves, at this stage, motivated by such exclusively domestic concerns.

One of the reasons they cared so much about foreign policy was, as we have seen, that it could be seen as a manifestation of national character. As William James saw so clearly, the real differences between "the party of red blood" and the party of "pale reflection" turned on the questions of what constituted ideal character and how it might be fostered. Deficiencies in the program of pacifism with respect to character development "set the militarist imagination strongly, and to a certain extent justifiably, against it."[75] While Lodge can be faulted for the lack of any really consistent ideological position, domestic or foreign, certain allegiances and preoccupations were ever present.[76] If he and Roosevelt had one message which they wanted to get across to the American people, it was the need to cultivate personal and national character. One unbroken thread which spans the years from Lodge's "True Americanism" oration to Roosevelt's *Autobiography* is their desire to see the country produce "young men with ardent convictions on the side of the right," men to whom "the great refusal" is impossible when their people or their country call them.[77]

A "character of force" was deemed a prerequisite for dealing with all problems, domestic and foreign. Lodge was intent on the reestablishment of "the principles which . . . will enable us to strive and conquer as in the olden times."[78] But what exactly were the qualities and principles he wanted to resurrect? And by what standard did he judge their value? There is a good hint in Lodge's description of those principles as the ones which will enable us to strive and conquer. His was a historicist definition of ideal character. The English-speaking people had attained a position of dominance in world affairs by means of their possession of "a character of force." Its results could "be estimated by the place which the English speech and the English race hold today in the world, and by the magnitude of the states they have erected

75. Fredrickson, *The Inner Civil War*, p. 234; James, "The Moral Equivalent of War," p. 464.

76. See John P. Mallan, "The Warrior Critique of the Business Civilization," *American Quarterly* 8 (Fall 1956): 221n. Mallan is, however, measuring Lodge against an ideal standard—that of a genuine "aristocratic" conservative tradition, which was never politically feasible in the United States.

77. Roosevelt, *An Autobiography* (New York, 1920), p. 23; Lodge, "True Americanism," p. 23.

78. Lodge, *Frontier Town*, p. 28.

and the wealth and power they control."[79] Character was what brought success and reputation in history.

Were, then, the martial qualities the only ones that mattered? Not entirely. Lodge thought of success in history in terms other than mere physical domination; "true national greatness" could also be measured by achievements in government and civilization and ultimately, in something of a circular argument, by the possession of "character." Character had a necessary military dimension, and Lodge would not have quarreled with Roosevelt's dictum that "it is better for a nation to produce one Grant or one Farragut than a thousand shrewd manufacturers or successful speculators."[80] But in *Hero Tales* they carefully explained that the men they extolled were ones "who joined to the stern and manly qualities which are essential to the well-being of a masterful race the virtues of gentleness, of patriotism, and of lofty adherence to an ideal."[81]

As David Burton has discovered, "character occupied a critical place" in their philosophy of imperialism. Their very search for character started them on the path to imperialism. Character could not exist in isolation. It had to be tested and demonstrated in adversity. As Lodge put it in his essay on Charles Russell Lowell: "still better and finer than a mere idealist . . . was a man of action, eager to put his ideals into practice and bring them to the test of daily life."[82] Lodge's only complaint about his great-grandfather, George Cabot, was that he had not done more and he seems to have tried to organize his own life so as to be immune to that charge.[83] Mere activism, however, was not enough. Great work could only be accomplished by those who "believed most fervently in their cause, their country and themselves."[84] By those standards Lodge and Roosevelt certainly qualified.

The problem was to find an arena in which to test and develop their, and the nation's, character. Lodge bridled both against his times

79. Lodge, *Studies in History*, p. 113. What should be obvious from such remarks is that Lodge enjoyed basking in the reflected light of the British Empire far too much to be as anglophobic as the Mugwumps accused him of being.

80. David H. Burton, *Theodore Roosevelt: Confident Imperialist* (Philadelphia, 1968), p. 34.

81. Roosevelt and Lodge, *Hero Tales from American History*, p. ix.

82. *Ibid.*, p. 227.

83. Lodge to Albert J. Beveridge, June 25, 1917, Beveridge Papers, Library of Congress (hereafter cited as Beveridge MSS).

84. Lodge, *Speeches and Addresses*, p. 8.

(comfortable times were not ones that made a nation great) and against the tendency inherent in American politics to pay too much attention "to small matters of legislation, too much . . . to economic questions, and too little attention to those great and far-reaching issues on which the future of the republic depends."[85] With the Civil War experience always in the back of their minds, they sought another ordeal to try the national character and provide a measure of national greatness. What they disdained in their private lives they wanted the nation to disdain also. The enemy was "materialist complacency."[86] The antidote was nationalism. As Lodge claimed:

Now, there is a great deal more than that [business questions] in the life of every great nation. . . . [our] flag is a great deal more than the sign of a successful national shop. . . . I never will admit that . . . [it is] merely the symbol of a land where I can live in rich content and make money.[87]

Better than materialism and the exaggerated fear of war that often accompanied it were national honor and a sense of duty to humanity.[88] In short, theirs was but a modified version of the standard idealist critique of industrial society.

They embraced a vigorous foreign policy and later imperialism in the hope that it would do an "incalculable amount" for American character.[89] They were certainly not oblivious to economic and strategic considerations, but Lodge's exclamation that "we hold the other side of the Pacific, and the value to this country is almost beyond imagination" clearly carried a double meaning. He was jubilant because "we have risen to be one of the great world powers,"[90] but he was also happy that "we have set up as an ideal something before our young men nobler than a successful speculator."[91] As Richard Leopold has concluded, theirs was "an unripe imperialism" whose roots were more emotional than economic or strategic.[92] America's problems were

85. Lodge, *Hero Tales*, p. 234; Lodge, *Speeches and Addresses*, p. 193.
86. See Mallan, "The Warrior Critique of the Business Civilization," pp. 216–30.
87. Lodge, *Speeches and Addresses*, pp. 285–87.
88. *Ibid.*, p. 307.
89. Morison, ed., *Letters of Theodore Roosevelt*, II, p. 1104.
90. Cited in Allan Nevins, *Henry White: Thirty Years of American Diplomacy* (New York, 1930), p. 136.
91. Clipping from an unidentified paper, Oct. 6, 1898, Scrapbooks, Lodge MSS.
92. "The Emergence of America as a World Power: Some Second Thoughts," in John Braeman et al., eds., *Change and Continuity in Twentieth-Century America* (Columbus, Ohio, 1964), p. 13.

those of the soul, and both great power status and imperialism were seen as instruments of salvation.

Lodge and Roosevelt wanted to change the course of American history. Rather suddenly in the 1890s they acquired an audience. What had been a personal solution became momentarily a possible national solution. In the Gilded Age there had been little room in the American pantheon for their aristocratic and anti-industrial ethos. As long as things were going well, as long as prosperity reigned at home and America seemed to be outdistancing the other nations economically, "materialist complacency" was bound to dominate. Under such conditions it was impossible to obtain a hearing for an alternative value system. Lodge and Roosevelt did not like to see the American people dominated by such a spirit but in the 1880s they publicly acquiesced in what seemed the inevitable.

Yet privately they never accepted it for themselves. Their attitude resembled nothing so much as "that of a lettered class living under a tyranny."[93] They were young and brash and knew from their study of history that the country had sometimes been moved by other forces. Still, "the tempo of their age was all against them."[94] Lodge witnessed Boston's failure of nerve and the ineptitude of its liberal Republican reformers.[95] No great ideal had followed on that of the War and a spirit of listlessness had infected upper-class Boston. Some who found the cult of materialism oppressive simply despaired and withdrew into their own world, seeking solace in theories of decadence.[96] But Lodge began to look beyond the limits of Boston and its increasingly conventional framework of thought. He took more seriously perhaps than did Henry Adams himself the latter's advice that "anything which takes a man morally out of Beacon St., Nahant, and Beverly Farms, Harvard College and the Boston press, must be in itself a good."[97] Against his Boston background Lodge can only be viewed as an innovator. Practically alone among New England politicians of his day he as-

93. John Jay Chapman's phrase, cited in Josephson, *The President Makers*, p. 22.
94. Brooks, *New England: Indian Summer*, p. 198.
95. See Martin Green, *The Problem of Boston* (New York, 1966), pp. 118–19. Lodge's judgment, however, was not that Boston had become culturally self-satisfied but rather, like Parkman's, that it had become emasculate.
96. Henry Adams, *The Life of George Cabot Lodge* (Boston, 1911), pp. 6, 13; John Higham, "The Reorientation of American Culture in the 1890's," in H. John Weiss, ed., *The Origins of Modern Consciousness* (Detroit, 1965), p. 35.
97. Ford, ed., *Letters of Henry Adams*, I, pp. 267–68.

sumed a national perspective. He made his own political opportunities; he stated what he wanted and proceeded to go after it with irrepressible energy.[98] Along with Roosevelt he "embarked upon a search for new doctrines, for a new ideology of leadership," and for "fresh sources of energy."[99]

It was a lonely search. Part of the extraordinary intimacy of Lodge and Roosevelt was due to the fact that for so long they had only each other. They chose the path of struggle and since their talents were by no means meager they soon developed a sense of their own power. When their time came, when in the wake of economic depression there developed a strong reaction against urban-industrial culture, they had something particularly appealing to offer. When they began to pound home the message that a new spirit was needed so that the nation might succeed in the world, their audience was the more receptive because they themselves seemed possessed of the sense of power and direction which was so wanting elsewhere.[100]

Much of their persuasiveness came from the sheer scope of their vision and from the dexterity with which they interwove the elements of domestic and foreign policy. But perhaps most important was the fact that theirs was a gospel of hope instead of despair:[101]

The continent has been conquered, and now the people's mind is turning to the fact that while we were engaged in this great work other things have been neglected—that we have heeded too little the importance of preserving in every way our institutions, of standing by American principles everywhere, at home and abroad, of putting the United States in the place where they belong in the great family of nations. . . .

The American spirit is reviving throughout the country in the last ten years. It means not only the preservation of every institution, the upholding of every American principle—it means Americanism, true Americanism, true patriotism here at home and wherever the flag floats in the most distant area.[102]

98. *Harper's Weekly* 37 (Jan. 21, 1893), editorial. Despite the outrage which this produced among his Mugwump critics he knew that there was a new politics and that he could no longer expect opportunity to come to him.

99. Josephson, *The President Makers,* p. 24; Higham in Weiss, ed., *Origins of Modern Consciousness,* p. 35.

100. Lodge, *Speeches and Addresses,* p. 293.

101. See, for example, Lodge's "Address at the Academy of Music" (Philadelphia, 1900), p. 26, in which he dwelled on the point that "the gospel of America is hope" and "the Republican party . . . appeals to hope."

102. Clipping, the New York *Advertiser,* Nov. 28, 1895, Scrapbooks, Lodge MSS.

Such rhetoric filled a deep-felt national need. In fact it was so well received that Lodge and Roosevelt began to believe that their efforts might result in a new national commitment, that there actually was a sentiment in the American people "above and beyond their love of peace" and desire to accumulate wealth.[103] They agreed with Mahan that in an assertive foreign policy and in expansion the nation had finally found "a regenerating idea" or at least the means of pulling itself back together.[104] They had much yet to learn.

II

Several writers have commented on the nebulous quality of the imperialism of Lodge and Roosevelt. Charles Beard judged them to have been "almost equally vague with respect to the essential character of the 'imperialism' to which they gave their hearty endorsement."[105] E. Berkeley Tompkins has described their writings as "an interesting potpourri of chauvinism, mysticism, Social Darwinism, and historical determinism."[106] However, that has not deterred other observers from claiming that for Lodge "territorial expansion . . . found its justification largely in the control which it would give over markets and trade routes."[107] Beard himself thought he had fingered that "essential character" when he wrote that Lodge "had a rather pragmatic outlook on the imperialist game: it was good for business."[108]

I myself would shrink from a categorical description of Lodge's imperialism. I have attempted to show that his outlook made him susceptible to imperialism, but that is not to say that he subscribed to a comprehensive and consistent imperialist ideology. One can find quotations to support most any claim as to its "essential character." Consequently, all such claims must be regarded with suspicion. In fact that whole debate may be sterile. It tends to deny what may be the most important fact about Lodge's imperialism, namely that it was eclectic and opportunistic. He was dissatisfied with things as they were and had some general ideas about the direction in which he wanted to see Amer-

103. *Cong. Record*, 55th Cong., 2nd sess., 1898, p. 3783.
104. A. T. Mahan, *Retrospect and Prospect* (Boston, 1902), p. 17.
105. "Roosevelt and Lodge," *New Republic* 43 (June 17, 1925): 103.
106. *Anti-Imperialism in the United States: The Great Debate, 1890–1920* (Philadelphia, 1970), p. 166.
107. Julius W. Pratt, *Expansionists of 1898* (Baltimore, 1936), p. 232.
108. "Roosevelt and Lodge," p. 103.

ican society go, but he was ever searching, whether for a "new ideology of leadership," "fresh sources of energy," or simply for the argument or act that would move the American people to support his views. His imperialist ideology never received a full statement until after 1898 and only a few years later it fell into desuetude. Its nature can be fully grasped not by internal analysis but only in relation to events.

No one has ever undertaken to discuss the imperialism of Lodge or Roosevelt without reference to the influence of either Alfred Mahan or Brooks Adams, and with good reason. Their influence was substantial, but by reserving until now its discussion, I have attempted to show that Lodge did not need their impetus in order to embark on the road that led to imperialism. One of the consequences of his eclecticism and opportunism was an extraordinary receptivity to new ideas and arguments. Lodge was introducing the ideas of Mahan and Adams into his Senate speeches only months after their publication. No sooner had he read Benjamin Kidd's *Control of the Tropics* than he was writing that the future of the country was going to turn on that issue.[109] However, the point is not that Kidd, or for that matter, Mahan or Adams, exerted such influence over his thinking, but rather that he found their arguments useful in moving the country to support a program whose general nature he had already determined for himself.

A consideration of the question of influence contains many pitfalls. By way of illustration, the conclusion of a recent student of Roosevelt's imperialism is that "there was no influence more critical in the formation of the explicit imperialist attitudes of Theodore Roosevelt than his personal and scholarly experience of the American West" and that "Lodge added nothing distinctive to Roosevelt's imperialist outlook."[110] That may be true, but it at least raises the question of how Lodge, who had a New Englander's disdain for the West, arrived at the same imperialist outlook.[111] It indicates that there may have been a number of paths thereto, and it suggests that Lodge and Roosevelt may have exercised considerable influence upon one another. David Burton almost admits as much when he concedes that Lodge's "friendly agreement

109. Lodge to Stephen O'Meara, Nov. 28, 1898, Lodge MSS.
110. Burton, *Theodore Roosevelt: Confident Imperialist*, pp. 35, 69–70.
111. He was accused (and with some justification) of never going West of the Hudson except to represent the interests of New England in Washington and at Republican National Conventions. See especially Nicholas Murray Butler, *Across the Busy Years: Recollections and Reflections* (New York, 1939–40), I, pp. 288–89.

often reassured TR in his own views."[112] Agreeing on the basics of what ailed American society, each could bring to their relationship the fruits of his own experience and in so doing serve to confirm the other's views. My own reading of their relationship is that they exercised great influence upon one another and that beside that influence, especially in the area of foreign policy where they were *always* in basic agreement, all others pale in comparison. It was an extraordinary friendship, practically unique in the annals of American politics. Roosevelt once wrote that Lodge "was my closest friend, personally, politically, and in every other way, and occupied toward me a relation that no other man has ever occupied or ever will occupy." Lodge, in turn, valued Roosevelt's opinion "more than anyone else's."[113] This mutual trust and affection should be borne in mind when assessing the influence of other individuals and points of view on Lodge's thinking.

Julius W. Pratt thought that Lodge's speeches in the Senate on naval construction and annexation embodied the whole Mahan philosophy.[114] On the other hand Grenville and Young have discovered that in 1892, when Mahan was already looking outward, Lodge's preoccupations were almost exclusively domestic and have concluded therefrom that Mahan's influence only became apparent gradually.[115] This contrasts sharply with John Garraty's assertion that Lodge was a quick convert to Mahan's point of view.[116] Though seemingly contradictory, the evidence supports all these interpretations. Hence a careful consideration of time and context is required.

Pratt's assertion is true for the period 1895–1900 and if one remembers that Lodge never paid much attention either to Mahan's neo-mercantilism or to his muscular Christianity. As the formality and infrequency of their correspondence suggest, Lodge and Mahan were not personally close. But Lodge did hold Mahan's opinions in high regard; in fact he considered him the "greatest authority living or dead on naval warfare."[117] The emphasis is informative. On questions of naval construction and strategy Lodge and Roosevelt were much indebted to Mahan's suggestions. But to say that Lodge followed Mahan

---

112. Burton, *Theodore Roosevelt: Confident Imperialist*, p. 35.
113. *Correspondence of Roosevelt and Lodge*, I, pp. 25, 280.
114. Pratt, "The 'Large Policy' of 1898," p. 241.
115. *Politics, Strategy and American Diplomacy*, pp. 220–21.
116. *Lodge*, p. 147.
117. Lodge to Mahan, Oct. 19, 1898, Mahan Papers, Library of Congress.

closely on those matters does not mean that reading Mahan led him to support a larger navy and expansion. Lodge was advocating a stronger navy and had at least a Federalist's interest in expansion in 1884 when Mahan was still an American copy of a "little Englander," who opposed expansion, feared strong central government, and advocated free trade.[118] Lodge did not need, in short, to undergo the great conversion experienced by Mahan. He used Mahan's ideas to supplement his own, and the fact that he absorbed them into his own outlook gradually suggests that his intellectual development in this area had a logic of its own. He would have opted for a powerful navy and for the annexation of Hawaii with or without Mahan.

The gingerly process by which Lodge incorporated Mahan's ideas into his own arguments (it was as if he were trying them out) also suggests that Lodge was responding to forces other than Mahan's ideas. It was five years from 1890 when Mahan sent him a complimentary copy of *The Influence of Sea Power upon History* to 1895 when in his speeches on Hawaii and naval policy he took up "the whole Mahan philosophy." In the meantime he slowly vented Mahan's ideas and made them a part of his essentially Federalist argument for a larger navy and for expansion. Grenville and Young have interpreted this to mean that Lodge "did not grasp at first the full significance or application of Mahan's doctrine of sea power."[119] That may be true, but it is also well to point out that Lodge had an acute sense of tactics. And needless to say the situation in 1895 differed greatly from that which had prevailed in 1890. In 1890 the issue was an appropriation for three "sea-going coastline battleships" (the contradictions involved in the name suggest the delicacy of the political situation) and Lodge's plea was traditional. He stressed the relationship between diplomacy and force, the lessons of the War of 1812, and wanted not an offensive navy, which "might bring us into needless conflict with the other nations of the world, but . . . one which is true to the American policy and the American idea of a Navy."[120] It was a major turning point in American naval history, but the authorization passed the House by only a vote of 139 to 104.[121] The next year his argument on the naval bill was

118. Capt. W. D. Puleston, *Mahan: The Life and Work of Captain Alfred Thayer Mahan, U.S.N.* (New Haven, 1939), pp. 67–72, 129.
119. *Politics, Strategy and American Diplomacy*, p. 219.
120. *Cong. Record*, 51st Cong., 1st sess., 1890, pp. 3169–70, 3268.
121. *Ibid.*, p. 6495.

much the same, but he now added the injunction (he had in the meantime read Mahan's book): "naval power, as every one knows who has studied history, has had, from the days of Hannibal, more to do with determining the fate of nations than almost anything else."[122] Mahan's influence is clear, but perhaps of even more interest Lodge chose not to elaborate the argument further; he mentioned the Mahanian thesis but then went back to talking about the War of 1812.

Other arguments which he was later to make so much of were introduced in the same manner. In 1891 he pointed out that Great Britain is "drawing about this country a cordon of forts and bases of supply for a navy manifestly for use in case of war."[123] What was one argument among many in 1891 became a theatrical production four years later when he had a large map studded with Maltese crosses brought into the Senate Chamber.[124] It was heavy-handed but it worked, whereas in 1891 it might have been counterproductive. Similarly, in 1892 he introduced the Mahanian argument that "the development of commerce has followed naval supremacy" and generally argued that "commerce can not be guarded except by a navy."[125] But not till 1895 was this argument fully developed. Then the plea that "commerce follows the flag," that a powerful navy is "one of the essential conditions of a great and world-wide commerce," took on new significance. Reflecting the increasing public interest in such matters generated by the depression, he could now clinch his argument by adding, and "of that commerce we do not today have our proper share."[126] Mahan's thesis of the historical importance of sea power was employed in much the same fashion. First mentioned in 1891, it was not fully elaborated until 1895. By then Hawaiian annexation was a realistic expectation and Lodge wanted "to take the first step toward finally establishing our control." To that end he now alleged that

The sea power has been one of the controlling forces in history. Without the sea power no nation has been really great. Sea power consists, in the first place, of a proper navy and a proper fleet; but in order to sustain a Navy we must have suitable posts for naval stations, strong places where a navy can be protected and refurnished.[127]

122. *Ibid.*, 51st Cong., 2nd sess., 1891, p. 1804.
123. *Ibid.*
124. The map is reproduced in Lodge, *Speeches and Addresses*, pp. 182–83.
125. *Cong. Record*, 52nd Cong., 1st sess., 1892, p. 3362.
126. *Ibid.*, 53rd Cong., 3rd sess., 1895, p. 3107.
127. *Ibid.*, p. 3082.

From coastline battleships to far-flung naval stations in five years! It required a virtual revolution in American political and strategic thinking. Lodge was in the vanguard but he was careful not to get so far out in front as to endanger his ability to lead. He tailored Mahanian doctrine to the exigencies of politics; he was not a hypocrite, but he did know how to wait.

No discussion of Mahan's influence would be complete without reference to the question of whether Lodge's thinking on foreign policy issues was governed primarily by considerations of strategic advantage. On one proposition most observers are agreed. There was relatively little *Realpolitik* in the Senate debates on imperialism; the emphasis was on "Manifest Destiny" and the anticipated commercial advantages. This has been viewed as a reflection of the public's interest in the latter and indifference to matters of national strategy.[128] Lodge himself did not shrink from admitting that commercial advantage also constituted a form of *Realpolitik*, but that was an argument to which many Americans turned a deaf ear. It was a matter of tactics, and Lodge, although governed in his own decisions by the criteria of *Realpolitik*, knew that the public was indifferent to what he found persuasive, and tailored his arguments accordingly. Certainly the manner in which he introduced the Mahanian arguments suggests that he was trying to get the public to see the importance of such considerations. It is equally clear that he was not successful in that regard and that the foreign policy legacy of the McKinley years was "a confusion of purpose shrouded in moral ambiguities."[129]

In the same vein historians have written that "nothing is more futile than to attempt to understand the Spanish-American War in terms of a rational calculation of self-interest," and concluded therefrom that "moral abstraction . . . was substituted for the political realism which had circumscribed previous American diplomacy."[130] Such charges raise the question whether Lodge himself might have been "unrealistic" in his thinking or whether circumstances rendered a "realistic" policy improbable. The answer in both cases is a qualified affir-

---

128. Richard E. Welch, Jr., *George Frisbie Hoar and the Half-Breed Republicans* (Cambridge, Mass., 1971), pp. 238–39; Osgood, *Ideals and Self-Interest*, p. 51.
129. Foster R. Dulles, *The Imperial Years* (New York, 1956), p. 164.
130. A. E. Campbell, *Great Britain and the United States, 1895–1903* (London, 1960), p. 187; Norman Graebner, ed., *Ideas and Diplomacy: Readings in the Intellectual Tradition of American Foreign Policy* (New York, 1964), pp. 339–40.

mative. A "realistic" foreign policy is a slippery goal when in a democracy public opinion is oblivious to matters of long-term planning. In the face of the American public's disinterest in questions of foreign policy and their lack of appreciation of the role of power in international politics, Lodge's effort to enlist American idealism in the cause of American nationalism was not unrealistic in terms of domestic politics. A similar answer can be given to the charge that he had no feel for the realities of international politics and failed to recognize that Britain was a satiated power.[131] Realism in the sense of what was politically possible dictated an anti-British policy; under American circumstances it was long practically a *sine qua non* of having any foreign policy at all. One type of realism precluded another.

Moreover, those like Lodge who preached a concern for the realities of international politics were motivated not by actual threats to American security, but rather by national egoism and a romantic attachment to power.[132] Such a judgment, however, ought to be tempered by three considerations. First, Lodge actually thought English aggrandizements were beginning to threaten American security.[133] Secondly, he, like Mahan, had derived an appreciation of the realities of power from historical study. Thirdly, much depends on with whom he is compared. Contrasted with Hoar and the Half-Breed Republicans, who made an artificial, if traditionally American, distinction between foreign affairs and foreign commerce, Lodge emerges as a supreme realist. England was, as he emphasized, America's rival for the world's trade, and the Navy was "an integral part of our foreign policy and an essential element in our commercial policy."[134]

On the other hand he was scarcely a classic *Realpolitiker*; the infusion of American moralism and romanticism in his thinking was too strong. He was never fundamentally troubled by a choice between the pursuit of national interest and the cause of humanity; he had too

131. Campbell, *Great Britain and the United States*, p. 34.
132. Osgood, *Ideals and Self-Interest*, pp. 28, 31. Osgood claims, with considerable justification, that "in the 1890's national security was a thin reed for supporting a preparedness movement of the dimensions envisaged by America's most vocal nationalists."
133. Grenville and Young, *Politics, Strategy and American Diplomacy*, p. 77.
134. *Cong. Record*, 53rd Cong., 3rd sess., 1895, pp. 3084, 3108. Given the expansion of trade that occurred in the 1870s and 1880s when the American navy was very weak, it can be effectively argued that the volume of American foreign commerce actually bore little relation to the strength of the American navy.

intense a belief in the American mission in history. In explaining why Americans ought to side with the Cubans he declared that "it is a matter of sentiment, and . . . right sentiment has and ought to have a large part in the affairs of men." Such sympathy was distinctively American and to abandon it would deny our historical birthright and destroy our faith in our own Republic.[135] These views were so basic to his approach to foreign policy that they survived even his profound reaction against Wilsonian idealism. Less than a year before his death he wrote in judgment of Metternich: "He is to me one of the worst men that history has to show; his ability . . . was very great, but his methods were mean, without any foresight, without a touch of feeling or sentiment."[136] Lodge, as have many Americans, thought there was a higher realism, that in practical idealism Americans had the solution to all questions of state.

Even more difficult to assess than the influence of Mahan is that of Brooks Adams. Brooks was a long-time friend who became part of the family in 1889 upon his marriage to Evelyn Davis, the sister of Lodge's wife Nannie. His correspondence with Lodge was sporadic but in volume it ranks second only to his much more intimate correspondence with his brother Henry.[137] Lodge and Brooks were at loggerheads on many of the issues of the day but they usually agreed on foreign policy, and it may be no coincidence that their correspondence was heaviest when foreign policy issues came to the fore as in the 90s and during the fight over the League of Nations.

Brooks, the eccentric of the group, was clearly so regarded. Roosevelt even thought he was "a little unhinged."[138] This complicates an assessment of his influence. Lodge, perhaps for family reasons, shied away from any systematic comment on Brooks's publications. Roosevelt,

135. Lodge, *Certain Accepted Heroes*, pp. 264–66. One is reminded here of the similar judgment of Mahan, who once wrote: "The sentiment of a people is the most energetic element in national action. Even when material interests are the original exciting cause, it is the sentiment to which they give rise, the moral tone which emotion takes, that constitutes the greater force. Whatever individual rulers may do, masses of men are aroused to effective action—other than spasmodic—only by the sense of wrong done, or of right to be vindicated. For this reason governments are careful to obtain for their contentions an aspect of right which will keep their people at their backs" (*The Interest of America in International Conditions* [Boston, 1910], p. 168).

136. Lodge to W. P. Cresson, Dec. 15, 1923, Lodge MSS.

137. Thornton Anderson, *Brooks Adams: Constructive Conservative* (Ithaca, N.Y., 1951), p. 194.

138. Morison, ed., *Letters of Theodore Roosevelt*, I, pp. 620–21.

[93]

however, did review Brooks's *Law of Civilization and Decay*, and Lodge's reaction was probably similar. Roosevelt sympathized with Brooks's military and imaginative man and found the attributes of his new economic man most distasteful. Although he accepted Adams's evaluation of these types, Roosevelt could not accept Brooks's economic determinism and was outraged by his conclusions. For Roosevelt, the idea that national development was a function of economic life was totally unacceptable. Wealth would not corrupt American life because men of character (like Lodge and himself) would arrest that corruption; the destiny of the nation *could* be influenced for good or evil.[139] As long as the "economic forces" (the financial interests) opposed their vision of the future, economic determinism was anathema.

Nevertheless, Lodge found many of Brooks's ideas useful; they often supported his own case. The idea in *Civilization and Decay* that the concentration of political power paralleled the concentration of economic power was taken over immediately. In Lodge's first major article on foreign policy we read that

The tendency of modern times is toward consolidation. It is apparent in capital and labor alike, and it is also true of nations. Small States are of the past and have no future. . . . The great nations are rapidly absorbing for their future expansion and their present defence all the waste places of the earth. It is a movement which makes for civilization and the advancement of the race. As one of the great nations of the world, the United States must not fall out of the line of march.[140]

Similarly, Lodge turned to his own uses Brooks's ideas about the power of the financiers and his propensity for contrasting the interests of the money lenders with those of civilization. Such notions fitted nicely with Lodge's advocacy of an assertive and anti-British foreign policy and with his prejudices against State Street. In 1894 he accused the British of making financial war on the rest of the world and at the height of the Venezuelan crisis he castigated England for trying to create a financial panic in the United States to further its own foreign policy ends.[141] A few months later, in advocating American interven-

139. Morison, ed., *Letters of Theodore Roosevelt*, II, p. 1492; Roosevelt, *American Ideals*, pp. 325–26.
140. Lodge, "Our Blundering Foreign Policy," p. 17. See also the *Cong. Record*, 53rd Cong., 3rd sess., 1895, p. 1984.
141. *Cong. Record*, 53rd Cong., 2nd sess., 1894, p. 4528; 54th Cong., 1st sess., 1895, p. 259.

tion in Cuba, the conditions which prevailed in England were employed in the form of an admonition not to let it happen here. Resistance was still possible (and strongly advocated), but it is interesting to see how much economic determinism Lodge could accept.

But, Mr. President, Lord Salisbury obeys a stronger force, a mightier will, than his own. In the last resort, the power which controls in Europe and in England is the great power of money and of the money lender. The money lenders do not care how many Armenians are butchered; . . . but they do fear that if England moved to rescue the wretched Armenians values might be disturbed and Ottoman bonds decline. . . . Is our civilization in the United States to break down as the civilization of western Europe has broken down before Armenia?[142]

Brooks was also useful because of his interest in instructing Americans in the implications of their new international position.[143] His thoughts on the growing interdependence of the United States and Britain and on the need for the U.S. to join the competition for the "seat of empire" in Eastern Asia closely paralleled Lodge's own. But there is no evidence that Brooks shaped Lodge's thinking in these matters.[144] Both ideas were prefigured in a letter that Lodge wrote to Henry White urging the importance of Anglo-American cooperation in the Far East.[145] But if it is difficult to tie any particular policy directly to Brooks's influence, it may still be correct to say that he made "a significant impression" on Lodge.[146] The influence of Brooks was particularly pronounced in one area. His influence can best be gauged by the fact that he took a man who was "non-commercial in goals and standards" much further down the road to economic determinism than he ever wanted to go.[147] After the war, Brooks's economics and Lodge's nationalism no longer appeared to be at cross purposes; Brooks effected

142. *Ibid.*, 54th Cong., 1st sess., 1896, p. 1972. The number and intensity of the protests against his proposals that he received at this juncture from the business leaders and bankers among his constituents could only have served to confirm his worst suspicions.

143. Anderson, *Brooks Adams*, p. 85.

144. See Brooks's articles, "The Spanish War and the Equilibrium of the World," *The Forum* 25 (August 1898), and "Commercial Future: The New Struggle for Life Among Nations," *Fortnightly Review* 71 (Feb. 1899).

145. Lodge to Henry White, Jan. 31, 1898, White MSS.

146. William A. Williams, "Brooks Adams and American Expansion," *New England Quarterly* 25 (June 1952): 217.

147. Richard Hofstadter, "Manifest Destiny and the Philippines: The Psychic Crisis" in Edwin C. Rozwenc and Kenneth Lindfors, eds., *The United States and the New Imperialism* (Lexington, Mass., 1968), p. 70.

their merger in *America's Economic Supremacy*.[148] Once again Lodge could believe that economic forces and American principles were working in tandem. Recommending Brooks's book, he now assured the economist Charles A. Conant that "the line in your preface in which you say that in this age the economic tendencies are those which are finally dominant . . . in the affairs of the world is a great truth, which is too much overlooked."[149] In his public speeches he began to forge the same links between the "economic forces" and American power that were the staple of *America's Economic Supremacy*:

This is an age in which the economic forces more than ever predominate. We have entered upon a world competition, . . . we are moving faster than anyone else, we have greater resources and a more energetic and capable people . . . ; we are already one of the three or four leaders and a great world power.[150]

In the end, however, *America's Economic Supremacy* only led Lodge, as it did Brooks himself, back to his familiar appeals for preparedness and greater social efficiency. In 1901 Lodge gave an important and neglected speech on army reorganization which is pure Brooks Adams.[151] His approval of Brooks's theory of the economic origins of war is a measure of how much economic determinism Lodge could accept when economics were serving to increase American power and even providing an argument for its further augmentation.

We have expanded far beyond our own markets commercially, and we are breaking into every market in the world. . . . We are marching fast toward the economic supremacy of the world.

But does anyone suppose that the other people like it? They are gasping for breath in all parts of Europe. . . .

. . . if anyone will take the trouble to look back into the history of modern times, since the great economic movements began, he will see how many of the wars came originally, never ostensibly but actually from economic causes. . . .

. . . we occupy a great position economically. We are marching on to a still greater one. . . . but dazzled by its splendor, do not forget its perils. . . .

148. Lodge sent the book to President McKinley with the message that "it seems to me one of the most brilliant and interesting discussions of present economic conditions and of the policy of expansion which I have seen" (Lodge to McKinley, Oct. 22, 1900, Lodge MSS).

149. Lodge to Charles A. Conant, Nov. 21, 1900, Lodge MSS.

150. Clipping from the Boston *Herald*, Nov. 10, 1901, Scrapbooks, Lodge MSS.

151. Lodge even wrote to Brooks to tell him that he was "the chief, if not the only, begetter of it" (Lodge to Brooks Adams, Jan. 8, 1901, Lodge MSS).

I wish to see the United States so prepared that under these new conditions she will always be safe by sea and by land.[152]

Any discussion which shows that Lodge came to believe he was living in an "economic" age inevitably raises the question whether he may not have advocated expansion primarily from economic motives. The question is a difficult one. Personally Lodge was "non-commercial in goals and standards"; his imperialism bore the traits of what Joseph Schumpeter called "pre-capitalist" imperialism.[153] No one who reads his correspondence and speeches can question his preoccupation with national prestige and power or his overriding interest in remaking the national character. Moreover, the "honor" he and Roosevelt valued so highly could only lose its absolutist character, once economic questions came to dominate international intercourse.[154]

Still, as Walter LaFeber has observed, "to interpret American expansion into the Pacific and Caribbean as expansion for merely strategic objectives distorts the true picture: they were strategic means to obtaining and protecting objectives which they defined as economic."[155] The argument need not be posed in either-or terms. Lodge was determined to be a modern man. He "committed himself in theory and practice to the modern sources of wealth" and served his political apprenticeship in an era when the business of America was indeed business.[156] He prided himself on an ability to face facts and did not shrink from acknowledging the relationship between economic and political power. In fact, he was the first to remind his colleagues that goods did not move on sentiment, and that the United States and Britain competed for the world's trade.[157] He recognized that the international power struggle had both a political *and* an economic dimension, and precisely because he saw the relationship between the two there is no point in arguing that his objectives were "merely strategic." It was, for example, easier for him as a high tariff advocate to accept the fact that the inter-

---

152. *Cong Record*, 56th Cong., 2nd sess., 1901, p. 637.
153. *Imperialism and Social Classes* (New York, 1951).
154. Charles Beard, *The Idea of National Interest* (New York, 1934), p. 19.
155. Rozwenc and Lindfors, eds., *The United States and the New Imperialism*, p. 82.
156. Abrams, *Conservatism in a Progressive Era*, p. 33; Richard E. Welch, Jr., "Opponents and Colleagues: George Frisbie Hoar and Henry Cabot Lodge, 1898–1904," *New England Quarterly* 39 (June 1966): 183.
157. *Cong. Record*, 53rd Cong., 3rd sess., 1895, p. 3084; 57th Cong., 1st sess., 1902, p. 4036.

national power struggle had an economic dimension than it was for free-traders, whose economics supposedly precluded that struggle and led to universal peace. As Lodge saw it, every nation was selfish, and England preached free trade out of self-interest. The prosperity (and even the civilization) of the U.S., on the other hand, depended on continued protection, and it could not permit itself the luxury of being influenced by self-serving British opinion.[158] But to recognize the importance of economics is not to define one's own objectives as economic. National power might be augmented in several ways (trading arrangements were one means among many), and a concern for its augmentation and even preservation dictated a concern for the health of the body, whether economic or politic, on which it was based. If Mahan advocated imperialism to arrest "a degenerating body economic,"[159] Lodge looked to an assertive foreign policy and eventually to imperialism as a means of curing America's political and social ills and arresting what he regarded as a deterioration in the American character.

In the abstract, any number of quotations could be educed to demonstrate that Lodge conceived of imperialism as primarily an economic enterprise. He wrote of "that vast trade with the East from which we must draw our future prosperity," argued that "this extension will help us industrially," and came to look upon the Philippines as "a great opportunity for the investment of surplus capital."[160] All these statements, however, were made in support of the retention of the Philippines, and all post-date the American seizure of Manila. Prior to Dewey's victory Lodge never evinced any particular interest in the Philippines. It is important to distinguish between arguments that were used prior to the war with Spain in order to create an imperialist *élan,* and those which were employed to rally domestic support for subsequent administration policy. The distinction, however fine, is necessary to an understanding of American imperialism.

Another difficult question is the extent to which Lodge was influenced by Darwinian theory and applied it to international relations. Lodge's familiarity with Social Darwinism is not at issue nor is the fact that he

158. Lodge, *Speeches and Addresses,* pp. 102, 122, 152.

159. Walter LaFeber, "A Note on the 'Mercantilistic Imperialism' of Alfred Thayer Mahan," *Mississippi Valley Historical Review* 48 (March 1962): 679.

160. Lodge to Mr. (E. B.?) Hayes, May 19, 1898; to George (Lyman?), June 13, 1898; and to William H. Taft, Nov. 22, 1900; Lodge MSS.

employed Darwinian imagery. He commonly declared that "in the process of evolution we have seen the nation grow and expand," and then converted that general statement into the admonition that "a nation may be able to fight, trade and organize, and yet, if unable to expand and spread, will not endure."[161] He delighted in the contrasts between expansion and stagnation, advancement and regression, which were the staple of all imperialists, but stopped short of making the systematic application of Darwinian doctrine to international relations featured in Mahan's work. If only for political reasons Lodge would never have written, as did Mahan, that everything was a part of the "struggle for life," that our own protective system was but "an organized warfare."[162]

Social Darwinism, though theoretically a neutral element in the battle between laissez faire individualism and purposive state action, was in the American environment a liability for Hamiltonians like Lodge and Roosevelt who supported state action in many areas.[163] As TR observed in commenting on Benjamin Kidd's *Social Evolution*, progress had scarcely been greatest where the struggle for life was keenest.[164] Lodge, arguing for immigration restriction, denied that the best necessarily survive, and insisted on restating the proposition in the form of "a question of the survival of the fittest to survive."[165] They were at pains to introduce the concept of guided evolution, which on the domestic scene accorded more closely with their Hamiltonian conception of government, and which on the international stage was not incompatible with an idealistic imperialism. Their viewpoint is the more understandable when seen as the converse of that of the American popularizer of Social Darwinism, William Graham Sumner, who opposed all state interference with individual struggle, whether government planning, military expenditure, or imperialism. If progress were dependent on the attainment of "a high degree of social efficiency," social efficiency became a vehicle for avoiding the uncontrolled conflict implicit in popular conceptions of the Darwinian struggle and for reintroducing the ele-

161. Lodge, "Address" of March 17, 1902, "A Record of the Dedication of the Monument on Dorchester Heights," p. 52, Massachusetts Historical Society; Lodge, *Fighting Frigate*, p. 268.

162. Mahan, *The Interest of America in Sea Power* (London, 1898), p. 18.

163. See Richard Hofstadter, *Social Darwinism in American Thought* (Philadelphia, 1944).

164. Roosevelt, *American Ideals*, p. 297.

165. *Cong. Record*, 57th Cong., 1st sess., 1902, p. 4040.

ment of morality. Character and idealism were integral parts of their conception of social efficiency, and theirs was a Social Darwinism tempered by a strong streak of American moralism. When Lodge spoke of all social and national efficiency being dead in Spain, he was clearly making a moral judgment.[166]

The Whig theory of history with its belief that the most advanced point in time represents the stage of highest development was a nice complement to a theory of evolution which suggested a passage from the simple to the complex and from a lower to a higher stage of civilization.[167] Introduce a Whiggish belief in progress and leaven it with the Romantic historians' moral assurance as to their ability to identify the forces of progress and you have Lodge's belief that the civilization of the United States was the highest yet attained, and a strong justification for American expansion.[168] So conceived, the Darwinian conflict encompassed the more traditional and historically grounded struggle between competing doctrines, forms of government, and even civilizations. And so viewed, the conflict between the United States and Spain could be regarded both as "natural and organic" and as an inexorable historical conflict between Spanish colonial despotism and American free government.[169]

As a result it is difficult to single out one element such as Social Darwinism and claim that it was determinant. This difficulty is compounded by the fact that Lodge, owing to his opportunism, was often deliberately vague on the question of causation. Living in an age of great change and sometimes doubting man's ability to direct events, Lodge flirted with determinism but was unable to isolate the determinants. The result was the frequent invocation of "the relentless world-forces which shape the destinies of mankind."[170] These forces were the more inexorable when they seemed to be taking the United States where Lodge wanted it to go. Such thinking was, of course, scarcely unique with Lodge, but all that can be said for it was that it was a sign of the times.

Alfred Mahan, Brooks Adams, the popularizers of Charles Darwin—

166. Lodge, *The War with Spain* (New York, 1899), p. 71.
167. Richard M. Weaver, *Ideas Have Consequences* (Chicago, 1948), p. 1.
168. Lodge, *Early Memories*, pp. 50, 218. In moments of detachment America was only the leader of "scientific civilization," but on the hustings that distinction was generally overlooked, and even in the cited work he lay claim to the superiority of the American race.
169. Lodge, *The War with Spain*, p. 4; Lodge, *Story of the Revolution*, p. 567.
170. Lodge, *The War with Spain*, pp. 2, 228.

all were of assistance in getting Lodge to where he wanted to go. But "where he wanted to go" was not a constant but rather a function of time and events. Lodge was a practical and a political man, sensitive both to limitations and to opportunities. If any one factor determined his imperialism it was probably the political one. At the very least we have in his case an interesting demonstration of the interplay between the ideology and the politics of imperialism.

III

Too much attention has been paid to the machinations of a small aristocratic clique and too little to the political context in which Lodge and his "co-conspirators" operated. In 1891 Lodge published an article, "The Political Issues of 1892," in which he failed even to allude to an issue of foreign policy.[171] Arguing for the 1892 naval appropriation, he carefully limited his appeal to that for "an efficient navy . . . large enough for defense, not large enough to tempt us to aggression or attack."[172] In both cases his arguments befitted the most orthodox of Republicans. This is the more surprising as foreign policy had figured in the last two Presidential campaigns,[173] and there was a growing appreciation of American power and influence.[174]

In early January of 1893 Lodge was elected U.S. Senator by the Massachusetts legislature, thereby realizing his ambition to sit in "the seat of Webster and Sumner." Shortly thereafter news reached the United States of an uprising against the native queen of the Hawaiian Islands and of the new government's desire for annexation. Lodge, his own political future assured, could now turn his attention to national issues. As "a prominent Republican Senator" (not identified but, from

171. *The Forum* 12 (Sept. 1891): 98–105.

172. *Cong. Record*, 52nd Cong., 1st sess., 1892, p. 3362.

173. The 1884 Democratic platform had made an issue of the Republican party's "British" policy and in 1888 the Republicans, seizing on an inadvertent and extremely ill-advised declaration of support for Cleveland by the British Minister, Lord Sackville-West, had been able to turn the tables and pin the pro-British label on their opponents. In the same vein they added a complaint about the Administration's "weak and unpatriotic treatment" of the fisheries dispute with Canada (Kirk H. Porter and Donald Bruce Johnson, eds., *National Party Platforms, 1840–1964* [Urbana, 1966], pp. 68, 82).

174. See Ernest May, *Imperial Democracy* (New York, 1973), pp. 5–6. In 1892 the major European powers raised their legations in Washington to the status of embassies, and Mulhall's *Dictionary of Statistics* showed the United States surpassing the European countries by nearly every economic standard.

the language employed, most probably Lodge) told the Washington correspondent of the Boston *Journal*:

The time has come when the United States has an opportunity to secure Hawaii without asking for it, and to provide a means by which its great interest in the Pacific Ocean and on the Pacific coast can be protected. In my judgment, it is wise in the United States to do this as a means of self-protection. There can be no question that if the United States shall not accept the proposition . . . those islands will fall under the control of the British Empire. . . .[175]

Harrison, though a lame duck, sent the treaty of annexation to the Senate, but President-elect Cleveland let it be known that he favored delay. Cleveland soon withdrew the treaty and sent to Hawaii an investigatory commission headed by a prominent opponent of expansion. Lodge, as befitted a freshman Senator, kept silent. During 1893 even Mahan's comments on Hawaii were tentative. He suggested that holding Hawaii would require a great extension of American naval power and wanted to be sure it would be forthcoming.[176] When the commission's report which suggested American complicity in the revolution was released, even the staunchly Republican New York *Tribune* decided that it might preclude annexation.[177] The expansionists had been outmaneuvered. Initially able to cloak expansionism in the rhetoric of piety, of support for a Christian and republican revolt against a tyrannical Queen, they soon had to acknowledge that Cleveland had preempted the "moral" position.

Not content with heading off expansion, Cleveland had seen political advantage in tying the Republicans to an "immoral" policy. The result was his December 18, 1893 message to Congress excoriating the activity of Minister Stevens and the Navy under his Republican predecessor. "The manner of Cleveland's rejection of annexation insured that the conduct of foreign policy would be handicapped by political strife for years to come."[178] Lodge confided to his diary his disgust with the President's "grotesque and miserable" Hawaiian policy and soon published his views.[179] But he was remarkably restrained at first. Still hoping

175. Boston *Journal*, Jan. 31, 1893.
176. Mahan, *The Interest of America in Sea Power*, pp. 32, 53.
177. May, *Imperial Democracy*, p. 23.
178. Grenville and Young, *Politics, Strategy and American Diplomacy*, pp. 41, 103.
179. Lodge Journal, entry for Jan. 22, 1894, Lodge MSS.

for Democratic votes for annexation and therefore reluctant to make Hawaii a partisan issue, he claimed that the "performance" was not a Democratic one (Democrats had always favored expansion) but rather that Cleveland's personal crusade "in behalf of a savage queen had humiliated the United States."[180] But unsure of its political effect, he did not dwell on the issue.

Meanwhile the panic of 1893 developed into the worst depression the United States had yet experienced. Economic questions commanded everyone's attention. Lodge's first major speech as a Senator was devoted to as philosophical and intellectual a defense as the tariff probably ever received in an American Congress. Lodge, like everyone else, was looking for a way out of the depression and became a convert to bimetallism, the international monetization of both silver and gold. This led him to propose that duties on English goods be doubled until such time as Britain should agree to the international use of silver.[181] It was as if he were giving his colleagues a lesson in the connection between economics and foreign policy.[182] It was a theme with considerable potential for getting Republican high-tariff and gold-standard conservatives to support an assertive foreign policy. Taking a cue from the philosophical implications of support for free trade outlined in his tariff speech, he claimed in the first article he devoted exclusively to foreign policy that the Democratic party had been "Cobdenized," that support for free trade and "abuse for the navy and sneers at any attempt to uphold the rights of the United States" went hand in hand.[183] The moral for the Republican business community was, of course, the reverse. Support for the tariff implied support for other governmental action— an assertive foreign policy, a powerful navy, and territorial expansion. We have heard so much of late of the expansionism inherent in free trade and the open door concept that we tend to forget that Lodge's contemporaries often saw the matter quite differently.

Outraged by Cleveland's politicization of Hawaiian annexation and determined to exploit the growing public discontent with the Administration, Republicans began to explore ways of turning the Administra-

180. Lodge, "The Opportunity of the Republican Party," pp. 150–51.

181. *Cong. Record*, 53rd Cong., 2nd sess., 1894, pp. 3611–24, 4527.

182. The bimetallists were the internationalists. Their basic disagreement with the silverites was that they did not accept the notion that the United States could unilaterally reestablish silver.

183. Lodge, "Our Blundering Foreign Policy," pp. 14–15.

tion's foreign policy to their political advantage. As a corollary to Cleveland's blundering economic policy, Lodge began talking about his "blundering foreign policy." In February 1894 Lodge had seen foreign policy as one issue among many, but by September he was giving it top billing. He now complained that Cleveland had "a profound contempt for the doctrine that . . . continuity in the foreign policy of a great nation is desirable" and, becoming shriller, he insinuated that it was "always easy to give away something valuable, especially to England, to which this administration appears to be strongly attached."[184]

Encouraged by the success of such tactics manifested in the election of an overwhelmingly Republican Congress, Lodge eagerly awaited further opportunities to pin an "immoral" and "un-American" label on Administration foreign policy. Republican criticism of Cleveland's foreign policy soon became even more acerbic than their attacks on his tariff policy.[185] Lodge's next opportunity was afforded by the "brutal stupidity and cowardice of Gresham" in the matter of the surrender of two Japanese students who, during the Sino-Japanese War, had sought American protection from the Chinese.[186] It has been suggested that Lodge was motivated in his criticism of Gresham by a desire to obtain a seat on the Foreign Relations Committee.[187] He undoubtedly wanted (and shortly secured) such an appointment, but to concentrate on his personal ambition alone is to ignore the larger partisan purposes being served.

Lodge also sought a means of turning the Hawaiian issue back on Cleveland and reestablishing the moral authority of expansionism. Opposing forced annexation was one thing, but seeking to restore "a savage queen" was quite another, and Lodge now sensed that Cleveland had gone too far. He began to preach a heady gospel of expansionism, but interestingly its principal justification lay in an interpretation of the recent election results. The Democrats had once more, as in 1861, allowed the Republican party to become the sole defenders of American-

184. Lodge, "The Results of Democratic Victory," pp. 271–72, 277.
185. Pratt, *Expansionists of 1898*, p. 208.
186. *Correspondence of Roosevelt and Lodge*, I, p. 140; *Cong. Record*, 53rd Cong., 3rd sess., 1894, pp. xxvii, 578, 967.
187. Schriftgiesser, *The Gentleman from Massachusetts*, pp. 129, 134; George E. Paulsen, "Secretary Gresham, Senator Lodge, and American Good Offices in China, 1894," *Pacific Historical Review* 36 (May 1967): 142.

ism. Now willing to risk a political battle over Hawaii, Lodge announced that the American people would take Hawaii "as soon as they have an Administration which will not thwart their desires in that respect."[188] He proclaimed himself an expansionist and identified completely with Mahan's doctrines. But whether he had "evolved a new philosophy" or was merely adjusting to changed political circumstances remains an open question.[189]

His language was now frequently extravagant; he proclaimed the need for a "great" Navy, declared his opposition to seeing the American flag pulled down where it had once been run up, and thought Cuba would soon become "a necessity."[190] He saw an opportunity to lead and form opinion, but he did not throw caution to the winds. His expansionism was still remarkably limited in its scope, and he continued to emphasize its defensive aspects.[191] As he saw it, the United States either had to take Hawaii itself or get embroiled in difficulties with a major power (Britain or Japan). He stressed the Senate's declaration warning other nations to keep their hands off, and the consequent responsibility assumed by the U.S. "A widely extended system of colonization" did not interest him; that was "not our line." But he did want to "take and hold the outworks as we now hold the citadel of American power."[192] Though he looked forward to there being but one flag from the Rio Grande to the Arctic, he reiterated his opposition to any extension to the south, "for neither the population nor the lands of Central or South America would be desirable additions."[193] Similarly, though he wanted a "great" Navy he hastened to assure his listeners that a navy as large as England's would be "totally unnecessary."[194] Good politics presented opportunities but imposed limitations as well.

Other limitations were implicit in Lodge's own desires. The *sine qua non* of an assertive foreign policy was a rigid enforcement of the Monroe Doctrine, and events next brought that issue to the fore. Venezuela claimed that England was encroaching on its territory and, through the

---

188. *Cong. Record*, 53rd Cong., 3rd sess., 1895, pp. 622, 630.
189. Grenville and Young, *Politics, Strategy and American Diplomacy*, p. 223.
190. *Cong. Record*, 53rd Cong., 3rd sess., 1895, pp. 1213, 3108; Lodge, "Our Blundering Foreign Policy," p. 17.
191. Grenville and Young, *Politics, Strategy and American Diplomacy*, p. 223.
192. *Cong. Record*, 53rd Cong., 3rd sess., 1895, pp. 1211, 1213, 3108.
193. Lodge, "Our Blundering Foreign Policy," p. 16.
194. *Cong. Record*, 53rd Cong., 3rd sess., 1895, p. 3107.

mediating influence of William Lindsay Scruggs, found a champion in Lodge. It was easy for Lodge to believe in British perfidy, and it is an overstatement to claim that "on the Venezuelan question Lodge once again followed, rather than led, public opinion."[195] He himself characterized his actions as crying out "alone in the wilderness."[196] That cry was a forceful article, "England, Venezuela, and the Monroe Doctrine," whose appearance coincided with a declaration by the Chairman of the Republican National Committee that the Administration's weak foreign policy would be the chief issue in the ensuing campaign.[197] Lodge implied that the British incursion was yet another result of American neglect of foreign affairs and called upon his fellow citizens to either maintain the Doctrine or abandon their "rightful supremacy in the Western Hemisphere."[198] A month later he took his cause directly to Britain's leaders, and when Joseph Chamberlain took up the standard British theme of how fortunate the United States was "in being untroubled by any foreign policy," Lodge, though willing to concede that this was generally true "outside of the Americas," insisted that in the Western Hemisphere "we had a very definite one." There America had to be "supreme."[199]

To use the Doctrine as a basis for urging an assertive foreign policy was actually to limit one's horizons. At this juncture Lodge's vision extended only to "hemispherism" and to attribute to him a desire "to create an American overseas empire is to misunderstand him."[200] The first proposition of American foreign policy was that

The United States did not propose to entangle itself in the questions of Europe or Asia. Beyond the limits of the American hemisphere all that we desire to do is to guard the American citizen and the American property wherever it may happen to be. . . . [But] we are the head and the supreme leader in this hemisphere, and we must not suffer our position to be abated one jot.[201]

195. Grenville and Young, *Politics, Strategy and American Diplomacy*, pp. 225–26.

196. Lodge to Anna Cabot Lodge, Dec. 18, 1895, Lodge MSS.

197. May, *Imperial Democracy*, p. 33. This was also the year of the Corinto affair and the Armenian massacres, both of which figured in the campaign.

198. Lodge, "England, Venezuela, and the Monroe Doctrine," *North American Review* 160 (June 1895): 653, 657–58.

199. Lodge to Anna Cabot Lodge, July 16, 1895, Lodge MSS.

200. Grenville and Young, *Politics, Strategy and American Diplomacy*, p. 229. The imputation is Pratt's in *Expansionists of 1898*, p. 232.

201. Clipping, New York *Advertiser*, Nov. 28, 1895, Scrapbooks, Lodge MSS.

An important landmark on the road to an imperial future, this would also prove a convenient and defensible posture on the road back.

Given the role which issues of foreign policy were coming to play in American domestic politics, the question arises of the extent to which those issues were artificially created. It was a question posed by Lodge's critics and one he felt compelled to answer.

Great political questions, whether foreign or domestic, cannot be created from nothing by any man. . . . they spring from existing conditions; they come from the social, economic, or political development of mankind. . . . the great powers of Europe have reached out in all directions and seized the waste places of the earth. . . . it was this advance which brought the European movement into contact with American interest. We had nothing to do with it. The aggression was not ours.[202]

This land seizing did not concern the United States as long as it was confined to Africa and Asia, but by 1895 "it had become apparent that unless we were prepared to see South America share sooner or later the fate of Africa it was necessary for us to intervene."[203] His view that the European powers were engaged in a worldwide contest for raw materials, markets, and prestige was certainly in accord with the facts of the late nineteenth century.[204] His apprehension lest the Western Hemisphere become another Africa, though unwarranted, appears to have been honest.[205] It was never an impossibility, and the absence of American concern would probably have made it more likely. Lodge was reacting to events, not creating those events, and in this sense there was nothing contrived about the issues he was trying to make. On the other hand, the nature, and sometimes the timing, of his reactions had more to do with the exigencies of domestic politics than he was willing to admit. The foreign policy issues he raised were not artificial in origin, but neither were they considered on their merits alone.

He learned as he went along. The relationship between foreign policy and domestic politics was a many-faceted one. A balance was not easily struck. From the Venezuelan crisis he drew the lesson that domestic unity and the steadfastness in policy which was its companion

202. Lodge, *Certain Accepted Heroes*, pp. 235–36, 239.
203. *Ibid.*, pp. 237, 244.
204. See chapter one, "A World of Empires," of David Healy's *U.S. Expansionism* (Madison, 1970) for a good overview of the international setting.
205. It was a staple of both his speeches and his private correspondence. See, for example, his *Speeches and Addresses*, pp. 234–35, and letters to Mr. Blackwell, Dec. 23, 1895, and to Henry (Higginson?), Dec. 26, 1895, Lodge MSS.

were an important ingredient in the achievement of foreign policy success.[206] But such domestic unity was usually fleeting, and he often found his foreign policy goals in conflict with his domestic political aspirations. He was nothing if not agile. Whereas in 1895 he thought Cuba would become "a necessity" for the U.S., after the insurrection broke out and the Cubans began to demand their independence he made a quick retreat. Morality as manifested in good politics now demanded support for Cuban independence, and Lodge was henceforth to deny that he ever favored annexation and to emphasize the higher ground of "Our Duty to Cuba."[207]

Lodge chafed under such limitations but paid careful attention to them. He preached a new doctrine, but his position was so precarious that he felt the necessity of tailoring that doctrine to the dictates of American public opinion. There was no point in winning a battle only to lose the war. Just a few months before the declaration of war on Spain he reiterated his opposition to taking anything beyond our hemisphere.[208] Though he was concerned about the future of China and personally wanted "to say to England that we would stand by her in her declaration that the ports of China must be opened to all nations equally or to none," he had to acknowledge that "our foreign policy is always more hap-hazard than I like to see it."[209]

The imperialism of both Lodge and Roosevelt was nurtured in their reaction against this haphazardness and what they regarded as the "irresponsibility" of American policy toward Cuba. In early 1893 Roosevelt lamented to Speck von Sternberg how difficult it was to arouse the nation and began to "question whether anything but a military disaster will ever make us feel our responsibilities and our possible dangers."[210] Privately he even admitted his admiration for "the imperialist instinct" (which seemed an embodiment of the qualities and policies he desired), while expressing his disheartenment over

206. Grenville and Young, *Politics, Strategy and American Diplomacy*, p. 228; Lodge to Frank L. Sanford, Dec. 29, 1895; George (Lyman?), Dec. 21, 1895; and Henry (Higginson?), Dec. 21, 1895, and Jan. 23, 1896; Lodge MSS.

207. Lodge, "Our Duty to Cuba," *The Forum* 21 (May 1896): 278–87; Lodge to General Draper, Dec. 20, 1897, Lodge MSS. However, he never entirely gave up the thought of ultimate annexation. See a letter of June 13, 1898, to a Mr. Ward, Lodge MSS.

208. Lodge, "The American Policy of Territorial Expansion," *The Independent* 50 (Jan. 13, 1898).

209. Lodge to Henry White, Jan. 31, 1898, White MSS.

210. Morison, ed., *Letters of Theodore Roosevelt*, I, p. 764.

the lack of it which his fellow Americans exhibited.[211] Lodge was particularly concerned lest his compatriots neglect "the responsibility which we assumed when we announced to the world that no one [else] should be allowed to interfere in the island; the proposition that it is none of our business is precisely what the South said about slavery. . . ."[212] Up to the verge of war it was this inaction and "irresponsibility" that Lodge emphasized. It was a good tactic. It was an argument that went to the heart of America's moral professions. It pointed up the need for what he had always advocated. Its antitheses—preparation, decision, and a practical and responsible idealism—these were the major themes of his April 13, 1898 speech on Cuba and the essence of his approach to foreign policy.

If two years ago we had recognized the belligerency of the Cuban insurgents they would have been able to raise money, . . . and open a port; they would have won their independence . . . and we never should have been involved.
. . . if we had today, as we ought to have, twenty battle ships and a hundred torpedo boats, there never would have been a Cuban question; . . . the contest would have been so hopeless that it never would have been entered upon. . . . If we had clung to the old faiths, if we had kept our Navy and our defenses as Washington advised, if we had looked a little further ahead into what the Monroe doctrine meant, we should not be standing on the verge of war today.[213]

If one is looking for continuity in Lodge's approach to foreign policy, here it is. Whatever the crisis these were the elements to which he had reference; preparation and timely policy formation were his panaceas.

Lodge's approach to foreign policy was moulded in an exceptionally political environment. He knew where he wanted to go (and conceived of his own ends as "ideal") but he also understood American politics and knew that the "idealism" of American public opinion was not the same as his own. Roosevelt reflected their *modus operandi* when he candidly wrote:

I wish we had a perfectly consistent foreign policy, and that this policy was that ultimately every European power should be driven out of America, and every foot of American soil, including the nearest islands in both the Pacific

211. Roosevelt to W. R. Clowes, the British naval expert, Jan. 14, 1898, quoted in Howard K. Beale, *Theodore Roosevelt and the Rise of America to World Power* (Baltimore, 1956), p. 68.
212. Lodge to Henry (Higginson?), March 9, 1898, Lodge MSS.
213. *Cong. Record*, 55th Cong., 2nd sess., 1898, pp. 3782–83.

and the Atlantic, should be in the hands of independent American states, and so far as possible in the possession of the United States or under its protection. . . . Now, our people are not up as yet to following out this line of policy in its entirety, and the thing to be done is to get whatever portion of it is possible at the moment.[214]

It was this practical and political approach which caused Lodge to be sometimes a "Hawaiian" and at others a "Cuban." It was this same approach and concern for his own ability to survive and continue to fight the battle that led him to stress Executive-Congressional unity on Cuba.[215] As Roosevelt observed, Lodge realized "that if the President and Hoar stand one way [on Cuba] and he another, his own republican party will throw him out of the Senate next year."[216] If before the war he and Roosevelt never advocated a full-fledged imperialism, that was a function of the limitations imposed by successful politics. There was simply no occasion for it. Similarly, if their own thinking was inchoate and they could not make up their minds whether American intervention in Cuba was a matter of national self-interest or of duty to humanity, it was because the political environment was such that they needed both arguments to move the nation and were never forced to choose between them.[217]

Suddenly in war and in Dewey's Manila Bay victory they had their opportunity. Even though Dewey's presence in the Far East was a result of Roosevelt's planning, the evidence supports Howard Beale's contention that the taking of the Philippines was not part of a well-thought-out Far Eastern policy.[218] Lodge made no significant reference (publicly or privately) to the Philippines before the war, and apparently "the prospect of retaining the islands did not occur to him until *after*

214. Morison, ed., *Letters of Theodore Roosevelt*, I, p. 746.
215. *Cong. Record*, 55th Cong., 2nd sess., 1898, p. 3782; Lodge to Anna Cabot Lodge, April 3, 1898, Lodge MSS.
216. Morison, ed., *Letters of Theodore Roosevelt*, I, p. 812.
217. Lodge to Henry (Higginson?), March 9, 1898, Lodge MSS. Lodge, of course, found their reconciliation in the American mission in history.
218. Beale, *Roosevelt and the Rise of America*, p. 62. Roosevelt had developed and imparted to McKinley a plan for use "if things looked menacing about Spain." One, but not a major, aspect of that plan called for the Asiatic squadron to "blockade, and if possible take Manila" (*Correspondence of Roosevelt and Lodge*, I, pp. 278–79). But even before Roosevelt became Assistant Secretary of the Navy, naval officers had formed contingency plans for attacking the Philippines in the event of war with Spain. See J.A.S. Grenville, "American Naval Preparations for War with Spain, 1896–1898," *Journal of American Studies* 2 (April 1968): 33–47.

news of Dewey's victory had reached the United States."[219] Some observers found the sudden turn of events too much to comprehend. "You have a new game to play," Henry Adams wrote to John Hay, "[and I] don't quite feel as though I knew the value of the cards or of the players."[220] Not so Roosevelt or Lodge. If they did not conspire "to utilize the impending crisis with Spain to launch the United States on a career of colonial expansion," they *were* quick to seize the opportunity presented by what Mahan called "the preparation made for us" in the Philippines.[221] They looked upon the war as an opportunity for gaining support for the powerful fleet they had long desired and as a chance to impress upon the American people the truth of what they had long preached. The 'Large Policy' should be viewed in this context. It was not just a policy of territorial expansion; they were also sensitive to what they saw as an opportunity to bring about a revolution in American thinking about foreign policy. It was an opportunity unlikely to present itself again. Therefore Lodge was in "no hurry to see the war jammed through." As he wrote to Roosevelt, who was already in Tampa with his regiment:

We shall come out better if we take our time. . . . We ought to take Porto Rico as we have taken the Philippines and then close in on Cuba. Let us get the outlying things first. The Administration I believe to be doing very well and to be following out a large policy. The one point where haste is needed is the Philippines, and I think I can say . . . that the administration is grasping the whole policy at last.[222]

In short, here was an opportunity to effect most of the changes in American life that Lodge and Roosevelt had long dreamed of being able to institute. Their minds ran in many directions. They could conceive of the war and expansion bringing about a panoply of changes which they thought would be good for the country, just as the opponents of the war and of expansion feared that in their wake would follow a series of unwelcome changes in both America's foreign and domestic politics. If Senator Hoar feared the effect of imperialism on America's domestic institutions, Lodge welcomed it. The relationship among the various

219. Grenville and Young, *Politics, Strategy and American Diplomacy*, p. 230.
220. Ford, ed., *Letters of Henry Adams*, II, pp. 175–76.
221. Pratt, "The 'Large Policy' of 1898," pp. 220–21; William E. Livezey, *Mahan on Sea Power* (Norman, Oklahoma, 1947), p. 23.
222. *Correspondence of Roosevelt and Lodge*, I, pp. 299, 302.

elements in their program was complex and ever changing.

Writing as a historian Lodge chose to attach particular significance to one development: "the questions of the acquisition here and there of territory upon which markets rest or defence depends are details; the great fact is the abandonment of isolation" and the assumption of a world role.[223] Here at last, in Lodge's view, was an opportunity to effect a workable fusion of American power and American idealism. As a practical matter the organization of American power seemed to be dependent upon the assumption of international responsibility. Under American conditions imperialism and altruism necessarily went together.[224]

The opportunities were manifold and their exhilaration great. Lodge found England's support of the American position during the Spanish-American War especially heartening and began to dream of the Anglo-American supremacy to which his racial views had always made him susceptible:

The millions who speak the English tongue in all parts of the earth must surely see now that, once united in friendship, it can be said, even as Shakespeare said three hundred years ago: 'Come the three corners of the world in arms, and we shall shock them.'[225]

For a while all seemed possible, and it was in this atmosphere that Lodge and Roosevelt began to give imperialism a full explication. Roosevelt's famous "Strenuous Life" and "Expansion is Peace" statements date from this period. Lodge began to turn his history into a tract for imperialism. His *Story of the Revolution* may be the most military-centered account of the struggle for American independence ever writ-

---

223. Lodge, *Story of the Revolution*, p. 574; Lodge, *The War with Spain*, pp. 193, 235–36.

224. Since the outbreak of World War II "isolationism" has been a bugbear for American historians. Thus we have Karl Schriftgiesser proclaiming that Lodge's philosophy of expansionism was founded upon a dual belief in isolation and imperialism (*The Gentleman from Massachusetts*, p. 146) and E. Berkeley Tompkins (*Anti-Imperialism in the United States*, p. 286) denying that the anti-imperialists were isolationists. The anti-imperialists were, strictly speaking, probably not isolationists (isolationism has always been more of a tactic than a goal in itself), but one can not read the major pamphlets of the anti-imperialists (such as George Boutwell's "Isolation or Imperialism") or the Democratic platform of 1900 with its condemnation of "Republican involvement in world politics" without concluding that the anti-imperialists were the ones wielding the isolationist argument and that, in the context of the day, Roosevelt and Lodge were the internationalists.

225. Lodge, *Story of the Revolution*, pp. 568–71.

ten, and in his *War with Spain* he first voiced the full range of Darwinian and determinist arguments for American expansion.

They had great plans. They hoped to make of American imperialism a model imperialism, an agent of international reform and a means of elevating the tone of American life. They wanted to believe that the country was embarked on a career which would be "beneficial to the world and honorable to ourselves."[226] Withal they were motivated by a concern for both their own and the nation's reputation. They were determined to differentiate American imperialism from British imperialism. Lodge regarded the Jameson raid as "a sordid speculation," and Roosevelt thought the British were beginning to shirk the burdens of empire.[227] Somehow they thought they could enjoy the benefits of imperialism without incurring its liabilities. Lodge thought that dealing with the Spanish cessions would tend to "elevate and enlarge the whole tone and scope of our politics." He even imagined that the Philippines would be governed by "a class of men precisely like those employed by England in India."[228] They entered on an imperial venture with the intention of acting as political mentors to their charges, of training them "in the principles of freedom," insisting (with some truth) that the other colonial powers would never have been so troubled to introduce self-government.[229] "Above all things," Lodge wanted the United States to "be free ... from the slightest suspicion even that there is jobbery or corruption or that we are trying to get into those islands to exploit for the benefit of individuals or of corporations."[230]

Imperialism was a challenge whose acceptance could portend a new era in American history.

Now is the accepted time. I do not want this generation to fail in the task which has been imposed upon it: I do not want our children and our children's children reaping a bitter harvest which has grown from our mistakes or our cowardice. . . .

I want them to be able to say of us that we saw that the United States

226. Mahan to Lodge, Feb. 9, 1899, Lodge MSS.
227. *Correspondence of Roosevelt and Lodge*, I, p. 220; Morison, ed., *Letters of Theodore Roosevelt*, III, pp. 116–17.
228. Lodge to Mr. Haskell, Dec. 1, 1898, Lodge MSS; Lodge to the Rev. Endicott Peabody, Aug. 17, 1898, Houghton Library, Harvard University.
229. Burton, *Theodore Roosevelt: Confident Imperialist*, p. 37; Lodge, *Speeches and Addresses*, p. 349; Lodge, "Shall We Retain the Philippines?" *Collier's Weekly*, Feb. 10, 1900, p. 3.
230. *Cong. Record*, 55th Cong., 3rd sess., 1899, p. 2810.

could not be turned into a gigantic Switzerland or Holland, that it could not be a hermit nation hiding a defenceless, feeble body within a huge shell; that it could not be shut up and kept from its share of the world's commerce until it was smothered by a power hostile to it in every conception of justice and liberty when it might have prevented such a fate.[231]

For a brief moment they captured the imagination of perhaps a majority of the American people. But a belief in their own purposes did not blind them to the facts of American political life. They proceeded with considerable caution and worried about initial impressions. Lodge knew the country would demand "success in government" in its dependencies, and was therefore both alarmed and depressed by the drift of affairs in the Philippines and Cuba. He set great store in retaining "the confidence of the country."[232] Roosevelt had already expressed the same fears in a letter to Secretary of State Hay:

A series of disasters at the very beginning of our colonial policy would shake this administration, and therefore our party, and might produce the most serious and far-reaching effects upon the nation as a whole, for if some political cataclysm was the result, it might mean the definite abandonment of the course upon which we embarked—the only course I think fit for a really great nation.[233]

Nor could they entirely shed the pessimism born of years of crying in the wilderness. They never forgot that their interests and standards were not universally shared. Even at the height of the war enthusiasm Roosevelt quipped to Lodge that "the average New York boss is quite willing to allow you to do what you wish in such trivial matters as war and the acquisition of Porto Rico and Hawaii provided you don't interfere with the really vital questions [like patronage]. . . ."[234] Roosevelt was elected Governor of New York in the fall of 1898 by only a narrow margin in a campaign handicapped by public preoccupation with state "canal scandals" and by the apathy with which the electorate viewed the recent war.[235] By January he was confessing to Lodge a growing realization that "this huge materialistic community [New York] is at bottom, either wrong or half-hearted on the Philippines question."[236]

231. Boston *Herald*, Nov. 1, 1899.
232. Lodge to Roosevelt, July 12, 1899, Roosevelt MSS.
233. *Correspondence of Roosevelt and Lodge*, I, p. 406.
234. *Ibid.*, I, p. 334.
235. Morison, ed., *Letters of Theodore Roosevelt*, II, p. 888.
236. *Ibid.*, II, p. 924.

They knew their politics too well to expect that they could have things their own way for very long. For all their excitement, on the political front they proceeded with circumspection. Under the influence of Mahan, who considered public feeling about the Philippines to be "doubtful" and confessed that even from the standpoint of American advantage he had not fully adjusted himself to the idea of taking them, Lodge backtracked from his original enthusiasm for taking all of the Philippines.[237] Mahan was concerned lest the American people fail to support the increased military expenditures which expansion would entail and inclined to hold no more than Luzon. With his assistance Lodge worked out a rather ingenious arrangement designed to limit both the domestic and international liabilities of acquisition. On August 11, 1898, Lodge presented this plan to Acting Secretary of State William Day:

I see very plainly the enormous difficulties of dealing with the Phillipines [*sic*], and am by no means anxious to assume the burden of possession outside of Luzon—if we go as far as that—for I assume that as a matter of course we shall retain Manila. . . .

The only practical solution that occurs to me is that we should take the whole group as an indemnity for the war, and then cede all the islands except Luzon to England in exchange for the Bahamas and Jamaica and the Danish Islands, which I think we should be entitled to ask her to buy and turn over to us. This would relieve us of the burden of administering that great group in the East . . . and would leave us in the Phillipines [*sic*] associated with a friendly power with whom we should be in entire accord.[238]

However realistic in terms of American politics and interests, such a proposal could not have had much appeal for England. The British were interested in a strong American presence in the Far East, not in having to protect an American outpost. Lodge's idea was never seriously entertained, but it does throw light on the nature of his commitment to expansionism. When convinced that the people had made up their minds to take the Philippines and when reassured by the election returns, Lodge returned to his previous insistence on taking all of the islands.[239]

Meanwhile Lodge was confronted with two significant hurdles. In both cases he found it politic to conceal his long-range designs and the

237. Mahan to Lodge, July 27, 1898, Lodge MSS.
238. Lodge to Judge Day, August 11, 1898, Lodge MSS.
239. Lodge to Cushman Davis (Chairman of the Senate Foreign Relations Committee and a member of the Peace Commission), Oct. 31 and Nov. 18, 1898, Lodge MSS.

extent of the revolution in American foreign policy he hoped to effect. His first task was to prevent an open rupture in the ranks of the Republican party in Massachusetts (where anti-imperialist sentiment ran strong), for he himself was up for reelection in January, 1899. To that end he worked out a tacit agreement with Senator Hoar to maintain unity at home and confine their debate over imperialism to the national arena. The platform adopted by the Republican State Convention went no further than to declare that the people freed from Spanish tyranny should not be returned to Spain, and to express approval of the conduct of the Administration.[240] The ensuing state elections produced a large Republican legislative majority, and Lodge's own reelection routinely followed.

Circumspection was also the route to ratification of the peace treaty. Lodge's tactics provide an interesting and revealing contrast to those employed to the same end by Wilson some twenty years later. Lodge issued no ringing call for an imperial future; he made only one short speech in support of ratification and spent his time working behind the scenes to influence the votes of undecided colleagues. In that one speech he concentrated on the "practical" matters at hand and went no further than he had to. His principal argument, that the treaty committed the United States to "no policy, to no course of action whatever in regard to the Philippines," begged the ultimate question. Such matters would have to await the receipt of more information about conditions there. It was "impractical" to reject the treaty; it would mean a continuation of the state of war and humiliation for the American people who would be branded "a people incapable of great affairs or of taking rank . . . as one of the greatest of the great world powers."[241]

In the end the American people barely escaped being judged "unfit as a nation to enter into great questions of foreign policy"; the treaty was ratified by the Senate on February 6, 1899 with but one vote to spare. Lodge confided to Roosevelt that "it was the closest, hardest fight I have ever known and probably we shall not see another in our time where there was so much at stake."[242] American imperialism was off to a shaky start.

240. Welch, "Opponents and Colleagues: George Frisbie Hoar and Henry Cabot Lodge, 1898–1904," pp. 186–88.
241. *Cong. Record*, 55th Cong., 3rd sess., 1899, p. 959.
242. *Correspondence of Roosevelt and Lodge*, I, pp. 368, 391.

Victories did not preclude setbacks. Most galling was probably their inability to convert the war experience with its lessons as to the danger of unpreparedness into support for an expansion of American military might. No sooner was the war over than Lodge was complaining about the action of the Senate in "putting ships out of commission deliberately at such a time as this."[243] Roosevelt was also "very much disappointed" and lamented "that we should find such difficulty in learning our lessons: it was bad enough to have the session pass by without any effort to reorganize the Army . . . but I did not expect to see the Navy gone back on, and especially not by the Senate." In reply Lodge could only suggest that they had obtained some of the things they wanted.[244]

It was not till a year after the war that Lodge fully revealed his hand. In the meantime he had been able to bolster his control of the party in Massachusetts and no longer had much to fear from the Anti-Imperialists.[245] In a speech before the Republican Club in Boston on October 31, 1899 he threw down the gauntlet. He dropped all pretense that the American presence in the Philippines might be only temporary and had nothing but scorn for those who advocated the "great refusal":

I am opposed to turning these islands over to any other nation. I believe that we can give to those people a larger measure of peace and happiness, of freedom and prosperity than any other nation in the world, for I believe in the capacity, in the honesty and the good faith of the American people. I think, therefore, that it is our duty to stay there, and a nation, like a man, must not fail in its duty.[246]

This was followed by a speech in the Senate on the seventh of March, 1900 (the 50th anniversary of Webster's famous speech), which has been called "the most detailed brief" imperialism ever received in America.[247] However, the speech is open to a number of interpretations. It was less a paean to imperialism as such than a careful refutation of the objections of those who "proceed on the theory that we are engaged in the perpetration of a great wrong."[248] His emphasis was more on the undeniable assertion that expansionism had long been a fact of American life than on the necessity of America's participating in the

243. *Cong. Record*, 55th Cong., 3rd sess., 1899, p. 2725.
244. *Correspondence of Roosevelt and Lodge*, I, pp. 393–95.
245. Welch, "Opponents and Colleagues," p. 196.
246. Boston *Herald*, Nov. 1, 1899.
247. Welch, *George Frisbie Hoar*, p. 261.
248. Lodge, *Speeches and Addresses*, p. 358.

international power struggle. His greatest concern was to undercut what Louis Hartz has described as the "ironic 'Americanist' outburst against imperialism."[249] The only way to stem the attacks of the Anti-Imperialists was to establish imperialism's "American" credentials and its moral authority. Lodge gave up none of his usual arguments for expansionism and he was still unwilling to distinguish between the requirements of duty and interest.[250] But he was also coming to realize that "the questions involved in the future management of these islands and in our policy in the Far East are of a nature to demand the highest and the most sagacious statesmanship."[251] It was in some ways a temperate and thoughtful speech. Even the unfriendly *New York Times* noted that

In the recent past, especially in the last two years, he has been . . . sobered by the responsibilities brought by the crowding events of the time. He has met with more reserve and caution the questions of the actual present than he showed in anticipation of them.[252]

Like Webster fifty years earlier, Lodge was searching for a means of reestablishing national unity. Imperialism was no longer a great adventure but a sobering responsibility, "one of the penalties of greatness." The stridency was gone from his voice, and his preoccupation with responsibility contained as always the seeds of his doubt, in this case second thoughts about the extent of the American people's commitment to imperialism. While affirming his faith in the "power" of the American people to meet their responsibilities, he seemed to leave open the question of their willingness.[253] When the cheering stopped the problems inherent in the American approach to matters of foreign and defense policy, and for which imperialism was supposed to have been an antidote, still remained.

Lodge was coming to realize that it was a two-way street; imperialism could effect changes in American society, but the exigencies of domestic politics could also affect the nature of American imperialism. What would happen to even the most altruistic of imperialisms in the wake of a declining public interest in foreign policy? Could that interest be

---

249. *The Liberal Tradition in America* (New York, 1955), p. 289.
250. Lodge, *Speeches and Addresses*, p. 367.
251. *Ibid.*, p. 319.
252. *New York Times*, March 9, 1900, editorial.
253. Lodge, *Speeches and Addresses*, pp. 357–58.

sustained? If not, how could America's new international posture be maintained? Mahan had taught another lesson, one that went beyond questions of naval strategy. It was that "in our country national policy, if it is to be steadfast and consistent, must be identical with public conviction."[254] And Mahan was worried:

Our difficulty at present does not proceed from outside conditions, but from those internal to our own national habits of thought, which in the past have been distinctly averse to studying external political problems, and even to admitting their existence, until pressed home upon our consciousness by an immediate emergency. Startling as has been the effect produced upon public sentiment by the recent exigency which threw the Philippines upon our hands, it must be remembered that a mental temperament evolved and ingrained by generations of acceptance . . . must tend to revert, as passing time dulls the sharp impression and lively emotions that followed the war with Spain.[255]

In order to obtain even a modicum of what they wanted, Lodge and Roosevelt were forced to give a number of hostages to public opinion, so many in fact that it raised the question whether imperialism could do for the country what they supposed it might and whether it could take the form they originally envisaged. Lodge had to compromise and limit his imperialism from the moment it came close enough to realization to become a political issue. In arguing for the retention of the Philippines he was forced into many concessions. He had to assert that "we shall never admit . . . [them] within our tariff, we shall never make their people part of the citizenship of the United States"; we shall never make them "either economically or politically part of our system."[256] Even more serious, given what led Lodge to embrace imperialism in the first place, he could not publicly admit that possession of the Philippines would have "the slightest effect" upon the size of the American navy.[257]

Initially he had moved the American public to support his vision of the future by appealing to their altruism, but in the course of the 1900 election campaign he was forced to shift ground and admit that "while we regard the welfare of those peoples as a sacred trust, we regard the

254. Mahan, *The Interest of America in Sea Power*, p. 118.
255. Mahan, *The Problem of Asia* (Boston, 1900), pp. 130–31.
256. Lodge, "Shall We Retain the Philippines?" p. 3; Lodge, *Speeches and Addresses*, p. 324.
257. Lodge, *Speeches and Addresses*, p. 356; *Cong. Record*, 56th Cong., 1st sess., 1900, p. 5402.

welfare of the American people first."[258] 1900 was to prove just as much a watershed as had 1898. The politicians judged the American people to have lost their enthusiasm for empire and word was passed among Republicans to soft-pedal the issue. In compliance Lodge wrote an article, "The Results of a Bryan Victory," in which he made no direct reference to either imperialism or foreign policy.[259] Neither McKinley's nor even Roosevelt's campaign in 1900 was such that a Republican victory could be interpreted as a triumph for imperialism.[260] But Lodge felt constrained to try; *after the fact* he sought to interpret the returns as evidence that:

the hypocritic ravings about imperialism and militarism fell upon deaf ears, and for weal or woe the American people, wisely and triumphantly as I believe, have decided that the United States should play its great part among the nations of the earth. There is no retreat from this decision, and it is this which renders this election epoch-making and puts it in that small company with which the names of Washington and Lincoln are forever associated.[261]

He must have known that he was engaged in a charade, but decisions from which there was no retreat had been made. Even the Democratic platform of 1900 proposed "a declaration of the nation's purpose to give the Filipinos, first, a stable form of government, second, independence, and third, protection from outside interference."[262] A means of bringing American purposes and American power into closer concert had still to be found. A well-defined foreign and strategic policy were still wanting. The United States had, indeed, become a great power and incurred a great power's responsibilities. But the imperialism which had been thought to offer a solution had only added a new dimension to the problem.

258. *Official Proceedings of the Twelfth Republican National Convention* (Philadelphia, 1900), p. 88.
259. *Harper's Weekly* 44 (Sept. 8, 1900): 837.
260. May, *American Imperialism*, p. 212; Thomas A. Bailey, "Was the Election of 1900 a Mandate on Imperialism?" *Mississippi Valley Historical Review* 24 (March 1937): 43–52.
261. Clipping from the New York *Sun*, Nov. 24, 1900, Scrapbooks, Lodge MSS.
262. Porter and Johnson, eds., *National Party Platforms*, p. 113.

Chapter Four

Theodorus Pacificus

In the summer of 1899 Lodge confessed to Roosevelt that he was content ("I have shot my bolt. . . . I go no higher") and that he had "but two great desires—one to see my country succeed in these vast problems and emerge gloriously on the great world stage where she has set her conquering foot; the other is to make you President and I think it can be done."[1] At the time neither appeared very likely (the U.S. Army was bogged down in a war in the Philippines and Roosevelt doubted he could even be reelected Governor of New York), but in Lodge's mind their realization was already fatally linked. As he envisaged the scenario, Roosevelt would "take the War Department," "command the confidence of the country," and "bring the Philippine war to an end." For these services he would be awarded the Presidency.[2]

Despite the euphoria engendered by the easy victory over Spain those like Lodge, who under the tutelage of Mahan and Cecil Spring Rice were attuned to the realities of the new international situation, had reasons for concern. The United States was not the only power emerging at this time; the international system was also having to accommodate the aspirations of Germany and Japan and was no longer very

1. Lodge to Roosevelt, July 12, 1899 (the second of that date), Roosevelt MSS.
2. *Ibid.* The appellation used as the chapter title, though much in keeping with Lodge's vision, was actually bestowed on Roosevelt by Cushman Davis in 1895. The context was originally domestic (Roosevelt's performance as Police Commissioner), and Davis was being mischievous (*Correspondence of Roosevelt and Lodge*, I, p. 180 [Sept. 22, 1895]).

stable. America had stepped on to the great world stage, but just how much glory would attend thereto was still something of an open question.

With Dewey's victory in Manila Bay, traditional American foreign policy had become irrelevant. It became commonplace to argue, as did Roosevelt on many occasions, that Americans could no longer choose whether they would play a great part in the world's affairs—only whether they would play it well or ill.[3] In *The Story of the Revolution*, which appeared in late 1898, Lodge was confident what that part would be:

Isolation in the United States has been a habit, not a policy. It has been bred by circumstances and by them justified. When the circumstances change, the habit perforce changes too, and new policies are born to suit new conditions.[4]

But exhortation was not necessarily conviction, and Lodge had long been impressed by the idea that habits of thought formed over a long period of time were almost indestructible.[5] He knew too much history to expect that the prevalent Jeffersonian ideas about foreign and defense policy would disappear as rapidly as conditions had changed. The problem was one in political education and it called for the most skillful management.

Foreign policy, even under the best of circumstances, was democracy's most difficult problem. The absence of policy and of the need for any had long obscured the difficulty. Suddenly and under unfavorable circumstances (in a context where foreign policy issues had become a plaything of domestic politics) a policy was needed. The more pessimistic of Lodge's coterie doubted the problem could be met. As Henry Adams expressed it:

. . . under amiable McKinleys or Napoleonic Bryans, how are we to deal with a united Europe bent on mastering Asia, which means the world? Our people are not even at a point to begin asking questions. They can't even manage the Philippines. They don't want to think about it, and they're quite right.[6]

3. Archibald Cary Coolidge, *The United States as a World Power* (New York, 1912), p. 374.

4. Lodge, *Story of the Revolution*, p. 575.

5. Henry Adams and Lodge, "Critical Review of von Holst's *Constitutional and Political History of the United States*," p. 341.

6. Ford, ed., *Letters of Henry Adams*, II, p. 234.

Referring to policy with respect to the Philippines, Lodge confided to Taft that "there is a curious apathy apparent in this part of the country and it seems very difficult to make people understand what enormous issues there are at stake on this election."[7] At the moment when the United States needed a policy to support the role in world politics it assumed as a result of the Spanish-American War, popular support for that more active role appeared to be dwindling. If Adams in his cynicism was inured to such events, Lodge, who had so recently given expression to his faith in the people (in *The War with Spain* he held that in the great crises of American history the popular instinct had "always been true and right"), felt the problem acutely. Not only the "glorious emergence" of the United States but even the fate of the Republican party could depend on its successful resolution. The situation seemed to place a premium on the type and style of national leadership that Lodge had long admired.

The classic formulation of the problem of the conduct of foreign policy in a democracy appears in Alexis de Tocqueville's *Democracy in America*.

Foreign politics demand scarcely any of those qualities which are peculiar to democracy; they require, on the contrary, the perfect use of almost all those in which it is deficient. . . . a democracy can only with great difficulty regulate the details of an important understanding, persevere in a fixed design, and work out its execution in spite of serious obstacles. It cannot combine its measures with secrecy or await their consequences with patience. These are qualities which more especially belong to an individual or an aristocracy, and they are precisely the qualities by which a nation, like an individual, attains a dominant position.[8]

In the late nineteenth century it had not been customary to attach much significance to these warnings. As James Bryce (Tocqueville's successor as observer of subjects American) remarked: "The evil would be more serious were it not that in foreign policy, where the need for continuity is greatest, the United States have little to do." America still sailed "upon a summer sea."[9]

Yet the problem was inherent in American conditions and had attracted the attention of the Federalists from the start. Hence, it was an

7. Lodge to Taft, Sept. 3, 1900, William H. Taft Papers, Library of Congress.
8. Alexis de Tocqueville, *Democracy in America*, ed. Phillips Bradley (New York, 1948), I, pp. 234–35.
9. James Bryce, *American Commonwealth* (London, 1889), I, pp. 66, 303.

important part of Lodge's intellectual inheritance. Hamilton had been apprehensive lest sensibility become "an overmatch for [foreign] policy." Washington had not only to fight the British but "an inborn and a carefully cultivated dread of standing armies and military power," a feeling which "was turned most unreasonably against our own army, and carried in that direction to the verge of insanity."[10] Lodge carried these concerns in his intellectual baggage, but saw in them only a difficult, and not an insurmountable, problem. Had he lived longer he too might have come to Walter Lippmann's unhappy conclusion "that the prevailing public opinion has been destructively wrong at the critical junctures . . . too pacifist in peace and too bellicose in war."[11] But Lodge was a child of the nineteenth century, and, accordingly, Cleveland's message on Venezuela elicited this hopeful response:

. . . far from showing that a democratic government is dangerous, I think his [Cleveland's] attitude and the response of the people to it show that a democracy is capable of standing up for their rights in a question of foreign policy, which is the most difficult thing for a republican government to manage with conformity and vigor.[12]

Nor did he then admit the validity of Bryce's contention that American institutions were unsuited for the government of dependencies.[13] It was a lesson he learned only slowly. He had his own eyes fixed firmly on China and the importance of developing an Eastern policy, but even though he found his attention diverted by "continual efforts to pass resolutions about the Boers and on other subjects with which we ought not, as a government, to meddle unless we mean to take positive action," he still thought "we shall learn in time what our new responsibilities and our new relations with the world offers and requires [sic]."[14] With the right kind of leadership the problem was still soluble.

10. Lodge, *Alexander Hamilton*, p. 259; Lodge, *George Washington*, I, p. 324; Lodge, *Story of the Revolution*, p. 513. The same message was a prominent feature of Mahan's writings. In *The Interest of America in Sea Power* (p. 258) he deeply lamented the fact that "in democracies . . . policy cannot long dispute the sceptre with sentiment."

11. *Essays in the Public Philosophy* (Boston, 1956), pp. 23–24.

12. Lodge to John C. Ropes, Jan. 18, 1896, Lodge MSS.

13. James Bryce, "The Policy of Annexation for America," *The Forum* 24 (Dec. 1897): 391–92.

14. Lodge to J. E. Chamberlin, May 4, 1900, Lodge MSS. He thought the Chinese question far outweighed anything else in importance and was "the gravest and most difficult question which this or any other generation has confronted" (Lodge to W. W. Rockhill, Jan. 10, 1901, and to Brooks Adams, June 29, 1900, Lodge MSS).

Lodge and Roosevelt chafed under the limitations imposed by these conditions, but could look upon them as simply another factor in the American political equation, one which was both a guide to action and a reminder of what could not even be attempted. The American people, in Roosevelt's observation, suffered from a sentimental humanitarianism which deprived them of the ability to look very far in either time or space and this made it difficult to do well in foreign affairs:[15]

This people of ours simply does not understand how things are outside our own boundaries; of course I do not desire to act unless I can get the bulk of our people to understand the situation and to back up the action; and to do that I have got to get the facts vividly before them.[16]

That might yet be managed. They neither despaired of finding a solution nor contemplated an antidemocratic one.[17] As Lodge once asked John Morse, after due reference to all of democracy's shortcomings, "what is there better?" Nonetheless Lodge, reflecting the experience of a lifetime, chose his words carefully when in 1923 he wrote: "Foreign relations are a very difficult subject; the people at large only understand them on a few salient points and deal with them on very broad lines."[18]

Nor had Tocqueville exhausted the American democracy's disabilities in the realm of foreign policy. Had he observed the pernicious influence which domestic politics had come to exercise on foreign policy in late nineteenth century America he would have been even less sanguine. Partisanship in matters of foreign policy was a luxury which free security permitted Americans to afford and one in which they had freely indulged.[19] The opposition party tended to be opportunistic rather than consistent or constructive.[20] Platforms on foreign policy issues were

15. Morison, ed., *Letters of Theodore Roosevelt*, V, p. 721.

16. Roosevelt quoted in Beale, *Roosevelt and the Rise of America*, p. 455.

17. Roosevelt chose to keep some of his actions on the world stage hidden from the American people. His rule of thumb was that of making no arrangements for which he did not think he could eventually secure the support of the American people. When he resorted to secrecy he usually did so in an effort to compose world differences in a manner that would leave the U.S. free of responsibilities and commitments. See Bradford Perkins, *The Great Rapprochement: England and the United States, 1895–1914* (New York, 1968), p. 103; and Raymond A. Esthus, *Theodore Roosevelt and the International Rivalries* (Waltham, Mass., 1970), p. 3.

18. Lodge to John T. Morse, Jr., April 7, 1921, and to Robert L. O'Brien, Nov. 10, 1923, Lodge MSS.

19. Dulles, *The Imperial Years*, p. 18.

20. A perfect example is Bryan the anti-imperialist once complaining while Roosevelt was President that "there is a tendency under this administration to

often but a collection of platitudes and illogicalities.[21] The Democratic platform of 1900 roundly condemned Republican imperialism, but declared strongly for the "strict maintenance of the Monroe Doctrine" and denounced the Hay-Pauncefote (Canal) treaty as "a surrender of American rights and interests not to be tolerated by the American people."[22] Obtaining an advantage in domestic politics was everyone's primary concern. Bryan seemed impervious to the international repercussions of his campaign oratory and was prone to blame all the country's ills on England. The animus of the silverites defeated the first Anglo-American arbitration treaty, and even the principled anti-imperialist Carl Schurz was not above playing on popular hostility toward England.[23]

Though often guilty of similar political opportunism, Lodge was helped to a realization that it was dangerous by the fact that the Republican party was charged with managing this new and difficult situation. But, unlike many of his contemporaries, he also realized that the United States had committed itself to policies which, acting alone, it could never successfully carry out. For this reason he particularly lamented the fact that "an administration which undertakes to respect and fulfill treaty obligations to England is an inviting object of attack."[24] His friend Elihu Root had similar concerns and told Secretary Hay that "diplomacy, as viewed from the opposition American standpoint, has but two phases: if we agree with any Power on any subject there is a secret alliance; if we disagree there is a conspiracy to get up a war and foist a soldier on the back of every American laborer."[25] In the opinion of Lodge's circle, this problem was compounded by the fact that when the Democratic party did act on conviction in matters of foreign policy, it still dwelt in Jefferson's court.[26] In the same platform in which the Democrats proposed to guarantee the independence of the Philippines, they approved of Jefferson's *wholesome* doctrine

allow the Monroe Doctrine to acquire a moth-ballish flavor" (Dulles, *The Imperial Years*, p. 254).

21. Tyler Dennett, *John Hay: From Poetry to Politics* (New York, 1933), p. 257.

22. Porter and Johnson, eds., *National Party Platforms*, pp. 113, 115.

23. Ray Ginger, ed., *William Jennings Bryan: Selections* (Indianapolis, 1967), p. 51; Perkins, *The Great Rapprochement*, pp. 29, 53.

24. Lodge, *Fighting Frigate*, p. 40.

25. Quoted in Dennett, *John Hay*, p. 312.

26. The expression is Mahan's and is contained in a letter to Roosevelt of July 1, 1911, Mahan MSS.

("Peace, commerce and honest friendship with all nations; entangling alliance with none"), earnestly protested "against the Republican departure which has involved us in *so-called* world politics, including *the diplomacy of Europe* and *the intrigue and land-grabbing of Asia*," and especially condemned "the ill-concealed *Republican alliance* with England."[27] It was against this background that Lodge stressed the importance of developing an Eastern policy and vented his fear of the foreign policy consequences of Bryan becoming President.[28] And it was in this atmosphere that Roosevelt and Lodge, on the accession of Roosevelt to the Presidency, were to test their long-held views regarding the conduct of American foreign policy.

Lodge guided Roosevelt's career from the start. It is generally acknowledged that he secured Roosevelt's appointment as Assistant Secretary of the Navy, but less attention has been given to his role in Roosevelt's accession to the Presidency.[29] Lodge toyed with the possibility as early as 1895 when Roosevelt was only a Police Commissioner in New York. He was taken with Roosevelt's ability "to impress the popular imagination" (an ability which he himself did not have) and told him that while "I do not say you are to be President tomorrow; I do not say it will be—I am sure that it may and can be."[30] Lodge also talked Roosevelt into accepting the Vice-Presidency and giving up the Governorship of New York, the argument being that he would be in a better position for the Presidency if he could get out of the maelstrom of New York politics with his reputation still intact.[31] For whatever reason (and it was probably a combination of the fact that they were in perfect agreement on foreign policy issues and that Roosevelt's ability to "impress the popular imagination" was such a valuable and timely asset), by 1899 Lodge had already made the fateful link between the United States' success in world politics and Roosevelt's accession to the "greatest office man can now hold on earth."[32] One member of Lodge's immediate circle, his brother-in-law Brooks Adams, had such faith in

27. Porter and Johnson, eds., *National Party Platforms*, p. 115. Italics mine.
28. Lodge to James Ford Rhodes, June 19, 1900, Rhodes MSS; Lodge to Henry White, June 29, 1900, quoted in Nevins, *Henry White*, pp. 170–71.
29. See Roosevelt, *Autobiography*, p. 224, and Anna Roosevelt Cowles, ed., *Letters of Theodore Roosevelt to Anna Roosevelt Cowles* (New York, 1924), p. 207, for Roosevelt's appreciation of what Lodge did for him.
30. *Correspondence of Roosevelt and Lodge*, I, p. 179 (Sept. 22, 1895).
31. *Ibid.*, I, p. 404 (July 1, 1899); II, p. 462 (Aug. 7, 1915).
32. Lodge to Roosevelt, Sept. 15, 1901, Roosevelt MSS.

Roosevelt that he confessed to Lodge his feeling that Roosevelt's coming to the Presidency would mark "the turning point in our history," "the moment when we won the great prize."[33]

It is not my intention to deal with the particulars of Roosevelt's foreign policy. Rather my concern is with his approach to foreign policy (an approach shared by Lodge) and the manner in which he conducted it (a manner which met with Lodge's heartiest approval). It was not that they had a set of specific policies ready and waiting to set into motion; it was more a matter of attachment to a certain style and to certain first principles.[34] Their solution to the problem of the conduct of foreign policy under the peculiarities of the American situation followed from that.

Neither is it my purpose to demonstrate that Lodge played a crucial role in determining Roosevelt's policy in any given instance. They thought so much alike that Lodge's approval of Roosevelt's course of action flowed less from the responsibility that comes from participation in the formulation of specific policy than from basic agreement on what needed to be done and on how it might be accomplished. When in 1912 they parted political company for the only time in their lives, Roosevelt made a point of saying that it was only with respect to internal politics that their views had begun to drift apart.[35] Their correspondence also reveals that they were able to heal that breach by emphasizing anew their agreement on foreign policy.[36]

To stress their agreement on the basics of the conduct of foreign policy is not, however, to imply that Lodge, during Roosevelt's presidency, was only a passive observer. He was actually Chairman of the Senate Foreign Relations Committee in all but name.[37] Moreover, his intimate relations with Roosevelt were "unchanged" by the latter's entry

33. Brooks Adams to Lodge, Oct. 26, 1901, Lodge MSS.

34. Their description of that policy under Roosevelt differed little from what they had always wanted American foreign policy to be—namely "able, vigorous, dignified and in the highest degree successful" (Porter and Johnson, eds., *National Party Platforms*, p. 140).

35. *Correspondence of Roosevelt and Lodge*, II, p. 425 (March 1, 1912). The point of their continuing to agree on foreign policy even in the face of what he calls "totally different political philosophies" is also made by Lawrence F. Abbott in "More Rooseveltiana," *Outlook* 139 (April 29, 1925): 646.

36. *Correspondence of Roosevelt and Lodge*, II, pp. 429–30, 434, 438–39 (Dec. 31, 1912; Feb. 27, Sept. 17, 22, 1913).

37. Philip C. Jessup, *Elihu Root* (New York, 1938), I, p. 545.

into the White House,[38] despite the fact that "their positions were gradually and perhaps unconsciously reversed and Roosevelt grew to be the leader while Lodge became the follower and disciple."[39] Roosevelt continued to discuss "almost every move" he made in politics with him.[40] In the realm of foreign policy Roosevelt particularly esteemed Lodge's views:

he was of all our public men the man who had made the closest and wisest study of our foreign relations, and more clearly than almost any other man he understood the vital fact that the efficiency of our navy conditioned our national efficiency in foreign affairs. Anything relating to our international relations, from Panama and the navy to the Alaskan boundary question, the Algeciras negotiation, or the peace of Portsmouth, I was certain to discuss with Senator Lodge.[41]

There is also Alice Roosevelt Longworth's probably apocryphal story of her father telling a foreign diplomat who had inquired as to his opinion on a certain subject: "Go to Senator Lodge and talk with him; there is no one who knows my mind better or whom I trust more."[42] Lodge influenced Roosevelt on a number of points (especially with regard to tactics), but all I mean to show is that Lodge was close enough to Roosevelt to know how the various foreign policy problems which arose during Roosevelt's tenure were handled and that his judgment as to Roosevelt's success in dealing with them was, however prejudiced, also well informed. His attachment to the "Rooseveltian solution" was the greater for his having lived with it closely and for its being intimately bound up with their personal reputations and with the validity of what they had so long been preaching.

38. Roosevelt, *Autobiography*, p. 383. When TR went to Africa in 1909 Lodge asked rather plaintively in a letter: "do you realize that in twenty-five years I have never [before] been without seeing you or hearing from you for more than a few days at a time . . . ?" (*Correspondence of Roosevelt and Lodge*, II, p. 337 [June 21, 1909]).

39. Abbott, "More Rooseveltiana," p. 646.

40. Morison, ed., *Letters of Theodore Roosevelt*, VI, p. 935.

41. Roosevelt, *Autobiography*, p. 383. Lodge's role can also be assayed from the fact that he was the first person (ahead of Secretary of State Hay) to learn that it was the Japanese who had invited Roosevelt's mediation toward ending the Russo-Japanese War (*Correspondence of Roosevelt and Lodge*, II, p. 131 [June 5, 1905]) and that he was chosen to voice in London Roosevelt's personal commitment to a tacit American, British, and Japanese alliance (William H. Harbaugh, *Power and Responsibility: The Life and Times of Theodore Roosevelt* [New York, 1961], p. 273).

42. William J. Miller, *Henry Cabot Lodge* (New York, 1967), p. 9.

My argument is unaffected by the fact that there is some truth in Tyler Dennett's assertion that Roosevelt found much of his foreign policy already made for him.[43] The "Rooseveltian solution" reflected the conditions of the American situation and those conditions had in some way to be met. Both his predecessors and his successors had to grapple with many of the same problems. If John Hay found it necessary to devise a policy, such as the "Open Door," which reflected both America's material interests and its idealism, and if in so doing he had the approaching presidential election in mind, it was because there were aspects of the American situation which anyone charged with the conduct of foreign policy could not ignore.[44] On the other hand, Roosevelt played a role in international politics which probably went beyond anything his predecessors could even have imagined and played that role in a manner uniquely his own. Most observers agree that the personal element was an important one, that in many ways Roosevelt imposed himself and his ideas on his countrymen and upon the world's leaders by the sheer force of his personality. One close student of Roosevelt claims that the personal equation was so decisive "that the unfolding drama of American foreign relations from 1902 is essentially the story of the vigorous interplay of Roosevelt's personality and the surging mainstream of events."[45] Even if one concedes that he inherited the basic outlines of policy, there seems to be no denying that his method and manner of conducting foreign policy were both highly personal and innovative.[46]

II

The Rooseveltian solution was constructed under particularly adverse conditions. As Howard K. Beale has claimed, it would be another forty years before Americans accepted the active participation in world decisions for which Roosevelt felt we shared responsibility.[47] He and

43. Dennett, *John Hay*, p. 349.
44. Louis J. Halle, *Dream and Reality: Aspects of American Foreign Policy* (New York, 1958), p. 224; Dennett, *John Hay*, pp. 307–08.
45. Harbaugh, *Power and Responsibility*, p. 183.
46. It was, for example, Roosevelt's conduct of the office that led Wilson to revise his estimate of the Presidency and to develop a new appreciation of the power which flowed from control of the nation's foreign policy. Contrast Wilson's *Constitutional Government in the United States* with his earlier *Congressional Government*.
47. Beale, *Roosevelt and the Rise of America*, pp. 253–54.

Lodge succeeded in the late 1890s in awakening in the American people a sense of power. They repeatedly stressed the relationship between power and responsibility, but the concomitant sense of responsibility was much slower to develop.[48]

As the Anti-Imperialists, historiographically speaking, have again come into their own, it has also become apparent that they influenced subsequent American foreign policy to a greater degree than traditionally recognized. The imperialist crusade of the late 1890s produced a strong counterreaction, and the American people soon began to devote their attention increasingly to matters of domestic reform.[49] Even Lodge had to shift gears. When he wrote in 1904 that "there are many public questions which affect the welfare of the United States, but there is none which goes so deep or in which the future is so much involved as it is in this," he was talking not about expansion, but rather about immigration restriction.[50] When he tried to explain to his friend Henry Higginson that no nation had "ever accomplished so much with Asiatic people as we have accomplished in these islands [the Philippines] in two years," Higginson insisted that "we have tried this Philippine experiment without success; . . . Hang the responsibility! Think of our own people . . . and let us cut stick."[51] After briefly complying with its "duty" the country wished, as after World War I, to return to "normalcy." Popular disillusionment with imperialism was in many ways the beginning of Lodge's political education. Not even Roosevelt could under such circumstances succeed in shaking the complacency of the bourgeois mind.[52] He and Lodge had to learn to live with the fact that the feeling that the United States had an important stake in international affairs was limited to a small segment of American society.[53]

No consensus prevailed even among those who felt that the new

48. See, *inter alia*, A. E. Campbell, *Great Britain and the United States, 1895–1903*, p. 206, who claims that American foreign policy of the 1890s reflected the fact that "American ideals were incompatible with the exercise of power, but not with a sense of power"; and Henry Steele Commager, *The American Mind* (New Haven, 1950), pp. 46–47, who draws attention to the "dichotomy of political and economic imperialism and moral and psychological isolationism."

49. Welch, *George Frisbie Hoar*, p. 287; Tompkins, *Anti-Imperialism*, pp. 255, 272; Osgood, *Ideals and Self-Interest*, pp. 18–19; Dulles, *The Imperial Years*, pp. vii–ix.

50. Lodge, "A Million Immigrants a Year," *Century* 67 (Jan. 1904): 469.

51. Lodge to Henry Higginson, May 12, 1902, and Henry Higginson to Lodge, May 9, 1902, Lodge MSS.

52. Mallan, "The Warrior Critique of the Business Civilization," p. 229.

53. Esthus, *Roosevelt and the International Rivalries*, p. 1.

pattern of world politics called for more active American participation. American opinion leaders generally extended their conceptions of domestic stability to the international sphere, but could not agree on the best means of fostering either domestic or international stability. There was some feeling that economic arrangements were central to the solution, but many sought that stability in "Americanism," while others sought it in the law, or in the pacifist impulse. The very period that saw the wave of nationalist sentiment rise to new heights also witnessed a phenomenal growth in the peace crusade.[54]

The methods proposed for organizing the world so as to make it safe for the American democracy varied greatly, but, nevertheless, there emerged a widespread feeling that peace and stability were the basic requirements. There was about this the suggestion of a satiated imperialism, but also of a longing for the stability of the previous era.[55] At the heart of Roosevelt's plans for the uses of power there lay "one common, revealing objective," stability at home and abroad, a concern similar to that of his predecessor who, under the guise of what Henry Adams called "McKinleyism," had sought the same ends by the promotion of combination and consolidation.[56] Lodge voiced this general feeling when he spoke in 1901 of the United States entering a new commercial and industrial epoch, and announced that "there is no nation in the world to which peace is so important as it is to the United States in order to secure ample scope for the great progress we are making."[57] His general declaration that "the policy and interest of the United States alike demand the peace of the world" evoked nearly universal acclaim, but there remained concealed under that rubric abiding philosophical differences as to how that peace might best be attained.[58]

Lodge and Roosevelt have usually been classed among those who

---

54. Carl Parrini, *Heir to Empire* (Pittsburgh, 1969), p. viii; Merle Curti, *Peace or War: The American Struggle, 1636–1936* (New York, 1936), p. 197. See also C. Roland Marchand, *The American Peace Movement and Social Reform, 1898–1918* (Princeton, 1972), especially Chapter I, "Up from Sentimentalism," pp. 3–38.

55. Osgood, *Ideals and Self-Interest*, p. 95; A. E. Campbell, *America Comes of Age: The Era of Theodore Roosevelt* (New York, 1971), p. 96.

56. John Blum, "The Republican Roosevelt," in Morton Keller, ed., *Theodore Roosevelt: A Profile* (New York, 1967), p. 173; Adams, *The Education*, pp. 373–74; Dennett, *John Hay*, p. 331.

57. Lodge, "Speech at the Dinner of the Middlesex Club, Nov. 9, 1901," p. 18, Speeches File, Lodge MSS.

58. *Cong. Record*, 59th Cong., 1st sess., 1906, p. 1470.

believed in power politics. They understood the uses of power in international relations and sought peace in concerts of power rather than in a legalistic or paper system.[59] Howard Beale contends that Roosevelt had a particularly noteworthy concern with power relationships; "he was intrigued with power, with the problems of power, and with rivalries for power."[60] And Roosevelt himself once confessed that he believed in power.[61] Often in American history that has been sufficient to condemn a man, and just as often it has obscured the truth. Roosevelt and Lodge sought not maximum power but rather maximum prestige and influence and sought that by means decidedly more political than military. They sought an accretion of American power (acknowledging that prestige and influence were aspects of power), but never solely for its own sake, and were always the first (as in the cases of Hawaii and Cuba) to admonish their fellow citizens (who seldom got the message) that there were no rights without concomitant duties.[62] The idea that power and responsibility went hand in hand was in fact the principal rationale for the Roosevelt Corollary to the Monroe Doctrine; as Roosevelt told George Otto Trevelyan "we cannot perpetually assert the Monroe Doctrine on behalf of all American republics, bad or good, without ourselves accepting some responsibility in connection therewith."[63]

To neglect the importance which they attached to prestige and to reputation is, as in the case of a failure to understand that they did not conceive of power apart from responsibility, to write the history of another era. Theirs was usually a conception of self-interest tempered, in accord with Hamilton's theory, with a due regard for reputation.[64]

59. John M. Blum, *The Republican Roosevelt* (Cambridge, Mass., 1954), p. 110.
60. Beale, *Roosevelt and the Rise of America*, pp. 449–50.
61. Bishop, *Theodore Roosevelt and His Time*, II, p. 94. The complete quote, however, is: "I believe in power, but I believe that responsibility should go with power."
62. See, for example, Roosevelt, *The Strenuous Life: Essays and Addresses* (Philadelphia, 1903), p. 271, and Roosevelt, *Autobiography*, p. 543.
63. Morison, ed., *Letters of Theodore Roosevelt*, IV, pp. 1133–34. The Corollary was a delayed response to Lord Salisbury, who in his reply to Secretary Olney had claimed that "The Government of the United States is not entitled to affirm as a universal proposition, with reference to a number of independent states *for whose conduct it assumes no responsibility*, that its interests are necessarily concerned in whatever may befall those states simply because they are situated in the Western Hemisphere." See Henry James, *Richard Olney and His Public Service* (Boston, 1923), p. 116. Italics mine.
64. Wolfers and Martin, eds., *The Anglo-American Tradition*, pp. 146–47.

Shortly after McKinley's assassination Lodge reminded Roosevelt that Bacon had once stated "that foreign nations are a present posterity."[65] As the period of Republican ascendancy was drawing to a close he warned a Congress about to terminate the Russian treaty in an unfortunate, demagogic fashion that "as Mr. Jefferson said, it is well that we should act with respect to the opinion of mankind; we ought to make our standing before the world as strong as possible."[66] Lodge had his own definition of what it meant to be a world power. In assessing Roosevelt's achievements in foreign policy he put it this way:

A world power we had been for many long years, but we had at last become a world power in the finer sense, a power whose active participation and beneficent influence were recognized and desired by other nations in those great questions which concerned the welfare and happiness of all mankind.[67]

Their solution to the problem of the conduct of foreign policy in a democracy also required a detailed understanding of both international and domestic politics and put a premium on political talent. As Roosevelt explained it:

. . . among free peoples . . . it is only in very exceptional circumstances that a statesman can be efficient, can be of use to the country, unless he is also (not as a substitute, but in addition) a politician. . . . [Lincoln] was superior to Hamilton just because he was a politician and was a genuine democrat and therefore suited to lead a genuine democracy.[68]

They understood that their political talents often had to be employed in the domestic and foreign arenas simultaneously, that they had to be directed both toward developing support at home and toward organizing the world so as to minimize the difficulties under which American democracy labored in its foreign relations. A successful American foreign policy could be naught put political, and necessitated paying at least as much attention to domestic as to foreign conditions. When laying down the ground rules for American policy, rules which seem at first glance to be a response to external conditions, Lodge was also looking back over his shoulder and taking into account the exigencies of domestic politics and the peculiarities of the American situation.

65. *Correspondence of Roosevelt and Lodge*, I, p. 503 (Sept. 12, 1901).
66. *Cong. Record*, 62nd Cong., 2nd sess., 1911, p. 480.
67. *Ibid.*, 63rd Cong., 2nd sess., 1914, p. 6455.
68. Morison, ed., *Letters of Theodore Roosevelt*, V, pp. 351–52.

Lodge gave his most detailed interpretation of the Rooseveltian solution in 1913 when, speaking to the Naval War College, he expounded the three American policies which would "make most strongly for the maintenance of the world's peace."[69] If one does not regard the list as exhaustive (Lodge was more candid about the ingredients of successful statesmanship than about those which made for good politics), these remarks provide a good insight into Lodge's philosophy of international relations. Though by this time his experience in the conduct of American foreign policy encompassed two decades, the surprising thing about this speech is how little it contained in the way of new ideas. The Federalist wisdom he had long cherished still seemed singularly appropriate to the American situation.

He introduced their solution by emphasizing that it was "not to be found and cannot be included in any general arbitration treaties." His first point was that "it should be the particular care of those charged with the responsibility of the nation's foreign relations to be ever on the alert and to anticipate the development of questions which may lead to international differences."[70] Foresight was so necessary because the people were "shortsighted" when it came to international affairs.[71] A corollary concern was the avoidance of a situation "into which a friendly nation might stumble and from which such a nation would find it difficult to withdraw."[72] Lodge wanted Secretary of the Navy John Long to send a cruiser to La Guaira in 1901 because he was worried about German efforts to get possession of the Margarita Islands, which, if successful, "would put us in a very embarrassing position and might lead to war."[73] The same considerations motivated him in 1912 to persuade the Senate to declare (in what became known as the Lodge Corollary to the Monroe Doctrine) that "by the word 'colonization' we also cover action by companies or corporations or by citizens or subjects of

69. Lodge, "Speech on International Arbitration Before the Naval War College, Feb. 13, 1913," p. 7, Speeches File, Lodge MSS.
70. *Ibid.* This closely follows TR's own description of what his foreign policy was based on, namely "the exercise of intelligent forethought and of decisive action sufficiently far in advance of any likely crisis to make it improbable that we would run into serious trouble" (*Autobiography*, pp. 548–49).
71. Roosevelt, *Autobiography*, p. 581; Morison, ed., *Letters of Theodore Roosevelt*, V, p. 782.
72. Lodge, "Speech on International Arbitration," p. 7, Lodge MSS.
73. Gardner W. Allen, ed., *The Papers of John Davis Long, 1897–1904* (Boston, 1939), pp. 365–66.

a foreign State which might do . . . what the Monroe doctrine was intended to prevent."[74] He not only wanted to prevent the Japanese from seizing land on the Mexican coast, but wanted "to prevent it at the start so that there may be no difficulty on their part in getting out without humiliation or any sense of compulsion or retreat."[75] Regarding it as "the part of wise policy and wise diplomacy to anticipate," he sought to anticipate both the moves of foreign governments and American reaction thereto.[76] Experience taught him that the latter was particularly difficult to predict or to control and that this was both a danger to peace and a source of weakness. He had drawn a twofold lesson from the first Venezuelan crisis: that "there is nothing which so weakens our position as the lack of knowledge of just what we mean when we speak of the Monroe doctrine," and that the situation had been improved "by defining our position because that does away with restlessness and uncertainty."[77]

One way of solving the problem of the conduct of foreign policy in a democracy was to get everything carefully spelled out, to combat the dangers of uncertainty and inconsistency by firmly committing the American democracy to fundamental policies and then impressing those upon the minds of foreign leaders. America required a "well-settled foreign policy" and the importance of attaining it was matched only by the difficulty of so doing. Some years after the need first arose, Lodge was still warning his countrymen that they could "no longer go on without a well-settled foreign policy," that it was "high time that the American people generally should understand our Eastern policy and adhere to it, as they understand and adhere to Washington's policy of neutrality in the affairs of Europe, or to the Monroe doctrine."[78] Lodge's concern for the development of a "well-settled foreign policy" closely paralleled Mahan's interest in "the clear expression of national purpose," which when "accompanied by evident and adequate means to carry it into effect" was "the surest safeguard against war."[79] Once a

74. Thomas A. Bailey, "The Lodge Corollary to the Monroe Doctrine," *Political Science Quarterly* 48 (June 1933): 220–39; *Cong. Record*, 62nd Cong., 2nd sess., 1912, p. 5661.

75. Lodge to Barrett Wendell, April 8, 1912, Lodge MSS.

76. *Cong. Record*, 62nd Cong., 2nd sess., 1912, p. 5661.

77. Lodge to Henry (Higginson?) and to Rawle (?), Jan. 20 and 21, 1896, and to Barrett Wendell, April 8, 1912, Lodge MSS.

78. Lodge, "Our Foreign Policy," pp. 103–04.

79. Mahan, *The Interest of America in Sea Power*, p. 157.

course of national conduct had been agreed upon, then one could proceed as per Elihu Root's description of Roosevelt's conduct: "He did not think of the international situations which demanded action as being mere occasions of the moment, but he treated each situation with which he dealt as an incident to a national course of conduct."[80] To be successful such a policy required widespread understanding of its basic principles, both at home and abroad. This led Lodge to insist that the Monroe Doctrine be "rigidly upheld," and probably also led him to oppose Mahan's proposal for making the Monroe Doctrine coordinate with U.S. security interests by restricting its operation to the Caribbean area.[81] Subtlety, flexibility, and innovation had to be sacrificed to the end of preventing any misunderstanding (either at home or abroad) of what American policy entailed.

Even more important, in Lodge's opinion, was "the strict observance of all treaties existing with other nations." Why did Lodge attach so much importance to such an obvious tenet of good international relations? He answered part of that question when he stated that "the nation that disregards its treaty obligations will soon find the world unwilling to enter upon agreements with it and, what is far worse, will also find itself constantly embroiled with other nations in regard to questions of good faith and upright dealing which are more likely than any others to bring on war."[82] The other part of the answer lies in the importance which he attached to maintaining the country's honor and good name and the gentleman's code by which he arrived at the course which would best protect that honor.[83] Reputation was such an important commodity that Lodge could "never consent to subjecting the United States . . . to [even] the imputation of bad faith."[84] Reputation was central to Roosevelt's success (both at home and abroad) and had

80. Elihu Root, "Roosevelt's Conduct of Foreign Affairs" in Hermann Hagedorn, ed., *The Works of Theodore Roosevelt* (New York, 1925), XVIII, pp. xi–xii.

81. Lodge, "Speech at the Middlesex Club, Nov. 9, 1901," p. 18, Lodge MSS; *New York Times*, Nov. 10, 1901; *Correspondence of Roosevelt and Lodge*, I, p. 487 (March 30, 1901).

82. Lodge, "Speech on International Arbitration," pp. 9–10, 15, Lodge MSS.

83. See, for example, his article on "International Copyright," *The Atlantic Monthly* 66 (Aug. 1890): 264–70, wherein he argued that the United States should become party to international copyright agreements principally on the ground that it was necessary to the "country's honor and good name"; "It does not become the United States, holding high place in the forefront of the nations, to stand like a highway robber beside the pathway of civilization. . . ."

84. Lodge to James Ford Rhodes, Sept. 4, 1912, Rhodes MSS.

been secured, in his own description, by never deviating from the principle of having "the Nation behave toward other nations precisely as a strong, honorable, and upright man behaves in dealing with his fellow-men."[85] In their unwillingness to draw a distinction between private man and public man they had come a long way from Machiavelli, but nevertheless their code was capable of masking considerable belligerence and of producing a blinding self-righteousness. But it also had its redeeming features. It helped to keep Lodge, who certainly wanted to annex Cuba, from seeking to effect those desires. It was his conviction that "we made a certain promise to them and that promise must be carried out in the presence of a doubting world, keeping it as no nation has ever kept its word before."[86]

Two forms of behavior were under their code particularly blameworthy: promising to do what one could or would not do in the end, and assuming a posture which in any way smacked of hypocrisy. It was precisely these two errors into which the American democracy seemed most likely to fall. Lodge was careful in all matters affecting international relations to commit the American Government "only so far as the Government could redeem its pledges."[87] From the first he regarded the arbitration movement as one fraught with problems for the United States and preferred no treaty to one whose provisions were likely to be disregarded. When the question of arbitration first came before the Senate in 1897 he wanted the treaty to be "in such shape that it can stand any strain which . . . may be put upon it."[88] He thought it more honest and fair to say frankly what we would do in a given contingency rather than to obscure fundamental problems with words or platitudes, and regarded his efforts to amend the far-reaching Taft arbitration treaties as ones designed to make the treaties "at least reasonably truthful."[89]

Lodge, it is true, often took a conservative view of man's ability to change his ways and of democracy's capacity for conducting foreign

85. Roosevelt, *Autobiography*, pp. 417–18.
86. Lodge to A. E. Cox, Dec. 15, 1900, Lodge MSS; Boston *Herald*, Oct. 9, 1902.
87. William Lawrence, *Henry Cabot Lodge*, p. 60.
88. Lodge to Prof. J. B. Thayer, Jan. 19, 1897, and to Curtis (Guild?), Feb. 6, 1897, Lodge MSS.
89. Lodge to Henry White, Dec. 18, 1900, Lodge MSS; Lodge to Roosevelt, June 14, 1911, Roosevelt MSS. Lodge describes making them "at least reasonably truthful" as "our end."

policy in such a way as to guard American integrity and reputation.[90] In his behalf, however, it should be noted how widespread among the American public was the illusion that in arbitration they had found a means of preventing future wars.[91] Under American circumstances skepticism was often the better part of wisdom. It was neither easy nor popular to deflate such illusions, but Lodge and Roosevelt saw this as their personal duty. Someone, in Lodge's view, had to take the long-range and statesmanlike approach, what with the clergy and the Chambers of Commerce "all writing and resolving in favor of the treaty without knowing or caring anything about the terms except that they should be large and comprehensive" and with the Irish just as "irrational and careless" in their opposition.[92] When Roosevelt first raised the subject of the Taft arbitration treaties with Lodge he termed entering into such treaties "a lie—because our people neither could nor would observe it," and appealed to Lodge's integrity, claiming that "your past forbids you to be guilty of the hypocrisy of voting for such a treaty." It was "the kind of thing that led to 'National dishonesty.' "[93] Accordingly, Roosevelt made the claim that "no moral movement is permanently helped by hypocrisy" the crux of his argument against the treaties.[94] More than an exaggerated sense of honor underlay their insistence that the American people could not afford to make a promise they might not keep. The interests of peace and of a successful foreign policy were also involved. Lodge thought lasting peace could not be promoted "by pretense or by cloudy or furtive devices" and felt that "no greater disaster could befall the cause of peace than to make a promise in a treaty designed to promote peace which we know will not be kept in certain contingencies."[95]

Conscious of the vagaries of public opinion, Lodge never felt (especially after seeing how quickly the American public turned away from

90. See, for example, Lodge, *The Democracy of the Constitution*, p. 46.

91. Henry Adams, caustic as ever, called arbitration the "last refuge of the feeble-minded" (Ford, ed., *Letters of Henry Adams*, II, p. 569). But outside their own restricted set such views were rarely heard.

92. Lodge to Roosevelt, June 3, 1911, Roosevelt MSS.

93. *Correspondence of Roosevelt and Lodge*, II, pp. 404–05, 409 (June 12, Sept. 12, 1911).

94. Roosevelt, "The Peace of Righteousness," *The Outlook* 99 (Sept. 9, 1911): 68, and "The Russian Treaty, Arbitration and Hypocrisy," *The Outlook* 99 (Dec. 30, 1911): 1047.

95. *Cong. Record*, 62nd Cong., 2nd sess., 1912, p. 2604.

their initial avid embrace of imperialism once the Filipinos did not welcome American forces with open arms) that the public could be relied upon to sustain a "well-settled policy." Throughout his life he looked to "good faith" and to the reputation of nations rather than to public opinion as a means of providing the continuity of policy and predictability of action conducive to peace among nations.[96] He held strong opinions on the Canal Tolls issue because it had led to a widespread feeling in Europe that the United States was duplicitous and could not be relied upon, despite its posing as the champion of international arbitration, to submit to arbitration a dispute which was so clearly an arbitrable one. He warned the Senate that

they have come to believe that we are not to be trusted; that we make our international relations the sport of politics and treat them as if they were in no wise different from questions of domestic legislation. . . . It is not well for any country, no matter how powerful, to be an outlaw among the nations. Not so many years ago there were people in England who used to speak with pride of her "splendid isolation," but they soon found out that while isolation might be splendid, it was in the highest degree undesirable.[97]

Roosevelt avoided such situations by giving substance to American verbal offerings.[98] This, in the opinion of his partisans, was the cornerstone of the Rooseveltian solution. They felt he conducted the foreign relations of the United States in such a manner that "the governments of other countries came to understand that he meant what he said"; thus he created an impression of resolution and purpose which "raised the prestige of the United States to a height it had never before attained."[99] Reputation and good faith were more important than any

96. See especially his speech to the Washington Arms-Limitation Conference, the full text of which was carried in the Washington *Star* of Dec. 10, 1921.

97. *Cong. Record*, 63rd Cong., 2nd sess., 1914, p. 6455. Robert Osgood claims (*Ideals and Self-Interest*, p. 104) that Wilson "delighted liberals and outraged Rooseveltian nationalists with a novel exhibition of self-denying morality when he . . . ask[ed] on grounds of national honor for the repeal" of the tolls provision of the Canal Act. Lodge and Root, however, fully supported Wilson (*Cong. Record*, 63rd Cong., 2nd sess., 1914, pp. 3603–04, 6453–56). Actually Lodge and Roosevelt had for some time favored submitting the issue to arbitration (*Correspondence of Roosevelt and Lodge*, II, pp. 438–39 [Sept. 17, 22, 1913]; Roosevelt to the editor, *The Outlook* 103 [Jan. 18, 1913]: 111) and precisely because they believed the U.S. had a moral obligation to arbitrate the question if Great Britain insisted and because they considered it a matter of national honor.

98. Tyler Dennett, *Roosevelt and the Russo-Japanese War* (Garden City, N.Y., 1925), p. 333.

99. Root, "Roosevelt's Conduct of Foreign Affairs," p. xxvi; Lewis Einstein, *Roosevelt, His Mind in Action* (Boston, 1930), p. 127.

particular issue and no matter how lightheartedly the United States had entered into an agreement, or how strenuously Roosevelt and Lodge had opposed their so doing, once the engagement was contracted it acquired an importance greater than its intrinsic one and had to be fulfilled.[100] It was an attitude basic to Lodge's approach to foreign policy; in fact it pervaded his thinking on all issues of public policy. The man who opposed all but the most limited arbitration treaties insisted that those in force be fulfilled to the letter, and the man who opposed prohibition in the belief that it would lead to widespread hypocrisy voted for its strict enforcement. Sometimes American democracy had to be protected from itself.

The third and most important of the policies which, in Lodge's view, the nation should adopt for the preservation of its peace was "the maintenance of a complete defense against armed aggression."[101] In this strategy he saw a new urgency "for today great wars are fought in a few months, while it takes years to build modern ships and cast rifled guns."[102] But the wisdom of preparation was scarcely new to either Roosevelt or to Lodge. To understand the emotional and intellectual capital they invested in this issue, one must view the matter in its historical context.

As Harold and Margaret Sprout have demonstrated, the political alignments which grew out of the Jefferson-Hamilton split "foreshadowed the future politics of American naval development in general."[103] Roosevelt first went into print to instruct his generation in the lessons of the War of 1812, and Lodge devoted a large portion of his writing to the same purpose. They were convinced from their reading of American history that "intelligent foresight in preparation and known capacity to stand well in battle are the surest safeguards against war."[104] American history was but the story of how the Jeffersonians' gossamer theories had been "crushed in the iron grasp of facts."[105] The wisdom of preparation was as old as the difficulty of getting it accepted. Even in 1921

100. See, for example, *Correspondence of Roosevelt and Lodge*, II, pp. 438–39 (Sept. 12, 1913); and Stephen Gwynn. ed., *Letters and Friendships of Sir Cecil Spring Rice* (Boston, 1929), II, pp. 185–86.
101. Lodge, "Speech on International Arbitration," p. 15, Lodge MSS.
102. Lodge, *Fighting Frigate*, p. 19.
103. Harold and Margaret Sprout, *The Rise of American Naval Power, 1776–1918* (Princeton, 1967), p. 24.
104. Roosevelt and Lodge, *Hero Tales from American History*, p. ix.
105. *Cong. Record*, 58th Cong., 3rd sess., 1905, p. 3495.

Lodge chose a Federalist example to make the point that to disarm in the midst of an armed world was, as Hamilton said in his Report on Manufactures, as idle as to talk about free trade in a protective world.[106] The problem was perennial and particularly American, and the Roosevelt who, as President, wrote to Elihu Root exclaiming "Oh, if only our people would learn the need of preparedness, and of shaping things so that decision and action can alike be instantaneous" differed little from Roosevelt the imperialist or from Roosevelt the militant World War I interventionist.[107] They opposed whatever "tended make us rely less on our own strength and fighting force" and saw their duty as one of counteracting the American proclivity for placing too much faith in laws and panaceas.[108] They never expected the problem to go away, but as long as Roosevelt was in command they could feel that some progress was being made, that the nation was slowly being led to believe in self-reliance and preparedness.[109]

Lodge gave recognition to Roosevelt's talents in this area when he secured Roosevelt's appointment as Assistant Secretary of the Navy and when, in 1899, he confessed that he thought the Secretaryship of War the post best suited to Roosevelt.[110] The object of their endeavors in this, to them, absolutely crucial area of preparation was, and by force of circumstance had to be, twofold: they had to fit the defense needs of the United States to the changing international situation, but, and this was the greater task, they also had to find a means of impressing those needs upon the American people. The dual nature of this operation comes through clearly in Roosevelt's confession in his *Autobiography* that though he thought sending the battle fleet around the world had given the Japanese pause and had been his "most important service" to peace, his prime purpose was to "stimulate popular interest and belief" in the U.S. Navy.[111]

The Lodgian rationale for preparedness looked, in short, to both the domestic and international aspects of the American situation; American

---

106. Lodge to L. A. Coolidge, Aug. 25, 1921, Lodge MSS.
107. Morison, ed., *Letters of Theodore Roosevelt*, IV, p. 731.
108. Roosevelt quoted on the arbitration treaty of 1897 in Beale, *Roosevelt and the Rise of America*, p. 91; and Lodge speaking on the Taft arbitration treaties in the *Cong. Record*, 62nd Cong., 2nd sess., 1912, p. 2605.
109. Morison, ed., *Letters of Theodore Roosevelt*, IV, p. 731.
110. *Correspondence of Roosevelt and Lodge*, I, p. 430 (Dec. 16, 1899).
111. Roosevelt, *Autobiography*, pp. 592–95.

defense policy could only be successful if it conformed to both those conditions. The maintenance of a "complete defense against armed aggression" was for Lodge the more imperative because weakness invited attack, and because "when weakness in military or naval preparation is coupled with great wealth and with an aggressive spirit [as in the U.S.] the temptation to attack is much increased."[112] The safety of the United States lay in its navy; the fleet represented both its peace and its power. Interestingly, however, Lodge did not think the United States needed a navy as large as that of Great Britain.[113] The security of the United States rested on a navy of optimum, not maximum, size and increments which might threaten international agreement or turn the public against navalism were counterproductive. Fortunately, conditions were also such that the United States required only a small army. In Roosevelt's words, the country had to rely on the navy because "our form of government is not one suitable for military exertions."[114] But the reason the United States could follow its natural proclivities in this direction was that it had "no neighbors of great military force" and would, in Lodge's view, "have none so long as we maintain the Monroe Doctrine."[115] The Monroe Doctrine, so conceived, reflected both internal and external aspects of the American condition.

Preparedness was also a means of effecting the nation's other foreign policy goals. The navy, in Lodge's view, was an important instrument of diplomacy. The navy had kept the Germans out of Venezuela and given the United States a say in the fate of China; the fleet in its voyage around the world did "more to promote peace than anything that has been done" and demonstrated the truth of Lord Nelson's adage that his "seventy-fours" were the best negotiators in Europe.[116] Not even the

---

112. Lodge, "Speech on International Arbitration," p. 15, Lodge MSS. Or as he put it in 1904: "No position could be worse than that of a nation which, like ours, is rich and aggressive if it is left unarmed and undefended" (*Cong. Record*, 58th Cong., 2nd sess., 1904, p. 2734). The same theme was also a staple of Rooseveltian rhetoric and came apparently from Brooks Adams, whom Roosevelt quoted as saying that if "we show ourselves 'opulent, aggressive and unarmed,' the Japanese may some time work us an injury" (*Correspondence of Roosevelt and Lodge*, II, p. 135 [June 5, 1905]).

113. *Cong. Record*, 58th Cong., 2nd sess., 1904, p. 2734.

114. Morison, ed., *Letters of Theodore Roosevelt*, IV, p. 1049.

115. Lodge, "Speech on International Arbitration," p. 16, Lodge MSS.

116. *Cong. Record*, 58th Cong., 3rd sess., 1905, p. 3498, and 60th Cong., 2nd sess., 1909, p. 2546.

objects of the peace societies could be promoted from weakness. Roosevelt felt that he "would have been powerless to speak for peace" if it were thought that he wished peace "because the nation I represented was either unable or unwilling to fight if the need arose."[117] Similarly, Lodge was convinced that the United States could not promote disarmament from weakness and even believed large armaments were coincident with peace. Only with its own peace assured could the United States labor successfully for the peace of the world.[118] Preparedness became in their view the *sine qua non* of having any American foreign policy at all; as Roosevelt told his last Congress:

No friendliness with other nations, no good will for them or by them, can take the place of national self-reliance. Fit to hold our own against the strong nations of the earth, our voice for peace will carry to the ends of the earth. Unprepared, and therefore unfit, we must sit dumb and helpless to defend ourselves, protect others, or preserve peace.[119]

Lodge, reviewing Roosevelt's conduct of U.S. foreign policy, had this answer for those who had been alarmed by his combativeness and apparent militarism. The Rooseveltian solution had worked.

There never has been an administration . . . when we were more perfectly at peace with all the world, nor were our foreign relations ever in danger of producing hostilities. But this was not due in the least to the adoption of a timid or yielding foreign policy; on the contrary, it was owing to the firmness of the President in all foreign questions. . . . Thus it came about that this President, dreaded at the beginning on account of his combative spirit, re-

117. Quoted in Dennett, *Roosevelt and the Russo-Japanese War*, p. 333. See also the classic exchange of letters between Roosevelt and Carl Schurz upon the successful conclusion of the Portsmouth Conference. Schurz had high praise for Roosevelt's efforts: "the true mission and the immense moral influence of this republic as the great peace power of the world, have never been so strikingly and beneficently demonstrated as they have been demonstrated by you." But when he used this as a springboard for urging upon Roosevelt the cause of disarmament, Roosevelt rejoined that "if I had been known as one of the conventional type of peace advocates I could have done nothing whatever in bringing about peace" (*Correspondence of Roosevelt and Lodge*, II, pp. 195–200). Lodge so approved of Roosevelt's reply that he later printed the exchange in the *Correspondence* and at the time declared: "I was delighted with your letter to Schurz; it represents, of course, what you and I have talked over so many times; it is a good thing to have the opportunity to put it once to a man like Schurz." Lodge's comments are contained in a letter to Roosevelt of Sept. 17, 1905, Lodge MSS, but were omitted from the version printed in the *Correspondence*.

118. *Cong. Record*, 61st Cong., 2nd sess., 1910, p. 6725; Lodge, "Speech on International Arbitration," p. 18, Lodge MSS.

119. Quoted in Dulles, *The Imperial Years*, pp. 240–41.

ceived the Nobel prize in 1906 as the person who had contributed most to the peace of the world in the preceding years, and his contribution was the result of strength and knowledge and not of weakness.[120]

III

Foresight, the cultivation of good faith, and preparedness—those were the basics of Lodge's public prescription for the conduct of American foreign policy. But as a good politician he was not so candid about the kind of knowledge and the political and managerial abilities which the American situation seemed to require. However, if one reads between the lines his views on these subjects can also be ascertained, for they too were an integral part of the Rooseveltian solution.

The first requisite for a foreign-policy manager was an understanding of both domestic and international politics. It was "his wide and accurate historical knowledge" which, in Lodge's opinion, fitted Charles Sumner "peculiarly for the treatment of international questions." And it was Webster, who by anyone's reckoning took a highly political approach to his diplomatic responsibilities, whom Lodge thought "singularly well adapted for the conduct of foreign affairs."[121] In the formulation of an "American position" one had always to look both ways; both an intimate knowledge of American and of international history and politics were essential.

We are again coming to understand the importance of a statesman knowing his own country, of taking into account its domestic structure and politics and being aware of its special weaknesses.[122] Perhaps the greatest weakness of American society in this period when it came to the conduct of foreign policy was, as a British Ambassador to the U.S. once observed, the fact that "everything in this country is subservient to politics."[123] In the American context it was a luxury to look at foreign

120. Lodge, *The Senate of the United States, and Other Essays and Addresses, Historical and Literary* (New York, 1921), pp. 135–36.

121. Lodge, *Early Memories*, p. 287; Lodge, *Daniel Webster*, p. 261.

122. For an interesting discussion of this aspect of statesmanship see Stephen R. Graubard, *Kissinger: Portrait of a Mind* (New York, 1973), p. 20. Graubard summarizes Kissinger's thinking on the subject thus: "The statesman who ignored the internal weaknesses of his society or exaggerated its strengths, whether measured by the determination of the people or their unity, neglected the rudiments of his political profession."

123. Sir Michael Herbert quoted in Beale, *Roosevelt and the Rise of America*, p. 119.

policy in any way other than its effect on domestic politics. By the time Roosevelt became President he and Lodge already had behind them a long history of viewing foreign policy issues from the standpoint of domestic political advantage. They knew first hand the basic problems, the animosities between the various ethnic groups (animosities which seemed to find their easiest, and perhaps safest, outlet in foreign policy issues) and the often contradictory desires of the American body politic (a people who were intensely nationalistic and yet quite unmilitary).[124] They had seen foreign policy become a major weapon for the political "outs" and rarely redound to the benefit of the "ins." They felt that the country needed "to make up its mind definitely what it wishes and not to try to pursue paths of conduct incompatible one with the other," but the nature of the American political system and of the American body politic bespoke the difficulty of its doing so.[125]

As W. Stull Holt long ago discovered, the U.S. Senate invariably took a political approach to foreign policy—even to the peace treaty of 1898, the first important treaty approved by the Senate in twenty-five years.[126] This situation drove John Hay to despair. "Diplomacy is impossible to us," he complained, "no fair arrangement between us and another power will ever be accepted by the Senate"; "they will reject . . . any treaty whatever, on any subject, made with England; I doubt if they would accept any Treaty of consequence with Russia or Germany; the recalcitrant third would be differently composed, but it would be on hand."[127] Roosevelt shared Hay's forebodings, but drew a more practical lesson.

It is hard to get any treaty through the Senate. There is always sure to be a considerable minority anxious to reject it so as to embarrass the administration, and a smaller minority anxious to do anything against England. With those two elements in view, I want to be dead sure a treaty is all right before making an effort to get it through.[128]

124. Though as a politician he never dared say so, Lodge viewed politics against the same Massachusetts background as did Henry Adams and probably shared in private the latter's view that American politics "had always been the systematic organization of hatreds" (*The Education*, p. 7).

125. Roosevelt, *Autobiography*, p. 580.

126. *Treaties Defeated by the Senate* (Baltimore, 1933), p. 165 *et passim*. Lodge was the floor manager in that one successful effort.

127. [Henry Adams, ed.], *Letters of John Hay* (Washington, 1908), III, pp. 156–57, 185.

128. Morison, ed., *Letters of Theodore Roosevelt*, III, p. 66.

Nor was the problem confined to treaties; it affected every aspect of American foreign policy. The composition and prejudices of the American population were a standing invitation to demagoguery. In the poignant language of Hay, who being less a politician suffered the situation more acutely than Roosevelt or Lodge:

Even that lightweight blatherskite Bryan, calls us imperialists in one breath, and in the next attacks us for not being imperial enough. They expect us to make Russia honest and Germany unselfish; to insult England every hour and make certain of her cooperation whenever it is needed; to keep China whole and to smash her to pieces. . . .[129]

True, "a politician of extraordinary ability is not necessarily God's gift to a nation."[130] Yet the situation at the turn of the century did call for political and managerial abilities of the highest order. The foreign policy preached by Mahan, for all its emphasis on strategic considerations, also reflected American conditions and involved respect for, and close attention to, public opinion.[131] Roosevelt acknowledged that basic Mahanian wisdom when in 1901 he expressed the belief that public men could never lead the country "much further than public opinion had prepared the way."[132] In the solution according to Roosevelt and Lodge no foreign policy initiative was taken without due consideration to its effect on domestic opinion and on their own political fortunes. Domestic politics had to come first; without a domestic base of support none of their larger goals were realizable. Lodge suffered in reputation because of this; he was so devoted to the fishermen of Gloucester that Root chided him for being "the Senior Senator from the fishing grounds," and an observer of his actions on a larger stage recalls his determination as a member of the Alaskan Tribunal "to exact a pound of flesh."[133] But Lodge, as Root well knew, could not politically afford to support a treaty unsatisfactory to Massachusetts' sea-going voters. Similarly, a genuine compromise settlement of the Alaskan boundary dispute would

129. [Adams, ed.], *Letters of John Hay*, III, pp. 195–96.

130. Gerald W. Johnson, review of John Garraty's *Lodge* in *The New Republic* 129 (Nov. 16, 1953): 18.

131. Livezey, *Mahan on Sea Power*, pp. 28–29; Puleston, *Mahan*, pp. 160–61; Dulles, *The Imperial Years*, p. 231; Mahan, *The Interest of America in Sea Power*, pp. 118, 126, 258.

132. Quoted in Dulles, *The Imperial Years*, p. 239.

133. Jessup, *Elihu Root*, II, p. 85; William Phillips, *Ventures in Diplomacy* (Boston, 1952), p. 12.

have crippled Roosevelt severely (there being no chance that the Democrats would have supported such an "invidious" agreement with England). A reputation of standing up for "American" interests was necessary to political success and both Lodge and Roosevelt knew how to play that game.[134]

A balance between their interest in developing strong domestic support and their interest in stable international relations was difficult to strike. Lodge's maneuverings often earned him suspicions similar to those voiced by Henry Adams with respect to the Senate's handling of the Hay-Pauncefote treaty—that Lodge was cutting Hay's throat for the sake of the German and Irish vote.[135] But even the canal project had "to be sacrificed to the implacable machine," had to be postponed until after the election because under American conditions "domestic politics weighed more heavily than international comity."[136] It was, in Lodge's judgment, a burden which they could not have carried in the campaign.[137] Care had to be taken to keep any potentially divisive foreign policy issue out of election campaigns for fear it would upset the delicate party balance.[138] Once a treaty was "all right" and the campaign was over, as in the case of the second Hay-Pauncefote treaty, they could then turn their talents and resources to securing its ratification. Lodge made their *modus operandi* explicit in a letter to Roosevelt urging that:

> ... *all* questions of patronage must be kept in abeyance and must wait until the English treaty ... is out of the way. Such an attitude will help the treaty I know. I hope Morgan proved amenable. Your seeing all these Senators and especially asking them to lunch is most wise and effective.[139]

134. Jessup, *Elihu Root*, II, p. 85; Perkins, *The Great Rapprochement*, p. 172. The classic example is probably Roosevelt's Perdicaris telegram. It should not be imagined, however, that either man was governed entirely by political expediency. On the one occasion when Roosevelt seemed to be surrendering his convictions to political considerations (when he agreed in the 1904 campaign to push for far-reaching arbitration treaties) Lodge opposed him strenuously. See Holt, *Treaties Defeated by the Senate*, pp. 211–12.

135. Ford, ed., *Letters of Henry Adams*, II, pp. 267–68.

136. Charles S. Campbell, Jr., *Anglo-American Understanding, 1898–1903* (Baltimore, 1957), p. 198.

137. Lodge to Henry White, April 3, 1900, Lodge MSS.

138. See, for example, Lodge's advice to Roosevelt re the dangers of postponing the Alaskan boundary dispute in a letter of July 1, 1903, Roosevelt MSS.

139. *Correspondence of Roosevelt and Lodge*, I, p. 507 (Oct. 17, 1901).

Roosevelt and Lodge knew all the tricks of their trade—how to exploit the political system, how to dramatize their "Americanism," and how to manipulate the prejudices of the various ethnic groups so that each acted as "an antiscorbutic to the others."[140] Both were as devoted to a tacit Anglo-American alliance as was John Hay, but neither suffered from his reputation for Anglophilia. Roosevelt was adept at the art of gesturing—of following a mobilization of the navy against Germany in the Caribbean with a massing of troops against alleged British encroachments on the Alaskan border—and developed it into a consummate skill, both in domestic politics and on the larger world stage.[141] As he saw the situation: the American people

acquiesce entirely when I refuse to permit any attitude hostile to England to be taken whether in connection with Ireland or in connection with Germany, but they would rebel, and from their standpoint quite justifiably, if I took an attitude which was supposed to favor England at the expense of Ireland or Germany.[142]

Roosevelt had both a talent and a reputation such as to enable him to accomplish what few others, under the circumstances, would even have attempted. Whether one puts it positively and says "no one has ever understood popular psychology so well" or conveys a note of derision as did Richard Hofstadter when he called Roosevelt "the master therapist of the middle classes," the point remains that Roosevelt was a politician of extraordinary ability.[143] The answer to Morton Keller's question why the Roosevelt who "went about his policy-making with considerable subtlety of style and purpose" was so long "regarded as a classic American innocent" is that the two were linked, that the pose was a means (and perhaps a necessary one) to the larger policy purpose.[144] It was a highly personal solution to the problem of the conduct of foreign policy under American circumstances, and one which required Roosevelt's considerable talents. This is attested by the fact that it did not survive him. Once Roosevelt was out of the way the Midwestern Republican progressives, whose constituencies were un-

---

140. Morison, ed., *Letters of Theodore Roosevelt*, VI, p. 1104.

141. Dennett, *John Hay*, pp. 384, 388.

142. Morison, ed., *Letters of Theodore Roosevelt*, II, pp. 1436–37.

143. Einstein, *Roosevelt, His Mind in Action*, p. 88; Hofstadter quoted in Keller, ed., *Roosevelt: A Profile*, p. ix.

144. Keller, ed., *Roosevelt: A Profile*, p. ix.

concerned with foreign policy matters, drifted into political opposition, and the United States into isolation, with Taft fearing to have anything to do with the second Moroccan crisis.[145] It was only from an unusual position of power (after his overwhelming victory in 1904) and by the most careful exercise of his political talents that Roosevelt was able to accomplish much in the area of foreign policy. His ability to defy the Senate on the Santo Domingo treaty as well as the success of the Portsmouth Conference and of his intervention at Algeciras rested on this base.[146]

But many things even a Roosevelt could not do. For all his ability and agility he could not overcome certain patterns in the American approach to foreign policy. He and Lodge bridled at these restrictions, sought to remove them to the extent they were able, and yet knew that insofar as they could not remove them they had to take them into account.[147] Their complaints bore a remarkable consistency over the years. Isolationism and indifference to foreign policy were the greatest problem. As Roosevelt put it, there was precious little appreciation of the interdependence of modern nations; "on this continent we are as naturally insular, or parochial, as ever the English were in the old days when compared with the rest of Europe."[148] Lodge, reviewing his own work in the area of foreign relations, could only lament that "these things are not of the least interest to the masses."[149]

Particularly disturbing was "the tendency to conduct our foreign affairs by agitation and clamor," what Roosevelt called the tendency to "combine the unready hand with the unbridled tongue" (a tendency which manifested itself in those who sought every occasion to insult the Japanese and yet at the same time wanted to cut naval appropria-

---

145. John Milton Cooper, Jr., "Progressivism and American Foreign Policy: A Reconsideration," *Mid-America* 51 (Oct. 1969): 267–70; Dulles, *The Imperial Years*, p. 301; Osgood, *Ideals and Self-Interest*, p. 103.

146. Holt, *Treaties Defeated by the Senate*, pp. 228–29.

147. If Roosevelt failed to inculcate in the American people the basic lessons of international politics (Osgood, *Ideals and Self-Interest*, p. 77), it was probably because he realized that could only come as the product of painful experience (Morison, ed., *Letters of Theodore Roosevelt*, VII, pp. 295–96). Roosevelt accepted the situation philosophically: "the business of an active politician is not to complain of defects which cannot be changed, but to do the best he can in spite of them" (Gwynn, ed., *Letters of Spring Rice*, I, p. 479).

148. Roosevelt quoted in Nevins, *Henry White*, p. 294.

149. Lodge to Roosevelt, Sept. 14, 1910, Roosevelt MSS.

tions).[150] On the same par was the nation's proclivity for making extravagant promises and then not worrying much about their performance. As Roosevelt wrote to Lodge with respect to the Taft arbitration treaties: "I think the treaty will give immense satisfaction and be very popular, and if ever any need comes for executing it the people will repudiate it with the most cheerful lightheartedness; we are a funny nation."[151] Roosevelt in office was in a position to neutralize, if not necessarily overcome, this tendency for American foreign policy "to go in zig-zags."[152] But when he no longer had Roosevelt to rely on, Lodge's own attitude became increasingly defensive. In reference to the Taft arbitration treaties, he told Roosevelt "I am sure that I have the situation now where nothing serious can happen and as for the rest I care very little."[153] If he could not overcome certain tendencies he would at least render them as harmless as possible.

The weaknesses of American society when it came to the conduct of foreign affairs weighed heavily in all their decisions. The process by which they came to abandon their vision of an imperial future is an interesting case in point. As Roosevelt put it: "The Philippines present . . . a very hard problem because we must consider it in connection with the country's needs and ideas also, and with what it is reasonable to expect as a permanent policy of this country with its alternating system of party control."[154] Limits upon action were implicit not only in the American political system and their own regard for public opinion, but also, and this was especially important in the liquidation of imperialism, in their concern for the health and reputation of the American national experiment. Under American conditions good politics was often good statesmanship.

150. Lodge to Roosevelt, Jan. 8, 1912, Roosevelt MSS (the letter appears in the *Correspondence*, II, pp. 420–21, but this phrase is omitted there); Roosevelt, *Autobiography*, p. 580. No theme appears with more regularity in Roosevelt's writings. It was to him the most incomprehensible of all political positions. See also Morison, ed., *Letters of Theodore Roosevelt*, IV, pp. 930, 1169; VI, p. 1127; and *Correspondence of Roosevelt and Lodge*, II, pp. 133–35 (June 5, 1905).

151. Morison, ed., *Letters of Theodore Roosevelt*, V, p. 274. Root's commentary on the importance attached to making the "liberal" gesture was even more caustic: "Think of rational people being contented to get a treaty passed together with an authorized written construction of it which explains that it does not mean what it says it does" (Jessup, *Elihu Root*, II, pp. 276–77).

152. Roosevelt, *Autobiography*, p. 579.

153. Lodge to Roosevelt, Jan. 13, 1912, Roosevelt MSS.

154. Quoted in Beale, *Roosevelt and the Rise of America*, p. 456.

Lodge was never converted to anti-imperialism. He remained convinced that native peoples had to be aided toward self-government and that they retrograded when left alone; with respect to Santo Domingo he once remarked that "it is no credit to us or to civilization that such a condition should exist in one of the most fertile and beautiful islands in the world."[155] Yet he came gradually to accept the wisdom of the "Olney compromise"—that a policy worthy of America's strength and maturity did not necessitate becoming a colonizing power on a large scale.[156] Lodge made his adjustments and was not in 1906, like Albert Beveridge, still ranting on as if it were 1899.[157] Lodge never entirely gave up on expansionism. In 1905 he suggested to Roosevelt the acquisition of Greenland, but the very suggestion showed how much his ideas had changed.[158] Greenland was as different from the Philippines as could be imagined. It was in the Western Hemisphere, practically unpopulated, and unlikely to present the administrative problems which had plagued the United States in the Philippines and Lodge as Chairman of the Senate Philippines Committee. Lodge made these adjustments not because they were in his opinion "right" in the abstract, but because other convictions dictated their necessity. The process of loosening the imperial attachment was gradual, and bore the imprint of many considerations both domestic and foreign.

Disengagement from the Philippines was nearly complete in ten years and need only be sketched here in its barest outlines: as early as 1901 Roosevelt expressed the hope of getting out and privately stated his belief that the loss of supremacy in the Philippines would not necessarily be fatal;[159] by 1903 Lodge admitted the people "have lost all interest" in imperialism and declared his opposition to the annexation of any more islands;[160] in the next few years they looked to a relation-

155. Lodge to Charles Francis Adams, Jr., May 1, 1906, Lodge MSS; *Cong. Record*, 59th Cong., 1st sess., 1906, p. 1472.

156. Richard Olney, "Growth of Our Foreign Policy," *Atlantic Monthly* 85 (March 1900): 290–91.

157. John Braeman, *Albert J. Beveridge: American Nationalist* (Chicago, 1971), pp. 66–67.

158. *Correspondence of Roosevelt and Lodge*, II, p. 120 (May 12, 1905).

159. Morison, ed., *Letters of Theodore Roosevelt*, III, pp. 105–06; Gwynn, ed., *Letters of Spring Rice*, I, p. 344.

160. Quoted in Dulles, *The Imperial Years*, pp. 223–24. In Roosevelt's ever colorful language this was expressed as his having "about the same desire to annex" another island "as a gorged boa constrictor might have to swallow a porcupine wrong-end-to." See Morison, ed., *Letters of Theodore Roosevelt*, IV, p. 734.

ship with the Philippines similar to that with Cuba;[161] by 1907 Roosevelt regarded the Philippines as a grave liability and in 1910 Lodge publicly acknowledged that he considered the abandonment of plans for large expenditures for the fortification and defense of the Philippines to be a "wise" step.[162] In a famous letter to Taft in 1907 Roosevelt revealed the pressures and considerations which influenced their course:

There is just one point as to which I feel uneasy, and that is the Philippine question. We have continually to accommodate ourselves to conditions as they actually are and not as we would wish them to be. I wish our people were prepared permanently, in a duty-loving spirit, and looking forward to a couple of generations of continuous manifestation of this spirit, to assume the control of the Philippine Islands for the good of the Filipinos. But as a matter of fact I gravely question whether this is the case. Even in the West Indies, which are right under us here at home, and where anything that happens is brought home close to us, and where we are at an enormous advantage compared with foreign powers in dealing with any situation, it is exceedingly difficult to get this people to take a proper view of any emergency that arises. . . . it is impossible, for instance, to awaken any public interest in favor of giving them tariff advantages; it is very difficult to awaken any public interest in providing any adequate defense of the islands; . . . This leads me up to saying that I think we shall have to be prepared for giving the islands independence of a more or less complete type much sooner than I think advisable from their own standpoint, or than I should think advisable if this country were prepared to look ahead fifty years and to build the navy and erect the fortifications which in my judgment it should.[163]

The relation of American democracy to empire was but another aspect of the problem of the conduct of foreign policy in a democracy. Public opinion was an important curb on their appetite for further expansion, but it took more than that. It took, in fact, many years of unproductive effort and bitter experience to bring them to the virtual abandonment of the Philippines. The hardest pill to swallow was the public's failure to understand what the colonial problem entailed and their lack of interest in practical (especially tariff) arrangements to benefit the islands.[164] They were disillusioned by the attitude of most

---

161. Morison, ed., *Letters of Theodore Roosevelt*, V, p. 401.

162. Morison, ed., *Letters of Theodore Roosevelt*, V, pp. 761–62; *Cong. Record*, 61st Cong., 2nd sess., 1910, p. 6588.

163. Morison, ed., *Letters of Theodore Roosevelt*, V, pp. 761–62.

164. Jessup, *Elihu Root*, I, pp. 221, 363, 369–70; Lodge to Taft, April 24, 1906, Taft MSS; Harbaugh, *Power and Responsibility*, p. 186.

of their countrymen toward the Philippines, and what started in Lodge as an inherited skepticism about democracy's ability to conduct its foreign affairs began in these years of disappointment to harden into cynicism. A note of bitterness crept into his acknowledgment that the concerns to which he had devoted so much of his life, such as his work on the Philippines, were "of remote interest to the voters of the United States."[165]

Still he was a political realist and never a man to shy from the facts of a given situation. He took the events of these years in stride and in so doing developed an even deeper appreciation of what under American conditions was possible in the realm of foreign policy. Two factors were important in assisting him to keep his balance and perspective. As long as Roosevelt was President there was still hope for improvement. Moreover, his concern about the fragility of the American experiment gave him pause. A statesman could not long pursue a course counter to the public inclination without damaging the whole political fabric. As he put it even in the heyday of imperialism when he thought that the capacity of the American people knew few bounds: "faith and belief in our country are the most precious possessions that we have; anything which tends to lower or weaken that faith is a deadly injury."[166] From his perspective restoring the confidence of the American people in their national Government had entailed enormous sacrifices, but as he told Roosevelt in 1908 "popular confidence in the government is all we have in reality to sustain the Republic."[167]

Whether their concern was the immediate one of securing votes or the more statesmanlike preoccupation with retaining both domestic and foreign confidence in the American Government, one cannot but be impressed by the profound sense of limitation with which Lodge and Roosevelt assessed their ability to do what they wanted in the area of foreign policy. A respect for those limitations was a central aspect of the Rooseveltian solution. Imperialism was a chastening experience, it is true, but their concern with effecting a balance between American rhetoric and American performance antedated their disillusionment

165. Lodge, "Speech at Symphony Hall, Jan. 3, 1911," p. 7, Lodge MSS.
166. Boston *Herald*, Nov. 1, 1899.
167. Lodge to Roosevelt, July 2, 1908, Roosevelt MSS. The context for this remark was what Lodge regarded as Roosevelt's great achievements in the domestic arena, but he was also going to the heart of the whole Rooseveltian solution.

with imperialism. The humanitarians who sought American intervention in Armenia in 1895 to stop the massacres being perpetrated by
the Turks had been instructed by Lodge in the relationship between
policy and America's actual ability to influence events in that corner
of the world.[168] European diplomats, even those as close to American
conditions as Spring Rice, tended to overestimate the ability of American leaders to overcome the isolationism and indifference to foreign
affairs which held sway among the American populace, and had to be
reminded that "Asia is the very place where America could least help
you." Even Mahan, who like Spring Rice was urging Anglo-American
cooperation in China, had recalled to his attention the fact that "as yet
our public opinion is dull on the question of China."[169] However re-
sentful he was about finding it necessary to delay until "even the blind-
est could see," Roosevelt was ever cognizant of the limitations imposed
by that circumstance.[170] He did not intervene in Haiti because the people
could not be "waked up" and in the Orient he proceeded cautiously
because he realized that "as yet . . . we cannot fight to keep Manchuria
open." He thought the stakes there momentous and told Secretary
Hay that he wanted "in Manchuria, to go to the very limit I think our
people will stand," but recognized therein a profound and abiding
limitation.[171] Even the success of the Portsmouth Conference did not
turn his head; as he told Spring Rice: "I certainly do not intend to go
into peace-making as a regular business. It is quite enough to keep this
nation on an even keel and to prevent its being led into doing anything
out of the way on the one hand, or showing weakness on the other."[172]

An appreciation of the limitations on their action was also implicit
in their historical perception of policy. They had an almost Burkean
sense of policy, a feeling that changes in national policy could be effected only gradually and that only a policy deeply ingrained in the
consciousness of the people could withstand the vagaries of public

168. Lodge to a Mr. Porter, Dec. 2, 1895, Lodge MSS.
169. Morison, ed., *Letters of Theodore Roosevelt*, II, p. 1051; III, p. 23.
170. Quoted in Dulles, *The Imperial Years*, p. 264.
171. Morison, ed., *Letters of Theodore Roosevelt*, III, pp. 478, 532; IV, p. 770.
172. Gwynn, ed., *Letters of Spring Rice*, II, p. 11. See also a provocative article
by Raymond Esthus, "Isolationism and World Power," *Diplomatic History* 2
(Spring 1978): 117–29. Esthus emphasizes the continuing strength and vitality
of the isolationist tradition, and shows how much it served to limit Roosevelt's
options.

opinion. As Lodge expressed it when discussing Washington's supposed injunction against "entangling alliances":

It is not worthwhile to discuss whether this policy strictly enforced is absolutely wise or not. The American people for more than a hundred years have not only believed in its wisdom, but have faithfully observed it, and there is no immediate probability that it will ever or ought ever to be departed from.[173]

For the same reason they revered the Monroe Doctrine. At least when hemispheric issues were at stake the average American had "something in the way of traditional national action" to which appeal could be made as a precedent.[174] The rationale for their *modus operandi* is best summed up in Roosevelt's reply to Spring Rice's appeal for closer Anglo-American relations and more active American participation in world politics:

Personally I appreciate to the full the difficulty of committing oneself to a course of action in reliance upon the proposed action of any free people [here TR included the British] which is not accustomed to carrying out with iron will a long-continued course of foreign policy. It would be well nigh impossible, even if it were not highly undesirable, for this country to engage with another to carry out any policy, save one which had become part of the inherited tradition of the country, like the Monroe Doctrine. Not merely could I, for instance, only make such an engagement for four years, but I would have to reckon with a possible overthrow in Congress, with the temper of the people, with many different conditions. In consequence, my policy must of necessity be somewhat opportunist. . . .[175]

The American situation required that primacy be accorded to domestic politics. Still the exigencies of the international situation when Roosevelt assumed the Presidency were such as to place considerable responsibility on his shoulders. The trick was to strike a balance between the requirements of the international situation and the limitations inherent in American conditions. Therein lay Roosevelt's special value. He was, in Henry White's opinion, so successful because he was the

---

173. Lodge, *Frontier Town*, p. 269. Lodge, of all people, should have been aware that Washington's injunction was against "permanent alliances" and that "entangling" was a Jeffersonian elaboration thereon. Later, when trying to elicit American support for the Allied cause in World War I, he learned to appreciate the difference.
174. Morison, ed., *Letters of Theodore Roosevelt*, V, pp. 761–62.
175. Gwynn, ed., *Letters of Spring Rice*, I, pp. 442–43.

only American leader "who combined the qualities of an able politician at home with those of an equally good diplomatist abroad."[176] He always looked both ways and the point he most wanted to impress upon his successor was "that we must very seriously consider both domestic and foreign conditions as regards the retention of the islands [the Philippines]."[177] This involved an assessment of future American intentions and capabilities as well as of future Japanese intentions and capabilities. Another example of his simultaneously looking to both the domestic and foreign ramifications of policy was his rationale for sending the fleet around the world.[178] Sensing, at a time when few of his contemporaries were attuned to world developments, that the United States could no longer live in isolation undisturbed by the pressure of foreign aspirations, "it was the capital effort of his life" to reconcile these facts "in some dark way or other, to the prevailing platitudes, and so get them heeded."[179] This required his knowing his own country and according a general primacy to domestic politics, but that would have availed him little if he had not also had a good understanding of the changing world scene.

He had, in short, to present the world to the American people in such a way as to make it understandable, but in so doing not lose his own firm grasp on the realities of the international situation. As Lodge advised Roosevelt when the latter was looking for a successor to Hay as Secretary of State, "he must know Europe and understand world politics, the relations of nations and the balance of equilibrium of the powers."[180] To understand domestic politics, as in their opinion Bryan later so sadly demonstrated, was not enough. There was general agreement that the United States had an interest in peace, but few shared their feeling that peace could now be better assured by an active participation in world politics than by continued abstention. Among their generation they were singular in their perception of international trends and in the attention they devoted to their study. The Lodge who seldom ventured west of the Appalachians went to Russia in 1901 to ascertain

176. Quoted in James Ford Rhodes, *The McKinley and Roosevelt Administrations* (Port Washington, N.Y., 1965), p. 279.
177. Morison, ed., *Letters of Theodore Roosevelt*, V, pp. 761–62.
178. Roosevelt, *Autobiography*, pp. 592–95.
179. H. L. Mencken, "Roosevelt I," in Keller, ed., *Roosevelt: A Profile*, p. 63.
180. *Correspondence of Roosevelt and Lodge*, II, p. 160 (July 2, 1905).

"how soon they will reach the point of dangerous and destructive rivalry."[181] The Lodge who in 1896 wanted to go it alone, and thought all Europe except for Russia was hostile to the United States, soon became an avid promoter of Anglo-American rapprochement.[182] Unlike many of their fellow nationalists who shared their eagerness to play at power politics (Beveridge, for example), they were neither ignorant of the rules nor adverse to playing with a partner.[183] They understood how world power was structured and were quick to adjust their thinking to the changing patterns of international politics. The principal new reality was that the acquisition of the Philippines had transformed the United States "from a geographically isolated continental Power into a scattered empire with a strategic problem virtually insoluble without recourse to alliances"; security for the Philippines and commercial equality in China required that careful attention be given to the balance of power in the Far East and by that route to the general European balance upon which that in the East was contingent.[184] In enunciating the Open Door policy, Hay, like Monroe before him, had spoken without the power to back up his words, and the major task Roosevelt inherited was that of establishing some semblance of balance between American purposes and American means in the Far East.[185]

They conferred a high priority on strategic considerations and this often led them to what were for many Americans unpalatable conclusions. Seeing that American interests were affected by the European balance of power, they readily conceded that the strength of Great Britain was of concern to the United States.[186] Lodge believed the downfall of the British Empire would be "something which no rational American could regard as anything but a misfortune to the United States" and called to the attention of his fellow Senators the fact that Britain

181. Lodge, *Fighting Frigate*, p. 259.

182. *Cong. Record*, 54th Cong., 1st sess., 1896, p. 6048.

183. Osgood, *Ideals and Self-Interest*, p. 73.

184. Harold and Margaret Sprout, *Rise of American Naval Power*, pp. 230, 245.

185. Grenville and Young, *Politics, Strategy and American Diplomacy*, pp. 308–09; Graebner, *Ideas and Diplomacy*, p. 344.

186. This was the wisdom of practically the entire "realistic" coterie. See, for example, Mahan, *The Problem of Asia*, pp. 16–17; *The Interest of America in International Conditions*, pp. 75, 80–81; and Brooks Adams, *America's Economic Supremacy* (New York, 1947), pp. 70–71. Obviously there was also an emotional and cultural component to this viewpoint.

was helping to maintain the Monroe Doctrine.[187] The same recognition of the reality of power came through in Roosevelt's admonition to Taft that "the 'open-door' policy . . . completely disappears as soon as a powerful nation determines to disregard it, and is willing to run the risk of war rather than forego its intention" and in his own determination, knowing that the power to implement the American ideological preference for strengthening China would never be forthcoming, to conciliate Japan.[188] The same perspective is also apparent in Lodge's insistence that offering the good offices of the United States in order to prevent a European war was not only the country's "highest duty" (an interest in peace for its own sake was endemic to the thinking of so many Americans) but also its "wisest policy," and in Roosevelt's recognition that should England prove incapable of maintaining the European balance of power it would be incumbent upon the United States to assist her.[189] Only a few Americans looked at world politics in this manner, and to state that after Roosevelt's Administration "realism went on the defensive" is but to say that things reverted to their normal condition.[190]

However, this should not be taken to mean that Roosevelt's policies were always "realistic." Under American circumstances many of the options available to a European *Realpolitiker* were closed. Under American conditions a completely "realistic" policy could not engender sufficient public support and was therefore quite "unrealistic." The resistance to foreign alliance and to military expenditure and the ideological preferences of the American people were severely limiting factors. All these considerations dictated the need for an indigenous kind of realism, for a formula which, though basically realistic in its perception of international trends, also paid its obeisance to American ideological preferences and to domestic political conditions.

187. *Correspondence of Roosevelt and Lodge*, I, p. 446 (Feb. 2, 1900); Henry White to Lodge, Jan. 20, 1903, Lodge MSS. White had drawn Lodge's remarks to Lord Lansdowne's attention and it is quite possible they were intended for that purpose.

188. Morison, ed., *Letters of Theodore Roosevelt*, VII, p. 190; Walter V. and Marie V. Scholes, *The Foreign Policies of the Taft Administration* (Columbia, Mo., 1970), pp. 247–48.

189. Lodge to Henry Higginson, Feb. 1, 1906, Lodge MSS; Beale, *Roosevelt and the Rise of America*, p. 447.

190. Osgood, *Ideals and Self-Interest*, p. 101.

IV

A number of other characteristics served to set the Rooseveltian solution apart. It was, as had been their interest in imperialism, as readily defined by what it was not as by what it was, as much by their determination not to do certain things as by any positive program. Theirs was a foreign policy solution haunted by the ghosts of American history and their own earlier experiences and, consequently, one never designed to appeal to "the pale pink people."[191] It was a policy which found justification in the character of those who opposed it and in the nature of the policy they proposed to put in its place. While complaining to Lodge in 1901 that the last two years had shown that British statesmen were capable of committing the wildest follies, Roosevelt readily admitted that "the attitude of the entire Bryanite party, plus creatures like Mason in our own party, and the Godkin-Parkhurst-Atkinson type of mendacious mugwump, shows the same thing in us."[192] Particularly antipathetic were, in Roosevelt's ever colorful language, "the small body of eunuchs" who consistently oppose all actions in the national interest and the "professional international humanitarians . . . with their utterly maudlin confusion of right and wrong, . . . and their deification of feeble inefficiency, tempered by futile aspirations toward a vague general beneficence"—people who made him "feel somewhat as if we were all threatened with death by drowning in an ocean of weak tea with too much milk and sugar."[193]

The historical attitude of the Democratic party on foreign policy matters ran a close second. Lodge's partisanship, strong in any case, only became more intense when he contemplated what happened the last time the Democrats had controlled the nation's foreign relations.[194] Roosevelt was haunted by the same historical images—determined never to pursue a "Buchananlike" course and ever alert lest we "grow sentimental and commit some Jefferson-Bryan-like piece of idiotic folly."[195] Lodge shared this perspective, and when war in the Balkans

191. A term used by Frank Basil Tracy in a favorable piece, "Henry Cabot Lodge," *New England Magazine* 33 (Nov. 1905): 300.

192. *Correspondence of Roosevelt and Lodge*, I, pp. 485–86 (March 27, 1901).

193. Morison, ed., *Letters of Theodore Roosevelt*, III, p. 663; VII, p. 281.

194. Lodge, "Why Theodore Roosevelt Should Be Elected President," *North American Review* 179 (Sept. 1904): 326.

195. *Correspondence of Roosevelt and Lodge*, II, p. 234 (Sept. 27, 1906); Roosevelt quoted in Beale, *Roosevelt and the Rise of America*, p. 353.

seemed likely in the fall of 1908 he was sure all sorts of difficult questions would arise and confessed he would "feel pretty anxious if they were in the hands of Mr. Bryan and his cabinet."[196]

Much of this was inevitable and but the result of the manner in which approaches to foreign policy had become entwined in domestic politics. Unfortunately, the behavior of their political opponents was often such as to confirm them in their views. The tragedy of the situation was that it led not to rational discussions of policy differences but to a judgmental posture inimical to mutual understanding or even to a communication of views. All too easily Taft became a "floppy-souled creature" in Roosevelt's eyes and all too easily Taft came to believe that Roosevelt was not in favor of peace.[197]

The Rooseveltian solution also put a premium on leadership. Both Lodge and Roosevelt believed in the politics of leadership. Roosevelt once even admitted to an English friend that he believed in an "imperialist democracy."[198] Lodge never lost his early Federalist distrust of democracy and was an unrelenting believer in government by qualified and personally distinguished representatives. Revealing was his recommendation of Ralph Waldo Emerson's essay on "Character" to Roosevelt in 1905.[199] Emerson stressed the power inherent in personal character and declared that "the men who carry their points do not need to inquire of their constituents what they should say, but are themselves the country which they represent."[200] In the realm of foreign policy the ear-to-the-ground politician was even less justified than in domestic affairs. Lodge never tired of ridiculing statesmen who followed the wisdom of Mr. Pickwick:

'Slumkey forever!' roared the honest and independent.
'Slumkey forever!' echoed Mr. Pickwick taking off his hat.
'Who is Slumkey?' whispered Mr. Tupman.
'I don't know,' whispered Mr. Pickwick in the same tone.
'Hush, don't ask any questions. Its always best on those occasions to do what the mob do.'

196. Lodge to Roosevelt, Aug. 8, 1906, and Oct. 9, 1908, Roosevelt MSS.
197. Morison, ed., *Letters of Theodore Roosevelt*, VII, p. 465; Archie Butt, *Taft and Roosevelt: The Intimate Letters of Archie Butt* (Garden City, N.Y., 1930), II, p. 753; Henry F. Pringle, *The Life and Times of William Howard Taft* (New York, 1939), I, p. 748.
198. Morison, ed., *Letters of Theodore Roosevelt*, VII, p. 112.
199. *Correspondence of Roosevelt and Lodge*, II, p. 177 (Aug. 21, 1905).
200. Emerson, *Essays* (Second Series) (Cambridge, Mass., 1903), pp. 89, 91.

'But suppose there are two mobs?' suggested Mr. Snodgrass.
'Shout with the largest,' replied Mr. Pickwick.
Volumes could not have said more.[201]

Its great men and not its institutions had made America great; that part of the Federalist outlook (a view derived more from Hamilton than from John Adams) Lodge never lost. No institutional framework could guarantee peace. Peace was elusive and would, in Lodge's opinion, always be better preserved by "enlightened men" than by formalized abritration procedures.[202] Roosevelt's success in leading the country to accept a more active role in world politics and his success in preserving world peace were but further proof of the value of strong leadership. Lodge had a romantic conception of leadership, but it seemed to him that in the American experience the only men who had been able to lead —able to induce the people to give voluntarily what could seldom be commanded—were those, like Roosevelt, to whom the people had formed a "romantic" attachment.[203] But even someone who took a more objective view than Lodge would have had to admit that Roosevelt's was a hard act to follow.

All these were important and identifying characteristics of the Rooseveltian solution. But at its heart lay a cluster of ideas and beliefs ordinarily more familiar to students of America's intellectual history than to students of its foreign policy. Those ideas and beliefs are generally grouped under the umbrella of "practical idealism," and Roosevelt was perhaps its foremost spokesman. Like most of his fellow Americans he believed in ideal norms and in the essential morality of the universe and found support for those beliefs not so much in philosophy or religion but in history, in American achievements, and in the promise of the American future.[204] Implicit in this view was the naive suggestion that the American national state was a "practical" means of effecting an ideal end. When it came to foreign policy this easily gave rise to the

201. *Cong. Record*, 62nd Cong., 2nd sess., 1912, p. 2598. The occasion was a major speech on the Taft arbitration treaties. The same Dickensian illustration was later used against Wilson. See Lodge, *War Addresses* (Boston, 1917), p. 168.
202. *Cong. Record*, 62nd Cong., 2nd sess., 1912, pp. 2604–05.
203. See Lodge's eulogy of Roosevelt in *The Senate of the United States*, especially pp. 153–58, where Lodge explains the fact that Roosevelt "had the largest personal following ever attained by any man in our history" in terms of Roosevelt's personal attractions, his courage, his "generous humanity," and the fact that he had about him "a touch of the knight errant."
204. Henry May, *The End of American Innocence*, pp. 14, 17–18.

belief that idealism could be reconciled with self-interest. As we have seen, Lodge sought to justify his intense nationalism in just this manner: the American national state was man's last and best hope on earth, and if it was to fulfill its mission the state itself had to be made strong and secure. If one can credibly view one's own state or people as an agent of civilization and moral progress, then, of course, the burden of choice as to foreign policy is appreciably lightened. As Roosevelt assured the British, speaking at Oxford in 1910: "It is the highest duty of the most advanced and freest peoples to keep themselves in such a state of readiness as to forbid to any barbarism or despotism the hope of arresting the progress of the world by striking down the nations that lead in that progress."[205]

Abstractly, of course, insuperable difficulties are involved in the application of practical idealism to the field of international relations. As Norman Graebner so cogently put it: "A nation cannot pursue simultaneously its national interest and what it imagines to be the cause of humanity, for a nation and its ideology are not synonymous."[206] But often under American conditions it has seemed incumbent upon a statesman to try. The lesson of the American historical experience was that nationalism and idealism, if properly blended, could be made to reinforce one another; as Roosevelt told Lyman Abbott in 1900, "if Lincoln had not consistently combined the ideal and the practicable the war for the Union would have failed, and we would now be split in half a dozen confederacies."[207] The special appeal of practical idealism in this regard was that it served to postpone arguments about ultimate ends and allowed one to focus on tactics.

Certain options were obviously closed. A European-style *Realpolitik* was, as we have seen, impossible. The belief that democratic nations could choose between power politics and a moral foreign policy was too widespread.[208] Lodge and Roosevelt thought they knew better. The

205. Hermann Hagedorn, ed., *The Americanism of Theodore Roosevelt* (Boston, 1923), pp. 231–32. For an account particularly sensitive to the moral strain in Roosevelt's approach to foreign policy see Frederick W. Marks, III, "Morality as a Drive Wheel in the Diplomacy of Theodore Roosevelt," *Diplomatic History* 2 (Winter 1978): 43–62.

206. Graebner, *Ideas and Diplomacy*, p. viii.

207. Morison, ed., *Letters of Theodore Roosevelt*, II, p. 1133.

208. Hans J. Morgenthau, *In Defense of the National Interest* (New York, 1957), p. 13. Or as Wolfers and Martin (*The Anglo-American Tradition in Foreign*

wisdom of the Federalists bespoke the fact that a nation's form of government did not necessarily bear a relation to the nature of the foreign policy it pursued, and the American historical experience argued that the nation's existence (or the luxury of having any foreign policy at all) depended on its ability to defend its interests.[209] Still, in the American democracy foreign policy could not long be conducted without the support of the people, and that support usually depended upon their being convinced that national policy conformed to high moral standards. But at the same time no American political leader could afford, in the atmosphere of assertive nationalism which prevailed around the turn of the century, to subject himself to the charge that he was surrendering the interests of the United States to some other power (and especially not to England). The situation required both a moral foreign policy and one that paid close attention to the national interest, just the type of foreign policy that had traditionally worked best under American conditions. As Hans Morgenthau once observed, "between John Quincy Adams' moral principles and the traditional interests of the United States there was hardly ever a conflict; they . . . fit the interests as a glove fits the hand."[210] The foreign policy successes of the years just previous to Roosevelt's accession to the Presidency, Cleveland's Venezuelan Message and Hay's Open Door Note, rested on the same combination of moralism and concern for American interests. The pattern was set long before Roosevelt took office, but that did not make his task any the easier. To attempt to revisit the Adamsian (or Federalist) solution in an era when American interests were becoming more widespread, and when American moral pretensions were also correspondingly greater, was no simple matter. Adams had been closer to the original Federalist conception of combining preparedness with a determination to mind one's own business, while Roosevelt, under pressure from a public opinion that wanted to combine nonpreparedness with meddling in the affairs of other states, could only seek "in some dark way" to combine preparation with meddling.

To emphasize the political necessity of a solution which combined

---

Affairs, p. xx) put it: English and American thinkers developed a "philosophy of choice" in international relations, which was bound to be ethical, while Continental thinkers continued to be preoccupied with a "philosophy of necessity."

209. See, for example, Hamilton's comments in the 6th Federalist (Clinton Rossiter, ed., *The Federalist Papers* [New York, 1961], p. 56).

210. Morgenthau, *In Defense of the National Interest*, p. 22.

self-interest with moralism is not, however, to charge either Lodge or Roosevelt with hypocrisy in the matter. Like Macaulay they made a virtue of sharing the predominant views of their culture. Not much time need be spent in demonstrating that Lodge and Roosevelt were intense nationalists. That is generally acknowledged. What needs emphasis is the other side of the equation—the fact that they were men of high personal ideals and men who recognized the force and power of American idealism. Lodge knew that it was "only the men of ideals who in the long run can move and guide the people," and they judged one another and their contemporaries by those standards.[211] Roosevelt complained that Serge Witte (the Russian diplomat) was "totally without high ideals" and explained his position to Trevelyan as follows: "Inasmuch as I personally think that practical politics are a most sordid business unless they rest on a basis of honesty and disinterested sentiment (though of course I appreciate to the full that with the disinterested sentiment there must also go intelligent self-interest) I could not help feeling much contempt for the excellent Mr. Witte."[212] In short, Roosevelt's interest in raising the ethical standard of national action and Lodge's in assuring "our moral supremacy" in this hemisphere were not just flights of rhetorical fancy, but an integral part of their definition of American foreign policy.[213] Of course, they were fooling themselves, but what was unsuccessful in the realm of philosophy because it masked an attempt to impose American values had, nevertheless, both historical and political resonance.

Such idealism, however qualified, had to operate from a base of power. This is where they parted company from so many of their countrymen. Idealism in international relations was not a self-fulfilling proposition. Little could be accomplished from a position of weakness.

---

211. *Cong. Record*, 60th Cong., 1st sess., 1908, p. 4907.
212. Morison, ed., *Letters of Theodore Roosevelt*, V, p. 23.
213. Roosevelt's Sixth Annual Message to Congress quoted in Osgood, *Ideals and Self-Interest*, p. 89; Lodge to Elihu Root quoted in Jessup, *Elihu Root*, I, p. 488. This deserves emphasis because some observers have had difficulty reconciling what they consider Roosevelt's "basically Realist" approach to foreign policy with the high moral tone he always assumed. See for example, Osgood, *Ideals and Self-Interest*, pp. 89, 106. Osgood can only state that: "Although Roosevelt's approach to international relations was Realistic, he was far from being a cynic; while recognizing the primacy of self-interest he did not draw any rigid antithesis between ideals and self-interests as ends of national action." Elsewhere, however, Osgood insists that "realism remained the province of those least inhibited by ethical restraints."

Roosevelt tended to view the role of the United States in world affairs in much the same manner as he regarded his own domestic leadership. As he told Lodge:

I believe in the perpetuity of the American Republic, partly because we as a people give our heartiest admiration and respect, not to the mere strong man, regardless of whether he is good or bad, nor yet to the weakling of good purposes, but to the strong man who uses his strength disinterestedly for the public good; and our greatest national asset is that of this type, the Timoleon and Hampden type, we have produced the greatest examples that the world has ever seen in Washington and Lincoln.[214]

Transfer the arena to international relations and you have the belief that "our chief usefulness to humanity rests on our combining power with high purpose."[215] The lesson of the American historical experience (the Revolution and the Civil War being the major cases in point) was the agreeable belief that moral force and physical force were complementary. Applying the same wisdom to international relations resulted in the conviction that influence came most readily to the "just man armed" and that only from that position could one really work for world peace.[216] It was a neat little package; only by effecting a combination of the interests of the American national state with those arising from the idealism of her citizens could American foreign policy be successfully conducted and only then could world peace be ensured, a peace, it just so happened, which was also in the interest of the United States. Lodge favored Roosevelt's intervention in the first Moroccan crisis because the peace of the world was of first importance to the United States and declared it "a melancholy thing indeed if the moral influence of the United States could not be exerted for such a purpose."[217] Roosevelt had managed to strike just the balance between self-interested nationalism and idealism which served best to unite the country behind him and permit a maximum assertion of American influence. Lodge was so taken with the success of the Rooseveltian solution that he declared in triumph that "we are the strongest moral force—

214. Morison, ed., *Letters of Theodore Roosevelt*, VI, pp. 1135–36.
215. Roosevelt, "The Peace of Righteousness," p. 70.
216. *Correspondence of Roosevelt and Lodge*, II, pp. 135, 197 (June 5 and Sept. 8, 1905).
217. Lodge, "The Monroe Doctrine and Morocco," *Harper's Weekly* 50 (March 10, 1906): 333, 352.

also physical—now extant, and the peace of the world rests largely with us." But, never losing sight of the inherent difficulties, he quickly added: "so far you have saved the situation."[218]

Fortunately, the interests and the ideological preferences of the United States were complementary. American leaders of the period never faced the problem, as did those of France for example, of selling to liberals at home an alliance with a reactionary, autocratic power. It was a rapprochement with England that American interests semed to require and this caused no problem for Lodge, who tended to see things in terms of the fate of English civilization and was culturally anti-German, or for Roosevelt, who foresaw an Anglo-American combination dominating the world in the interest of civilization.[219] The Rooseveltian solution and the active role in world politics which it permitted rested, then, on propitious circumstances, on the fact that England and France could be regarded as "natural" allies (in both the ideological sense and in the sense that they had common interests).[220] For this reason the American populace was spared the agony of having to reconsider their approach to foreign policy and for this reason the Rooseveltian solution was politically feasible. Foreign policy has always been easiest for the United States when the nations who stood in the way of the realization of American interests could also be regarded as the opponents of freedom and civilization (when, as Lodge put it, the conflict was "between the military socialism of Russia and Germany and the individualism and freedom of the United States and England.")[221] Such enemies were made for America. They allowed American nationalism and American

218. *Correspondence of Roosevelt and Lodge*, II, p. 171 (July 25, 1905).

219. Gwynn, ed., *Letters of Spring Rice*, I, p. 250; Beale, *Roosevelt and the Rise of America*, p. 81. Lodge not only thought that Germany was "the hostile spirit" (Lodge to John Hay, Sept. 30, 1898, Lodge MSS) but had a strong cultural bias against Germans. See John Garraty, "Henry Cabot Lodge and the Alaskan Boundary Tribunal," *New England Quarterly* 24 (Dec. 1951): 477, 479.

220. Lodge to Elihu Root, July 7, 1905, Elihu Root Papers, Library of Congress. As Lodge explained it to Roosevelt. "I am very anxious that we should do all we can to draw France toward us. France ought to be with us and England—in our zone and our combination. It is the sound arrangement economically and politically. It will be an evil day for us if Germany were to crush France" (*Correspondence of Roosevelt and Lodge*, II, p. 162 [July 2, 1905]). Nor was this merely a reflection of the growing entente between France and England. Already in 1899 Lodge was working toward bringing France "into our combination where she belongs" (Lodge to Henry White, Nov. 19, 1899, White MSS).

221. Lodge, *The War with Spain*, p. 236.

idealism to march on hand in hand and were therefore conducive to the formulation of American policy and the mobilization of American power.

Only from our perspective are the weaknesses of their solution so readily apparent. From their perspective the Rooseveltian solution worked well. Most of their contemporaries would have agreed. If Roosevelt's own assessment of his Presidency was self-congratulatory, there was nevertheless some truth in his assertion that when he left the Presidency not one shot had been fired in seven and a half years against a foreign foe and that "we were at absolute peace and there was no nation in the world with whom a war cloud threatened, . . . or from whom we had anything to fear."[222] What Lodge had no way of knowing was whether theirs was a permanent solution to the problem of the conduct of foreign policy by the American democracy or whether its success was due in part to the fact that the United States was still, in Bryce's words, sailing "upon a summer sea."

It was a time of hope, of confidence, and of belief in moral progress. The nineteenth century had seen, in Roosevelt's view, "a real and great advance in the standard of international conduct," and he looked forward to even greater improvement in the twentieth century.[223] Democracy no longer presented the difficulties they once thought it might; the more Roosevelt saw of the Czar, the Kaiser, and the Mikado the more content he was with democracy. Events had given the lie to the dire prognosis implicit in Henry Adams's *Democracy*.[224] Roosevelt, like Lodge's Federalist heroes, had made democracy work, both at home and in the conduct of the nation's foreign policy. There was every indication that the wisdom of his solution would be grasped by his successors. It was especially difficult to imagine that the progress of the nineteenth century (and with it the basis for the Rooseveltian solution) might be suddenly shattered by the outbreak of war in Europe. Lodge

222. Roosevelt, *Autobiography*, p. 602. The ellipsis replaces the phrase "no nation in the world whom we had wronged," a claim which many of Roosevelt's opponents (thinking of the Philippines and of Colombia) would have vigorously contested. While he did make the claim and never wavered in its assertion, the last phrase in the sentence hints at a preoccupation with relations with the other great powers and here, most would have agreed, Roosevelt was punctilious.

223. Morison, ed., *Letters of Theodore Roosevelt*, V, p. 640. See also Roosevelt, *Autobiography*, pp. 532–33.

224. *Correspondence of Roosevelt and Lodge*, II, pp. 152, 189–91 (June 16, Sept. 2 and 7, 1905).

and Roosevelt, though more cautious than their contemporaries, had never been anxious about the actual physical security of the United States.[225] Though he had been warned that the balance of power in Europe was collapsing and that military predominance had passed to the Central Powers, Lodge could not really imagine the ultimate catastrophe and seemed in 1913 to endorse Lincoln's warning that the destruction of the American democracy could only come from within.[226]

Still he had his fears that the Rooseveltian solution (both in domestic and foreign politics), being in its nature both fortuitous and contingent, might come undone. He recognized how important Roosevelt's personality and talents had been and told him in 1907 that "I wish most deeply you could be President again for the next four years; I am sure that it would be best for the country."[227] Henry Adams was right when he wrote that Lodge had a "true 'idee fixe' " about Theodore; and as both the domestic and foreign policy aspects of the Rooseveltian solution came unraveled under Taft, as domestic antagonisms grew and the nation's ability to influence events abroad shrank, Lodge's thoughts turned increasingly to the possibility of returning to the Rooseveltian solution.[228] In his letters to Theodore he began to emphasize, as he had many years earlier, that the "one positive feeling among the American people is for you."[229] There was even a subtle change in his overall view of progress. In 1904 he felt that the civilization they had inherited was being pushed beyond its former limits and that a process of steady evolution had again begun, but by 1912 he was taking a darker view, contrasting current attitudes with the more sanguine conceptions prevalent in his youth and expressing the fear that industrial civilization might be about to break down.[230] Many influences worked to produce this change in his overall outlook (with the prospect of the

225. Osgood, *Ideals and Self-Interest*, p. 83.
226. Gwynn, ed., *Letters of Spring Rice*, II, p. 161; Lodge, *Democracy of the Constitution*, pp. 136–37.
227. Lodge to Roosevelt, Sept. 24, 1907, Roosevelt MSS.
228. Ford, ed., *Letters of Henry Adams*, II, p. 530. This must have been particularly galling to Lodge because he had pledged at the 1908 Republican National Convention that "the great services of the President to the world's peace will be continued by the party he led" (Lodge, *Speeches and Addresses*, p. 416). Actually Taft washed his hands of the second Moroccan crisis and concentrated his efforts in the international arena on just those initiatives (the arbitration treaties, for instance) most likely to arouse Lodge's ire.
229. Lodge to Roosevelt, April 19, 1910, Roosevelt MSS.
230. Lodge, *Frontier Town*, pp. 125–26; Lodge, *Early Memories*, pp. 214–15; Lodge to John T. Morse, Jr., Dec. 14, 1912, Morse MSS.

Democrats again occupying the White House near the top of the list), but not least among them was the fact that Roosevelt would no longer be conducting the nation's foreign policy. This came out clearly in February of 1914, when in the course of the Panama Canal Tolls debate Lodge declared that:

When the year 1909 opened, the United States occupied a higher and stronger position among the nations of the earth than at any period in our history. Never before had we possessed such an influence in international affairs. . . . [In the intervening years] this great position and this commanding influence have been largely lost.[231]

231. *Cong. Record,* 63rd Cong., 2nd sess., 1914, p. 6455.

Chapter Five

The Heir of
Jefferson and Buchanan

By his own admission Henry Cabot Lodge was "a pretty rigid Republican and party man," and one can well imagine that he looked with anything but favor upon the elevation to the Presidency of only the second Democrat since the Civil War.[1] Nevertheless, he scarcely knew Woodrow Wilson and, as John Garraty suggests, if he disliked and distrusted him in March of 1913, there was as yet no personal antagonism involved.[2] Lodge's detractors have usually claimed that his intense, personal animus against Wilson influenced his stand on what, like the League of Nations, were critical questions of state. The implication is that Lodge's ideas are therefore not worthy of serious consideration. This has been a comfortable position for Wilsonians because it has allowed them to avoid discussion of the problems inherent in the Wilson-

---

1. *Cong. Record*, 63rd Cong., 2nd sess., 1914, p. 3603. Lodge and Roosevelt had, as we have seen, an abiding distaste for the methods by which Jefferson and Buchanan had conducted America's affairs of state. Their historical reputations were a matter of lifelong concern, and Lodge was always ready to welcome "help in the good work of putting Jefferson in his proper place" (Lodge to Roosevelt, Aug. 20, 1906, Lodge MSS). Association with Jefferson and Buchanan became a convenient shorthand for categorizing all those who did not follow in the Federalist or Lincolnian tradition, and as Woodrow Wilson began to stake out a course contrary to their predilections and at odds with the "Rooseveltian solution," he soon fell victim to the same associations. The identification of Wilson with Jefferson and Buchanan appears frequently in their correspondence, and the precise language of the title of this chapter is taken from a letter from Roosevelt to Frederick Scott Oliver, July 22, 1915 (Morison, ed., *Letters of Theodore Roosevelt,* VIII, p. 949).

2. Garraty, *Lodge,* pp. 295, 297.

ian approach to the conduct of American foreign policy. On the other hand, defenders like Lodge's grandson have only admitted "that there was political hatred for limited periods of time" and have insisted that "could never have been a motivation for Lodge's decision on policy."[3] Such an "either-or" proposition cannot be sustained. There are times in all our lives when our assessment of someone's motives and our feelings about their personal integrity influence our judgments on the programs which that individual advances. A clearer definition of what constitutes "hatred" might be helpful, but the question can, I think, best be resolved by a close look at the events and issues which drove such a wedge between Lodge and Wilson and revealed that they had not only different philosophies of international relations, but even different views about what determined the course of history.

Their differences went far deeper than those of electoral politics; they were inherently intellectual and reflective of two very different value systems. Anyone who has observed the relationship between professors subscribing to contradictory schools of historical interpretation, or between men who are convinced that they alone have the perfect prescription for peace, will not be surprised to find that personal feelings are not easily excluded from such matters and that one's image of the values, motivation, and personal integrity of one's intellectual opposite do inevitably influence the manner in which the ideas and policies which he or she advocates are received. However, there are limits to the benefits to be derived from discussing the relationship between Lodge and Wilson abstractly. It was only over time and in response to discrete historical events that they came to discover how basic and far-reaching their differences were. I hope to be able to show just how their differences came to the fore and began to have such a deleterious effect on the country's foreign relations.

What I would do is look at Wilson through the eyes of Lodge. In no other way can Lodge's course of action, so long the subject of so much misinformation and misinterpretation, really be understood. Or to put it another way, I refrain from passing the judgment that Lodge's view of Wilson was one-sided, not because I dispute it, but because such a judgment has tended to preclude a consideration of Wilson's policy from a point of view critical enough to make Lodge's reactions at least

3. *Ibid.*, p. 312.

understandable, if not justifiable.[4] Of course, the suggestion implicit in my approach is that sometimes there was good reason for Lodge to feel the way he did about Wilson's foreign policy.[5] If by such means I happen to focus attention on some of the problems inherent in the Wilsonian approach to foreign policy and show the range and variety of factors which have influenced American conceptions of the nature and purpose of foreign policy, those will be ancillary benefits. It is Lodge's story that I would tell.

Lodge had his doubts about Wilson even before he became President. During the campaign of 1912 he confided this opinion to his friend John Morse:

As to Wilson, I think he is a man of ability, but he has no intellectual integrity at all. A man may change one or two opinions for his own advantage and change them perfectly honestly, but when a man changes all the well considered opinions of a life time and changes them all at once for his own popular advantage it seems to me that he must lack in loyalty of conviction and he, I know, is totally deficient in loyalty to friends. I do not think he can be trusted in any respect. I think he would sacrifice any opinion at any moment for his own benefit and go back on it the next moment if he thought returning to it would be profitable.[6]

The point is not that Wilson's course lent itself to this kind of criticism, but that Lodge's criticism of the Presidential candidate of the Democratic party in the fall of 1912 was so restrained. Lodge was an unhappy man in 1912. Estranged from Roosevelt on a question of principle (his advocacy of the recall of judicial decisions) and unable to approve of TR's third party course, he was compelled to support Taft, but did so without enthusiasm. His initial relations with Wilson must be viewed in this context. His inclination to give Wilson the benefit of the doubt (and even in February of 1914 to attribute to him the wish to restore

4. *Ibid.*, p. 313.
5. Over the years Arthur Link has come to understand that the Wilsonian approach to foreign policy was not without its shortcomings. Link can usually excuse those shortcomings because he finds justification in Wilson's ultimate purposes (in his "Higher Realism"), but the very shortcomings he reveals go a long way toward explaining why Lodge became so suspicious of Wilson's motives and objects.
6. Lodge to John T. Morse, Jr., Oct. 11, 1912, Lodge MSS. The reference to Wilson's disloyalty to his friends can be traced to Lodge's friendship with his fellow classicist, Andrew West, whose enmity for Wilson, as a result of their dispute over the location and function of the Graduate School at Princeton, was legendary.

the nation to its former prestige) must be viewed in the context of his feeling that the Taft Administration had been "a ghastly failure" and his believing, as late as April of 1914, that Roosevelt was "bent on the destruction of the Republican party. . . ."[7]

Yet even in the absence of a viable alternative, Lodge was distressed by many aspects of "New Freedom" diplomacy. Arthur Link has described Bryan's spoilsmanlike administration of the State Department as "the greatest debauchery of the Foreign Service in the twentieth century" and has dealt more harshly with the diplomacy of Wilson's first two years than with that of any other period of his Presidency, decrying both Wilson's and Bryan's ignorance of the techniques and issues of foreign affairs and the general naiveté of New Freedom diplomacy.[8] Lodge's own reaction can only be adjudged comparatively mild when we take into account his life-long devotion to improving the caliber and working conditions of the Foreign Service, his great interest in foreign policy, and his emotional and intellectual attachment to the Rooseveltian solution.[9]

It was not that age had mellowed Cabot Lodge. He was in these years at the height of his abilities, but had little peace of mind. Winthrop Chanler, a long-time friend, captured a significant side of the somewhat embittered and increasingly pessimistic Senator when he wrote in 1913:

He shows his age by the whiteness of his hair and the intolerance of his political point of view as expressed privately. In public I should say he is better than ever as a speaker, broader, more eloquent, a skilled and veteran fighter. At home he is quite different, does not argue, gets more excited and vehement over trifles, this you know of old.[10]

7. *Cong. Record*, 63rd Cong., 2nd sess., 1914, p. 3603; Lodge to John T. Morse, Jr., n.d., but filed with the letters for 1914 and clearly written in that year, and Lodge to Brooks Adams, April 26, 1914, Lodge MSS.

8. *Wilson: The New Freedom* (Princeton, 1956), pp. 98, 278–80.

9. Lodge was perhaps the staunchest defender of the State Department's budget requests to be found in the U.S. Senate. Southern and agrarian Democrats, on the other hand, were usually opposed to higher salaries and more expensive housing for the nation's diplomats. Not even their latter-day conversion to Wilsonian internationalism or their espousal of the League of Nations changed this basic pattern. The incongruity is not as striking as it first appears. Long suspicious of ordinary diplomacy, they were naturally disposed to find favor with something which purported to take its place.

10. Gwynn, ed., *Letters of Spring Rice*, II, p. 186.

His was an intolerance born of a lifelong attachment (both intellectual and emotional) to a particular style of national leadership and to a particular resolution of the problem of the conduct of foreign policy in a democracy. It was an intolerance recently nourished by what he regarded as Roosevelt's extraordinary success in demonstrating the timeless wisdom of the Federalists. But it was also a viewpoint tinged by now with a bit of cynicism, a cynicism born of long observation of the vagaries of American public opinion and of the knowledge that, in the face of what Lodge regarded as irrefutable historical argument, "the Jeffersonian myth" lived on.[11]

Lodge's views and prejudices on the subject of foreign policy were in 1913 much the same as they had always been. They are set forth most clearly in his correspondence with Roosevelt. For example, they drew the same and predictable conclusions from Wilson's and Bryan's hesitancy on the Canal Tolls issue, both complaining that they were placing the United States in "an attitude of hypocrisy" and both castigating "the solemn jacks of universal arbitration" who "pay no attention to the neglect of these practical treaties [the renewal of the Root arbitration treaties] and are engaged in eulogizing Bryan's loose talk about universal peace."[12]

Harley Notter has shown that Wilson's views on the conduct of foreign policy were also determined, in essential outline, long before he became President, and it is tempting to view the conflict that developed between Lodge and Wilson as the inevitable result of conflicting philosophies of international relations.[13] But to do so would be to miss the dynamics of the conflict. For it was only in reaction to specific events, and not in abstract discussion of policy, that their contrasting philosophies were revealed and that the question of one another's integrity came into play. Within the context of their divergent philosophies and inevitable differences of opinion, the questions of just "when"

11. The ability of "the Jeffersonian myth" to survive all demonstration of the historical error of its central tenets was incomprehensible to Lodge's coterie and was good breeding ground for their pessimism about the ultimate fate of democracy. See, for example, Brooks Adams to Henry Adams, Oct. 6, 1904, Houghton Library, Harvard University.

12. *Correspondence of Roosevelt and Lodge*, II, pp. 438–39 (Sept. 17 and 22, 1913).

13. *The Origins of the Foreign Policy of Woodrow Wilson* (New York, 1965), p. v.

and "how" Lodge's opinion of Wilson's conduct of the nation's foreign policy deteriorated to the point where he came to question the motivation for the President's every move remain important ones. Answers must be found if we would understand Lodge's course of action and why differences over foreign policy sometimes cut so deep.

From the outset Lodge interpreted Wilson's political maneuverings as "flinching" and giving way on everything "the minute that he finds that there is any considerable body of voters opposed to it." He was also put off by the fact that the South seemed to be again in control in Washington.[14] But the administration of the State Department and the handling of foreign policy disturbed him most. He soon confided to Brooks Adams that he "did not think that they could get up an Administration which . . . would be feebler and less effective than that of Taft; but they have done so. The prevailing characteristic of this Administration . . . seems to be ignorance, and that is particularly apparent in the State Department."[15] Bryan's handling of the Japanese exclusion problem first elicited the probably inevitable comparison with TR's management of such sensitive matters and caused Lodge to wish they had some idea of what to do with the Navy and to fear that "by sheer feebleness and ignorance they may flounder into war." In fact Bryan bore the brunt of Lodge's criticism. Lodge found him to be "absolutely ignorant of everything relating to foreign relations," and particularly objected to his "making a series of loose speeches on universal peace and telling Japan that under no circumstances would we fight, which of course encourages them to extreme demands."[16]

The Administration's Mexican policy caused Lodge great concern, and for that reason his initial patience is the more remarkable. He was probably restrained by what he considered the dismal record of the Taft administration in that area. Even in July of 1913 (long after British officials were blaming Wilson's nonrecognition of Huerta for the chaos prevailing in Mexico) Lodge confined himself to demanding the protection of American citizens in Mexico and continued to blame Taft more

14. Lodge to Brooks Adams, May 22, 1913, Lodge MSS; and to John Jay Chapman, Sept. 9, 1913, Houghton Library, Harvard University.

15. Lodge to Brooks Adams, May 22, 1913, Lodge MSS. Lodge's old friend, and now British Ambassador to the U.S., Cecil Spring Rice shared this view, confiding to Sir Edward Grey his opinion that this was "the most incompetent government which America has ever had" (Peter Calvert, *The Mexican Revolution, 1910–1914: The Diplomacy of Anglo-American Conflict* [Cambridge, England, 1968], p. 189).

16. Lodge to Brooks Adams, May 22 and 28, 1913, Lodge MSS.

than Wilson.[17] An untutored observer might even be forgiven for detecting an incipient bipartisanship in Lodge's remarks on the Senate floor in August of 1913:

I regard the Mexican question as of the utmost delicacy and difficulty. I think the President of the United States is endeavoring to find a solution by which war may be avoided and order restored in Mexico. I wish to aid him in every possible way in bringing about that result. . . . I have tried to study the question; . . . and I see the utmost difficulty in determining on any policy.[18]

He also publicly supported Wilson's decision to wait on events, declaring: "Only two courses were open to the President—intervention and non-intervention—and I am sure that the sentiment of the country would not tolerate intervention."[19] Nor did this merely reflect the fact that the Republicans had no alternative to propose. Lodge was never enthusiastic about war with Mexico and felt that "everything must be done that can be done in honor to avoid it." He saw no alternative to a waiting policy when coupled, as it initially was, with a ban on the export of arms to either side. Even in private he was willing to give Wilson the benefit of the doubt, telling one friend, the President "is doing the very best he can, but he is entirely new at the business and has been feeling his way." Particularly pleasing to Lodge was Wilson's willingness "to dicuss the matter and to consider all suggestions," a practice which Wilson unfortunately soon discarded. Bryan was still the chief obstacle to a sensible policy; while admitting that his opinion of Wilson was declining, Lodge thought the situation might still be remedied by "a competent Secretary of State."[20]

However, behind the agreement of Lodge and Wilson on a waiting policy lay quite different attitudes toward the events unfolding in Mexico. John Garraty has described Lodge's attitude as one of cynicism, though a knowledge of Mexican history and of the end result of the revolution might as easily lead one to describe it as realistic.[21] Though

17. Calvert, *The Diplomacy of Anglo-American Conflict*, pp. 191–94; *New York Times*, July 23, 1913.
18. *Cong. Record*, 63rd Cong., 1st sess., p. 3388.
19. *New York Times*, Aug. 28, 1913, p. 2.
20. Lodge to Fred Shattuck, Aug. 26, 1913, and to William Sturgis Bigelow, Aug. 30, 1913, Lodge MSS.
21. Garraty, *Lodge*, p. 301. Even sympathetic Americans are no longer as enthusiastic about the Mexican revolution as they once were. In their complaints that the revolution merely substituted one elite for another and did not fundamentally

Lodge by no means agreed with all aspects of British policy in Mexico, his overall view of the situation corresponded closely to that of the British Foreign Office and especially to that of Spring Rice, his old friend and now British Ambassador to the U.S., to whom he confided his hope that "they have got a man now of the Diaz type who will do sufficient throat cutting to restore peace."[22] While acknowledging that seemed "an unpleasant thing to say," Lodge thought it "impossible to maintain order or any approach to decent government in Mexico upon any other terms."[23] While readily conceding that "neither the man (Huerta) nor his methods are desirable," he feared that to force Huerta out would only "increase the anarchy now existing and leave the situation worse than before."[24] As long as Wilson was content to play for time and to prohibit all arms shipments, and thus leading Lodge to believe that he had no idea of making his moral objection to Huerta a matter of public policy, Lodge felt he too could afford to wait.[25] If Wilson believed that the Huerta government was likely to fall, there was as much reason to believe that it would succeed. If Wilson was content to rely on public

---

alter the country's social structure they are beginning to sound a little like Spring Rice and Lodge. See, for example, John Womack, Jr., "The Spoils of the Mexican Revolution," *Foreign Affairs* 49 (July, 1970): 677–87.

22. Lodge thought there were "extremely valid" objections to the recognition of Huerta "wholly apart from his character and methods," principally the fact that his government was not sufficiently well established to merit recognition. He also expressed to Spring Rice the wish "that your country and France and the others had not been so quick to recognize Huerta, because I feel that if we could all act together we should have a much better chance of getting an established government" and pointed out that "the fact that Lord Cowdray secured large and profitable concessions from Huerta, on the ground that he had secured the recognition of his government, has done and is doing much harm." See Gwynn, ed., *Letters of Spring Rice*, II, p. 192; and an undated letter of Lodge to Spring Rice, in reply to the latter's letter of Aug. 22, 1913, and obviously written shortly thereafter, Lodge MSS.

Another indication of the close working relationship that rapidly developed between these two old friends (fellow imperialists and admirers of the Rooseveltian solution) is the fact that it was Lodge whom Spring Rice consulted on the question of whether the Mexican situation had deteriorated to a point where it warranted his interrupting his summer holiday and returning to Washington. See Gwynn, ed., *Letters of Spring Rice*, II, p. 192.

23. Lodge to Spring Rice, March 10, 1913, Lodge MSS.

24. Gwynn, ed., *Letters of Spring Rice*, II, pp. 192–93; Lodge to Spring Rice, n.d., but probably late August, 1913, Lodge MSS.

25. Lodge to Spring Rice, n.d., but probably late August, 1913, Lodge MSS. Lodge's precise language was: "Of course the moral ground that Huerta is a bad man who has obtained his place by force, murder and other Mexican methods, is not one to stand upon as a final proposition and the President told me that he had no idea of making any such objection a public one."

1. *Alexander Hamilton after the painting by John Trumbull—the portrait Lodge chose for the frontispiece of* The Works of Alexander Hamilton.

2. *The photograph of Lodge that accompanied his article "Shall We Retain the Philippines?" in 1900.*

3. *The Senate Committee on the Philippines, which Lodge chaired, in 1902.* COURTESY OF THE MASSACHUSETTS HISTORICAL SOCIETY.

4. *Theodore Roosevelt as he appeared in Lodge's* The War with Spain.

5. *Sir Cecil Spring Rice (1914),*
British Ambassador to the United States
and Lodge confidant.

6. No friends of Wilson—Lodge, General Leonard Wood, and Dean Andrew West at the Princeton University commencement exercises, 1916.

7. *Lodge at his home in Nahant, 1916.*
COURTESY OF THE MASSACHUSETTS HISTORICAL SOCIETY.

8. *A. Lawrence Lowell (above)
and Lodge (right) as they appeared
in publicity photographs for their
"Joint Debate on the
Covenant of Paris,"
March 19, 1919.*

9. *A pro-League cartoon by Lute Pease which depicts the strength of public sentiment for the League, but which in retrospect also says something about the naive optimism of its proponents. From the* Newark Evening News, *reprinted in* Current History, *April 1919.*

10. *A cartoon by Bert R. Thomas meant to be critical of the Senate, but which also approximates Lodge's conception of the American public's commitment to internationalism. From the* Detroit News, *reprinted in* Current History, *January 1920.*

"WHERE DO WE GO FROM HERE?"

11. *A cartoon by Nelson Harding,*
rare for its recognition of the responsibility
both Lodge and Wilson bore for the defeat
of the League Covenant. From the Brooklyn Eagle,
reprinted in The Outlook, *January 7, 1920.*

opinion to do the job, Lodge, having less faith in its efficacy, was content to let him.

The first matter to cause Lodge to revise his opinion of Wilson's conduct of American foreign policy was one of Wilson's many violations of the rules of good diplomacy when it came to Mexican affairs, his instructions to his special agent Lind.[26] It was to Roosevelt, a pattern to occur with increasing frequency, that Lodge poured out his changing feelings:

The way in which the Mexican business has been handled is melancholy. Wilson's instructions to Lind seem inconceivable. To open negotiations with the head of a government and put to him as the first condition that he should abdicate is something new in diplomacy. Of course Gamboa took full advantage of it and slapped our faces. Those instructions were never seen by John Bassett Moore. They were concocted by Bryan and Wilson. You can have no conception of Bryan's ignorance, and he has reached a point where he cannot learn. . . . Wilson, who is the narrowest partisan that I have ever seen in the White House, and whose attitude is that of a schoolmaster towards his boys, is singularly ignorant, in a way which surprises me about foreign relations. . . .[27]

Roosevelt, in character, came back even a little stronger:

Bryan is, I really believe, the most contemptible figure we have ever had as Secretary of State, and of course Wilson must accept full responsibility for him. I regard Wilson with contemptuous dislike. He has ability of a certain kind. . . . But he is a ridiculous creature in international matters.[28]

In September 1913 Lodge developed ulcers and this kept him away from Washington for some time. In his absence Wilson's Mexican policy developed in a way that could only have been incomprehensible to Lodge. In November Wilson issued a statement to the diplomatic corps that did precisely what he had told Lodge he would not do. The statement called the Huerta regime a menace to the peace of the Hemisphere and threatened that "if General Huerta does not retire by force of circumstances it will become the duty of the United States to put him

26. See, for example, Philip H. Lowry, "The Mexican Policy of Woodrow Wilson," diss. Yale, 1949, p. 74.
27. Lodge to Roosevelt, Sept. 8, 1913, Roosevelt MSS.
28. Morison, ed., *Letters of Theodore Roosevelt*, VII, p. 747. Morison claims that Lodge "did not oppose Wilson's decision not to intervene only because he felt that the nation was unprepared to intervene." Lodge actually said that "we were not prepared to urge intervention, and if intervention is to come the country certainly is not ripe for it now" (Lodge to Roosevelt, Sept. 8, 1913, Roosevelt MSS). "Preparedness" has a political as well as a military dimension.

out. . . ."[29] To compound matters Wilson thereby established a pattern which plagued him in so many of his diplomatic dealings; his first notes were strong and ominous, but the subsequent ones dribbled off into futility. He threatened and then when his wishes were not met he took no action. Huerta came as a result to believe that Wilson was bluffing and was even able, interpreting Wilson's threat as but another manifestation of *Yanqui* imperialism, to use it to solidify his own position.[30] Not even the lifting of the arms embargo to permit shipments to Huerta's principal rivals, Carranza and Villa, seemed to help, and it soon became evident that Wilson had painted himself into a corner. Lodge appreciated this and was content, at a time when Huerta was getting stronger and when he and Wilson were working hand in hand on the Canal Tolls issue in an effort to improve Anglo-American relations, to let Mexican matters drift until such time as they would catch up with the Administration. In assessing the situation in March Lodge predicted that Wilson would soon have to bite the bit.

In an international complication the first and most fundamental rule is that one should keep one's hands free, so as to be able to take advantage of any and all contingencies as they arise. Instead of doing that, Mr. Wilson proceeded to tie his hands by refusing to recognize Huerta on the wrong ground. . . . In this way the President has got himself so entangled that he cannot be extricated except at the cost of either personal humiliation, which will reflect on the United States—or intervention, which he wishes to avoid at all hazards.[31]

Given the choice, Wilson, taking advantage of the Tampico incident, chose intervention, but not without a serious clash with Lodge over the purposes of that intervention, and not without making himself look ridiculous. In the terse words of one student of Wilson's Mexican policy:

He had entangled himself so that he was forced to an act of war, ostensibly to make Huerta salute the flag, really to deprive Huerta of some munitions, and, behind it all, to assist the Constitutionalists. But Huerta never saluted the flag; he continued to receive munitions; and the Constitutionalists became Wilson's bitter enemies.[32]

29. Garraty, *Lodge*, pp. 297, 303.
30. Both Philip Lowry ("The Mexican Policy of Woodrow Wilson," p. 74) and Howard F. Cline (*The United States and Mexico* [Cambridge, Mass., 1953], p. 150) make this point.
31. Lodge to John T. Morse, Jr., March 17, 1914, Lodge MSS.
32. Lowry, "The Mexican Policy of Woodrow Wilson," p. 125. The similarity

The Mexican crisis of 1914 marked a sharp turning point in Lodge's attitude toward Wilson.[33] Their initial clash came on what was almost a philosophical question, the grounds on which the intervention of one country in the affairs of another might be justified.[34] Wilson wanted Congress to authorize hostilities against Huerta by name. Lodge regarded that as an unwarranted and undignified declaration of war against an individual which left the country to go to war "in silence as to the real and only truly justifying international grounds."[35] The Senator was particularly anxious to avoid being put in a position where he might appear "to pick and choose between the factions which tear Mexico asunder" and thought that the proper course for the nation as a whole. Moreover, he warned the Administration that the seizure of Vera Cruz, call it what they might, would be armed intervention and that it would be resisted. That was all the more reason there should be no doubt as to American objects.

If we are to intervene for any cause or at any point in Mexican territory, I want it to be done on broad sufficient grounds. . . . I want to lift it up from the level of personal hostility and place it on the broad ground of great national action, taken in the interest and for the protection of American lives in a foreign country, and for the purpose of restoring peace and order, if we can, to the unhappy people just across our border. . . . I want to place it upon a ground where we shall all be content to have it rest.[36]

Lodge wanted the intervention to accord with prevailing standards of international law, standards which did not allow for the perhaps finer

---

between Lowry's indictment of Wilson's policy and Lodge's as detailed in a major speech on Mexico during the 1914 campaign (see the Boston *Herald*, Oct. 28, 1914, p. 6) and in a subsequent speech in the Senate on Jan. 6, 1915 (see Lodge, *War Addresses*, pp. 4–17) is striking.

33. Garraty, *Lodge*, p. 305.

34. It is still debatable whether an intervention cast in Wilsonian morality and liberalism (helping the "good guys") or one patterned on Lodge's more tangible objects (the protection of American lives and property) is more "justifiable." The American answer has so often been to blur the distinction. There is also the related and pertinent matter of which is the more limiting, the more likely to lead to a rapid termination of the intervention.

35. Lodge, *The Senate and the League of Nations* (New York, 1925), p. 14.

36. *Cong. Record*, 63rd Cong., 2nd sess., 1914, pp. 6966–67. After the fact he put his views even more sharply: "The United States had properly but one object in Mexico and that was to restore peace and order; . . . the policy adopted by the President was to get Huerta out of office. That was not the policy for the United States to take up. To substitute one Mexican for another as President of Mexico was not worth a drop of blood from the veins of an American sailor or soldier" (Lodge to Langdon Mitchell, Dec. 2, 1914, Lodge MSS).

distinction which Wilson felt able to draw. From the Administration's refusal to allow the authorizing resolution to instruct the President to protect the lives and property of American citizens, Lodge drew the perhaps not unwarranted conclusion that the Administration was acting in concert with Villa and Carranza and feared that requiring the protection of American lives in areas where they were in control would complicate its relations with them. Worse to Lodge than anything else in the framing of our Mexican policy was "this putting us in the attitude of an ally of Pancho Villa," and he attempted to arrest that development by calling for the immediate reinstitution of a complete embargo on *all* arms shipments to Mexico.[37]

But though he felt that the Administration's management of the Mexican business had been "incredibly bad," it was still against Bryan, whom he regarded as Villa's "chief supporter," that Lodge's principal fire was directed.[38] But for one small matter, his views might not have passed beyond those of the previous year when he felt that Wilson needed only a competent Secretary of State. True, there had been a serious breach on policy (and one that brought their different conceptions of international morality into play), but the more lasting effect probably flowed from Lodge's observation of Wilson's conduct in a crisis situation. As he told the story in *The Senate and the League of Nations*, when he and Senators Stone and Shively called at the White House shortly after the bloodletting at Vera Cruz:

We found Mr. Wilson in a state of great agitation and very much disturbed. He had never meant to have war. Owing to his misinformation he was taken completely by surprise by the fighting at Vera Cruz and he was thoroughly alarmed. . . . What struck me most in the conversation was the President's evident alarm and his lack of determination as to his policy. He evidently had not thought the question out or in any way determined beforehand what he would do in certain very probable contingencies. . . . It must have been clear to everybody that armed resistance was likely to occur; but it was only too obvious that the President had made no preparation in his own mind for this most probable event.[39]

37. *Cong. Record*, 63rd Cong., 2nd sess., 1914, pp. 7123–24.
38. Lodge to Brooks Adams and to Curtis Guild, April 26, 1914, and to Ellerton James, April 29, 1914, Lodge MSS.
39. Lodge, *The Senate and the League*, p. 18. Lodge was not alone in his observations. Others had much the same impression of the crisis' effect on Wilson. See Link, *Wilson: The New Freedom*, p. 402.

However, the only contemporary evidence of such a feeling is a brief reference to the President's having been "thoroughly frightened by Vera Cruz." Possibly in this case, as in the matter of Wilson's personal vendetta against Huerta, Lodge "at the moment . . . did not grasp its full significance or realize the light it threw upon Mr. Wilson himself."[40]

The President's indecision respecting Mexican matters acquired its full significance only when Lodge found Wilson taking a stand on the European war which was less pro-Ally and less forthright than that which he himself advocated. In this retrospective sense the Mexican crisis of 1914 did color Lodge's feelings towards the President. Above all it prompted the virtually inevitable contrast between his behavior and conduct of the nation's foreign relations and those of Roosevelt. Both of Lodge's major attempts to explicate that contrast, *War Addresses* and *The Senate and the League of Nations,* take Wilson's Mexican policy as their starting point.

II

Woodrow Wilson was not always the champion of internationalism. When he led the Democratic party to support an "international" position, that "marked as much of a reversal for the Democrats as opposing it did for the Republicans."[41] The Republican party had forged the rapprochement with England, and Roosevelt had brought the United States into the innermost counsels of the powers of Europe. Central to the Rooseveltian solution were two propositions: that the interests of peace and civilization were best served by a close relationship among the Great Powers and that noninterference in European affairs, as Mahan put it in 1910, did "not imply absence of concern in them, nor . . . involve heedlessness of the fact that the shifting of the balance in Europe may affect our interests and our power throughout the world."[42] This led to an interest in international stabilization (as Roosevelt told Baron von Eckhardtstein in 1912, the U.S. was becoming "more and more the balance of power of the whole globe") and to certain more tangible concerns (Roosevelt felt that "if Germany should overthrow

40. Lodge, *The Senate and the League,* pp. 15, 20.
41. John Milton Cooper, Jr., *The Vanity of Power: American Isolationism and the First World War* (Westport, Conn., 1969), p. 160.
42. *The Interest of America in International Conditions,* p. 178.

England and establish the supremacy in Europe she aims at, she will be almost certain to want to try her hand in America").[43] Consequently, it was only natural that they paid close attention to the policies of the various European states (Roosevelt told Lodge, for instance, that German war plans contemplated "flank marches through both Belgium and Switzerland") and tried to encourage the determination and preparation of England and France.[44]

Distressed by the recrudescence of isolationism under Taft, Lodge found the acceleration of that trend under Wilson even more worrisome. The go-it-alone attitude in China (the withdrawal from the Powers' banking consortium) exemplified this trend, and it may explain why Lodge attached such importance to the Canal Tolls issue, involving as it did a demonstration of concern for the opinions of Europe and a means of soothing ruffled Anglo-American relations. But if Wilson, in Lodge's opinion, did the right thing on the Canal Tolls issue, he followed it with a definition of America's world role which seemed the very antithesis of the Rooseveltian achievement. Wilson offered as a counter to Roosevelt's still rather imperialistic internationalism what can probably best be described as "self-righteous isolationism." Speaking in May of 1914, Wilson explained that Washington had urged the avoidance of entangling alliances "because he saw that no country had yet set its face in the same direction in which America had set her face." According to Wilson, those conditions had not changed: "We cannot form alliances with those who are not going our way; . . . those who are right, those who study their consciences in determining their policies, those who hold their honor higher than their advantage, do not need alliances."[45] A more explicit denial of the Rooseveltian concern to cultivate a concert among the Great Powers and of the proposition that the United States had a security interest in European developments could scarcely be imagined. Yet neither Lodge nor Roosevelt rose to meet Wilson on the abstract issue. The Chief Executive might, as Roosevelt had demonstrated, involve the United States in European

43. Baron Hermann von Eckhardtstein, *Die Isolierung Deutschlands*, quoted in Edward H. Buehrig, *Woodrow Wilson and the Balance of Power* (Bloomington, 1955), p. 154; Morison, ed., *Letters of Theodore Roosevelt*, VII, p. 423.

44. *Correspondence of Roosevelt and Lodge*, II, p. 409 (Sept. 12, 1911).

45. James Brown Scott, ed., *President Wilson's Foreign Policy* (New York, 1918), p. 45.

affairs (however surreptitiously), but the political climate was still such that no one with a sense of political reality would have thought of proposing more formal arrangements. Wilson by marrying American isolationism to the strong inclination of Americans to believe in their own superior morality had staked out a seemingly unassailable position. The Wilsonian and Rooseveltian approaches to the conduct of American foreign policy rested on quite different philosophical foundations, but it took the cataclysm of the First World War to bring their disparity into focus, to move the discussion from the abstract to the policy level, and permit Lodge and Roosevelt to make their case.

The initial American reaction to the war was in keeping with Wilson's May statement. Walter Weyl described it best:

Believing thus in our intrinsic peacefulness, it was in no spirit of humility that we met the outbreak of the Great War. We did not put ourselves in the place of the fighting nations, and acknowledge that in their circumstances we too might have been struggling in the dust. Rather we boasted of our restraining democracy, and of our perfect co-operative union, which protected us from European anarchy. . . . Our compassion for the peoples of Europe was tinged with a bland, self-righteous arrogance.[46]

Abstention from the European conflict, particularly an abstention based on a belief in a superior morality such as Wilson preached, precluded an active interest in either international justice or in American security, concerns which had been central to the Rooseveltian solution.[47] Neutrality itself was not the immediate issue, for neutrality in 1914, as Edward Buehrig has written, was "no mere personal preference of Wilson's"; it was but the traditional and expected American posture toward Europe.[48] The real question was whether neutrality would mean only abstention or be used to serve other interests.

The outbreak of war found Lodge in England, where so often in the period from 1895 to 1914 he spent a part of the summer. The war caused him to cancel plans to visit France, but he did not hurry home and did not arrive in New York until the 23rd of September.[49] He was in London the day the cabinet decided on war, and his favorable opinion

---

46. *American World Policies* (New York, 1917), p. 32.
47. Edward H. Buehrig, "Idealism and Statecraft," *Confluence* 5 (Autumn 1956): 253.
48. Buehrig, *Wilson and the Balance of Power*, p. 272.
49. Boston *Herald*, Sept. 24, 1914.

of Lloyd George seems to have derived from his role in forcing that decision.[50] Writing in retrospect Lodge confessed that:

The crowding events of those days as they came upon us in London, so near to the scene of action and involving as they did the safety of the British Empire, made an impression upon all who watched the developments of the days as they passed, which no one, I think, could ever forget. My sympathies were from the very first strongly with the Allies. I believed then, as I have continued to believe ever since, that nothing less was at stake on the result of the conflict than the freedom and civilization of the Western world.[51]

John Garraty considers Lodge's position in August of 1914 to have been "no different from that of a majority of Americans who felt favorably disposed toward France and England, and unfriendly toward Germany" but did not believe that America should enter the war. However, Garraty also concedes that Lodge was so pro-Ally that he was quick to see Wilson as pro-German.[52] As we examine the evidence it is well to keep a few distinctions in mind. Lodge shared the shock and disbelief that was the reaction of most Americans to seeing a major war break out in Europe after so long an interlude of peace, an interlude easily productive of the thought that the nineteenth century was the beginning of a new and better era in human history. Only the year before, he had expressed the opinion that the United States was more likely to succumb to internal than to external danger, and he could never quite rid himself of the feeling that "this awful war [was] the greatest calamity to humanity and civilization ever known."[53] In this, as in his general sympathy for the Allied cause, he was in line with the thinking of most of his countrymen. But if, as he subsequently claimed, Lodge thought that "the freedom and civilization of the Western world was at stake on the conflict," then his sympathy for the Allies was based on propositions that many Americans were reluctant to accept: namely, as Corinne Roosevelt Robinson wrote of the feelings of her brother Theodore, that the Allies were fighting our battles, that not only American security, but even the survival of American values, depended on an Allied victory.[54] That would have given to his sympathy for the Allies

50. Lodge to Roosevelt, March 20, 1918, Lodge MSS.
51. Lodge, *The Senate and the League*, p. 25.
52. Garraty, *Lodge*, pp. 306–07.
53. Lodge to Corinne Roosevelt Robinson, Oct. 10, 1914, Houghton Library, Harvard University.
54. *My Brother Theodore Roosevelt* (New York, 1921), p. 279.

a dimension which, except in Genteel New England, was unusual among Americans in the early stages of the war. It would also help explain his increasingly bitter feelings toward Wilson, who was not at all of the same mind.

Lodge's first public utterance on the war was a statement given to a correspondent of the New York *Sun* in London, a statement which was cleared with the British government and probably even timed to accord with their plans. As Lodge subsequently explained his action:

> Being most anxious not to embarrass the British Government in any way, I spoke to my friend, Lord Harcourt, then Secretary for the Colonies, about it, and he was very anxious that I should make such a statement as I proposed to make just at that critical time. I felt at the moment a keen regret that the United States had not made a protest as to the invasion of Belgium and the breach of her neutrality.[55]

After due obeisance to the feeling that the United States was outside the circle of war, and expression of hope that it would remain so, Lodge came quickly to the point. What interested him (and the British Government) was the shape American neutrality would take. Lodge called upon his fellow Americans to remember that "we have a national duty to perform; that duty is the observance of strict neutrality as between the belligerents. . . ." What bothered Lodge (and in turn the British Government) were the Administration's departures from previous American practice. He did not understand how the Administration could consider permission to private persons to lend money to France to be spent on the purchase of supplies in the United States, an impairment to strict neutrality, "while at the same time it appears to think it is consonant with honest neutrality to give $25,000,000 of the public money outright to Germany for ships which Germany cannot use."[56] He was a long way from advocating American participation in the war (an obviously untenable position politically), but he *was* quick to see that strict neutrality would work to the advantage of the Allies, and eager to have it do so.

A further insight into his initial reaction is provided by some observations in the diary of John Jay Chapman, who was also in London and reported under the heading of August 26:

55. Lodge, *The Senate and the League*, p. 29; or see the New York *Sun* of August 23, 1914; or the reprint of his statement in the *Cong. Record*, 63rd Cong., 2nd sess., 1914, p. 14199.
56. Lodge, *The Senate and the League*, p. 26.

Lodge was interesting. He gave me a letter to Haldane. . . . Lodge quoted Haldane 'The fight is to put an end to Prussian Militarism and if we win it must mean disarmament.' That is all we need—spoken solemnly by the whole Administration. Lodge is not satisfied with Wilson and Bryan—too much German in it. Wilson still says he will buy the boats. If he does Lodge will attack him. . . . L. says he couldn't get me an interview with Wilson—a letter from him would be waste paper.[57]

There was no immediate break between Lodge and Wilson, but the outbreak of war and their respective reactions brought an important new dimension, and added a new strain, to their relations. As Lodge later put it: "I, at least, became more and more dissatisfied with his policy and ceased to have any confidence in his conduct of our relations during the trying and eventful years which followed the beginning of the war in 1914."[58]

Upon arrival in New York on the 23rd of September, Lodge issued another statement, which again was all the British could have asked. He suggested that all peace talk now was the work of German agents and said:

We must eliminate from our minds any idea of a speedy peace, which will leave everything in the same condition as it existed in July. . . . Either Germany will dictate the peace or the Allies. If Germany conquers France, England, or Russia, she will dominate Europe and will subsequently seek to extend that domination if she can to the rest of the world.

Great Britain, France and Belgium believe that they are fighting the battle of freedom and democracy against militarism and autocracy, the battle for public laws against the laws of the sword, and for the right of small nations to exist. . . . All the Allies are determined that they will put an end to the conditions which made the hideous calamity of this war possible. They will fight on until that purpose is accomplished. . . . It is for us to maintain our neutrality and at the right moment use all our influence for peace that will be lasting. . . . No other peace is worth having.[59]

So early did Lodge express the conviction that the only peace worth having would be one pursuant to an Allied victory and so early did he fear and seek to head off pressures for another type of settlement! Though resigned to American neutrality, and the more easily because he was confident the Allies would be ultimately victorious, he believed

---

57. M. A. DeWolfe Howe, *John Jay Chapman and His Letters* (Boston, 1937), p. 284.
58. Lodge, *The Senate and the League*, pp. 30–31.
59. *New York Times*, Sept. 24, 1914, p. 5.

from the outset that the United States had both a moral and a security interest in an Allied victory. That alone could make the peace a lasting one and, while operating within the bounds of neutrality, that was *the* condition which the United States ought to promote. Wilson, on the other hand, did not publicly recognize that the United States had either a moral or a security interest in an Allied victory. The accepted explanation for this is that he assumed such a posture so as to be better able to mediate the conflict and bring about peace.[60] But the point I would make is that Wilson was interested in arranging a peace per se while Lodge thought a "lasting peace" could only be based on an Allied victory. Lodge later asserted that he had believed from August 1914 that it was inevitable that the United States "should be engaged" in the conflict.[61] Though there is not sufficient contemporary evidence to support such a claim, it *is* clear that he early placed an Allied victory above both peace and America's keeping out of the war.

Roosevelt's initial reaction was less straightforward. As Howard Beale has observed, given the fact that the entente with England during Roosevelt's administration was so close, "it would have been surprising had he not felt we should enter World War I on Britain's side."[62] He came rather quickly to that position, but his immediate reaction was less pro-Ally than that of Lodge. The outbreak of war found Roosevelt in the United States and about to embark on a campaign to save some vestige of the Progressive party in the 1914 congressional elections. He was in close touch with American opinion and, as Robert Osgood notes, his initial reticence on the subject of America's duty to intervene gives "a clue to the public's attitude as well as his own."[63] He told an English friend that the country was "emphatically in favor of England, France and Belgium; yet curiously enough . . . very lukewarm as regards Russia and Serbia," and he expressed to Hugo Muensterberg the opinion that the "several nations engaged . . . are, each from its own standpoint,

60. This is certainly Arthur Link's view. See, for example, *The Higher Realism of Woodrow Wilson and Other Essays* (Nashville, 1971), p. 136; or *President Wilson and His English Critics* (Oxford, 1959), p. 9.
61. *Cong. Record*, 65th Cong., 1st sess., 1917, p. 1440.
62. *Roosevelt and the Rise of America*, p. 171. In this connection it is interesting to note Lodge's thankfulness that rapprochement had proceeded so far that there were no outstanding issues to plague Anglo-American relations (Charles G. Washburn, "Memoir of Henry Cabot Lodge," *Proceedings of the Massachusetts Historical Society* 58 [April 1925]: 342).
63. *Ideals and Self-Interest*, p. 137.

right under the existing conditions of civilization and international relations."[64]

At first Roosevelt did not think of the war as part of his ongoing crusade for international righteousness. Rather, he viewed it as an object lesson for Americans and drew from it precisely those lessons which had long since become conventional with him. He scoffed at Bryan's belief in his conciliation treaties at a time when the most solemn international engagements were proving worthless, and warned that the United States would be trampled by the huge, straining combatants unless it prepared and made it dangerous for them to do so.[65] Roosevelt took pains to point out that American immunity had nothing to do with superior morality, but was solely a function of the Monroe Doctrine. And he again drew attention to democracy's historic problem, the fact that "free peoples have generally split and sunk on that great rock of difficulty caused by the fact that a government which recognizes the liberties of the people is usually not strong enough to preserve the liberties of the people against outside aggression."[66] Given his penchants, he naturally looked for a basis for some forthright American action and hoped that Wilson would at least do something to demonstrate America's interest in the conflict. He first toyed with the idea of a protest against the war contributions being levied on Belgium and then moved on to suggest that there was "even a possible question whether we are not ourselves . . . violating obligations which we have explicitly or implicitly assumed in the Hague treaties" by not protesting the violation of Belgium's neutrality.[67] His hesitancy stemmed from obligations to

64. Morison, ed., *Letters of Theodore Roosevelt*, VII, pp. 794–95, 809.

65. "The Foreign Policy of the United States," *The Outlook* 107 (August 22, 1914): 1011–13. As he expressed it, "there are certain lessons of continuing National policy which we as a Nation should draw from this contest."

66. "The World War: Its Tragedies and Its Lessons," *The Outlook* 108 (Sept. 23, 1914): 169, 176.

67. Morison, ed., *Letters of Theodore Roosevelt*, VII, p. 810; "The World War: Its Tragedies and Its Lessons," p. 175. The latter charge soon became the central point in Roosevelt's campaign against Wilsonian inaction, and for a more assertive neutrality. There can, I think, be little quarrel with Robert Lansing's finding that legally there was doubt "whether this Government should act in regard to a violation of The Hague Conventions unless the rights of the United States or its citizens are impaired by the violation" (Memorandum to President Wilson, Nov. 23, 1914 in *Papers Relating to the Foreign Relations of the United States, The Lansing Papers, 1914–1920* [Washington, 1939], I, pp. 35–36). The Administration never filed even a protest. But whether the U.S. had a moral obligation to protest is another matter, and, in light of Wilson's subsequent attempt to establish the League of Nations on the basis of international moral obligation, a particularly

his fellow Progressives, many of whom had long been in the forefront of the American peace movement, and from his growing despair over the fact that the Administration "only too well represents the American people."[68] However, in private he began to complain vigorously about the shortsightedness, the ignorance, and the cowardice of the American people when it came to foreign affairs.[69] The self-righteousness of the pacifists really got under his skin, and he wanted the American people to appreciate how "grim [a] comment on the professional pacifist theories [it was] . . . that our duty to preserve peace for ourselves may necessarily mean the abandonment of all effective effort to secure peace for other unoffending nations. . . ."[70]

Whatever the reasons for his initial hesitancy, Roosevelt moved rapidly toward Lodge's pro-Ally position. The essential point, and one that brought him close to the position espoused by Lodge, was the declaration in a September 23 *Outlook* article that "a peace which left Belgium's wrongs unredressed and which did not provide against a recurrence of such wrongs . . . would not be a real peace."[71] The decisive factor, as in Lodge's case, appears to have been his association

---

interesting one. Roosevelt's attitude quickly coalesced around the proposition that "it is wicked hypocrisy for us ever to talk of entering into another Hague convention unless we in good faith strive to secure the carrying out of the Hague convention into which we have already entered. . . . The unselfish thing for this nation to do is to protest at this moment against the wrong done to Belgium" (Roosevelt to Andrew Dickson White, Nov. 2, 1914 in Morison, ed., *Letters of Theodore Roosevelt*, VIII, pp. 827–28). So early did the attitudes which were to govern his approach to the League of Nations arise!

68. Roosevelt quoted in Russell Buchanan, "Theodore Roosevelt and American Neutrality," *American Historical Review* 43 (July 1938): 777. Roosevelt's developing pessimism accords well with Arthur Link's finding that "the most important development in the American reaction to the war before the spring of 1915 . . . was the dilution of the pro-Allied sentiment" (*Wilson: The Struggle for Neutrality* [Princeton, 1960], p. 12).

He did not make a public and direct criticism of the President for his failure to protest the violation of Belgian neutrality until five days after the election (see Harbaugh, *Power and Responsibility*, p. 473). He explained his hesitancy to Lodge as a product of his not wanting to embarrass his friends before the election (*Correspondence of Roosevelt and Lodge*, II, p. 449 [Dec. 8, 1914]). He claimed to have told those supporters he would only hold off until after the election and would then smite the President with a heavy hand and, indeed, he was rejoicing only a few months later to be free of all connections to party, and able to go his own way (*Correspondence of Roosevelt and Lodge*, II, p. 456 [Feb. 18, 1915]).

69. Morison, ed., *Letters of Theodore Roosevelt*, VII, p. 816; VIII, p. 817.

70. "The World War: Its Tragedies and Its Lessons," pp. 172–73. The dilemma remains to this day a real one.

71. *Ibid.*, p. 169.

with and respect for prominent Englishmen and his inability to resist their appeals, couched as they were in the moral idealism of Anglo-American civilization and in a language which sounded almost Rooseveltian. Their English friends did not mince words. Rudyard Kipling told Roosevelt he was "aghast" at the inaction of the United States and found it " 'almost incredible' that the United States, which had always stood out against such 'horrors,' should now maintain silence."[72] George Otto Trevelyan continually impressed upon Lodge the impact of American opinion on Allied morale and was totally unable to understand Wilson's saying that questions as to right and wrong could only be examined at the end of the conflict.[73] To many Englishmen this was but a self-serving evasion, and they long remained convinced that Wilson "did not begin to understand what the war was all about."[74]

Believing that the United States had a moral and security interest in an Allied victory and finding that so few Americans shared this view, Roosevelt and Lodge opened their hearts more readily to their English friends than to their own countrymen. Roosevelt told Spring Rice (initially under the injunction of secrecy) that had he been President he would have called attention to the guaranty of Belgium's neutrality and declared that the Hague treaties imposed "a serious obligation which I expected not only the United States but all other neutral nations to join in enforcing." He added that he would have been willing to back up such a statement and believed that had he been President (an important qualification) the American people would have followed him.[75] Similarly, in reply to Trevelyan Lodge declared that "the country understands pretty well that the liberty and democracy in which we believe and our future material and political interests are involved in the success of the allied countries" and expressed his fear that Wilson belonged to that small class of university professors who were under the influence of German thought.[76]

The importance of their English connections can also be seen in the close friendship which developed between Lodge and the British Ambassador, Spring Rice, in these trying years. As Lodge explained it,

72. Buchanan, "Theodore Roosevelt and American Neutrality," p. 779.
73. Sir George Otto Trevelyan to Lodge, Oct. 27, 1914, Lodge MSS.
74. Link, *President Wilson and His English Critics*, p. 7.
75. Roosevelt to Spring Rice, Oct. 3, 1914, in Morison, ed., *Letters of Theodore Roosevelt*, VIII, p. 821.
76. Lodge to Trevelyan, Nov. 13, 1914, Lodge MSS.

"he had insisted as a matter of hygiene, that Spring Rice should come to him daily at the close of the afternoon and 'unpack his heart with words'—saying the worst that he could against America for its abstention."[77] Afterwards he wrote of his feeling that Spring Rice "found it a comfort to be with someone to whom he could open his heart without reserve."[78] We may reasonably assume that the opening of hearts was not all on one side and that Spring Rice found in Lodge not only comfort, but important support for the Allied cause. The exact nature of those conversations and how closely they concerted their actions will probably never be known, but the similarity of their views was remarkable. This harmony was not for any want of Spring Rice's devotion to England's cause. Spring Rice had sneered that "we [the United States] were no nation, just a collection of people who neutralize one another" and, reminded "of the souls in Dante who were neither for God nor for God's enemies, but for themselves," had determined that a nation which had done nothing to prevent the crime would never be allowed to prevent the punishment.[79]

Lodge and Roosevelt poured out their true feelings to their English friends, but they remained seasoned American politicians. What was clear to any student of the American scene was that there was scarcely any sentiment for American participation in the war.[80] Even Spring Rice did not expect that and suggested in early 1915 that were the U.S. to go to war with Germany there would be "a strong probability of civil war."[81]

Under such circumstances Lodge and Roosevelt had to consider carefully the means of facilitating an Allied victory. Circumspection was imperative. Lodge, Roosevelt, and those close to them like Root—all saw the necessity. Root explained to Lord Bryce that he did violence to his feelings by keeping quiet, but thought it the wisest course as it allowed him to exercise influence on practical matters and to speak

77. Gwynn, ed., *Letters of Spring Rice*, II, p. 215n.

78. *Ibid.*, II, p. 435. Spring Rice was a poet of sorts and a further indication of the closeness of his relations with the Lodges can be found in the poem "In Memoriam A. C. M. L." written about Lodge's wife Nannie and privately printed by Lodge in 1918. See Cecil Arthur Spring Rice, *Poems* (London, 1920), pp. 124–68.

79. Thomas A. Bailey, *Woodrow Wilson and the Great Betrayal* (New York, 1945), p. 23; Gwynn, ed., *Letters of Spring Rice*, II, pp. 240–42.

80. Link, *Wilson: The Struggle for Neutrality*, pp. 17–18.

81. Gwynn, ed., *Letters of Spring Rice*, II, p. 254.

from the tactically important "American point of view."[82] Given the mood of the country, the charge that they wanted to get the country into the war could easily prove fatal to their cause.[83] Roosevelt was vague on how America should intervene on behalf of Belgium because he felt that if he advocated all that he wanted, he "would do no good among our people, because they would not follow me." As ever he felt constrained to take into account the fact that "our people are short-sighted, and they do not understand international matters."[84] Lodge, long an admirer of Lincolnian tactics—"carry[ing] his people with him, step by step," was governed by much the same considerations.[85] Admitting to Trevelyan that the U.S. should have protested the violation of Belgium, he nevertheless pointed to the "difficulties which beset a country where there are large foreign groups," and declared he could not afford to have his name "connected with anything which would give the Administration the opportunity to say that the Republican leaders were trying to make the country depart from its attitude of neutrality."[86]

Prepared for a lengthy struggle, Lodge determined to move the country, issue by issue, in the direction dictated, to his way of thinking, by considerations of both morality and security.[87] His object at this stage, however, was an Allied victory and not American entry into the war. "I should regard it as little less than a crime," he stated, "to force this country into this war, in which its own interests are not immediately involved." But, unlike Wilson, he did not stop there, but added "however much they may be involved in the future." That, of course, was contingent on the course of the war and the degree of Allied

82. Jessup, *Elihu Root*, II, pp. 321–22.

83. This was exactly the charge which Wilson was to use so successfully in the 1916 election campaign and one which was quick to surface. Taft, for example, wrote to a confidant as early as Feb. 28, 1915, that he believed "Lodge and Roosevelt would get us into war if they could" (Taft to Gus Karger, Taft MSS).

84. Morison, ed., *Letters of Theodore Roosevelt*, VIII, pp. 829–30. Roosevelt also thought the British shortsighted, but less so, comparing their difference from the Americans in this regard to "the comparative widths of the Channel and the Atlantic Ocean."

85. Roosevelt and Lodge, *Hero Tales from American History*, pp. 284–85.

86. Lodge to Trevelyan, Dec. 12, 1914, Lodge MSS. See also a letter of Lodge to Francis B. Chadwick, March 27, 1915, in which he stated: "I would simply destroy my usefulness if I came out and took sides" (Lodge MSS).

87. Lodge to J. D. H. Luce, Dec. 28, 1914, and to Lord Bryce, Jan. 14, 1915, Lodge MSS.

success.[88] Believing as he did in an eventual Allied victory, he felt justified in taking the long-range view.[89] Intervention might be eventually necessary, but that could be left to events; his immediate object was to be of all possible assistance to the Allied cause.

His course was attended by much frustration. His position was often uncomfortable both morally and politically. He and Roosevelt were convinced that Wilson and Bryan "were temperamentally incapable of developing an honorable policy toward the war," that their course of conduct made a mockery of the "whole international code of gentlemenly behavior" which had been the essence of the Rooseveltian solution, but they found themselves being warned not to make an issue of the Administration's foreign policy.[90] Roosevelt did not do so publicly until after the election, and Lodge did so only circuitously.

Limiting his comments on the war in Europe to such generalities as its calamitous effect on Western civilization (yet, nevertheless, making the point that "we are a large and integral part" of that civilization), Lodge continued to reserve his harshest comments for Wilson's Mexican policy. By the late summer of 1914 as the chief object of the Administration's policy appeared to be that of deposing Carranza and enthroning Pancho Villa, the absurdity of its "moral" intervention was becoming manifest.[91] The Administration's Mexican policy became an important issue in its own right, but it took on added significance because Lodge thought Wilson's handling of the Mexican problem symbolic of the shortcomings of his approach to foreign policy and therefore a useful surrogate issue. The nature of Lodge's denunciation of Wilson's course in Mexico at Worcester on October 27, 1914 (and

88. Lodge to Francis B. Chadwick, March 27, 1915, Lodge MSS.

89. Lodge to J. D. H. Luce, Dec. 28, 1914; to Herbert St. John Mildmay, Jan. 12, 1915; and to Lord Bryce, Jan. 14, 1915; Lodge MSS.

90. *Correspondence of Roosevelt and Lodge,* II, pp. 447–49 (Dec. 7, 8, 1914); Osgood, *Ideals and Self-Interest,* pp. 138–39. Osgood places Roosevelt's coming to this conclusion at "the end of November." But as early as the 16th he was telling Hiram Johnson "it would be impossible to stigmatize too harshly Wilson's attitude in foreign affairs" (Morison, ed., *Letters of Theodore Roosevelt,* VIII, p. 846).

91. Arthur S. Link, *Woodrow Wilson and the Progressive Era, 1900–1917* (New York, 1954), p. 129. See also Robert E. Quirk, *The Mexican Revolution, 1914–1915* (Bloomington, 1960), pp. 282–83. Quirk speaks of Wilson's and Lansing's "strange affinity for Villa, the most lawless factional leader in the Mexican Revolution. . . . The worse Villa's spoliation became, the more the American government tried to find means to placate him." Lodge feared the Administration might pursue a similar policy in Europe and give way whenever the Germans appeared menacing.

his use of the issue through the Presidential campaign of 1916) indicates that it was a convenient means of attacking the philosophical bases of Wilsonian foreign policy, while continuing to advocate a policy of strict neutrality toward the war in Europe and avoiding the imputation that he wanted to involve the United States in that war in any way.[92] Particularly egregious, in Lodge's opinion, was the Administration's hypocrisy, its using the Tampico incident "as a pretext for more active interference against the Huerta government," and its tortuous course in choosing neither a policy of total abstention nor of efficient intervention, but one combining the worst features of both.[93] This put the United States in the morally reprehensible position of supporting one Mexican faction against another and had resulted in a situation where

we may have to fight with Mexican soldiers at any moment. We have got the wolf by the ears and seem unable to let go. Mexico is unpacified. These are the actual results of the peace policy of the President in Mexico. If that is an achievement in the interests of peace, if that is an international or diplomatic success, I do not know what constitutes peace or success in dealing with a grave international situation.[94]

Once the obstacle of Roosevelt's efforts on behalf of the Progressive candidates in the 1914 campaign was removed, he and Lodge, in their mutual frustration with the Administration and again, as in the early 1890s, finding themselves almost alone, turned increasingly to each another. Their personal relations, Lodge insisted to Trevelyan, had remained much the same after 1912, the only difference being that they ceased to talk politics. But in the course of the winter of 1914–15

92. Additional evidence that Lodge was attempting to make a connection between Wilson's Mexican and European policies can be found in his comment to Roosevelt that "the first phrase of your Mexican article exactly expresses what Wilson has been doing in regard to the European war—'furtive meddling'" (*Correspondence of Roosevelt and Lodge*, II, p. 451 [Jan. 15, 1915]). Lodge was also quick to claim that his Worcester speech had "more success" than any in the campaign (letter to Langdon Mitchell, Nov. 13, 1914, Lodge MSS).

93. This hypocrisy, Robert Quirk believes, proved the real undoing of Wilson's Mexican policy. "In insisting upon the morality of his acts, he aroused both the hatred and the scorn of the Mexicans—hatred over the invasion but a deep scorn for what they saw as his hypocrisy" (*An Affair of Honor: Woodrow Wilson and the Occupation of Vera Cruz* [Lexington, Ky., 1962], Preface).

94. Boston *Herald*, Oct. 28, 1914. He made essentially the same points after Congress reconvened. See his speech delivered in the Senate on Jan. 6, 1915, the first speech included in his *War Addresses*, pp. 3–19.

they were again "discussing politics in the old way."[95] The improvement in their relations was gradual and as always was built on profound agreement on foreign policy issues. Lodge heartily approved of TR's articles on neutrality and preparedness and agreed that our attitude in regard to the Hague Conventions had been "pitiful."[96] Soon he too was telling his correspondents that he had felt strongly at the beginning of the war that the U.S. should have "protested against the violation of Belgium and the sowing of mines on the high seas" and "put ourselves at the head of the neutral powers," thereby creating "a powerful force both for the protection of neutrals and the suppression of some of the worst features of the war."[97]

In this manner a hypothetical Rooseveltian alternative was formulated. Whether one considers it mythical depends on one's assessment of what Roosevelt could and would have done had he been President. Lodge never subscribed to the more extreme version. Only once did he express the idea that if Roosevelt had been President there would have been no war.[98] In more thoughtful moments he doubted whether American intervention before the Belgian frontier was crossed could have arrested further developments (he had little inclination to suggest the Germans would have been so reasonable), but he did feel that it would have put the U.S. in a strong position and "saved us many troubles."[99] To that extent Lodge believed in the Rooseveltian alternative, and this certainly helped smooth the way for his political rapprochement with Roosevelt.

But the improvement in their relations was rooted in perhaps even firmer ground, in their mounting despair over Wilson's conduct of the nation's foreign policy. Roosevelt declared to Lodge his feeling that "Wilson and Bryan are the very worst men we have ever had in their positions . . . worse then [sic] Jefferson and Madison." Lodge wholeheartedly agreed, saying that "Wilson and Bryan go beyond anything we have ever had, and there are certain persons who I think were pretty inefficient in the past."[100] Finding a sympathetic listener and

95. Lodge to Trevelyan, April 23, 1915, Lodge MSS.
96. *Correspondence of Roosevelt and Lodge*, II, p. 448 (Dec. 7, 1914).
97. Lodge to J. St. Loe Strachey, May 20, 1915; see also the somewhat weaker version to an American named Barton, May 13, 1915; Lodge MSS.
98. *Correspondence of Roosevelt and Lodge*, II, p. 483 (Feb. 9, 1916).
99. Washburn, "Memoir of Henry Cabot Lodge," p. 345.
100. *Correspondence of Roosevelt and Lodge*, II, p. 450 (Dec. 8, 11, 1914).

one to whom he could confide feelings that he otherwise had to restrain, Lodge soon declared that "I heartily dislike and despise" Wilson and "live in hopes that he will be found out by the people of the United States for what he really is."[101] Despite this new-found agreement, Lodge still worried about Roosevelt's intentions with regard to the Republican party and was relieved to hear that Roosevelt's preoccupation with Wilson's foreign policy had carried him to the point where he could declare that "I really believe that I would rather have Murphy, Penrose or Barnes as the standard-bearer of this nation in the face of international wrong-doing."[102] With that the Bull Moose was dead, and a partnership which had as its principal object the removal of Wilson from office was formed. The chance of Roosevelt's running as a Progressive candidate for the Presidency was thereafter more apparent than real, for in the background would always be Lodge warning him that "the only thing which could save Wilson would be your running as the Progressive candidate for President."[103]

Their animosity toward Wilson was nurtured and bred on significant differences with respect to the form American neutrality should take. Lodge and those of his persuasion had a definite historical image of the manner in which neutrality should be maintained, an image which accorded nicely with their present desires. As Elihu Root subsequently put it: "Ordinary knowledge of history—of our own history during the Napoleonic wars—made it plain that . . . neutral rights would be worthless unless powerfully maintained."[104] That was a history which Lodge had early taken to heart. The Federalists had maintained "a bold and strong neutrality, . . . ready to strike the first nation, no matter which it was, that dared infringe it," while the Jeffersonians had "left us to be kicked about at the mercy of the two great European powers."[105] The wisdom of his great-grandfather was that

101. Lodge to Roosevelt, Jan. 15, 1915, Lodge MSS.
102. *Correspondence of Roosevelt and Lodge*, II, p. 450 (Dec. 8, 1914).
103. Lodge to Roosevelt, Dec. 2, 1915, Roosevelt MSS. He continued: "It seems to me that feeling as you and I do our first duty to the country is to remove this Administration from power." Lodge even offered to take the post of Secretary of State (he had declined it when offered by Taft), "if the right sort of President came in."
104. Elihu Root, *Addresses on International Subjects*, eds. Robert Bacon and James B. Scott (New York, 1916), p. 435.
105. Lodge, *Alexander Hamilton*, p. 163; Lodge, *George Cabot*, p. 462.

neutral nations, and ours especially, must either submit to ruin or resist it, but if . . . we hesitate which to prefer, we are already half undone; for, if our indignation is not excited by the wounds which innocence and honor receive, public liberty must soon be lost, and private rights will speedily follow.[106]

But resistance depended on strength. As Hamilton had advised in the 11th Federalist: "A nation despicable by its weakness, forfeits even the privilege of being neutral."[107] History, ever a guide, was in this instance particularly relevant. Lodge never wavered in the view that "in dealing with questions where the underlying conditions, like human nature and international relations, are in their essence constant" much could be learned from those who had guided the country through its most vulnerable years.[108]

III

In the Federalist conception of foreign policy safety had depended on neutrality. But it had also depended on military preparedness; that alone could give force and sanction to neutrality. The historical rights of neutrals were ones which neutrals had been able to uphold by force of arms. The Federalist conception of neutrality could not be discussed without reference to the Federalist policy of national defense, a point Lodge drove home repeatedly in a 1916 Washington's Birthday speech: "the democracy of Washington was not to buy its safety by gold, still less by the surrender of its rights, but was to assure and make real its ideal of peace by 'arms and discipline.' "[109] Lodge's prescription for America's safety was much the same; in order to preserve an honorable peace "two things were necessary": the maintenance of a strict neutrality and preparation for national defense.[110]

The opening blast in the preparedness campaign was touched off in October 1914 by Representative Augustus P. Gardner, Lodge's son-in-law. Gardner made some sensational (but not necessarily unjustified) charges regarding the condition of the nation's defenses and claimed

106. Lodge, *George Cabot*, pp. 125–26.
107. Clinton Rossiter, ed., *The Federalist Papers*, p. 87.
108. Lodge, "Washington's Policies of Neutrality and National Defence," in *War Addresses*, p. 120.
109. *Ibid.*, p. 128.
110. "Speech at Norwell, Mass., Sept. 4, 1915," Lodge MSS.

that peace propaganda was blinding Americans to the reality of national insecurity.[111] Lodge himself was not so outspoken, but did urge his fellow Americans to remember that "in an armed and fighting world an unarmed nation is in a position of grave peril."[112] After the election, Lodge forced the tempo with some startling charges respecting the inefficiency of the country's armed forces and on December 7 he joined Gardner in introducing a resolution calling for a full inquiry into the state of the nation's defenses.[113]

There was no rush to the banner; in fact there was little popular enthusiasm for preparedness prior to the sinking of the *Lusitania* in early May of 1915. Until Gardner made his charges, there had been practically no public discussion of the effect of the war on American naval policy or of its bearing on the future security of the country.[114] The general reaction was that Gardner was unduly alarmed, an impression to which Wilson contributed by scoffing at his charges as "good mental exercise" and claiming that "talk of this sort has been going on ever since he was a boy of ten."[115]

Lodge and Gardner, however, represented a constituency which was much more pro-Ally than the country at large, an area of the country which had close cultural ties to England and had never received any appreciable German immigration. Gardner made so bold during the campaign as to announce himself as being "very strongly in favor of the Allies" and to declare the German cause an "unholy" one and "a menace to the principles of democracy." His district was "enthusiastically" with him on the subject.[116] Lodge was careful not to take such an unneutral position in public, but did not hide the fact that his sympathies, like those of most of the initial supporters of preparedness, lay strongly with the Allies.[117] But what was an asset in Gardner's reelection campaign in Massachusetts' Essex County was a liability in the nation as a whole (and even in the Irish wards of Boston) and this Lodge also understood. The charge that they wanted to prepare so that

111. *Cong. Record*, 63rd Cong., 2nd sess., 1914, pp. 16694, 16747.
112. *Boston Herald*, Oct. 28, 1914.
113. *New York Times*, Dec. 3, 1914; Senate J. Res. No. 202.
114. Harold and Margaret Sprout, *The Rise of American Naval Power*, pp. 317–18.
115. *New York Times*, Oct. 20, 1914, p. 1.
116. Constance Gardner, ed., *Some Letters of Augustus Peabody Gardner* (Boston, 1920), pp. 88–89.
117. Osgood, *Ideals and Self-Interest*, p. 200.

the United States might fight alongside the Allies was long to haunt the preparedness movement.

For this reason Lodge's rationale for preparedness was vague and easily countered. For him preparedness was a natural accompaniment to a policy of neutrality, but for most Americans neutrality was not an active but a passive policy. Not yet prepared to argue that there was an imminent threat to American security, Lodge could only claim that preparedness was the best way of keeping the peace.[118] However, his fervent belief in this was not sufficient recommendation to a populace among whom the idea that armaments themselves were the cause of war was widespread.[119]

The problem, as ever under American conditions, was to invest what one deemed the proper policy with a sense of moral urgency. If Lodge and Roosevelt blurred the issue and came to argue for preparedness in terms of the preservation of the nation's character and moral fiber (and as late as August of 1916 Lodge was hedging with the claim that our national character and respect "if not our national life" are at stake), that was probably more a function of their reading of the realities of American political life than of their own lack of security concerns.[120] Contrary to what Robert Osgood claims, Lodge issued a strong warning about the nation's vulnerability, and did challenge the nation's sense of detachment from the war.[121]

In these days of rapid movement and swift communications what possible defense could be offered to a military machine, organized to the highest point of efficiency, by an untrained people springing to arms which they have not got? The ocean barrier which defended us in 1776 and 1812 no longer exists. Steam and electricity have destroyed it.[122]

Moreover, he felt that Wilson and Bryan, while insisting we remain defenseless, were actually pushing the country into a position likely to bring either war or humiliation.[123] But until the war came closer to the

118. *Ibid.*, p. 205.
119. In language reminiscent of his "imperial" period, Lodge claimed in July of 1916 that an extensive building program would "be of more value to our peace than all the diplomatic notes that can ever be written" (*Cong. Record*, 64th Cong., 1st sess., p. 10926).
120. Boston *Herald*, August 20, 1916.
121. *Ideals and Self-Interest*, p. 205.
122. *Cong. Record*, 63rd Cong., 3rd sess., 1915, p. 1610.
123. Lodge to Roosevelt, Feb. 5, 1915, Roosevelt MSS. A good case can be made for this point of view. See Harbaugh (*Power and Responsibility*, p. 479), who be-

American people such arguments were notably ineffective, and as a consequence Lodge did have frequent resort to such arguments as:

I do not believe that virility, patriotism, and courage are so dead in the United States or so narcotized by commercialism and the talk of professional peace advocates that we could not get 500,000 young men, or five times that number, under proper conditions to make themselves fit and ready to come to the defense of the country. . . .[124]

He and Roosevelt laid claim to the moral leadership of the nation but were unable to wrest it from Wilson's hands. Once the argument had been joined in those terms and the American people did not rush to embrace the preparedness cause, Lodge became discouraged. His hatred for Wilson grew, and the issue of preparedness became symbolic of their different philosophical approaches to foreign policy. Thus did policy and personality merge, and when events subsequently demonstrated that early preparation would have been a wise policy the supposed Rooseveltian alternative took on added lustre.[125] Lodge can be criticized for failing to appreciate the difficulties under which Wilson was operating, as John Garraty asserts, but his criticism was not therefore necessarily inconsistent. If he bewailed the indifference of the American people, and at the same time attacked Wilson's hesitant advances toward preparation and eventually war, it was because he saw a connection between the two.[126] Wilson had made light of their concerns from the beginning and was, to Lodge's way of thinking, responsible for both the state of American opinion and the state of American defenses. Preparedness became, and in the American context necessarily so, not just a question of public policy but also one of moral leadership.

But in the Lodgian scheme, preparedness, for all its importance, was

---

lieves that "Wilson's decision to hold Germany to 'strict accountability' destroyed the premises on which his original opposition to preparedness rested, that is, the United States was not in danger of becoming involved in the war." Note, however, that Lodge made his critical judgment *before* Wilson issued his strict accountability note. The prejudice was there first, but the policy came to justify it.

124. *Cong. Record*, 63rd Cong., 3rd sess., 1915, p. 1609.

125. What Roosevelt would have been able to do had he been President can only be conjecture. But Wilson's long opposition to preparedness and the consequent state of the country's military when war finally came led to assertions that early preparedness would have kept us out of war or at least have shortened it and saved many lives. See, for example, Corinne Roosevelt Robinson, *My Brother Theodore Roosevelt*, p. 283; and Daniel H. Elletson, *Roosevelt and Wilson: A Comparative Study* (London, 1965), p. 131.

126. Garraty, *Lodge*, p. 336.

only the means to an end. As Lodge did not yet envisage American participation in the war, that end was a neutrality in keeping with the interests of the United States and with his conception of international morality. Under the cover of a supposed national agreement on a course of neutrality, there were from the outset profound differences between Wilson's passive, abstentionist conception and Lodge's belief that neutrality meant "the full performance of our duties as a neutral and an absolute insistence upon our rights as a neutral."[127] As those differences became manifest Lodge could not resist drawing the inevitable historical analogy:

Washington was not a phrase-maker. . . . When he declared the country to be neutral he meant that it really should be neutral and in that capacity should not only insist on every neutral right, but should also perform all neutral duties.[128]

As early as January of 1915 Lodge complained that Wilson's Administration had tried to help the Germans "in an underhand fashion," and the parallel between Wilson's actions and those of Jefferson whose "theory was to keep peace, at all hazards, to involve the country in no foreign connections, and yet at the same time, with marvelous inconsistency, to aid France and injure England to the utmost extent" probably did not escape him.[129]

The exact nature of American neutrality was not an academic issue, but a practical one which would redound to the considerable advantage of either the Allies or the Central Powers. There was no perfect middle ground. Each American decision was bound to help one of the belligerents. While everyone talked of neutrality, the precise definition of that neutrality was capable of arousing the deepest emotions and feelings. American neutrality in its historical precedents and the practices which then had the sanction of international law worked to the advantage of the Allies. The fact that Lodge discussed his first comments on the subject with British leaders indicates that he knew this was the case. Though obliged to move "so cautiously at the beginning," Lodge's devotion to the Allied cause was early quite complete.[130]

127. Lodge, "Speech at Norwell, Mass., Sept. 4, 1915," Lodge MSS.
128. Lodge, *War Addresses*, p. 122.
129. Lodge to Ellerton James, Jan. 6, 1915, Lodge MSS; Lodge, *George Cabot*, p. 460.
130. Lodge to Trevelyan, May 12, 1917, Lodge MSS.

The problem was the tactical one of finding the best means of serving Allied interests. Since Lodge was not in control of the nation's foreign policy, his strategy could only be piecemeal and defensive. He devoted himself—and "not without success—to preventing measures that would hurt the Allies."[131] Knowing that the status quo (that is, the traditional and generally accepted conception of neutrality) worked to the Allies' advantage, he sought to tie the Administration's hands by insisting that "our duties as a neutral require . . . that we should take no action which would change the conditions created by the war in favor of one belligerent as against another."[132] His British correspondents often expected more, but he urged upon them the advantage of his speaking from technically neutral ground. In reply he pointed out that "an honest neutrality is the most helpful thing to the Allies" and suggested that "the continued export of arms and munitions of war generally from this country is of greater importance to the Allies than a fleet and soldiers would be." It was important "that things should remain as they are." "With free exports from the United States the material advantage . . . [was] all with the Allies."[133] Only against this background of service and moral commitment to the Allied cause can Lodge's growing suspicion of Wilson's motives and his growing hatred for the man who had such a different set of priorities really be understood.

I have seen no treatment of Lodge which shows sufficient appreciation of the depth of his moral commitment to the Allied cause. It explains a great deal, including his opposition to Wilson's idea of a universal league and a "peace without victory." I can only suggest that historians may have been thrown off the track by Lodge's reputation as a twister of the British lion's tail, a reputation which the Mugwumps did so much to cultivate and which, never realizing the changes which had taken place in Lodge's attitude, still dominated their thinking in the war years. Thus we have Lodge's old adversary, Charles W. Eliot, complaining in 1915 about Lodge's selection as President of the Massachusetts Historical Society on the grounds that he was "a promoter of

131. Lodge to Moreton Frewen, April 24, 1916, Frewen MSS.
132. Lodge, "Speech at Norwell, Mass., Sept. 4, 1915," Lodge MSS.
133. Lodge to Moreton Frewen, April 24, 1916, Frewen MSS; Lodge to Col. Herbert St. John Mildmay, Feb. 6 and Sept. 7, 1915; to Frewen, Aug. 16, 1915; and to Trevelyan, April 7, 1916; Lodge MSS.

suspicion and distrust between [the] United States and Great Britain."[134] Walter Millis seemed to sense where Lodge's loyalties lay when he observed that Lodge's speeches often hinted "at a neutrality . . . less than absolute," but he was unable to understand that Lodge took such a stand not because he wanted war but because he thought the Allied cause a morally superior one.[135] John Garraty was on the track when he noted that Lodge very early placed the objective of an Allied victory above his belief that the United States should keep out of the war. But Garraty is not helpful when he indulges in the now hackneyed comparison between the "practical" Lodge and the "idealistic" Wilson. When discussing the question of neutral rights he insists that "Wilson made paramount the moral issue, Lodge the materialistic one."[136] Actually there is every reason to conclude that Lodge's views were as much the result of moral conviction as were Wilson's opposite ones. Contrary to what many Americans have wanted to believe, it is no simple matter to arrive at a definition of a "moral" or "idealistic" foreign policy. Actually the conflict between Wilson and Lodge makes more sense if viewed as a clash between men whose moral standards were in conflict. Lodge was convinced that the cause of international peace and justice would best be served by an Allied victory and thought in terms of what he could do to contribute to that end, while Wilson thought it could best be served by a compromise peace and placed the same emphasis on American abstention as Lodge placed on an Allied victory. Those were profound differences and help explain why Lodge would never concede the idealism of Wilson's course and why his reputation for idealism aroused in Lodge, as in Roosevelt, so much ire.[137]

Two developments engendered in Lodge the feeling that Wilson was morally obtuse. Particularly "painful" were the Administration's protests against British interference with American trade.

They observed a profound silence about the violation of neutrality in Belgium, and in China too for that matter, they said no word about the utter disregard of the Hague Conventions, to which we are signatories; and then find their voice as to the interference with American trade.[138]

134. Eliot to James Ford Rhodes, April 7, 1915, Rhodes MSS.
135. Walter Millis, *Road to War: America 1914–1917* (Boston, 1935), p. 218.
136. Garraty, *Lodge*, pp. 313–14.
137. See Osgood (*Ideals and Self-Interest*, p. 146), who speaks only of Roosevelt's reaction.
138. Lodge to Herbert St. John Mildmay, Jan. 12, 1915, Lodge MSS.

Lodge found this hypocritical and morally incomprehensible, and it early led him to charge that the Administration was using international questions to garner votes at home.[139] That was "a very dangerous business," and the suspicion as to Wilson's motives, once planted, never disappeared. It was there to blossom forth with renewed vigor whenever the President assumed a posture which could be regarded as inimical to the Allied cause.

But more than anything else it was Wilson's efforts to have the government purchase the German ships trapped in American harbors by the outbreak of war which aroused Lodge's indignation. This issue may have put Lodge and Wilson "on opposite sides of the fence once and for all."[140] The bill was couched in general terms (the U.S. had a very small merchant marine and did need ships), and Wilson never publicly admitted that he planned to purchase the German ships, but Arthur Link believes he intended to do so.[141] He refused to accept Lodge's amendment to the Ship Purchase Bill, which would have forbidden the shipping board from purchasing any ships owned by belligerents, and he never denied Lodge's charge (made in an effort to elicit just such a denial) that he intended to buy the German ships.[142] Lodge objected to the scheme for a number of reasons. He regarded the purchase of belligerent ships as "an unneutral act and almost an act of hostility," especially as it would give the Germans "thirty or forty millions of United States money in exchange for ships which they cannot possibly use and which are deteriorating every day." He also thought the idea was of German origin and discerned in Treasury Secretary McAdoo's business connections with the banking house of Kuhn, Loeb and Company, which was in turn allied with the leading German steamship lines, the only "intelligible reason" for its being pushed.[143] Moreover, the matter stirred other old prejudices; Lodge thought government entry into the shipping business would be a long step toward social-

---

139. Lodge to Henry Higginson, Dec. 31, 1914, Lodge MSS. Spring Rice shared Lodge's opinion and wrote to Foreign Secretary Grey that "it seems rather shocking that this country, and especially this very moral Government should only protest where its grossly material interests are affected, and for nothing else" (Gwynn, ed., *Letters of Spring Rice*, II, p. 255).

140. Garraty, *Lodge*, p. 308.

141. *Wilson: The Struggle for Neutrality*, p. 150.

142. *Cong. Record*, 63rd Cong., 3rd sess., 1915, p. 2092.

143. Lodge to Ellerton James, Jan. 6, 1915; to Roosevelt, Jan. 15, 1915; and to John T. Morse, Jr., Jan. 28, 1915; Lodge MSS.

ism.[144] But even worse, Lodge felt, was the Administration's misapprehension of the international situation.

I feel very strongly about the bill, because if they persist in buying the German ships and England, France and Russia decline to recognize the transfer of the flag—as they unquestionably will . . . —and the ships are sent to sea, they will be regarded by the powers I named as still being German ships, good prize and liable to capture or destruction. Now it is one thing to capture the ship of a private person, but it is a different thing to take a Government-owned ship and they will reach a point where either war or humiliation is upon us. Wilson apparently thinks that England, France and Russia will not persist—just as he thought that nobody would fight when he took Vera Cruz. He apparently does not realize that nations which are fighting for their lives do not stick at trifles.[145]

Such fears were not groundless. Arthur Link once wrote that: "It is certain the British would not have acknowledged the legality of the American government's purchase of the German vessels; moreover, the British would probably have seized the ships if the government shipping corporation had tried to use them in the Atlantic trade."[146] I am not so certain that Britain would have run the risk of antagonizing the U.S. over such a relatively minor matter. It is hard to believe that the British, who stood most to gain by increased cargo space for the Atlantic trade, would have done more than file a strong protest. Lodge, too, may have understood this, but he certainly gave every indication that he was firmly convinced that the Allies would seize the ships. That possibility, plus Wilson's refusal even to promise that the German ships would be kept out of the North Atlantic trade, prompted Lodge to make his first public personal attack on Wilson. He pointedly suggested that "any man who did not think the facts ought to be made to suit his will would have known that the people of Vera Cruz would fight."[147] Then two weeks later, exasperated with Wilson's attitude of "sic volo, sic jubeo," he compared the President to the Oxford don who maintained:

144. Lodge to Frederick H. Prince, Oct. 27, 1914, Lodge MSS; *Cong. Record*, 63rd Cong., 3rd sess., 1915, p. 2092.

145. Lodge to John T. Morse, Jr., Jan. 28, 1915, Lodge MSS. Note the parallel Lodge drew between Wilson's course in Mexico and what he feared would be his course with respect to the European war, a parallel which increasingly captured Lodge's attention.

146. *Woodrow Wilson and the Progressive Era*, p. 153n.

147. *Cong. Record*, 63rd Cong., 3rd sess., 1915, p. 2650.

My name is Benjamin Jowett;
    I'm the master of Balliol College.
Whatever is known, I know it.
And what I don't know isn't knowledge.

Turning on Wilson the full brunt of the sarcasm for which he had long been famous, he went on to declare that

when the President is approaching a new subject the first thing he does is to make up his mind, and when his mind is made up the thoughts which in more ordinary mortals are apt to precede the decision or determination of a great question are excluded; information upon the new subject is looked on as a mere impertinence.[148]

Wilson's greatest weakness, his inability to compromise, defeated him in this as in so many instances, but not before he had made for himself "finally and irrevocably an implacable enemy in the person of Henry Cabot Lodge."[149] Now believing Wilson to be "the most dangerous man that ever sat in the White House, except Buchanan, who was dangerous from weakness, while this man is dangerous from his determination to have his own way, no matter what it costs the country," he was soon confessing to Roosevelt that he "never expected to hate any one in politics with the hatred I feel towards Wilson."[150] His hatred was now so intense that he became incapable of any longer distinguishing between the man and the office, or between foreign policy and domestic politics, and this soon led him to an attempt to undercut the President's foreign policy. Writing to Trevelyan in April of 1915 Lodge declared it to be the President's hope "to rescue himself and his party by being the mediator who will end the war" and warned the Allies against allowing themselves "to be used as a makeweight in American politics."[151] This was an anomalous position for a super-patriot like Lodge as he would have been the first to complain if the shoe had been on the other foot. But his hatred for Wilson was now such that he could no longer even credit him with a desire to act in the national interest.

148. *Ibid.*, p. 3558.
149. Garraty, *Lodge*, pp. 311–12.
150. Lodge to Roosevelt, Feb. 19 and March 1, 1915, Roosevelt MSS.
151. Lodge to Trevelyan, April 23, 1915, Lodge MSS. It was not until the summer of 1916 that the Lodge-Trevelyan correspondence became a formal conduit for the exchange of views between Lodge and Foreign Secretary Grey, but one may reasonably suspect that the message got through long before that. See Trevelyan to Lodge, July 26, 1916, and Lodge's reply, Aug. 28, 1916, both in the Lodge MSS.

Wilson returned the feeling in kind. Long subject to a "tendency to equate political opposition with personal antagonism" and to doubt the integrity of any one who disagreed with him, Wilson came easily to the feeling that the struggle over the Ship Purchase Bill was a crucial test of his leadership.[152] Conceiving of himself as the champion of democracy as against special privilege, he looked upon Lodge and Root as sinister reactionaries who wanted to "bring back the days of private influence and selfish advantage." He determined to hit them "straight in the face, and not mind if the blood comes."[153] To put the onus for their deteriorating relationship primarily on Lodge's shoulders is unfair, for, as Josephus Daniels wrote, if Lodge "was very bitter in his antagonism to Wilson" and "hated him sincerely," he "was hated quite as deeply by Wilson in return."[154] Their growing antagonism was never strictly personal; it was also intellectual and political, the product of a clash between two strong-willed and self-righteous men, both convinced they knew what was best for the country and neither of whom suffered opposition lightly. The deterioration in their relations was also symbolic of growing divisions within the country over the proper American posture toward the war in Europe. That, as Alice Roosevelt Longworth later recalled, was what caused Americans in those days to so "cherish and nourish" their hatreds.[155]

The struggle over the Ship Purchase Bill had another important result. Ever since the outbreak of war gave a new primacy to foreign policy Lodge and Roosevelt had been drawn closer together. But it was on the Ship Purchase Bill that they again began working in tandem. It was in response to a suggestion from Lodge, for example, that Roosevelt wrote to Progressives like George Norris urging them to vote against the acquisition of the German ships.[156] It was a hard fight, fought on issues which demonstrated to TR that the Republicans were the only right-thinking party on foreign policy issues. Roosevelt's return to the fold was signaled by the fact that after the bill was killed

152. Link, *Wilson: The New Freedom*, pp. 69–70, and *Wilson: The Struggle for Neutrality*, p. 150; Robert Lansing, *The Peace Negotiations: A Personal Narrative* (Boston, 1921), p. 140.

153. Link, *Wilson: The Struggle for Neutrality*, p. 150; Garraty, *Lodge*, pp. 309–10.

154. *The Wilson Era* (Chapel Hill, 1944), I, p. 535.

155. *Crowded Hours* (New York, 1933), p. 260.

156. Lodge to Roosevelt, Feb. 5, 1915, Roosevelt MSS; Morison, ed., *Letters of Theodore Roosevelt*, VIII, p. 889.

Lodge spent a weekend at Sagamore Hill, his first such visit since 1911.[157]

IV

A philosophical question also aroused Lodge's ire, the more so when he realized that Wilson was not politically vulnerable on the issue and was both catering to and reflecting prevailing American prejudices. The problem was the degree of responsibility for events in other countries which the United States incurred as a result of its hemispheric policies, or more generally the extent of the responsibility which the United States owed to the international community in their efforts to reestablish the world's peace. There had always been imperialistic overtones to the international responsibility preached by Lodge and Roosevelt, but nevertheless the Rooseveltian solution had stressed America's obligations to the community of nations. The immediate cause for Lodge's quarrel with Wilson on this score was the latter's pronouncements on Mexican policy. But hovering in the background were the implications those pronouncements carried for American policy toward the war in Europe. Convinced, as is one recent student of Wilson's Mexican policy, that his actions had served to exacerbate the revolutionary temper and to encourage and prolong a devastating civil war, Lodge would not permit Wilson to absolve himself from that responsibility.[158]

For this condition of things and these atrocities Wilson is directly responsible. In order to get Huerta out he deliberately reduced Mexico to this condition, and having created this condition he says in his Indianapolis speech that they can fight for liberty in their own way, that there is bloodshed in Europe with which we do not interfere and there is no reason why Mexico should not have the same privilege. I do not think such a brutal declaration was ever made before by a man in high office in this country.[159]

The Mexican example was a good means of demonstrating the shortcomings of the Wilsonian approach to foreign policy because it did not carry with it, as did mention of the Administration's silence respecting the violation of Belgium, susceptibility to the counter charge of wanting

157. Morison, ed., *Letters of Theodore Roosevelt*, VIII, p. 886n.
158. Calvert, *The Mexican Revolution, 1910–1914: The Diplomacy of Anglo-American Conflict*, p. 301.
159. Lodge to Roosevelt, Feb. 11, 1915, Lodge MSS.

to involve the U.S. in the European war. Roosevelt soon went public with the charges Lodges had formulated.

This is the kind of language that can be used about Mexico with sincerity only if it is also to be applied to Dahomey and to outrages like those of the French Commune. It cannot in the long run be accepted by any great state which is both strong and civilized nor by any statesman with a serious purpose to better mankind. In point of public morality it is fundamentally as evil a declaration as has ever been put forth by an American President in treating of foreign affairs. . . .[160]

Roosevelt and Lodge believed that Wilson, in his preoccupation with keeping the country out of war and in assuming a morally neutral position, was destroying the American public's rather tenuous sense of duty and obligation toward the international community. As John Milton Cooper has observed, Wilson in this period coined what would later become isolationist watchwords and anticipated the basic arguments of the idealistic isolationists.[161] As late as 1916 the President could refer to the European War as "a drunken brawl in a public house," and could publicly state that Americans had no concern with the causes and objects of the conflict.[162] Arthur Link prefers to describe Wilson's course as that of "guiding the American people from provincialism toward world leadership and responsibilities"; but there is enough substance to Thomas Bailey's counter argument that Wilson taught only too well the lesson that the war in Europe was not our affair—and thereby encouraged America's traditional isolationist prejudices—to make it understandable why Lodge and Roosevelt found his actions so exasperating.[163] At the heart of Lodge's detestation of Wilson was his feeling that the President had increased the strength of the pacifist bloc, precisely the segment of American opinion that Lodge had long regarded as the chief obstacle to a greater American world role.[164] Actually the issue between Lodge and Wilson was more

160. Roosevelt, "Uncle Sam and The Rest of the World," *Metropolitan* 41 (March 1915): 12a.

161. *The Vanity of Power: American Isolationism and the First World War*, p. 37.

162. William L. Langer, "Woodrow Wilson: His Education in World Affairs," *Confluence* 5 (Autumn 1956): 186.

163. Link, *The Higher Realism of Woodrow Wilson*, p. 73; Bailey, *Woodrow Wilson and the Lost Peace* (New York, 1944), pp. 3, 20–22.

164. Lodge to Trevelyan, May 1, 1916, Lodge MSS. Even Walter Lippmann, still under the influence of the Rooseveltian solution, was arguing in 1915 that "the

over the character of the U.S.'s responsibilities than over their existence, but Lodge could not see it that way.

According to Lodge's own account, it was Wilson's response to the German torpedoing of the passenger liner *Lusitania* on May 7, 1915, that marked the point of no return in his opposition. Wilson's phrase 'too proud to fight' and his subsequent diplomatic correspondence, which, according to Lodge, evaded the issue and clouded it with words, destroyed the last vestiges of Lodge's confidence in him.[165] Lodge attached such importance to the *Lusitania* incident because Wilson's response seemed to confirm his worst fears about the President's approach to foreign policy and, perhaps of greater psychological import, because Wilson had muffed his first real opportunity to move the nation closer to a working partnership with the Allies.

Lodge's reaction should be viewed in the context of the fact that during the early period of the war interventionist sentiment was singularly absent among the great mass of the American people. Even after the *Lusitania* the interventionists remained "only a fractional minority."[166] At no time during the *Lusitania* crisis did Lodge urge going to war; in concentrating on the neutral rights issue he sedulously avoided even any suggestion of war in the national interest.[167] Insofar as he privately contemplated war, he still thought in terms of a conflict of resources rather than of men, claiming that "we could not, if Germany involved us in war, send great armies to France or Russia."[168] Nevertheless, he did advocate a much harder line against Germany than the Administration proposed and probably hoped that such a line would bring the United States psychologically closer to the Allies and perhaps eventually even into the war on their side. While confining his public remarks to a general affirmation of the right of American citizens to travel unmolested on the ships of belligerent nations, privately he declared that Germany would have to give assurance there would be no

---

policy of peace-at-any-price is a peril to internationalism" for it leads straight to isolation and away from the attempt to make a better and more peaceful world (*The Stakes of Diplomacy* [New York, 1915], pp. 217–19). Logically, of course, Lippmann was right, for an absolute pacifist must in the end be willing to sacrifice all his other values to his pacifism.

165. Lodge, *The Senate and the League*, p. 33.

166. Link, *Woodrow Wilson and the Progressive Era*, p. 177; Link, *Wilson: The Struggle for Neutrality*, pp. 17–18.

167. Harbaugh, *Power and Responsibility*, p. 477.

168. Lodge to J. Mott Hallowell, May 14, 1915, Lodge MSS.

further attacks on belligerent owned passenger ships and suggested "we must be prepared to take further steps if it is not given."[169]

However, he did not yet see war as the inevitable *dénouement*. Rather, he suggested measures such as breaking relations with Germany or taking possession of the German ships in American harbors as security for an indemnity.[170] He was disposed to favor forceful and decisive (but not nationally divisive) action in such circumstances. But when it became apparent that Wilson had no intention of doing anything that even approached what Lodge thought the situation demanded, but was "going to repeat his Mexican performance" and allow things to drift, Lodge came to what under the circumstances were for him all but inevitable conclusions.[171] His was a severe and simplistic indictment of Wilson, but one which acquired considerable currency in the Northeast and among pro-Ally Republicans. As Lodge put it:

The country was horrified, and at that moment the popular feeling was such that if the President, after demanding immediate reparation and apology to be promptly given, had boldly declared that the time had come when the rights and safety of American citizens were so endangered that it was our duty to go to war, he would have had behind him the enthusiastic support of the whole American people. He would have had it with more enthusiasm and fervor at that moment, I firmly believe, than he did when he finally went to war in 1917, because in the interval he had paltered with the issues . . . and had so confused the whole question that the mind of the people generally was not so clear upon our duty and the necessity of action as it was immediately after the sinking of the *Lusitania*.[172]

Lodge's argument can be readily dismissed as special pleading after the fact (the more so as at the time he said nothing about the country's "duty to go to war"). The country was very divided in 1915 and not yet prepared to pursue a policy based on force.[173] Wilson certainly would

169. Harbaugh, *Power and Responsibility*, p. 477; Lodge to Ralph B. Perry, May 13, 1915, Lodge MSS.

170. Lodge to Langdon Mitchell, May 22, 1915, Lodge MSS.

171. Lodge to Sen. William Borah, May 24, 1915; to Trevelyan, June 2, 1915; and to Sen. Frank Brandegee, June 11, 1915; Lodge MSS.

172. Lodge, *The Senate and the League*, p. 32. One is reminded of the judgment in Lodge's "The Last Forty Years of Town Government," in Justin Winsor, ed., *The Memorial History of Boston* (Boston, 1881), III, p. 208, that after the English had fired upon the national flag in 1806 "if Mr. Jefferson had at that supreme moment declared war and appealed to the country, he would have had the cordial support of the mass of the people not only in New England but in Boston itself."

173. Dexter Perkins, *Charles Evans Hughes and American Democratic Statesmanship* (Boston, 1956), p. 57.

have been hard pressed to secure the support of Bryan and his constituency for such a course. Yet the power of the President in his conduct of the nation's foreign policy, as Roosevelt had demonstrated, was great, and those who formulated the legend of the Rooseveltian alternative were not the only ones who believed that with the sinking of the *Lusitania* "the psychological moment was at hand."[174] There was considerable room for the honest reaction that "at last we are in."[175] Walter Lippmann was disturbed by the power which one individual had come to have over the destiny of the American Republic; "had Mr. Wilson wished war with Germany he could have had it"— "he could have used the Lusitania incident to make war inevitable."[176] And Joseph P. Tumulty has quoted Wilson himself as saying that "I am keenly aware that the feeling of the country is now at fever heat . . . ready to move with me in any direction I shall suggest."[177] Against this background Lodge's indictment of Wilson, and his feeling that it might have been otherwise, becomes an understandable, if still very much an oversimplified, accusation. In his disappointment, his hopes first raised and then dashed, it was easy to feel that "if our people had had the leadership of the President they would have followed him in any vigorous policy he might have adopted" and to believe, as did Roosevelt himself, that if Roosevelt had been President "the dignity and honor of the country would have been maintained."[178]

A corollary to the belief that Wilson had frittered away his opportunity and disintegrated public opinion was the belief that "if we had had a vigorous, effective policy from the beginning the Lusitania would not have happened."[179] In his increasing obsession with the idea of replacing Wilson, Lodge came easily to the belief that if Roosevelt had been President and Root Secretary of State there never would have

174. Corinne Roosevelt Robinson, *My Brother Theodore*, p. 288.
175. Alice Roosevelt Longworth, *Crowded Hours*, p. 238.
176. *The Stakes of Diplomacy*, pp. 15, 23.
177. *Woodrow Wilson As I Knew Him* (Garden City, N.Y., 1921), p. 233.
178. Lodge to Trevelyan, Feb. 1, 1916, Lodge MSS; *Correspondence of Roosevelt and Lodge*, II, pp. 483–84 (Feb. 9, 1916). Roosevelt went even further. As he told his English friend Arthur Lee, "the sad and irritating thing is that it is so much a matter of leadership. . . . I would from the beginning, if I had been President, have taken a stand which would have made the Germans either absolutely alter all their conduct or else put them into war with us. If the United States had taken this stand, in my judgment we would now have been fighting beside you" (letter dated June 17, 1915, in Morison, ed., *Letters of Theodore Roosevelt*, VIII, pp. 936–37).
179. Lodge to Langdon Mitchell, May 22, 1915, Lodge MSS.

been a *Lusitania* incident.[180] This was not, however, just a question of personality but also a reflection of Wilson's violations (both before and after the sinking of the *Lusitania*) of rules for the conduct of American diplomacy which had been an axiomatic part of the Rooseveltian solution. One of the first requisites was a reputation for probity and straightforwardness such that others might believe what one said, which, as both Roosevelt and Root pointed out, had not been the case with respect to Wilson's strict accountability note of February 10, 1915. Its effect had been negated by the Austrian Ambassador's receiving the impression that the note was intended primarily for its effect at home.[181] Something else one did not do, as Root put it in commenting on the first and second *Lusitania* notes, was to "shake your fist at a man and then shake your finger at him."[182] All this brought to Lodge's mind the by now inevitable parallel with Wilson's course in Mexico.

Wilson's Mexican policy failed so badly, it now seems the general consensus, because of his inability to wield the threat of armed intervention convincingly. He threatened and then did nothing to carry out those threats, with the result that even a weak opponent like Huerta believed that he was bluffing.[183] This is what Lodge meant when he wrote that "it is Mexico over again on a larger scale; he will try to drift off on a sea of diplomatic correspondence and will do nothing and never meant to do anything."[184] What Lodge could not know, but what he might have suspected, was that the Germans were reacting in much the same manner as had Huerta, and that Ambassador Bernstorff be-

180. Lodge to Frewen, Aug. 16, 1915, and to Root, Feb. 21, 1916, Lodge MSS; *Correspondence of Roosevelt and Lodge*, II, p. 483 (Feb. 9, 1916). Root himself felt that: "When the Gulflight was torpedoed and . . . Bernstorff's warning to the Lusitania passengers was published it was a certainty that our note [of strict accountability] was to be disregarded. Then was the critical time for our government to force into the German consciousness a realization that we were in earnest, if we were, and the failure to take any action at that time was incredible criminal incompetency. . . . If any man of ordinary practical sense and courage had been president then, the passengers on the Lusitania would be alive today" (Root to Lodge, Feb. 18, 1916, Lodge MSS).

181. Roosevelt, *Fear God and Take Your Own Part* (New York, 1916), pp. ii–iii; Elihu Root, "Roosevelt's Conduct of Foreign Affairs," in Hagedorn, ed., *The Works of Theodore Roosevelt*, XVIII, p. xxvi.

182. Wister, *Roosevelt: The Story of a Friendship, 1880–1919*, p. 344.

183. P. Edward Haley, *Revolution and Intervention: The Diplomacy of Taft and Wilson with Mexico* (Cambridge, Mass., 1970), p. 108; Cline, *The United States and Mexico*, p. 150.

184. Lodge to Sen. Frank Brandegee, June 11, 1915, Lodge MSS.

came "firmly convinced" as a result of Wilson's treatment of the *Lusitania* incident "that he would never initiate a war with Germany."[185] Such, in Lodge's opinion, were but the inevitable results of wholesale violations of the rules of diplomacy which had the sanction of American historical experience from the Federalists to TR. Roosevelt even went so far as to suggest that "if Abraham Lincoln, after the firing on Sumter, had announced that the Union people of the North might be 'too proud to fight' and had then for three months confined his activities to adroit and subtle diplomatic notes written to Jefferson Davis, by the middle of summer the American people *would* have refused to fight."[186]

However, a good case can be made that American interests were best served by Wilson's course and not by the alternative being pushed by Lodge and Roosevelt, that the President, seeing that American security was not immediately threatened, actually followed the more statesmanlike course and the one most in keeping with the national interest.[187] Whatever its merits, that is an argument that must rest uncomfortably on the shoulders of the Wilson who claimed to disdain such considerations and to find justification only in service to higher causes.[188] It is also an argument that serves to emphasize the moral commitment which motivated Lodge and Roosevelt in their opposition to Wilson and in their support of the Allied cause. Moreover, one can accept the argument fully and yet recognize that in adopting such a course Wilson was eroding the foundations of what little internationalism existed in the country and not laying the best basis for public acceptance of the degree of commitment to the international community

185. Count Bernstorff, *Memoirs* (New York, 1936), p. 143. Bernstorff, incidentally, also thought that if Wilson had broken off relations with Germany after the *Lusitania* "he would have had public opinion behind him to a far greater extent than was the case of 1917." See also Merlo Pusey, *Charles Evans Hughes* (New York, 1963), I, p. 358, for evidence re the continuing impression in high German circles that the United States "will continue to confine itself to the use of big words."

186. *Correspondence of Roosevelt and Lodge*, II, p. 469 (Dec. 20, 1915); Morison, ed., *Letters of Theodore Roosevelt*, VIII, p. 994.

187. Campbell, *America Comes of Age: The Era of Theodore Roosevelt*, pp. 106–07; Ernest R. May, *The World War and American Isolation* (Cambridge, Mass., 1959), pp. 436–37.

188. "The force of America," Wilson once asserted "is the force of moral principle . . . there is nothing else that she loves, and . . . there is nothing else for which she will contend" (quoted in John Morton Blum, *Woodrow Wilson and the Politics of Morality* [Boston, 1956], p. 84).

which he later proposed to assume under the auspices of the League of Nations.

With the sinking of the *Lusitania* public sentiment in the Northeast and particularly in New England became increasingly and more outspokenly pro-Ally. The ideological preparation for a "Second Holy War" was well launched.[189] Simplification was the order of the day; subtlety and complexity could only weaken commitment. As Lodge told Prof. McCook of Harvard: "The issue to me is very simple. It is whether democratic government, as it exists in England, France and the United States, can survive Prussian militarism."[190] Moreover, a fateful comparison began to gain currency. As Lodge soon told the appreciative Trevelyan: "In its essence this great war is the last great struggle of democracy and freedom against autocracy and militarism, and it will succeed, I firmly believe, as the North fighting in the same cause succeeded against the South."[191]

If the *Lusitania* incident brought a deepening commitment to the Allies, it also brought a concomitant pessimism, especially as time made it clear that the Administration had no intention of pursuing the matter forcefully and that the psychological moment had passed. In Roosevelt this reaction was almost immediate. He came to doubt his America and on May 14 declared that "I am sick at heart over the way Wilson and Bryan have acted toward Germany, and above

189. Not atypical of the comments pouring in upon Lodge were the following: Moreton Frewen exclaiming that "it is the greatest disaster in history that this prodigious crisis should have found a Democratic Administration on the Potomac"; John Jay Chapman denouncing Wilson as the one who "has caused the West to remain in ignorance of what the war is about" and declaring that "the loss of the moment when honor might have been struck from the American bosom is what I hate the man for"; and even Henry Lee Higginson claiming that "we cannot as yet interfere, and also we cannot be neutral—that is, you and I cannot; . . . [but] if our Revolution was worth while, if our fight in 1861 was worth while, if the whole English history for years and years has been worth while, or that of France or Italy, it is worth while to condemn absolutely and entirely the Prussian idea of government" (John Jay Chapman to Lodge, n.d. but certainly 1915, and Moreton Frewen to Lodge, June 3, 1915, Lodge MSS; Perry, *The Life and Letters of Henry Lee Higginson*, pp. 476–77).

190. Lodge to J. J. McCook, May 12, 1915, Lodge MSS.

191. Lodge to Trevelyan, June 2, 1915, Lodge MSS. In support of his contention that in March of 1917 Lodge abandoned all pretense of neutrality, John Garraty cites (*Lodge*, p. 333) a letter to James Ford Rhodes in which Lodge declared that "it is no longer a contest between England and France and their allies on one side; it is now a struggle for the existence of freedom and democracy against a military autocracy which reverts to barbarism." My point, as evidenced by the letter to Trevelyan I have cited, is that he felt that way much earlier.

all, over the way that the country, as a whole, evidently approves of them and backs them up."[192] In Lodge the reaction took a little longer but in the end was nearly as complete. For him the "melancholy thing" was "the apparently general feeling of satisfaction with Wilson so long as he keeps us out of war, without any reference to the methods by which he does it, and the same indifference on the part of the people to the humiliation of the long and pointless diplomatic discussion about the *Lusitania*. . . ."[193] Especially depressing was the fact that it was still "not wise to criticize the President in public, because then it is immediately supposed that you want to precipitate the country into war. . . ."[194] For Lodge, long concerned with the question of "social efficiency," the conduct and apparent values of the American people made a poor contrast with those of the Allies. "Nothing could be finer," he told Trevelyan, "than the way in which the aristocracy of England has sacrificed itself nor the way in which the workingmen of England have gone to the front. . . . There is something very splendid in the quiet and solidarity of the French."[195] Still he did not entirely despair. He continued to believe

that there is an American people still existent that will some day rise in indignation but it is a long and weary time coming and when one hears and reads such things as one does about peace and the wisdom of sacrificing everything else for it, one's heart sinks.[196]

Nor was the attitude of the American public entirely discouraging from Lodge's point of view. There was, as Wilson was also coming to see, a strange dichotomy in the public attitude, "a double [and in many ways contradictory] wish of our people, to maintain a firm front in respect of what we demand of Germany and yet do nothing that might by any possibility involve us in war."[197] Therein lay an opening for those committed to the Allied cause and therein lies a further expla-

192. Hermann Hagedorn, *The Bugle That Woke America* (New York, 1940), p. 75; Anna Roosevelt Cowles, ed., *Letters of Theodore Roosevelt to Anna Roosevelt Cowles*, p. 304.
193. *Correspondence of Roosevelt and Lodge*, II, p. 463 (Sept. 25, 1915).
194. Lodge to William R. Thayer, Sept. 16, 1915, Lodge MSS.
195. Lodge to Trevelyan, June 2, 1915, Lodge MSS.
196. Lodge to William R. Thayer, Jan. 19, 1916, Lodge MSS. Lodge's mood in these days, dark at any rate, was made even gloomier by the passing of his beloved wife, Nannie, in September of 1915.
197. Wilson to Bryan, June 7, 1915 quoted in Merle E. Curti, *Bryan and World Peace*, Smith College Studies in History, 16 (April-July, 1931), p. 211.

nation for the stress which Lodge and Roosevelt placed on national prestige and honor. Though the American reaction to the *Lusitania* crisis disappointed them, they could derive some satisfaction from the fact that Wilson had been compelled to put American national prestige behind the issue of strict accountability, and in so doing had greatly circumscribed his own diplomatic flexibility and taken another step in the direction in which Lodge and Roosevelt were determined to move the nation.[198]

Seeing that the values of the nation were in such obvious conflict, Lodge viewed his task as one of forcing the issue. To allow Wilson to monopolize American idealism was to lose the whole struggle. The idealism of peace could only be effectively countered by the ideology of duty and service, both to country and to the principles of Western civilization. Regardless of the occasion Lodge now contrived to introduce into his speeches the idea that peace was not a sufficient goal, that there were other and higher ends to be pursued in this world. In a speech at the presentation of the Widener Memorial Library to Harvard, he reminded his audience of the special importance of books "just now, when freedom of speech, and freedom of thought, when liberty and democracy are in jeopardy every hour" and quoted Milton, who knew that books "are as lively, and as vigorously productive as those fabulous Dragon's teeth; and being sown up and down may chance to spring up armed men."[199] A few months later, speaking at the unveiling of "the Soldier's Monument" at Brookline, Massachusetts, he found occasion to put the question directly: "The one dominant question is whether we believe . . . that there are rights and duties and faiths in defence of which men should be prepared to fight and give up their lives in battle." The answer on an occasion honoring the dead of the Civil War was self-evident and the message was, of course, that "unless we are ready to sustain and continue their work and in like need and stress follow their example, the monuments we raise to their memories are stone and bronze hypocrisies and the words we

198. Daniel M. Smith, "National Interest and American Intervention, 1917: An Historiographical Appraisal," *Journal of American History* 52 (June 1965): 22.

199. Lodge, *Two Commencement Addresses* (Cambridge, Mass., 1915), p. 43. Spring Rice, who was present, told Lodge how greatly he was stirred by the speech and two years later, when he was receiving an honorary degree from Harvard, he recalled the occasion by quoting what Lodge had then said, and declaring that then "I heard the words, and today I have seen the men" (Gwynn, ed., *Letters of Spring Rice*, II, pp. 291, 394).

utter in their praise ignoble lip-service." He wanted, as in the 1890s, to be able to recapture the spirit which had moved New England during the Civil War, the spirit immortalized by Emerson when he wrote:

> Though love repine, and reason chafe,
> There came a voice without reply,—
> 'Tis man's perdition to be safe,
> When for the truth he ought to die.'[200]

200. Lodge, *War Addresses*, pp. 54, 56–57.

Chapter Six

Force and Peace

Emerson's was the answer American history gave to the pacifist movement and to a President who declared we were "too proud to fight." It took one idealism to counter another. But acquiring the will to fight was not enough; the nation also had to acquire the means of doing so. Lodge, in commenting on the *Lusitania* incident, declared: "Of course the thing to do is to keep up the discussion about preparedness; I mean to say something about it at Union College. . . ."[1] It is vital to an understanding of Lodge's subsequent course to realize that it was against this background that he made (in his famous "Force and Peace" speech) a considerable commitment to the idea of a league of nations, a commitment soon to haunt him. However, then, and subsequently, his conception of a league and its purposes differed sharply from that of Wilson. Lodge's idea of a league was closely related to his efforts to foster an idealism of duty and sacrifice and to speed the process of American rearmament, to the end that the United States might eventually stand alongside the Allies.

Lodge was "by instinct and conviction" a nationalist; he had in 1917 "much the same conception of national duty and destiny . . . that he had in 1884." Consequently, there is some truth in the accusation, current even at the time, that "glad as he would have been to have had the United States long ago clash with Germany, it was as a nationalist

1. Lodge to Langdon Mitchell, May 22, 1915, Lodge MSS.

[221]

[rather than an internationalist] that he so felt."[2] Still, as we have seen, his was never a nationalism incompatible with a sense of duty to the international community. Such a duty was but one of the attributes of Great Power status. Lodge had a conservative's sense of duty—natural, spontaneous, and obvious. It found its model in the Concert of Europe more than in contractual arrangements which were dangerous because of their inflexibility and whose very existence denigrated a true sense of responsibility. Lodge's thoughts ran inevitably to the seeming willingness of Americans to contract solemn obligations to arbitrate everything in theory, and then in practice to refuse to go to arbitration whenever it appeared the judgment might go against the United States.[3]

Lodge, less receptive to new ideas, lagged far behind Roosevelt in taking up the idea of a league, but when he did so it was in the context of the Rooseveltian solution and in accordance with the concept of a league that Roosevelt had advanced. Consequently, a look at Roosevelt's plans is warranted. In his views on form Roosevelt was remarkably consistent; what fluctuated wildly were his notions about a league's feasibility at given points in time. In his original plan, advanced in 1905, the league was little more than an alliance of the Great Powers and a means of resurrecting the Concert of Europe.[4] His conception was always exclusionist, limited in membership and objects. He thought in terms of an organization of "civilized" nations that would "insist upon the proper policing of the world," a league such as might appeal to someone of an imperialistic turn of mind.[5] He envisaged a "combination between those great nations which sincerely desire peace and

2. Clipping of an editorial from the *Christian Science Monitor* of June 13, 1917, Scrapbooks, Lodge MSS.

3. See Warren F. Kuehl, *Seeking World Order: The United States and International Organization to 1920* (Nashville, 1969), pp. 156–57. The American record was a hypocritical one. Though both were strong proponents of arbitration, Taft refused to arbitrate the Canal Tolls dispute and Wilson peremptorily dismissed Huerta's request for arbitration of the Tampico incident. Other, and usually political, considerations seemed to carry more weight.

4. William Clinton Olson, "Theodore Roosevelt's Conception of an International League," *World Affairs Quarterly* 29 (Jan. 1959): 338; John Chalmers Vinson, *Referendum for Isolation* (Athens, Ga., 1961), pp. 10, 12–13. Another way of understanding Roosevelt's conception of a league is to employ the useful analogy between his views on the regulation of the domestic economy and his ideas about international cooperation suggested by Jerry Israel in *Progressivism and the Open Door: America and China, 1905–1921* (Pittsburgh, 1971). In this sense Roosevelt's conception of a league might best be described as cartel-like.

5. Olson, "Roosevelt's Conception of an International League," p. 330.

have no thought themselves of committing aggressions." But righteous intent was never sufficient qualification. Roosevelt's concern for "the establishment of some form of international police power, *competent* and *willing* to prevent violence as between nations" was an extension of his desire to see the United States and England manifest those characteristics.[6] Peace and security, thought Roosevelt, could only be achieved by preparedness and the acceptance of international duty and responsibility, the very characteristics which physically isolated powers like the United States and Britain had seldom manifested. In short, Roosevelt's conception of a league was inseparable from his plea that "it is the highest duty of the most advanced and freest peoples to keep themselves in such a state of readiness as to forbid to any barbarism or despotism the hope of arresting the progress of the world by striking down the nations that lead in that progress."[7] A league, then, was only feasible if the "civilized" powers were militarily strong and possessed of an imperialist *élan* sufficient to prevent a public reaction against the assumption of international responsibilities. A league, in Roosevelt's mind, was ever as much a means of getting the United States and England to assume the proper international posture as an end in itself. In fact, his conception of a league subsumed that posture; without it no league could be effective.

Consequently, it was natural that when Roosevelt considered the league idea in the context of American abstention from the World War he repeatedly stressed a league of "efficient, civilized nations" who were "willing and able to use and to furnish force," powers "who possess virile manliness of character and the willingness to accept risk and labor when necessary to the performance of duty."[8] "The first essential" in any scheme for world peace was to understand that nothing could be accomplished unless the contracting powers acted in precisely the reverse of the manner of Wilson and Bryan. "Such shortsighted and timid inefficiency, *and, above all such selfish* indifference to the cause of permanent and righteous peace" were antipathetic to

6. "International Peace," Roosevelt's Address before the Nobel Prize Committee, delivered at Christiana, Norway, May 5, 1910, in Hagedorn, ed., *The Works of Theodore Roosevelt*, XVIII, p. 415. Italics mine.

7. Roosevelt, "Address at Oxford University, June 7, 1910" in Hagedorn, ed., *The Americanism of Theodore Roosevelt*, p. 231.

8. Olson, "Roosevelt's Conception of an International League," pp. 346–47; Roosevelt, "Utopia or Hell," *The Independent* 81 (Jan. 4, 1915): 13, 16.

the concept of a league for the peace of righteousness. On the other hand, a league might

... prove entirely workable, if nations entered into it with good faith, and if they treated their obligations under it in the spirit in which the United States treated its obligations as regarded the independence of Cuba, giving good government to the Philippines, and building the Panama Canal; the same spirit in which England acted when the neutrality of Belgium was violated.[9]

Feeling there was "no higher international duty" than to safeguard industrious, orderly states like Belgium, and that it would never be possible to commit a clearer breach of international morality than Germany's conquest of Belgium, Roosevelt raised the issue of a league in the early months of the war as a goad to preparation and a more active American role in the conflict.[10] Not daring to advocate outright American participation in the war, but feeling like Root that the nations of the Triple Entente had for all practical purposes resolved themselves into an international police force, the league Roosevelt advanced was meant to move American public opinion toward his brand of internationalism.[11] His league was an alternative to Bryan's conciliation treaties and to the Administration's course of action in "refusing to make us a power efficient in anything save empty treaties and empty promises."[12] Bryan's treaties, based on the assumption that the conciliation process, when coupled with friendship and an innate desire for peace, would suffice for the settlement of all international disputes, offered an illusory security. Moreover, they were increasing the reluctance of the American people to assume any international responsibility that carried a commitment of force and compounding the already great obstacles faced by the preparedness advocates.[13] Under such circum-

9. Roosevelt, "Utopia or Hell," pp. 15–16. Italics in the original.
10. Roosevelt, "The World War: Its Tragedies and Its Lessons," p. 169; Roosevelt, *America and the World War* (New York, 1915), p. 109. Warren Kuehl (*Seeking World Order*, p. 179) professes to be puzzled why Roosevelt raised the issue at all and suggests that "perhaps his utterances revealed less of a commitment to international organization than a desire to find some issue with which to embarrass President Wilson."
11. Jessup, *Elihu Root*, II, pp. 312–13.
12. Roosevelt, *America and the World War*, p. 136.
13. Link, *Wilson: The New Freedom*, p. 283. In the campaign of 1914 (almost three months after the outbreak of war) Wilson praised the Bryan conciliation treaties for making the use of force unnecessary and still had such faith in the efficacy of public opinion as to predict that "after the light has shone on a dispute for a year, it will not be necessary to do anything" (Boston *Herald*, Oct. 25, 1914).

stances, Roosevelt felt compelled to offer an alternative and to insist
that Americans "clear the rubbish off our souls and admit that everything that has been done in passing peace treaties, arbitration treaties
. . . and the like, with no sanction of force behind them, amounts to
literally and absolutely zero."[14]

At this stage Lodge sympathized with Roosevelt's complaints, but
otherwise had little interest in the league idea.

> I have already written you about your "America and the World War". . . .
> I have re-read it throughout. Nothing can be truer than your main theme of
> the folly, if not wickedness of making treaties which have no force and no
> intent of enforcement behind them. I was away last summer when those fatu-
> ous treaties were put through by Bryan. If I had been here I should have re-
> sisted them.[15]

When Lodge finally took up the league idea, Roosevelt had already
abandoned it, but so united were they in their objects, and so understanding of each other's methods, that the league never became a matter of contention between them. They tended to look upon league advocacy as a tactic, as a means to other ends. More important than a
league were the attitudes and postures that would make it practicable.
If those were not forthcoming, then all talk of a league was to no purpose. If they were, then a league need not be contrived but would
develop out of a natural sense of duty.

The increasing currency of ideas for international organization which
were at odds with Roosevelt's own, coupled with his growing disappointment with the Administration and his despair over its popularity,
early caused Roosevelt to reconsider the league idea. Roosevelt's change
of heart was related to the growing appeal of league-like proposals
(especially that for a League to Enforce Peace) which placed far less
emphasis on preparedness and duty than Roosevelt deemed requisite
and to his growing conviction (matching that in international circles)
through February and March that the American government had no
intention of enforcing the threats made in its "strict accountability"
note.[16] Questioning his America, he began to see that in the prevailing
climate of opinion the league idea could be used to prevent the very

14. Roosevelt, *America and the World War*, pp. 102–03.
15. *Correspondence of Roosevelt and Lodge*, II, pp. 452–53 (Jan. 20, 1915).
16. For the changing German assessment of America's intentions in these
months see Link, *Wilson: The Struggle for Neutrality, 1914–1915*, pp. 356–57.

things—preparation and a sense of international responsibility—he had intended it to foster.

Taft, Wilson and Bryan stand on an absolutely and completely different footing from me in this matter, because they explicitly or implicitly propose to substitute paper agreements for the potential use of force and explicitly or implicitly treat those proposed paper agreements as reasons why America should not prepare to defend itself. Moreover, they treat their proposals as being immediately realizable, as offering immediate substitutes for war. . . .[17]

Soon Roosevelt was telling Lord Bryce that it was inopportune to go into further detail about a league. Such plans were likely to do only mischief "unless they make it clear beyond possibility of doubt that the prime duty at present is to insist upon putting into effect all treaties entered into; and therefore that the prime duty of the great free nations is to prepare themselves against war."[18] Yet what he called "this education of evil" seemed to be gaining in currency; his villains' list on this score encompassed not only Wilson and Bryan, but also Carnegie and Taft.[19] Taft's leadership of the League to Enforce Peace was an important factor in Roosevelt's distancing himself from it, not only because Taft was personally and politically offensive, but because his philosophy of international relations was so alien.[20] Roosevelt found it especially incongruous that the men agitating for a League to Enforce Peace "declined to say a word in favor of our fitting ourselves to go into defensive war . . . and yet they actually wish to make us at this time promise to undertake offensive war in the interests of other peoples. . . ."[21]

Lodge listened to Roosevelt sympathetically, but chose to follow a somewhat different course. His reaction to the League to Enforce Peace may even have been initially as adverse as that of Augustus Peabody Gardner, who rose in the House in January of 1915 to denounce "the new dream" of an international court and an international army to enforce its decrees, claiming that "Andrew Carnegie has given $10,000,000 as a fund with which to persuade the world that a flexible

17. Einstein, *Roosevelt, His Mind in Action*, p. 249.
18. Morison, ed., *Letters of Theodore Roosevelt*, VIII, pp. 913–14.
19. Roosevelt to Lodge, June 15, 1915, Lodge MSS.
20. See Pringle, *The Life and Times of William Howard Taft*, I, p. 931; and Olson, "Roosevelt's Conception of an International League," p. 351.
21. Roosevelt to E. A. Van Valkenberg, June 29, 1915, quoted in Wister, *Roosevelt: The Story of a Friendship, 1880–1919*, p. 336.

spine is a better defense than a mighty biceps." Experience and history were being forgotten. As fast as one dream was shattered by events, the income from Carnegie's money was paying men to invent new ones.[22] Like Roosevelt, Gardner feared that the various proposals emanating from the peace movement would serve, as historically they often had, to cut the ground from under the preparedness movement. But Lodge saw an opportunity where the others saw only a danger, an opportunity which stemmed from his position of leadership within the Republican party.

Lodge never joined the League to Enforce Peace; in fact he declined an invitation to attend an organizing dinner designed to enlist the support of leading public figures.[23] But he did recognize its potential influence and was therefore not prepared to write it off, the less so as the majority of its founders were prominent Republicans.[24] At a time when many of the leaders of the American progressive movement were lining up in the anti-preparedness ranks and renewing their repudiation of the idea of using power as an instrument of diplomacy, the League to Enforce Peace was at least proposing to "enforce" peace.[25] With a large segment of the American peace community seemingly abandoning its traditional stand and with the prospect of an ensuing split in its ranks, Lodge saw a potential ally in the League to Enforce Peace, an ally in the fight for preparedness, in his efforts to move the country toward support for the Allies, and perhaps even in his efforts to drive Wilson from office.[26]

The League was the more attractive because of the enemies it was making and the problems it was creating for the Democrats. Bryan was the one major political figure who had rushed to denounce it as a false attempt to fight militarism with militarism, and this in a negative way effected just the association between the league idea and the preparedness issue that Lodge desired.[27] The logic of the League's third

22. *Cong. Record,* 63rd Cong., 3rd sess., 1915, p. 2688. Gardner also asked his colleagues if they believed "that public opinion in this country would support any administration which involved the United States in a Mediterranean dispute in which we were not concerned? Ask yourselves whether you would vote the additional troops and the additional money for an international army."
23. Warren F. Kuehl, *Hamilton Holt* (Gainesville, Fla., 1960), p. 127.
24. Ruhl J. Bartlett, *The League to Enforce Peace* (Chapel Hill, 1944), pp. 55–56.
25. Link, *Woodrow Wilson and the Progressive Era,* pp. 180–81.
26. Vinson, *Referendum for Isolation,* p. 19; Harold and Margaret Sprout, *The Rise of American Naval Power,* p. 323.
27. Lawrence W. Levine, *Defender of the Faith: William Jennings Bryan: The*

article calling for the use of force, if not necessarily the politics of the League's leaders, meant, as Root was quick to perceive, "the maintenance of a vastly greater army and navy than we have now." It also pointed toward "the most absolute entanglement in the politics of Europe," for "if we are going to adopt such a policy as that we ought immediately to join the Allies in making war on Germany because of her violations of international law and treaty obligations in her treatment of Belgium."[28] Even if the United States did not enter the war there was the possibility of its association with the victors in a league. Lodge was informed by his correspondents of the drift of British opinion on the subject of a league and only recently had been told that Arthur Balfour placed great importance on having the United States participate in, and give its moral sanction to, any Peace Congress.[29]

While avoiding even the semblance of a commitment to the League's program, Lodge, under the weight of these considerations, endorsed the principle of putting force behind the world's peace, and tried to nudge the leaders of the League a little further along the road down which the logic of their proposals was leading them. Speaking at commencement exercises at Union College in June of 1915, he declared, in words that have often been interpreted as an endorsement of the type of league Wilson later advocated, that "the peace of the world can only be maintained, . . . as the peace of a single nation is maintained, by the force which united nations are willing to put behind the peace and order of the world."[30] This was little more than a logical extension of his long-held view that peace could only be maintained by strength

---

Last Decade, 1915–1925 (New York, 1965), p. 62. Spring Rice's initial reaction to the League to Enforce Peace was also one of considerable skepticism. He feared "that the moment such a proposal was made everyone would begin to quote Washington's warning against entangling [sic] alliances." He pointed to the strong American desire to mediate but to the absence of "the slightest indication that they would appear as guarantors of the peace which might result from their mediation." Even after Lodge's "Force and Peace" speech he went no further than to concede that "if defence becomes really a practical issue, it is not outside the bounds of probability that the United States might become a practical member of a league of neutrals to guarantee treaties of peace." See Gwynn, ed., *Letters of Spring Rice*, II, pp. 270, 297.

28. Root to A. Lawrence Lowell, Aug. 9, 1915, League to Enforce Peace Papers, Widener Library, Harvard University (hereafter referred to as League to Enforce Peace MSS).

29. Moreton Frewen to Lodge, June 3, 1915, Lodge MSS.

30. Lodge, "Force and Peace," *The Annals of the American Academy of Political and Social Science* 60 (July 1915): 210. Credit may even be due to Lodge for originating the phrase "united nations." See Cooper, *The Vanity of Power*, p. 61.

of arms. As at least one contemporary understood, the thrust of the speech was directed against those who opposed preparedness and advocated "peace at any price."[31] Putting force behind the world's peace was offered as an alternative to those who thought it could be done by words, who thought something could be accomplished "by people who are sheltered under neutrality, gathering outside the edges of the fight and from comfortable safety summoning the combatants to throw down their arms and make peace because war is filled with horrors and women are the mothers of men." What is apparent from the above and from his insistence on a "union of civilized nations" (Germany to his mind no longer qualified) is that Lodge contemplated American participation in a league of victors and conceived of the league as a means of getting the United States to stand with the Allies. Meanwhile, "the first step . . . toward the maintenance of peace," he insisted, was "for each nation to maintain its peace with the rest of the world by its own honorable and right conduct and by such organization and preparation as will enable it to defend its peace." Nothing in the speech marked a significant departure from the views about the conduct of international relations he had long held. He did not even believe that such a league was an immediate possibility but looked for it to grow organically "in the slow process of the years."[32]

Lodge was probably also attracted by the limited and "practical" nature of what the League's leaders proposed. A better name for it might have been the League to Enforce Conciliation. In both philosophy and method it was far removed from what Wilson later endorsed.[33] The approach and emphasis of the League (as set forth by A. Lawrence Lowell in the "Program of the League") was so conservative it seemed designed to appeal to men of Lodge's persuasion. Lowell offered no panacea, and was aware that the league question "bristles with difficulties."[34] He did not advance the hope of abolishing war and stressed the fact that members did not bind themselves to enforce the decision of the tribunal or the award of the council of conciliation, but only to

31. Henry White to Lodge, June 10, 1915, Lodge MSS.
32. Lodge, "Force and Peace," pp. 203, 210–12.
33. See, for example, Vinson, *Referendum for Isolation*, p. 16; and especially F. H. Hinsley, *Power and the Pursuit of Peace* (Cambridge, England, 1963), pp. 146–47.
34. Lowell quoted in Roland N. Stromberg, "The Riddle of Collective Security, 1916–1920," in George L. Anderson, ed., *Issues and Conflicts: Studies in Twentieth Century American Diplomacy* (Lawrence, Kansas, 1959), p. 148.

force the disputants to first resort to those processes. "The conceptions of international morality and fair play," Lowell argued, "are still so vague and divergent that a nation can hardly bind itself to wage war on another, with which it has no quarrel, to enforce a decision or a recommendation of whose justice or wisdom it may not be itself heartily convinced." Even dearer to Lodge's heart must have been Lowell's insistence that the league had "no connection with any effort to stop the present war" (that is, no intention of becoming involved in efforts to deprive the Allies of their expected victory) and that to join such a league would mean greater U.S. preparation, with a moderate estimate of the American contribution being about 500,000 men.[35]

In the interest of preventing a party rupture on the league issue, and thereby jeopardizing a Republican victory in the 1916 elections, Lodge tried to keep a foot in both camps, to occupy the middle ground between those who led the League to Enforce Peace and Roosevelt, who in despair over his inability to rally the people to his policies was becoming more critical of the league idea. Roosevelt, feeling that the nation's course represented "neither readiness for national self-sacrifice nor appreciation of true internationalism," declared that "a movement right in itself may be all wrong if made at the wrong time." He still thought that Leagues to Enforce Peace might ultimately prove feasible, but not "until nations like our own are *not* too proud to fight, and *are* too proud not to live up to their agreements."[36] Lodge, too, was discouraged. The objects which had initially attracted him to the League seemed no closer to realization, and he also began to question the values of the American people.

It is difficult to feel otherwise than gloomy as one contemplates these things. It does seem at times as if the one object of the people of this country was to get all the money they could individually and locally and sacrifice everything to the preservation of life, comfort and amusement. . . .

Of course, internationally, public opinion is worth nothing unless there is force behind it. I preached that doctrine last summer at the Union College, and I have been preaching it ever since, but I cannot see that it has much effect.[37]

35. A. Lawrence Lowell, "A League to Enforce Peace," World Peace Foundation Pamphlet Series, 5 (Oct. 1915): 5–7, 10, 17.
36. Roosevelt, *Fear God and Take Your Own Part*, pp. 81, 169, 188, 346. Italics in original.
37. *Correspondence of Roosevelt and Lodge*, II, pp. 470–71 (Jan. 11, 1916). Lodge

Thus did the idea of a league become enmeshed not only with the preparedness issue, with the question of a more pro-Allied stance, and with the effort to defeat Wilson, but also with Lodge's assessment of the American national character. The Senator's views on the feasibility of a league cannot, therefore, be discussed to further advantage in the abstract. Only a chronological narrative can show how his stand on the league varied with his prospects for attaining his other objectives and with his assessment of the American temper.

II

The winter of 1915–16 was for Lodge a time of brooding and questioning. Neither his efforts on behalf of the preparedness movement nor those designed to move the United States closer to the Allies had more than limited success. In fact, Anglo-American relations were deteriorating as the Administration stepped up its protests against British violations of the rights of neutrals and the English became convinced that Wilson would wage his reelection campaign on an anti-British line.[38] Lodge rose in the Senate on December 10, 1915 to try to squelch what looked like the opening salvo in that campaign, a speech by Senator Hoke Smith of Georgia detailing repeated British violations of American rights and calling for a Congressional investigation. Returning to the fray for the first time since his wife's death, Lodge insisted that such an investigation include all violations of American rights, not just those affecting American commerce. Finding the perfect rejoinder, he declared that "to me American lives are more important than American dollars; the body of an innocent child floating dead upon the water, the victim of the destruction of an unarmed vessel, . . . a more poignant and a more tragic spectacle than an unsold bale of cotton."[39] Lodge continued to

---

also recommended to Roosevelt an article by Brooks Adams in the *Yale Review* that took an even less sanguine view and revived the old Adamsian contrast between the "military" and the "commercial" man. Adams traced all the country's troubles to "the false standards of our people," asking, "Is it not logical for men to reason that if money is the only end in life, then peace at any price is a sound policy?" See Daniel Aaron, "The Unusable Man: An Essay on the Mind of Brooks Adams," *New England Quarterly* 21 (March 1948): 28.

38. Arthur S. Link, *Wilson: Campaigns for Progressivism and Peace, 1916–1917* (Princeton, 1965), pp. 35–36.

39. Lodge, *War Addresses*, pp. 62–63.

fear, however, that the price that Ambassador Bernstorff would exact for an apparent American diplomatic victory over Germany would "be to engage in a controversy with Great Britain with the danger of blundering into strained relations, if not war. . . ."[40]

Then there was the matter of the Administration's attempt to redefine the rights of armed merchantmen to give greater latitude and effectiveness to the submarine, a plan which would have helped Germany, and which the Administration only abandoned under heavy pressure from the Allies and those, like Lodge, who expressed incredulity over the Government's apparent readiness to surrender the long internationally sanctioned right of Americans to travel or ship goods on belligerent merchantmen. To those who sympathized with the Allies and were content with the traditional American interpretation it seemed both unfair and unneutral to try to change the rules in the middle of the game.[41] Such Administration maneuverings only served to increase the feeling, already widely held in Republican ranks, that Wilson's foreign policy was being "carefully directed at the preconceptions of the American public" and being pursued without regard for its effect on the course of the war in Europe.[42]

The Administration's popularity remained high; it did not appear to be vulnerable on any foreign policy issue except perhaps that of Mexico. Lodge continued to occupy a defensive position (fending off any change of position on armed merchantmen and fighting the imposition of an embargo). He was able to blunt hostile initiatives but seemed further than ever from moving the country to support a Rooseveltian international posture. Such conditions reinforced the doubts about America he had long entertained. He began to feel that "the spirit of the past" had but little effect on present attitudes. "It is disheartening to the last degree," he declared, "to see the indifference about preparedness, or national defence, or anything except keeping snug and warm, and making money, and going to see movies."[43] Once, during the Civil War and even as late as the Spanish War, it had been different, but now Americans seemed to feel there was nothing that could justify the sac-

40. Lodge to William R. Thayer, Jan. 15, 1916, Lodge MSS.
41. Lodge, *War Addresses*, pp. 108–09.
42. Beerits Memorandum, "The Presidential Campaign of 1916," Charles Evans Hughes Papers, Library of Congress.
43. Lodge to William Sturgis Bigelow, Jan. 15, 1916, Lodge MSS.

rifice of life. It was with a very heavy heart that he reported to Trevelyan "that the desire not to become involved in the war and to keep
the country at peace is very general."[44]

All Lodge's fears and frustrations with respect to the type of foreign
policy being pursued by the United States came to focus on Wilson,
the man ultimately responsible for its conduct. He now told Roosevelt
that his detestation of the Wilson Administration went beyond anything he ever expected to feel in politics, and confided to John Morse
that he had "but one political desire left," to turn Wilson out of power.[45]

The obvious alternative was Roosevelt. But Roosevelt's judgment
was that in assuming the role of national exhorter he had rendered his
own candidacy impossible. He warned Lodge that it would be "utterly
idle to nominate me if the country is in a mood either of timidity or of
that base and complacent materialism which finds expression in the
phrase 'Safety first,' " utterly useless "unless the country is somewhere
near a mood of at least half-heroism." Initially Lodge was encouraged
as to Roosevelt's prospects and replied:

I know how much there is to the 'Safety first' feeling, and I have been through
black depression on account of it, but until it is absolutely proved to the contrary I shall continue to believe that the great body of the people are in favor
of preparedness and are still patriotic and ready to fight for and defend their
country. I cannot give up that belief without utter despair in the future.[46]

But however tenaciously he clung to certain beliefs, Lodge remained a
political realist and began to doubt whether a majority of the people
were with Roosevelt, to develop the "horrid suspicion that the majority
of the people are not with his policies, or Root's, or mine." That was
precisely what the campaign would test.[47]

It was from the outset not only a campaign to defeat Wilson but also
a campaign to reform the thinking and values of the American people.[48]
The two were inextricably linked. Lodge struck a crusading note in

44. Lodge to Trevelyan, Jan. 11 and Feb. 1, 1916, Lodge MSS.
45. Lodge to Roosevelt, Feb. 1 and 9, 1916, and to John T. Morse, Jr., Feb. 16,
1916, Lodge MSS.
46. *Correspondence of Roosevelt and Lodge*, II, pp. 480–81, 484 (Feb. 4, 9, 1916).
47. Lodge to William Sturgis Bigelow, April 14, 1916, Lodge MSS.
48. At the beginning of the year Roosevelt had announced that the "prime
work for this nation at this moment is to rebuild its own character" (*Fear God
and Take Your Own Part*, p. 107).

launching his campaign for reelection at Lynn in March and carried it
through the election. He seems to have sincerely felt that this was the
most critical election the nation had faced since 1864. An ordinary
campaign was out of the question. In speeches which verged on the
traditional New England Jeremiad and at political gatherings which
often took on the trappings of revival meetings, Lodge sought to counter the idealism of peace with the idealism of duty and sacrifice:

But the question that the generations yet to come will ask of us is not
whether we have kept the peace, because that can be done very meanly and
very humiliatingly. What they will ask of us . . . is not merely whether we
have kept the peace but whether we have kept the faith. . . . Let us forever
dismiss from our minds the idea that the Nation's life depends on the preservation of our individual lives. The life of a nation lies in its ideals. If it
abandons its ideals of humanity and justice, if it casts aside its principles,
if it becomes tributary and subject, then the nation is dead even if its citizens
live on in a country when honor, hope and aspiration have fled.[49]

History taught that nations, like men, had to have a conscience and
a soul. This had once been supplied by the conception of life and duty
held by the "Fathers" and by the men, both North and South, who
fought the Civil War, men who felt "that there was something more
precious than life, comfort, safety, money-making, prosperity." This
"shining spirit of self-sacrifice" had made the nation great. Publicly,
Lodge expressed "no doubt that, once awakened, this same conception
would be dominant among the American people now. . . ."[50] But privately he had doubts, and these deepened as it became apparent that
he would have to choose among the various ends he was seeking, that
an all-out campaign for preparedness and for ranging the country (if
only morally) on the side of the Allies was no asset in his fight to un-
seat Wilson. His heart was clearly with Josiah Royce who, in a speech
Lodge had inserted in the *Congressional Record*, declared:

Our duty is to be and to remain the outspoken moral opponents of the
present German policy and of the German state so long as it holds this
present policy and carries on its present war. . . . We owe to those allies
whatever moral support and whatever financial assistance it is in the power
of this Nation to give. . . . let us be ashamed of ourselves that we can not

49. Lodge, "Speech at Lynn, March 16, 1916," Lodge MSS. Excerpts appeared in
the *New York Times* of March 17, 1916.
50. Lodge, *War Addresses*, pp. 134–35, 145–46, 185. See also his eulogy of the
late Senator Zebulon B. Vance in the *Cong. Record*, 64th Cong., 1st sess., 1916,
p. 9756.

even now stand beside Belgium and suffer with her for our duty and for mankind. . . .[51]

But Lodge as a prominent Republican could not go that far without incurring serious political disadvantage for his party. This fact, above all others, shaped the campaign of 1916.

It also had much to do with his attitude on the league question. That too varied with the requirements of the campaign and with his assessment of what the American people stood for in morals. Now again prominent in his rhetoric was the theme that, contrary to the teachings of the peace-at-any-price advocates, force alone protected civilization and permitted the enjoyment of the rights to which the American people had become so deeply attached.[52] Preparedness was a prerequisite for the security of any community, whether national or international; a nation which was unable to maintain its own peace could not possibly preach peace with any effect to others.[53]

His views on the form a league might take remained conventional; the only real hope for the establishment of general peace among nations was "to be found through the operations of law and of international tribunals, and above all, in some reasonable agreements among the greatest and most responsible nations for the maintenance of peace."[54] He noted the enthusiasm for the League to Enforce Peace, but confided to a friend that he was "fighting shy of it" because "they seem to want to bind us to all kinds of things which the country would not hold to" (as an example he cited possible international interference with immigration restriction) and because he had "great doubts about the soundness of anything of which Taft is the head."[55] When Lawrence Lowell wrote inviting him to speak at the League's first national assembly, Lodge neither accepted nor declined but sought to obtain more information in private discussions. Lodge hesitated even though Lowell

---

51. *Cong. Record,* 64th Cong., 1st sess., 1916, p. 4666.

52. Lodge, *War Addresses,* pp. 132–33.

53. Lodge, "An Explanation of International Law," *The Youth's Companion* 90 (March 23, 1916): 155.

54. *Ibid.* As Warren Kuehl observes (*Seeking World Order,* p. 171) "no other idea had appeared with greater frequency or consistency in the plans and discussions prior to 1914" than that "any agency should be built upon legal and judicial foundations."

55. Lodge to William Sturgis Bigelow, April 5, 1916, Lodge MSS. Seeing the country divide along lines of national origin during the war tended only to confirm Lodge in his advocacy of immigration restriction.

presented the League in a highly conservative manner, emphasizing the practical difficulties involved and that the League sought a means of maintaining the world's peace "without an obligation to espouse the quarrels of another nation." In reply Lodge declared:

I am in favor of putting some force behind international agreement and I made a somewhat elaborate address on that subject at Union College last Spring. . . . I have been hesitating about the Peace League because it has seemed to me, apart from any impracticability to which you refer, there was a grave danger . . . of committing us to certain propositions which would be impossible of fulfillment. That was done by President Taft in his arbitration treaties with France and England, and I do not want to have the country involved in any engagements which it could not live up to absolutely.[56]

Such a response was completely consistent with his long-held views. Yet a few weeks later he addressed the League's assembly and, some would say, lent his endorsement not only to the League to Enforce Peace but to the league idea in general. Actually neither he nor Wilson went as far on that occasion as supporters of the League of Nations later thought they had. For that reason it is important to look closely at what was said and at the context in which it was said. Such statements as Ray Stannard Baker's alleging that "since May 1916 the proposal for an international organization had been the central pillar of Wilson's peace programme," and Harley Notter's claiming that both the Republicans and Democrats committed themselves in 1916 to a future world association to guarantee peace, do not clarify, but rather obscure, what was going on.[57]

1916 was an election year and the First Annual National Assembly of the League to Enforce Peace, occurring a few weeks before the national nominating conventions, was a political event of some importance. The organization was one with considerable potential for exercising an influence in the campaign. Moreover, its political shape and ideas about international organization were still so amorphous that it could extend invitations to speak to both Lodge and Wilson and both, seeing a political opportunity, could accept.[58] Neither Lodge nor Wilson was yet will-

56. Lowell to Lodge, April 28, 1916, and Lodge's reply, May 1, 1916, League to Enforce Peace MSS.
57. Ray Stannard Baker, *Woodrow Wilson: Life and Letters* (New York, 1927–1939), VI, p. 416; Notter, *The Origins of the Foreign Policy of Woodrow Wilson*, p. 532.
58. An indication of the political significance which Wilson attached to the League's proceedings was his insistence on speaking last, thereby freeing himself

ing to write off the League or to abandon the hope of making it a vehicle for their ideas. The question of international organization was fraught with difficulties, but as long as the internationalists were concentrating on building support for the principle of international cooperation the campaigning politician could easily evade the thornier issues. Before December 1916 no prominent figure in either major party, except Bryan, took an explicitly anti-League stand. To do so would have been "something like being against peace and a better world," and both Lodge and Wilson, in their speeches before the League, were in a sense replying to Bryan.[59] But as only Bryan and his following were outside the pale, neither Lodge nor Wilson needed to depart from their long-standing views in order to appear to endorse the League.

The League was still oblivious to many a hard question, and a careful reading of the statements made at the First Assemblage reveals that behind the facade of adherence to a plan, specific enough in most respects, there were great differences of opinion respecting when such a League ought to be initiated and what obligations it would entail. Robert Osgood, referring to the speeches of Theodore Marburg and Newton Baker, once suggested that the thinking of most of those present was closer to that of Wilson than to that of Lodge, but anyone reading the distinctly pro-Ally speeches of John Bates Clark or Samuel Gompers could easily come to the opposite conclusion.[60] So too could one reading the statement of Frank Streeter, who proposed the adoption on a national scale of "the New Hampshire Way," the creation of an organization (like the one formed in his state) which combined in its purposes the twin ideas of preparedness and the League to Enforce Peace.[61]

Behind the facade of agreement on the principle of the need for some sort of international organization both Lodge and Wilson carefully hedged their commitments and thereby revealed that they were far apart in their ideas as to the nature, timing, and purposes of a league. Wilson avoided discussing the plan espoused by the League to Enforce

---

from the possibility of direct criticism and allowing him to tailor his address to the direction the Conference had taken. The usual procedure at such gatherings was for the President to speak first. See Lodge, *The Senate and the League*, pp. 62–63.

59. Osgood, *Ideals and Self-Interest*, p. 248; Hays, *Memoirs*, p. 221; Vinson, *Referendum for Isolation*, p. 19.

60. Osgood, *Ideals and Self-Interest*, pp. 246–47.

61. *Enforced Peace*, Proceedings of the First Annual National Assemblage of the League to Enforce Peace, Washington, May 26–27, 1916 (New York, 1916), pp. 184–85.

Peace and diluted his new-found internationalism (he did state that "we are participants, whether we would or not, in the life of the world") by continuing to claim that "with its [the war's] causes and its objects we are not concerned." His prescriptions for the world's peace were particularly difficult to grasp; he spoke of peace depending upon "a new and *more wholesome diplomacy*," upon "*some sort of agreement* among the great nations," "*some feasible method* of acting in concert," and called upon the nations of the world to "*in some way* band themselves together to see . . . that right prevails. . . ." [62] As if in response to the influence which the Bryanites exercised within his party, Wilson did not even unequivocally endorse the use of force. Robert Lansing testified that "after preparing his address he went over it and erased all reference to the use of physical force in preventing wars." [63] The result was that when the President came to his punch line ("I feel that the world is even now upon the eve of a great consummation, when some common force will be brought into existence which shall safeguard right") it was not clear to his listeners whether he was talking about military force or about the force of public opinion resulting from a great international conversion to the principles of peace and democracy.

Lodge was equally vague on details, but, glad to see that the League recognized that voluntary arbitration had been carried to its limits, agreed that "the next step is that which this League proposes and that is to put force behind international peace." He clearly meant military force for he went on to make the point about preparedness which had attracted him to the League in the first place: "we as a nation shall find it very difficult to induce others to put force behind peace if we have not force to put behind our own." [64] The success of a league would depend on recognition of the necessity for preparedness. There were other obstacles as well. Lodge thought it unlikely that all wars could be

62. *Enforced Peace*, pp. 159–161. Italics mine.
63. Robert Lansing, *The Peace Negotiations: A Personal Narrative*, p. 34. Lansing was opposed to military sanctions in principle and Colonel House, probably with one eye on Bryan, also advised glossing over the problems attendant to the enforcement of peace. See Vinson, *Referendum for Isolation*, p. 30.
64. The *New York Times* (May 28, 1916, I, p. 2) grasped the thrust of Lodge's speech and emphasized not his endorsement of the League, but rather his declaration, as paraphrased by the *Times*, that "if the plan of the league is to succeed there must be adequate national defense." It also described him as "striking a responsive chord."

stopped, pointed from his long experience to "the difficulties which arise when we speak of anything which seems to involve an alliance," and urged the wisdom of being "careful at the beginning not to attempt too much." But the most important (and most neglected) qualification of his support came at the outset when he announced: "I have been glad to learn that the League has laid down as a principle that it is not engaged in attempting to bring the war in Europe to an end, that its work lies beyond that war. . . ."[65] In short, his endorsement of the League was highly conditional and required scarcely any deviation from his lifelong prescriptions for the conduct of foreign policy.[66]

III

Meanwhile the campaign was taking shape. Just as Lodge attempted to arrive at an accommodation with the League to Enforce Peace, so too was he willing to compromise on the choice of a candidate. The price for the unavailability of Taft was the unavailability of Roosevelt, and Lodge began to flirt with the idea of picking "a mare with no record," someone who had taken no stand on the vital questions of the day.[67] Though he would have preferred the surety of Roosevelt, there was an overriding consideration.[68] He would "rather see Theodore in the White House than anyone else," he confessed, "but there is one thing that weighs with me more than all other considerations, to which I should cheerfully sacrifice myself or any interest that I have . . . and that is the defeat of Wilson. . . ."[69] Other compromises were required. Lodge and Borah, hoping to make it easier for Roosevelt to support

65. *Enforced Peace*, pp. 164–67.
66. Lodge closed his speech with a rhetorical flourish, urging his listeners onward and upward, claiming that it was in search for Utopias that all discoveries and progress had been made, and quoting Matthew Arnold's lines: "Charge again, then, and be dumb. / Let the victors, when they come, / When the forts of folly fall / Find your body at the wall." This occasioned Newton Baker's famous quip that when the time came to charge the forts of folly, Lodge was AWOL (Daniels, *The Wilson Era*, II, p. 468). What is revealing, though, is that Lodge chose a quotation so replete with military imagery as a means of inspiring his listeners to greater effort on behalf of the league. He was reinforcing the connection between the ability to employ force and a viable league that he had drawn minutes earlier.
67. Morison, ed., *Letters of Theodore Roosevelt*, VIII, p. 1039.
68. In a letter to William R. Thayer (June 3, 1916, Lodge MSS) Lodge called TR "the ablest master of foreign affairs that we have" and declared that if he were elected "the entire position of the United States in the world . . . would be changed . . . by the mere fact that he was to be President. . . ."
69. Lodge to William Sturgis Bigelow, May 26, 1916, Lodge MSS.

the Republican ticket, drafted a platform which called for universal military service, an army of 250,000 and a navy second to none. But sensitive to the strength of the agrarian-progressive opponents of preparedness, Lodge succumbed to pressure and rewrote the platform so as to delete those items. He was even forced to swallow a plank calling for "a straight and honest neutrality between the belligerents." Only in its denunciation of Wilson's Mexican policy did the platform begin to meet Lodge's views, and Lodge could only justify it by telling Roosevelt that "I did what I could."[70]

In a last-ditch maneuver Roosevelt sought to save the situation by securing the Progressive nomination (and then hopefully the Republican) for Lodge. This was offensive to the Progressives and has been incomprehensible to most historians, but it was nevertheless understandable that Roosevelt should at such a moment have turned to Lodge, for on the issues which Roosevelt now considered important they were of one mind. Lodge had, as Roosevelt told the Conferees of the Progressive Party, "a peculiarly close acquaintance with the very type of questions now most pressing for settlement."[71] Roosevelt's suggestion was met with derision, and the Progressives went on to nominate Roosevelt against his wishes. Though Lodge did not secure the nomination (and there is little evidence he considered it a real possibility), he did, with Roosevelt's refusal to run as a third party candidate and his endorsement of Hughes, bring to a successful conclusion a personal campaign of long standing.

The Republican National Convention produced one other interesting development. Despite the efforts of influential Republican members of the League to Enforce Peace, the platform made no mention of the League and limited its internationalist statement to the by now perfunctory "we believe in the pacific settlement of international disputes and favor the establishment of a world court for that purpose."[72] What-

70. Harbaugh, *Power and Responsibility*, pp. 481, 486–87; Link, *Wilson: Campaigns for Progressivism and Peace, 1916–1917*, pp. 4–5.
71. Harbaugh, *Power and Responsibility*, pp. 489–91; Morison, ed., *Letters of Theodore Roosevelt*, VIII, pp. 1061–62.
72. Porter and Johnson, eds., *National Party Platforms*, p. 204. The Democratic platform was considerably more forthcoming, claiming that "the circumstances of the last two years have revealed necessities of international action" and proclaiming it a duty of the U.S. "to assist the world in securing settled peace and justice." However, on the league idea the platform was deliberately vague, declaring only that "we believe that the time has come when it is the duty of the United

ever pressures may have emanated from the pacific and isolationist Middle West, Lodge also had a hand in this. His explanation to Taft was that

Your draft of a resolution came just after the subcommittee had completed its report. I had it offered in the full committee and it was finally taken in a much mutilated and unimproved form. I am sorry that we could not do better.[73]

However, William Short reported to Lowell that the tentative draft of the platform *had* contained an endorsement of the League's program and that provision had only been removed "at the insistence of Senator Lodge."[74] Similarly, Talcott Williams claimed to have learned from a member of the Committee on Resolutions (of which Lodge was Chairman) that Lodge "was more responsible than anyone else for the failure to include the League to Enforce Peace in the Republican platform."[75] In comment on this situation Ruhl Bartlett once wrote: "What reasons led Lodge, who supported the league up to the moment President Wilson endorsed it, to make the deletion can only be surmised."[76] It is, of course, an exaggeration to claim, on the basis of what they said at the League's National Assemblage, that Lodge "supported" the League *or* that Wilson "endorsed" it; but, Lodge *was* coming to have a change of heart and we may usefully speculate on its impetus.

In Lodge's mind the test of the practicability of American membership in a league remained strong public support for preparedness and the manifestation of an "internationalist" feeling sufficient to align the U.S., at least morally, with the Allies. Progressive Party platform statements supporting the league idea had been interwoven with "bristling demands for thorough military preparedness and vigorous defense of American rights."[77] Lodge's inability to secure a similar statement in the Republican platform may have stirred second thoughts about the

States to join the other nations of the world in any feasible association that will effectively serve those principles, to maintain inviolate the complete security of the highway of the seas for the common and unhindered use of all nations" (Porter and Johnson, eds., *National Party Platforms*, p. 196).

73. Lodge to Taft, June 12, 1916, Taft MSS.

74. William Short to A. Lawrence Lowell, July 18, 1916, quoted in Bartlett, *The League to Enforce Peace*, p. 57.

75. John H. Latane, ed., *Development of the League of Nations Idea: Documents and Correspondence of Theodore Marburg* (New York, 1932), I, p. 138.

76. Bartlett, *The League to Enforce Peace*, pp. 57–58.

77. *Ibid.*, p. 57.

country's willingness to live up to the obligations that membership in a league would entail. His doubts on this score were probably cultivated by his English connections. British opinion remained skeptical about American membership in a league, doubtful that, given what seemed the all-consuming desire of the American people to avoid war, American membership in a league of nations would be meaningful.[78] Spring Rice warned Edward Grey that the American Congress could never be depended upon to execute a pledge to impose sanctions. He also took what he considered to be the incredibly weak American performance in Mexico as further proof that "this country is by no means ready to assume obligations in the future in Europe in connection with the Peace Treaty."[79]

Impressed by the extent of pacifist and isolationist sentiment among Midwestern Republicans, Lodge may also have revised his estimates of the probability of defeating Wilson or have had second thoughts about what Wilson might be able to do with the league idea while still in office. It was probably already apparent to him that the thrust of the Democratic campaign (what Arthur Link aptly calls the "Campaigns for Progressivism and Peace") was to forge a link between reform at home and a compromise peace abroad. Moreover, the league idea was becoming increasingly popular with those on the left (especially in Britain) who saw a panacea in either a super-state or in popular control of foreign policy and avoided the implication (so crucial in Lodge's view) that a league would have to be maintained by force of arms.[80] Wilson's views, at this point, seemed to be closer to that group than to those of the League to Enforce Peace. In the campaign Hughes, not the President, specifically endorsed the League to Enforce Peace and made the point, which Wilson avoided, that "our preparedness will have proper relation to this end."[81] Last but never least was the question of the relationship of the league to a European peace settlement. Wilson's acceptance of the league idea coupled with his refusal to be pinned down on particulars probably increased Lodge's fear that the league might be

78. Link, *Wilson: Campaigns for Progressivism and Peace*, pp. 35–36.
79. Gwynn, ed., *Letters of Spring Rice*, II, pp. 334–35, 339.
80. A. J. P. Taylor, *The Trouble Makers: Dissent over Foreign Policy* (Bloomington, 1958), p. 141; Stromberg, "The Riddle of Collective Security," pp. 151–52. See especially Henry R. Winkler, *The League of Nations Movement in Great Britain, 1914–1919* (New Brunswick, N.J., 1952).
81. Stromberg, "The Riddle of Collective Security," p. 152; Beerits Memorandum, "The Presidential Campaign of 1916," pp. 26–27, Hughes MSS.

used as a means of depriving the Allies of what Lodge regarded as their deserved victory. His fear was not without foundation. Indeed, Arthur Link has concluded that "all the evidence of Wilson's thinking since the summer of 1916 . . . leads to the conclusion that he believed that American interests, to say nothing of the interests of mankind, would be best served by a draw in Europe."[82] Under the weight of all these considerations, it can not be surprising that Lodge wanted to keep his options, and those of the Republican party, open.

Only if one appreciates the depth of feeling and moral fervor with which Lodge approached the campaign against Wilson can one comprehend how he was affected by its direction and outcome. He felt that "a great crisis" was at hand, one which would "determine whether we are a country or not."[83] Voting for Wilson was a form of moral degradation; Lodge declared himself "sick at heart to think that there are several millions of American citizens who will vote for Wilson,"—"the worst Presidency this country has ever had, and I do not except Buchanan."[84]

Feeling as Lodge did it was particularly galling to find that Wilson, except in his Mexican policy, was not vulnerable on the issues to which Lodge attached such importance.[85] In the crisis ensuing from Villa's raids into the United States Wilson was even forced to consult the Republican leadership in Congress, and Lodge, thinking of his 1914 performance, reported never having seen "such a spectacle of incompetency, insincerity and utter timidity."[86] Torn, in Lodge's words, "between fear of losing votes and fear of war," Wilson wanted "to do just enough [sending Pershing into Chihuahua in pursuit of Villa but limiting his range] to allay public feeling and avoid war."[87] He did just that

---

82. Link, *Wilson: Campaigns for Progressivism and Peace*, p. 411.

83. *Correspondence of Roosevelt and Lodge*, II, p. 484 (June 2, 1916).

84. Lodge to Roosevelt, July 10, 1916, Lodge MSS; Lodge to Roosevelt, July 15, 1916, Roosevelt MSS.

85. Link, *Wilson: Campaigns for Progressivism and Peace*, pp. 102–03; Lowry, "The Mexican Policy of Woodrow Wilson," p. 151.

86. Lodge to Corinne Roosevelt Robinson, July 2, 1916, Houghton Library, Harvard University. Lodge had always been close to Roosevelt's family. Perhaps unconsciously seeking in Corinne the support he had once received from Nannie, his correspondence with her became quite extensive after Nannie's death. Corinne, whose views were strong and close to those of her brother, seems not only to have supported Lodge's every move but often to have egged him on.

87. Lodge, *The Senate and the League*, p. 22. Lodge urged the Mexican issue on Hughes and, though he still stopped short of advocating war with Mexico, he placed all the blame for Villa's raids on the Administration, accusing it of creating

and succeeded in defusing the Mexican issue by making it appear that a solution was at hand, though this was still far from the case.[88]

However, the real problem was that the Republicans, try as they might, seemed always to end up on the defensive on the foreign policy issue. The war issue was predominant, and Wilson's forces pitched their campaign to the theme: "He kept us out of war." With the aid of posters depicting the carnage of war and buttons proclaiming "War in Europe, Peace in America—God Bless Wilson" (note the isolationist implication) the Democratic campaign developed a strong emotional appeal. The cry "he kept us out of war," however effective, was decidedly opportunistic and involved, insofar as Wilson himself used it, considerable self-deception, since the choice between war and peace (as events soon demonstrated) was no longer Wilson's to make. Wilson himself initially avoided it, only to declare in the heat of the campaign that "the certain prospect of the success of the Republican party is that we shall be drawn in one form or other into the embroilments of the European war."[89]

If the Democrats made it appear that peace had only to be willed to be obtained, the Republicans countered with an equally simplistic approach to the problem of the maintenance of national prestige and honor, likewise assuming that the will was father to the fact. Slogan countered slogan and innuendo matched innuendo. Few campaigns in American history have been as bitter and few have revealed a deeper division in the American body politic. If the Democrats regarded peace as the great underlying issue, Lodge thought it was the fact that "Wilson has failed in Americanism and patriotism" and was "shifty and cowardly in dealing with our foreign relations. . . ."[90]

---

this situation "by breeding contempt in the Mexican mind" (Lodge to Charles Evans Hughes, July 6, 1916, Lodge MSS).

88. Cline, *The United States and Mexico*, pp. 182–83.

89. Pusey, *Charles Evans Hughes*, I, pp. 356–58; Link, *Wilson: Campaigns for Progressivism and Peace*, p. 106. Pusey holds that the campaign was the more dishonest because Wilson actually knew that war with Germany was imminent and unavoidable (pp. 356–58). Link strongly disputes this contention (*Woodrow Wilson and the Progressive Era*, p. 238), but later concedes that in view of the desperate bids for victory being made on both sides the preservation of neutrality was "nearly impossible at best" (p. 255). See also Tumulty, *Woodrow Wilson As I Knew Him*, p. 159, who offers as an excuse for Wilson's inaction re Mexico his not wanting to get involved there since "it begins to look as if war with Germany is inevitable."

90. Lodge to James B. Reynolds, Oct. 20, 1916, Lodge MSS.

A crusade-like atmosphere attended both the "Campaigns for Progressivism and Peace" and Lodge's efforts to restore the "old American ideals." The possibility of the latter, Lodge felt, was directly contingent on the removal of Wilson from office. The country needed a man who would "restore the country to the position of high influence which it held under the administrations of McKinley and Roosevelt." Under the Wilson Administration American traditions had been abandoned, American ideals lowered, the American spirit dulled, and the national courage depressed. The President had wasted three years by his reluctance and hesitation on the preparedness issue, and could never seem to grasp that it was "possible to keep the peace with honor and dignity and without humiliation." There was a persistence of inherited traits in parties as well as in men, Lodge declared. The same forces that opposed Lincoln in 1864 were now rallying to Wilson, and this meant that "our character as a people, our respect abroad, and our self-respect" were all at stake. However, the analogy with 1864 was weak in one central respect and this proved Lodge's greatest obstacle in the campaign. It was also the reason he so frequently resorted to slogan and to the generalities of patriotism. He was forced to admit that, contrary to 1864, the life of the nation was not actually at stake. To say the opposite was to invite the charge of wanting to precipitate war, and it was precisely there that Republicans like Lodge were most vulnerable.[91]

No campaign speech was complete without the claim that Wilson was "killing the soul of the American people." The Administration's course in dealing with the grave questions presented by events in Mexico and the war in Europe, the Senator repeatedly emphasized, had "tended to loosen the fibres of the American conscience."[92] The question he continually put to his audiences was why "in the grave and critical situation produced by war in Europe we have utterly failed to exert any influence and we have vacillated and oscillated and paltered in dealing with every issue and every wrong until we have incurred the scarcely veiled contempt of all the nations of the earth." It was because the Ad-

---

91. Lodge's formal statement to the Boston *Evening Transcript* of his reasons for wanting to see Hughes elected, copy, Lodge MSS; clippings from the Boston *Herald* of August 20, 1916, and from the Kennebec (Me.) *Journal* of Sept. 7, 1916, enclosed with letters from Lodge to Corinne Roosevelt Robinson, Houghton Library, Harvard University; Boston *Herald*, Oct. 7, 8, 24, 28, 1916.
92. Lodge, *War Addresses*, p. 171.

ministration's foreign policy was ever shifting as a result of being based on what was likely to bring it the most votes at the next election, on the Pickwickian principle of shouting with the largest mob.[93] It was also because, and this was perhaps the greater evil, "the appeal of the Administration has been made, not to the highest ideals or to the best aspirations of the American people, but to the material desires of our nature."[94] The printed word is not really an adequate means of conveying the sense of outrage and the intensity of the moral fervor which marked Lodge's campaign against Wilson in 1916. But, short of being able to hear his actual voice, the following account of a speech before the Republican Club at Harvard comes closest to conveying the emotion with which he and many of his constituents viewed that election:

But the enthusiasm culminated only at the end of the address, when the Senator, with an impressive gesture, both hands uplifted, summoned the youth of Harvard to aid in "the first duty" of the people—"to restore the American spirit to power in this nation, to bring back fidelity to the old traditions, to make it clear to all the nations of the earth that what we would proclaim above all other things is not that we 'have kept the peace,' but that 'we have kept the faith.' "[95]

The by-product of a close campaign that each side feels it has to win is always a good deal of bitterness and acrimony. Wilson eventually came right out and accused the Republicans of wanting to get the country into the war.[96] Roosevelt, always a match for anyone in terms of extravagant language, and taking his cue from the name of Wilson's summer house, blamed Wilson personally for the American lives lost at sea and in Mexico: "Those are the shadows proper for Shadow

93. This was one of Lodge's favorite quotations. Usually employed in the context of the relationship between democracy and the conduct of foreign policy, he had, as we have seen, wielded it against the supporters of Taft's far-reaching arbitration treaties.

The charge is not without substance. The British certainly felt there was a relation between the forthcoming election and Wilson's "get tough" attitude toward Britain. Arthur Link (*Wilson: Campaigns for Progressivism and Peace*) is ambiguous on the subject. He writes of Wilson's "giving additional proof of his unwillingness to play politics with foreign policy" (p. 78), but cites evidence which indicates that political considerations were involved in both the stepped-up protests against British violations of neutral rights (p. 28) and in the decision to keep Pershing's troops in Mexico (p. 55).

94. Lodge, *War Addresses*, pp. 167–70.

95. *Boston Herald*, Oct. 24, 1916.

96. Pusey, *Hughes*, I, p. 355.

Lawn; the shadows of deeds that were never done; the shadows of lofty words that were followed by no action; the shadows of the tortured dead."[97]

There was also the issue of the postscript which in the closing days of the campaign Lodge accused Wilson of adding to the note dispatched to Germany in protest of the sinking of the *Lusitania*. Lodge had never understood why Bryan resigned only after the weaker second note, and in late October he had received information from reliable sources that the President, in order to mollify Bryan, had written a postscript [actually it was an accompanying press release] to the protest note which greatly softened the stand he purported to be taking, and had been deterred from this course only by threats of resignation within his Cabinet.[98] The details of the controversy are not important here, but it added tension to the campaign and a bitter personal element to the relationship between Lodge and Wilson. Wilson made what appeared to be a categorical denial of the charge but was actually only a clever evasion. Seizing on a technical inaccuracy in Lodge's indictment, he managed to convey the impression that it was totally false. Lodge knew better; he had a telegram from Lindley Garrison (Secretary of War at the time of the incident) assuring him that he (Lodge) had "stated the facts regarding the proposed postscript to the Lusitania note."[99] The effect of this is best summarized by Daniel Elletson, who writes: "Lodge knew that Wilson had prevaricated and Wilson knew that Lodge knew and this increased the feeling of hostility between the two men."[100] It was to Lodge but another in a long series of reasons why Wilson should be defeated. But Wilson, his honor impugned, chose to consider it a personal affront. He added a personal element to what was already a bitter political controversy by refusing an invitation to share a platform with Lodge on a ceremonial occasion—refusing "to join in any exercise in which he takes part or to associate myself with him in any way"—and by excluding Lodge from a diplo-

97. Quoted in Elletson, *Roosevelt and Wilson*, p. 133.
98. Lodge to Henry White, June 12, 1915, White MSS. The contretemps is covered in detail in Link, *Wilson: Campaigns for Progressivism and Peace*, pp. 145–48; and in Garraty, *Lodge*, pp. 329–332; and the revealing correspondence between Wilson and Bryan can be found in *Papers Relating to the Foreign Relations of the United States: The Lansing Papers, 1914–1920*, I, pp. 400–404.
99. Telegram from Garrison to Lodge, Nov. 5, 1916, Lodge MSS.
100. Elletson, *Roosevelt and Wilson*, p. 134.

matic function in which, by virtue of his rank on the Foreign Relations Committee, he ought to have been included.[101]

But that was nothing to Lodge compared with Wilson's electoral victory. He took Wilson's success hard, and the fact that he survived his own first popular election and thereby retained his Senate seat was but small consolation.[102] James Ford Rhodes found both Lodge and Roosevelt "grievously disappointed at the result" and "bitterly critical" of Wilson whom they accused of having made us "a nation of cowards."[103] Lodge considered the reelection of Wilson a "calamity," but even worse, in his opinion, was the nature of the vote that turned the scale and what this revealed about the character of the American people:

The vote that turned the scale was cast by Republicans—the native American unchanging Republicans, chiefly of the country towns, supplemented by the Scandinavian Republicans of the Northwest. They went over to Wilson on the one cry that he kept us out of war, which was not only false but was a sordid and base appeal. The men who of all others were thought to be strongest in Americanism proved to be the weakest. . . . [They] had so far degenerated that they left the party, which they had never deserted before, because some of the leaders of that party appealed strongly to American traditions and demanded the protection of American rights. It causes one to have very gloomy thoughts about the future.

His mood was in fact so dark that he told Lord Bryce that "the depression caused to me by the nature of this deciding vote . . . will always endure."[104]

IV

In this mood Lodge was confronted with Wilson's proposals for a "peace without victory" and for a league of nations constructed on that basis. If "Wilson's victory proved that he had successfully fused 'the

101. Link, *Wilson: Campaigns for Progressivism and Peace*, pp. 147–48.

102. His opponent, John F. ("Honey Fitz") Fitzgerald was not regarded as a strong candidate, and though Lodge won handily, his margin of victory (about 30,000 votes) was not as large as many observers had anticipated. Lodge thought he might have doubled his majority if he had "refused to take the only line which I thought worth taking, a strong one against Wilson and his foreign policy and indifference to American rights" (Lodge to Lord Bryce, Dec. 21, 1916, Lodge MSS).

103. M. A. DeWolfe Howe, *James Ford Rhodes: American Historian* (New York, 1929), pp. 273–74.

104. Lodge to Lord Bryce, Dec. 21, 1916, and to Trevelyan, Dec. 23, 1916, Lodge MSS.

peace cause with the ideal of progressive democracy,'" that was for Lodge all the more reason to be suspicious.[105] Hard on the heels of his victory, Wilson did what Lodge had for some time feared and expected, he put out his "Peace Note," a major effort to effect a negotiated settlement of the European conflict.[106] That initiative, coming as it did on the heels of a similar German proposal, was received in Nahant in much the same spirit as in London and Paris. Lodge had all along believed there could be no peace worth having in Europe "unless the Allies win a decisive victory."[107] Moreover, he had come to share the view of Wilson, and the fears and suspicions that accompanied it, that was prevalent in British governmental circles, the feeling that Wilson was a man of weak and indecisive character who could not be relied upon.[108] This feeling frequently had a bitter edge to it. Spring Rice, in commenting on Wilson's course, quipped that: "the Good Samaritan did not pass by on the other side, and then propose to the authorities at Jericho a bill for the better security of the highroads."[109] More somber was a letter dated December 5, 1916 from P. H. Kerr (an associate of Lord Milner's who was about to become private secretary to Lloyd George) to Sir Horace Plunkett, of which Lodge received a copy:

> The war in Europe is fundamentally a struggle between brute force—militarism—and the very imperfect idea of world law—public right—which is already in existence. . . . We must prove that right and liberty are stronger than might *in this war*. . . . If, therefore, America attempts to act as peacemaker except from the starting point that France, Belgium and Serbia are to be restored and in some way compensated, she is fighting the battle of militarism against public right. . . .
> You know also that I feel that America is now in danger of becoming an enemy to freedom in Europe only second to Germany itself. . . . the fact that

105. Arno J. Mayer, *Political Origins of the New Diplomacy, 1917–1918* (New York, 1969), p. 346.

106. On Oct. 10, 1916, Lodge wrote: "I think, and I have some inside information, that Wilson is planning to play as his last card the offer of mediation in Europe and that he will ask for an armistice while the proposition is being considered; he is working, of course, in the interests of Germany but chiefly to elect himself" (Lodge to James B. Reynolds, Lodge MSS).

107. Lodge to Roosevelt, Jan. 26, 1917, Lodge MSS.

108. Link, *President Wilson and His English Critics*, p. 7.

109. Gwynn, ed., *Letters of Spring Rice*, II, p. 347. A more widely quoted variation on the same theme is Trevelyan's remark that Wilson "is surely the quintessence of a prig. What a notion that the nations of Europe, after this terrible effort, will join him in putting down international encroachments by arms, at some future time, if he is afraid to denounce such encroachments even in words now!" (quoted in Link, *Wilson: Campaigns for Progressivism and Peace*, p. 273).

she has failed to recognize officially that there is a moral issue in the war, makes it possible that she will be driven to suggest peace terms which would in effect involve the partial triumph of the militarist evil, on the humanitarian plea of saving life.[110]

Against this background Wilson issued his famous "Peace Note" asking the belligerents to state their terms and declaring, in an attempt to establish a basis for an accommodation, that "the objects, which the statesmen of the belligerents on both sides have in mind in this war, are virtually the same, as stated in general terms to their own people and to the world." Among these shared objects were that "each side desires to make the rights and privileges of weak peoples and small States . . . secure against aggression" (which in view of Germany's treatment of Belgium was going rather far) and that "each is ready to consider the formation of a league of nations to insure peace and justice throughout the world."[111] The full exposition of what Wilson had in mind did not come until his "Peace Without Victory" address to the Senate on January 22, but what the President seemed to be trying to do (and this came as no surprise to Lodge) "was to marry the concept of a liberal settlement to the plan for a league of nations."[112]

However, there are problems pursuant to designating a peace such as Wilson might have been able to arrange a "liberal" settlement. What may have seemed "liberal" to Americans may have appeared quite "illiberal" to Belgians and Frenchmen. In view of what Fritz Fischer has revealed about German war aims, is it not possible that a peace which would have satisfied the American progressive's criteria (interested as he was in peace per se) might, from a European point of view, have been inherently "unprogressive."[113] The application of such terms to a prospective international order can only breed confusion. What to some may have appeared a "liberal" compromise settlement may have been

110. The copy was an enclosure to Robert Grant to Lodge, Dec. 19, 1916, Lodge MSS. Grant reported that Kerr had "sent this to Sir Horace as he was starting for America with the object of having him show it to Wilson." My purpose in introducing Kerr's letter is not to suggest that Lodge was directly influenced by it (his own course was set some time before Grant's letter could have arrived), but rather to show the circles in England with whom Lodge was in contact and how closely his views coincided with theirs.

111. Ray Stannard Baker and William E. Dodd, eds., *The Public Papers of Woodrow Wilson* (New York, 1925–1927), IV, p. 404.

112. Link, *The Higher Realism of Woodrow Wilson*, p. 106.

113. *Germany's War Aims in the First World War* (New York, 1967).

viewed by others as a return to the balance-of-power system and therefore an eminently "conservative" settlement.

Lodge's reaction was quick and vehement. Wilson's peace note was
published on the morning of December 21. That same day Lodge wrote
to Roosevelt expressing his regret that he had gotten mixed up with the
League to Enforce Peace and declaring that he had "become perfectly
dissatisfied with it." At the same time he denounced the President's
peace note and thought it proof that Wilson was working hand in glove
with the Germans to save them from deserved punishment by the
Allies.[114] He also despatched a warning to England: "I sincerely trust
that the Allies will not be deluded into accepting him in any capacity
as mediator or peacemaker; it would be a fatal mistake."[115] Neither the
domestic nor the foreign political consequences (linked by Wilson in his
"Campaigns for Progressivism and Peace") of a successful Wilsonian
peace initiative were easy for Lodge to contemplate. Germany's peace
note had been a "cry of distress" and an "effort to obtain peace at a
moment most favorable to her," and now Wilson, thinking only of his
own political future, had come out with this demand for peace, a move
"distinctly hostile to the Allies" and "timed in such a way as to help
Germany in her proposal." The Allies should understand that Wilson
was not a disinterested party but a man with his own ends to serve, a
man who would betray them in a moment.[116]

All this had an important bearing on the league question. Apart from
the emphasis Wilson had placed upon it in his peace note, Lodge knew
from Lowell that Wilson was now "very much in earnest about the
League" and that Colonel House had suggested that the Senate's attitude be sounded.[117] Two months earlier Lodge's attitude had been the
characteristic one of reserve and skepticism, but Wilson's peace initiative converted it overnight into one of fear and loathing.[118] The change

114. Lodge to Roosevelt, Dec. 21, 1916, Roosevelt MSS.
115. Lodge to Lord Bryce, Dec. 21, 1916, Lodge MSS.
116. Lodge to Trevelyan, Dec. 23, 1916, Lodge MSS.
117. Lowell to Lodge, Dec. 20, 1916, League to Enforce Peace MSS.
118. On October 4 Lodge had given this assessment to Lord Bryce: "Certainly
the outlook for the relations of the different nations with each other after peace
comes is very dark. Nothing is more painful than the retrogression in all that concerns international law and the practices that have been slowly and painfully
adopted for making war less terrible. . . . What can be done with the league for
peace in the future I do not know. We must try our best, of course, when the times

is apparent in a series of letters to Lowell who, not easily put off, was now pressing Lodge for a decision. On December 22 Lodge told him that his feeling that it was unwise to press the League at the present time was strengthened because it had gotten mixed up in the public mind with the idea that we were trying to make peace now, a misunderstanding which Wilson's peace note had encouraged. On the 28th he advised Lowell that he thought the League movement was now "doing rather more harm than good" and that nothing further ought to be done about it until after the war. The issue was not so much the League's particular program, but what Wilson might do with an idea which had such innate popular appeal.

Crucial, then, were Wilson's motives in advancing his peace note and these Lodge now deemed to have been twofold: "first, to get himself into the position of mediator for his own glory and, second, to avoid the danger of a renewal of the submarine warfare."[119] The latter soon emerged as the more compelling reason as Lodge began to see in Wilson signs of "a state of fear as to what an extension of the submarine warfare may bring." As a result of that fear, Lodge concluded, Wilson was "very anxious for peace now at any price and on any terms"; he doesn't "care a particle how the war ends as long as it ends and he has a hand in the peace."[120] Lodge never expected Wilson to succeed, but revealing of his state of mind at this juncture, just after Wilson's electoral victory, is the fact that he did not expect the American people to take exception to Wilson's scheme.[121] He put his faith not in the

---

comes [sic] but the obstacles, as you point out, are enormous" (letter in the Lodge MSS).

119. Lodge to Lowell, Dec. 22 and 28, 1916, League to Enforce Peace MSS. Elihu Root also believed that Wilson's real purpose in the peace note "was to try to force peace upon the allies, so as to keep us out of trouble with Germany, . . . a contemptible position" (Diary of Chandler Anderson, Feb. 2, 1917, Anderson Papers, Library of Congress).

120. Lodge to Robert Grant, Jr., Jan. [6?], 1917, Lodge MSS.

121. The state of mind of Lodge's coterie on this subject is perhaps best summarized by Brooks Adams who declared: ". . . I have little doubt that Wilson represents pretty fairly the opinions of the bulk of the American people. They will support anything which promises, in their opinion, to keep them out of immediate trouble and spare them an effort" (Brooks Adams to Lodge, Jan. 16, 1917, Lodge MSS). Note also the bitterness and pessimism which marked Lodge's remarks on the occasion of the celebration of the 100th anniversary of St. John's Church in Washington, D.C. on Jan. 13, 1917: "If we take no inspiration from the memories in which we glory, if we neglect their teachings and are content with lower and more sordid levels, then, when we come into the presence of the past, instead of raising our voices in idle acclaim it would be more honest to avoid

American people, but rather in the idealism and fighting spirit of the Allies. "The President," Lodge felt, did "not understand one great condition of his problem: he cannot comprehend that the people of England, France and Russia had rather die than submit to Germany; he is unable to grasp the fact that for certain things men had rather suffer and die than accept prosperity and comfort at the price of a degrading peace." His optimism on this score was the more pronounced as he had reason to believe (probably from conversations with Spring Rice) that the Allies would "firmly but politely refuse to have anything to do with Wilson's peace initiative."[122]

The opposition of Lodge and Roosevelt, and of many prominent Republicans, to Wilson's plans for peace was nurtured in these anxious days when they feared that he might somehow be able to snatch victory from the Allies. The means Roosevelt and Lodge now chose to thwart Wilson's plans were in keeping with the complementary but different roles they had played all along in the effort to get the country to prepare and to take a more pro-Allied position. Reflecting no real difference in opinion but a natural and tactically sound division of labor, Roosevelt came forth with a blistering attack on the league idea, while Lodge carefully maneuvered to create a Congressional obstacle to Wilson's plans. Roosevelt called the leaders of the League to Enforce Peace "dupes" of Germany and implied that the league movement had Germany's support because it was linked to a peace advantageous to that country.[123] Taking for the first time a public stand in direct opposition to the League to Enforce Peace, Roosevelt declared his intention to fight the League's proposals:

Because under existing conditions, and at this time, and in view of past performances of most of the leaders of the movement, and especially in view of the actions of our Government and people during the last two and a half years, the agitation or adoption of the proposals would be either futile or mischievous.[124]

---

speech and rhetoric, to avert our gaze and pass on, free at least from the hypocrisy of lauding the honor and the glories of the past which we, by our indifference to their teachings and by our failure to sustain them, neither desire nor deserve" (Lodge, *War Addresses*, p. 242).

122. Lodge to Lowell, Dec. 28, 1916, League to Enforce Peace MSS.

123. Actually such a charge was without justification. Taft was embarrassed by the link which Wilson was attempting to forge between the league idea and peace without victory, for he too felt there could be no just peace without an Allied victory (Pringle, *Taft*, I, p. 934).

124. *New York Times*, Jan. 2, 1917. *The New Republic*, in language that was to

Lodge's opportunity came when Wilson sought Congressional endorsement of his peace note. Fearing the ends which Wilson's intervention might serve, Lodge now sought refuge in America's traditional policies. Lodge and Wilson both recognized the appeal of traditional isolationism, and neither of them seems to have hesitated to exploit it when it suited their purposes. Lodge was not willing to admit that "as the war now stands" the U.S., a nonbelligerent, had any national or legal concern in the terms of peace. Now wanting the country to be as neutral in entering upon negotiations of peace as during the operations of war, he declared his unwillingness "to have myself placed by my vote in the attitude of trying to help one side in the negotiations of peace against the other; and particularly I do not want to be ranged against the side which I personally believe is fighting the battle of freedom and democracy as against military autocracy." He also objected to the fact that portions of the peace note (those relating to the league) were concerned not with peace but with the future policy of the United States. Admitting that such a league was the only way to go beyond voluntary arbitration and declining to attack such a proposal on its merits, he nevertheless considered the abandonment of the country's historic policy (hemispherism and nonalliance) "a question of very great moment" and cautioned that "whatever we do in that direction, if anything is possible—which I very much doubt—must be done with the utmost care." That could be left to the future; Lodge had a more immediate objective and that came through clearly in his summary statement: "Above all nothing of the sort should be urged or pressed now before the conclusion of the present war."[125]

The ensuing debate was like a dress rehearsal for the later battle over the league plan Wilson formulated in Paris. The battle lines and the division of forces were in 1917 much the same as they were to be

become stock and trade for Wilsonians, thereupon charged that "this revolution in his [Roosevelt's] own opinions raises questions of consistency, of personal good faith and of readiness to act upon his own words much more substantial than those which he raises against the friends of a peace league." That is a debatable proposition and there is much to be said on both sides. But *The New Republic*, too intent on advocacy of a league to want to clarify the matter, then retreated to the remarkable generality that "the object which Mr. Roosevelt was trying to accomplish in 1915 is the same as that which Mr. Wilson is trying to accomplish in 1917" (*The New Republic*, 9 [Jan. 13, 1917]: 281–82). Their objects in advocating a league were never even remotely the same!

125. Lodge, "The Peace Note of the President, Speech Delivered in the Senate, Jan. 3, 1917," *War Addresses*, pp. 199, 204–05, 214–15.

two years later. Just as would be the case in 1919, Republican isolationists and Republican internationalists, though wishing to serve opposite ends, were able to agree on tactics. Borah sought to reaffirm traditional American isolationism and noninvolvement in European affairs per se, while Lodge was willing to see that traditional posture temporarily reaffirmed as a means of preventing a type of internationalism which to his mind was derogatory of the national interest and conducive to the imposition of a settlement which would deprive the Allies of victory.[126] So bitter was the opposition to giving a blanket endorsement to Wilson's peace initiative that the Democrats were forced to delete all reference to a league from the resolution approving of Wilson's note. Even then there were only 48 votes in favor, with 17 negative votes (Lodge's among them) and 31 abstentions.[127] In the words of one historian of the struggle over the league: "the fight for . . . the type league Wilson felt essential . . . was largely lost before he committed any of his celebrated 'mistakes' of 1918."[128]

Wilson, thus thwarted in his efforts to secure an open-ended endorsement of his plans for a league and fearing that resumption of submarine warfare was imminent, hastened to flesh out his plan for peace in an effort to recapture control over the events which now seemed to be so rapidly slipping away from him. Addressing the Senate on January 22, Wilson made perfectly clear what till then Lodge had only suspected, that as Wilson conceived it American participation in a league was to be dependent upon there being a "peace without victory":

. . . but we owe it to candor and to a just regard for the opinion of mankind to say that, so far as our participation in guarantees of future peace is concerned, it makes a great deal of difference in what way and upon what terms it is ended; the treaties and agreements which bring it to an end must

126. Cooper (*The Vanity of Power*, pp. 142–44, 154) is particularly good on, and sensitive to, the differences between the forces commanded by Borah and those who followed Lodge.

127. *Cong. Record*, 64th Cong., 2nd sess., 1917, pp. 736–37, 791–97, 892–97. The resolution as finally approved read: "Resolved, That the Senate approves and strongly endorses the request by the President in the diplomatic notes of December 18 to the nations now engaged in war that those nations state the terms upon which peace might be discussed." Lodge favored the substitute offered by Sen. Gallinger (Republican from New Hampshire): "Resolved, That the Senate of the United States in the interests of humanity and civilization expresses the sincere hope that a just and permanent peace between the warring nations of Europe may be consummated at an early day, and approves all proper efforts to secure that end."

128. Vinson, *Referendum for Isolation*, p. 35.

embody terms which will create a peace that is worth guaranteeing and preserving, a peace that will win the approval of mankind. . . .[129]

Lodge's conception of the ends to be served by American participation in a league was totally different. It was perhaps most succinctly expressed by Trevelyan who upon American entry into the war proclaimed that "the League of Peace is formed."[130] But the league Wilson now proposed was to be based on an indecisive outcome (when, according to Lodge, Europe's longest period of peace had come only after the complete Allied victory at Waterloo) and on a denial that a moral issue had ever been at stake in the war. In retrospect it is tempting to say that the League of Nations would have worked better on the basis of a "peace without victory" than in association with the Peace of Versailles. But the matter is a complicated one. Would, for example, such a league, erected after two and a half years of war, and based on what Germany was then willing to accept in terms of a settlement, ever have had any moral authority in England, France, or Belgium?[131] Moreover, if U.S. membership in a league was no longer to be a means of associating the U.S. with the Allies might it not, following Wilson's logic, have led to some sort of association with the Central Powers? This fear lurked behind the question Lodge posed to the Senate: "If peace without victory is to be a condition precedent of lasting peace to be maintained by the covenant in which we are to take part, how are we practically to compel or secure the existence of such a condition?"[132]

Lodge's primary concern was now, as in May of 1916, to prevent the proposal for a league from interfering with Allied prosecution of the war against Germany. As Warren Kuehl writes, he "cooled toward that organization [the League to Enforce Peace] when he thought it had become enmeshed in efforts to end the war through mediation, an unthinkable act in light of Lodge's belief that German autocracy had to be destroyed." But even Kuehl then goes on to state that Lodge "while not fully abandoning the ideal of a league . . . certainly qualified what had once been an endorsement."[133] Unlike many of Lodge's critics

---

129. Baker and Dodd, eds., *The Public Papers of Woodrow Wilson*, IV, pp. 408–09.

130. Trevelyan to Lodge, April 7, 1917, Lodge MSS.

131. Fischer, *Germany's War Aims*, pp. 280–84.

132. Lodge, *War Addresses*, pp. 252–53.

133. *Seeking World Order*, pp. 221–22. The historiographical trend has been all in the direction of recognizing, as I have attempted to show, that Lodge's attitude

Kuehl does not confuse endorsement of the League to Enforce Peace with endorsement of other and very different league ideas. His treatment is remarkably even handed, but even he forgets that Lodge had

---

on the League was affected by a wide range of public policy considerations (its relation to the preparedness movement, to cooperation with the Allies, and to what he considered a proper conclusion of the war). See, for example, Kuehl, *Seeking World Order*; Cooper, *The Vanity of Power*; and Osgood, *Ideals and Self-Interest*. The more traditional interpretations stressed Lodge's inconsistency on the question of a league and in assessing reasons therefore could never get much beyond the animosity which Lodge developed toward Wilson. For example, Thomas Bailey (*Woodrow Wilson and the Lost Peace*, p. 99), drawing no distinction between the League to Enforce Peace and the idea of a league of nations, once wrote that "Lodge had openly and enthusiastically supported the idea of the League of Nations before Wilson took it up, and when Wilson came out in favor of it, Lodge somersaulted over into the opposition camp." This is the more surprising as elsewhere Bailey admits the soundness of many of the criticisms voiced against Wilson's conception of a league. Even Lodge's biographer, John Garraty (*Lodge*, p. 346) reiterated the charge that "Wilson's warm support of the league idea helped prejudice Lodge against it." That is true enough if placed in the proper context. But Garraty ignores the fact that Lodge's opposition to the league idea in the winter of 1916–17 grew out of a fear that it might be used to deprive the Allies of victory and therefore leaves the impression that Lodge was governed by his personal feelings .

In the face of this trend toward an improved understanding of Lodge one recent article (David Mervin, "Henry Cabot Lodge and the League of Nations," *Journal of American Studies* 4 [Feb. 1971]: 201–14) reads almost like the speeches of those Wilsonian partisans who in 1919 thought the best defense of a league was to avoid the many difficult questions (both of policy and philosophy) inherent in its operation and to attack the opposition for its inconsistency and for allowing personal and political hatreds to intrude into questions of public policy. Making no distinction among the various league plans, and neglecting the possibility that Lodge could have had legitimate policy objections to both the timing and the nature of the league Wilson had in mind, Mervin claims that "at some time in the eight months between the end of May 1916 and the end of January 1917, Lodge swung violently from a public and apparently total commitment to *the league suggestion* [italics mine] to the strongly hostile position he took up in the Senate on 1 February 1917" (p. 203). He then goes on (p. 204) to identify Lodge's change of mind as "the first of a series of shrewd tactical manoeuvres aimed at preventing Wilson from emerging as 'the maker of peace,' and reaping the enormous electoral benefits that would surely follow from this." According to Mervin, personal hatred of Wilson and a preoccupation with partisan advantage were Lodge's sole considerations. In its own way, and especially in its failure to recognize that the relationship between personal and partisan feelings and the larger issues of public policy is by no means a simple cause and effect progression, Mervin's assessment is as simplistic as Lodge's own disclaimer (*The Senate and the League*, p. 23): "I never had the slightest personal hostility to Mr. Wilson; . . . my opposition . . . in connection with the war and the League rested entirely on public grounds." Surely a public man and his policies are not so readily separable (and less so in the case of a man like Wilson who, like Lodge himself, tried to create the impression that policy was a function of character). While there is always something to be gained by a reexamination of political rhetoric (in this case the charges of Wilson's most partisan supporters), surely that rhetoric is as revealing in what it does *not* say, as in the impressions which it endeavors to create.

attached an important qualification to his original endorsement. As Lodge now told Lowell in severing his last ties with the League to Enforce Peace:

Two years ago [sic] I was strongly inclined to think that we could do something in the direction of the League to Enforce Peace and I spoke to your meeting in Washington. I then uttered a warning against mixing up the League with the peace which is to end this war. Since then the League has become involved in one way or another in the popular mind, and now definitely by the President's action, with the peace which is to end the present war. To me this is most unfortunate and so far as I am concerned I do not feel that the League any longer represents my opinion. Moreover, the more I have considered the question and particularly since the utterances of the President in his address, I am forced to the conclusion that the League for Peace, as he proposes it, would be a very dangerous thing for this country or any other to enter into. I think that instead of promoting peace it would tend to breed war and would create a very perilous situation. I am not willing at this time, with the war in Europe still raging, to commit the country blindly and in the dark to general propositions when the essential points are in the details and the terms of the treaties, of which at this moment we know nothing.[134]

The idea of collective security raised substantial political and philosophical problems, problems which to this day have not been successfully resolved. Roland Stromberg once suggested the need for a new perspective on the struggle over the League; he thought "a better thesis may be that the idea of collective security, being faulty or at least terribly elusive, was the real villain of this famous drama."[135] Lodge's reply to Wilson's fervid appeal for support for the league idea was neither a partisan diatribe nor a personal attack on Wilson, but rather a searching, philosophical speech based on the proposition that "this is a matter which cannot be determined by verbal adherence to a general principle; everything here depends on the details." Unfortunately, it was a speech which was quickly overshadowed by events, lost in the excitement over

134. Lodge to Lowell, Jan. 30, 1917, League to Enforce Peace MSS. Lodge also wrote to Taft just after the President's speech, backing off from an invitation to speak together with Taft at Lynn by declaring: "I will say frankly, however, that the League to Enforce Peace has been involved in such a way with the peace which is to end the present war (a danger which I foresaw) that I think I should be out of place as a speaker, for I do not at all favor the use which the President has made of it and I do not think it ought to be mixed up in any way with the conclusion of the war in Europe" (Lodge to Taft, Jan. 23, 1917, Taft MSS).

135. "The Riddle of Collective Security, 1916–1920," in Anderson, ed., *Issues and Conflicts: Studies in Twentieth Century American Diplomacy*, p. 148.

the German note announcing a renewal of submarine warfare. It is indicative, however, of the importance Lodge attached to it, that he decided to give it even in the face of now radically changed circumstances.

It is a speech replete with questions, many of which the advocates of a league could not then, and never really tried to, answer. Lodge was particularly concerned to uncover the conditions which Wilson regarded as precedent to a lasting peace. Wilson had stated that peace could only rest upon universal acceptance of the idea that governments derive all their just powers from the consent of the governed, and Lodge asked the practical question "who is to decide whether the principle is recognized under the different governments of the world with whom we are to form the League of Peace? . . ." Wilson said any peace must rest on the freedom of the seas, and Lodge asked whether he intended to do away with the established rights of belligerents in wartime. Lodge agreed with Wilson that only "by a league for peace behind which is the organized major force of mankind" could the world advance beyond voluntary arbitration. But troubled by the ambiguity of that phrase, Lodge insisted there was no half-way house; such a league would either be a voluntary association or rest on force. Pointing out that "you cannot make effective a league for peace . . . by language or high sounding phrases," that "the forces of the league must consist of an army and navy," he went on to raise the important question of the size and command structure of such an international force. He sensed that Wilson was not prepared to grapple with the more difficult questions attendant to American participation in a collective security organization and, reflecting the deep pessimism which had settled on him as a result of the election, he now had grave doubts as to whether the American people ("a people altogether too prone to be satisfied with words") would even ask them. In a prophetic statement, he declared that he could

hear already the clamor of those who have been shrieking for peace at any price and denouncing all armaments, rising around us with the passionate demand that we shall immediately join a league for peace, about the details of which they neither know nor care, but which will compel the establishment of large naval and military forces and which may bring us into war in any quarter of the globe at any moment at the bidding of other nations.

Under these circumstances Lodge retreated to the conventional wisdom of the standpatters—"to bear the ills we have" rather "than fly to others we know not of." In such a "tortured and distracted world" he now saw "nothing but peril in abandoning our long and well-established policies." Several things *could* be done to promote peace: "the protection of our own peace against foreign attack," and "the rehabilitation and re-establishment of international law" among them. But Lodge closed with a warning for those he felt would be tempted by a peace advantageous to Germany: "We cannot secure our own safety or build up the lasting peace of the world upon peace at any price; the peace of the world, to be enduring, must be based on righteousness at any cost."[136] To any but the undiscerning, that could only have meant that he felt strongly that a legitimate and morally compelling international order could only be constructed on the basis of an Allied victory. It was a conviction that American entry into the war would fortify.

Lodge's speech was shunted to the back pages by the German announcement of renewal of submarine warfare, but Wilson—his own peace plans now shattered—also found himself in the grip of events. To Lodge this brought considerable consolation. As he told Trevelyan, "I have been haunted for months with the horrible fear that he would end by blundering us into the war on the German side; that danger at least is passed." The breaking of relations with Germany was an irrevocable act; Wilson was "now in the power of events, and a great gain has been made."[137] Lodge played an important role in getting the Senate to sustain the President in breaking with Germany, but he remained content to "cross the other bridges as we come to them."[138] His confidence came from the fact (not unrelated to his own and Roosevelt's efforts) that each succeeding crisis had seen American (and Wilson's own) prestige ever more deeply committed. As Daniel Smith so aptly put it: "the submarine issue had become a symbol of Wilson's [and America's] dedication to uphold international law and the rights of humanity."[139] Lodge's long campaign to make the American people see that their prestige and honor were at stake in the war was at last bearing fruit.

The Senator's new-found optimism had its base, however, in the logic of events and in his assessment of German intentions, not in any

136. Lodge, "The President's Plan for A World Peace, Speech Delivered in the Senate, Feb. 1, 1917," *War Addresses*, pp. 247–71.
137. Lodge to Trevelyan, Feb. 5, 1917, Lodge MSS.
138. Lodge to Wintie Chanler, Feb. 8, 1917, Lodge MSS.
139. "National Interest and American Intervention, 1917: An Historiographical Appraisal," p. 23.

reassessment of Wilson or of his hold on the American people.[140] Lodge definitely did not share the opinions of those who, after the break, thought the President would have the nation at war in a few days. He claimed to know his Wilson too well to be so misled:

Germany compelled Wilson to break with Germany, and he would not have done it if he possibly could have helped. . . . It all depends on Germany. If she adheres to her order—as I think she must—he will be obliged first to allow our merchantmen to arm. . . . If England breaks down this new attack there may be no sufficiently flagrant case of the destruction of an American ship and American lives to compel war. He may escape it. I think it is not improbable. His one desire is to avoid war at any cost, simply because he is afraid.

Germany forced Wilson to break and I think she is very likely to force him into war, but he will suffer pretty much anything before that happens.[141]

Lodge's estimate of Wilson's intentions and motivations at this point, however harsh, and however lacking in understanding of Wilson's problems and responsibilities, is, nevertheless, not without some foundation. Arthur Link believes that "at no time during this critical period did the President recognize the necessity for American intervention on idealistic grounds or because such intervention was necessary to protect the security of the United States; indeed, had he been a free agent he would probably have adhered to the course of armed neutrality. . . ."[142] But he was no longer a free agent. If only moral and economic considerations had been involved, he could probably have accepted ruthless submarine warfare, but in the background lay always the matter of the nation's honor and the not unrelated question of the prestige of his own Administration, and these now served to block his retreat.[143] This Lodge sensed and exploited mercilessly. As he told Roosevelt, "I am trying to do my best to bring about the situation that ought to exist, to rouse this country against Germany and force the President forward"; "he is in the grip of events and I want to drive

140. See, for example, Lodge to Henry Higginson, Feb. 2 and 10, 1917 (Lodge MSS), letters in which he predicted that Wilson's response would be no more than to write another solemn note.

141. Lodge to Roosevelt, Feb. 13 and 22, 1917, Lodge MSS. From their point of view it would seem that a better case could have been made for Wilson's political timidity rather than for his physical timidity, but it suited their prejudices to believe that Wilson's reluctance to go to war was somehow the result of physical cowardice.

142. *Woodrow Wilson and the Progressive Era*, pp. 277–78.

143. See especially May, *The World War and American Isolation*, p. 158.

him forward as far as I can."[144] Lodge determined to keep Congress in session, insisted on giving Wilson the power to arm American merchantmen, and was in the end successful, not so much from the force of his own efforts but because he had an ally in Germany. The Zimmermann telegram was by his own confession "of almost unlimited use in forcing the situation." He put in a resolution of inquiry which required either a Presidential authentication or denial of the Zimmermann telegram, and in so tying it to Wilson he was convinced that he "helped to alienate the Country from Germany and separate the President from Germany."[145]

To the end Lodge feared that Wilson would avoid war if he possibly could. In contrast he himself began to feel that going to war "would be our salvation."[146] That statement was not without political implications. Lodge regarded the Republican party as the nation's "fighting party," but his interests and values were by no means so narrow as to give full credence to such an interpretation.[147] What he meant thereby (and what is indicative of the spirit in which he approached the war) emerges clearly in his speech supporting Wilson's request for a declaration of war:

. . . there are, in my opinion, some things worse for a nation than war. National degeneracy is worse; national cowardice is worse. The division of our people into race groups, striving to direct the course of the United States in the interest of some other country when we should have but one allegiance, one hope, and one tradition, is far worse. All these dangers have been gathering about us and darkening the horizon during the last three years. Whatever suffering and misery war may bring, it will at least sweep these foul things away.[148]

While it is clear that he approached the impending hostilities with a sense of relief, it is not so easy to resolve the question of how long he

144. Lodge to Roosevelt, March 2, 1917, Lodge MSS.
145. *Ibid.*
146. Lodge to William Sturgis Bigelow, March 27, 1917, Lodge MSS.
147. Lodge to Roosevelt, March 20, 1917, Lodge MSS.
148. Lodge, *War Addresses*, p. 301. Lodge understood only too well how difficult a problem foreign policy was for the United States. The problem of the conduct of foreign policy in a democracy (bad enough from his point of view) was made the more intractable by the tendency of the body politic to divide into race groups "striving to direct the course of the United States in the interest of some other country" to which they owed at least an emotional allegiance. What Lodge did not, of course, admit was that his own view of the war (and that of so many of his New England constituents) was also subject to the influence of ethnic and cultural heritage.

had been working toward that end. At what point did his efforts to get the United States to align itself more closely with the Allies slip over into an effort to involve the U.S. in the war on their side? After the fact he told Trevelyan:

I have long been working toward this end and I am glad it has come, not merely because I think the future peace and safety and national character of my own country depend upon our going to war, but because I think it would be an eternal disgrace if our country did not join with those who are fighting the battle to preserve human freedom, popular government and modern civilization.

. . . nothing could be more satisfying than to have you realize what a joy it was to me finally to reach the end for which I have been laboring for almost three years. It looked at times so hopeless; I was obliged to move so cautiously at the beginning, but as I look back even the shortest step was in the right direction.[149]

However, as late as the 15th of February, he had written to the same correspondent that "if (as I hope and pray) England is so successful against the submarines that this last assault breaks down and there comes another period of quiet, as there has twice before, war may be avoided."[150] Now, as if to demonstrate that he had never entertained such thoughts, he published his *War Addresses* which, in covering the period from January 1915 to April 1917, seemed to say that Lodge himself had been at war for some time. His purpose was "to show my record for these two years and how I had been working steadily for the end which has come."[151] The claim deserves to be treated with skepticism because Lodge, unlike Roosevelt, was not really attracted by war per se, because he placed great store in the preservation of national unity, and because he had long thought that the objects to which he was devoted (an Allied victory and the maintenance of American prestige) could be achieved without resort to war. Still there is a discernible pattern in his *War Addresses*. From those pages rises the image of a man with an acute tactical sense engaged in an effort to move Wilson and the country along step by step. Indeed, his own description of the volume comes remarkably close to the impression which a comparison of its various speeches still imparts.

149. Lodge to Trevelyan, April 7, May 12, 1917, Lodge MSS.
150. Lodge to Trevelyan, Feb. 15, 1917, Lodge MSS.
151. Lodge to William Sturgis Bigelow, June 4, 1917, Lodge MSS.

I am conscious that the tone is very moderate in the earlier speeches, but it was intentionally so, for I was trying to work along from point to point and I did not want my influence here [Washington] discounted in the beginning by its being said that I was an unreasoning pro-Ally. I think, however, that the speeches are on a steadily ascending scale, not of merit but of intensity, until the point at which I was aiming was attained.[152]

Lodge thought his own course clear enough to lay before the public, and would have enjoyed doing the same with Wilson's. He and Wilson had, he felt, been working at cross purposes ever since the outbreak of war in Europe. The fact that he had prevailed and Wilson had finally been forced to declare war altered the pattern of their relationship very little. Lodge was quick to applaud the President's War Message but just as quick to insist that Wilson, "in character and intention," was "exactly what he was."[153] "In fact," he told Roosevelt, "if that message is right, everything he has done for two years and a half is fundamentally wrong."[154]

The public was still confused about what was at stake in the war, and for that state of affairs Lodge and Roosevelt continued to hold Wilson personally responsible.[155] Nor did Wilson's belated effort to picture the war as a crusade to make the world safe for democracy overcome (actually it only exacerbated) their suspicion that his aims in the war, as in peace—that his very conception of the relationship between "Force and Peace"—could never be reconciled with their own. Their indictment, often repeated in letters to friends and political allies, ran as follows:

The contrast between Wilson's conduct down to the declaration of war and his subsequent utterances cannot be overcome. The gulf is too wide to bridge. You [James M. Beck] dispose absolutely of the proposition that he was patiently waiting until the people were prepared mentally and materially, because down to April 2d he was not only failing to prepare them but he was leading them as strongly as he could in the opposite direction and the lukewarmness which existed in regard to the war was owing to the way in which he lowered the American spirit and confused the popular mind.[156]

152. Lodge to Roosevelt, May 28, 1917, Lodge MSS.
153. Lodge to William Sturgis Bigelow, April 7, 1917, Lodge MSS.
154. Lodge to Roosevelt, April 23, 1917, Roosevelt MSS.
155. See especially Daniel M. Smith, *The Great Departure: The United States and World War I* (New York, 1965), pp. ix–x.
156. Lodge to James M. Beck, Sept. 20, 1917, Lodge MSS.

As Raymond Robins said to me, 'Wilson has spent two and one half years dulling the conscience of our people and weakening their moral fiber, and then without any change in circumstances he reversed himself while running full speed; and naturally the machinery stops and an immense number of people are completely puzzled and find themselves wholly unable to get up any moral enthusiasm.' He won the election on the 'He kept us out of war' issue. ... the damage he did to our people morally and materially during the last three years will bear evil fruit for a generation to come. Moreover ... what is perfectly impossible, what represents really nauseous hypocrisy, is to say that we have gone to war to make the world safe for democracy, in April, when sixty days previously we had been announcing that we wished a 'Peace without victory' and had no concern with the 'causes or objects' of the war.[157]

That there was a great deal of inconsistency between the doctrine of isolationism which Wilson, albeit in the interests of peace, had long preached and his new-found internationalism, between a war in which the United States had no concern and one pictured as a great moral crusade, is hard to dispute.[158] There was certainly enough to make it understandable that Lodge would muse in his diary:

I wonder if the future historian will find him out? He has only to read and compare his messages and papers and follow his mistaken policy in order to discover him.[159]

They suspected, however, and with some prescience, that Wilson would now appear as the "great idealist of the war for Democracy." But that, as Roosevelt told Lodge, was a view which would be taken "in spite of the testimony of you and myself."[160]

157. Morison, ed., *Letters of Theodore Roosevelt*, VIII, pp. 1216–17. Such feelings were also prevalent in Great Britain. See Arthur Walworth, *America's Moment, 1918: American Diplomacy at the End of World War I* (New York, 1977), p. 5.

158. As Henry Adams put it: "Never could I have conceived that in a short three months we could have gone into a great war and adopted a conscription not unworthy of Germany, at the bidding of a President who was elected only a few months ago on the express ground that he had kept us at peace" (Ford, ed., *Letters of Henry Adams*, II, p. 643).

159. Lodge, *The Senate and the League*, pp. 79–80.

160. *Correspondence of Roosevelt and Lodge*, II, p. 526 (May 26, 1917); Lodge to Roosevelt, May 18, 1917, Lodge MSS.

Chapter Seven

Lodge and the Fourteen Points, or the Struggle over the Nature of American War Aims

Just as Wilson was heralding the formation of his "league for peace" Charles Evans Hughes warned that "it is not the part of wisdom to create expectations on the part of the people of the world which the Covenant cannot satisfy."[1] On that point Wilson would have differed, for Hughes's advice ran counter to the President's conception of political leadership. Believing that in international relations idealism could be a self-fulfilling proposition, Wilson saw his duty in inspiring the people to believe that they need no longer be content with human imperfection, that the war could be a war to end all wars and the league a means of ensuring perpetual peace. He first engaged and then ultimately commanded and personified the hopes and aspirations of millions both at home and abroad. Many Americans came to believe (no other word is as descriptive) in the League of Nations. Their acceptance of the League bore many of the marks of an act of faith rather than of careful analysis of the factors (other than faith) requisite for the successful operation of a collective security system. When their hopes did not materialize, when the Senate developed reservations with respect to American entry into the League and international relations returned to their normal desultory pattern, it was easier to believe that this state of affairs was the result of the machinations of "evil" men than to entertain the proposition that their own faith might have been misplaced. The corol-

1. Charles Evans Hughes, "Address to the Union League Club of New York City, March 26, 1919," Hughes MSS.

lary of the "self-righteous martyred saint attitude" adopted toward Wilson by his many disciples was the idea that the will of the American people had been frustrated by "a little group of powerful men" or, more specifically, by the "craft and acumen," "the consummate cunning" of Lodge, who almost single-handedly "beat back this enormous movement" and kept the United States out of the League.[2] Hence, the prominent place in American demonology which Lodge has long occupied.

Such interpretations vary in their sophistication, but share a common quality: their defense of Wilson and of his conception of a league rests primarily on impugning the motives and character of those who opposed him. That alone should be sufficient to arouse suspicion. Moreover, such criticism has inhibited rational consideration of the problems involved in the enforcement of peace, and it is precisely on that point that American thinking has tended to imprecision.[3] Apparently, as Lodge once suggested, we will always have with us "those who wish to have the world's peace assured by force, without using force to do it."[4] The conclusions of those who have made the most thorough study of the issues involved (John Chalmers Vinson's work on Article X and Warren Kuehl's careful comparison of Wilson's conception of a league with that of other prominent American internationalists) indicate that ideas did play an important, even determinant, role in the struggle over the league. It served the interests of many of those in-

2. Stromberg, "The Riddle of Collective Security, 1916–1920," in Anderson, ed., *Issues and Conflicts: Studies in Twentieth Century American Diplomacy*, p. 164; Alan Cranston, *The Killing of the Peace* (New York, 1960), p. ix; Kenneth Colegrove, *The American Senate and World Peace* (New York, 1944), pp. 78–80; Raymond B. Fosdick, "Comment on Article by James E. Hewes, Jr., Entitled 'Henry Cabot Lodge and the League of Nations,'" *Proceedings of the American Philosophical Society* 115 (Feb. 1971): 65. Though Fosdick's "Comment" testifies to the endurance of this interpretation, it reached its high water mark in the period 1943–45 when plans for American participation in another and quite different world organization were being formulated. None of the advocacy history of that period added much in the way of new information or argument, it all being based on Denna Frank Fleming's *The United States and the League of Nations, 1918–1920* (New York, 1932). It is distinguished principally by its vitriolic character and by the extremity of its charges. A few writers went so far in their advocacy as to blame Lodge for World War II and the deaths of the many Americans who fell in that conflict. See, *inter alia*, Schriftgiesser, *The Gentleman from Massachusetts*, p. 361; and Daniels, *The Wilson Era*, I, p. 472.

3. James E. Hewes, Jr., "Henry Cabot Lodge and the League of Nations," *Proceedings of the American Philosophical Society* 114 (August 1970): 245; Stromberg, "The Riddle of Collective Security," p. 147.

4. Lodge, *War Addresses*, p. 270.

volved to believe that the struggle was essentially one of partisan politics and personal hatred, but the real problem was that Americans could not agree upon the nature of the League they wanted or upon the arrangements necessary to make it work.[5]

Both Wilson and Taft occupied an uncomfortable position. As Walter Lippmann later recognized, "in them the idealism which prompts Americans to make large and resounding commitments was combined with the pacifism which causes Americans to shrink from the measures of force that are needed to support the commitments."[6] Wishing to minimize the exertions so important to the Europeans (the commitment to come to their aid with troops), hoping and often convincing himself that the United States would never in practice be called upon to fulfill its commitment to use force on behalf of the territorial integrity of other states, Wilson came to depict the League in a manner reflecting the isolationism to which it was the supposed antithesis.[7] Trapped by the contradictions inherent in their own desires (a contradiction laid bare by Borah when he pointedly asked "What will your league amount to if it does not contain powers that no one dreams of giving it"), it is perhaps understandable that when it came their turn to write the nation's history Wilsonians found it profitable to argue personalities and motives rather than issues.[8]

It also behooves us to be suspicious of those interpretations which depict Lodge as the villain of the fight over the League because that was the manner in which it pleased Wilson to view the struggle. Lodge was singled out by name in the 1920 Democratic platform for his alleged inconsistency on the League and peace issue, and "the Republican Senate" was condemned for "its refusal to ratify the treaty merely be-

5. Kuehl, *Seeking World Order*, p. 339.

6. *U.S. Foreign Policy: Shield of the Republic* (Boston, 1943), p. 31. Byron Dexter has also raised some important and troubling questions respecting the ultimate compatibility of pacifism and collective security. He helps explain why the American peace movement has been more internationalist in principle than in practice. See "The Liberal Values and Collective Security," *Confluence* 5 (Autumn 1956): 307–19. It was, as we have seen, the League to Enforce Peace's recognition of that incompatibility which helped attract Lodge to it in the first place.

7. Buehrig, *Woodrow Wilson and the Balance of Power*, p. 275. When addressing American audiences Wilson tended to depict Article X as little more than a self-denying ordinance, which is just what many of his advisers (especially Lansing) had long advocated. See Stromberg, "The Riddle of Collective Security," p. 159.

8. Borah quoted in Stromberg, "The Riddle of Collective Security," p. 159.

cause it was the product of Democratic statesmanship, thus interposing partisan envy and personal hatred in the way of peace and renewed prosperity of the world."[9] The objections to such an interpretation are manifold. Apart from the fact that it denigrates the role of ideas in the determination of human behavior, it remains a little too convenient. The Democrats found it politic to run against Lodge in 1918 and again in 1920, and Wilsonians have been doing so ever since.[10] Lodge was never a popular figure on the American political scene. Indeed, he presented an inviting target and outside New England his very virtues were readily converted into liabilities. As even the admiring Barrett Wendell noted, Lodge was "not sympathetic in either temper or in ad-

9. Porter and Johnson, eds., *National Party Platforms*, pp. 213–14. This has always been the interpretation favored by those close to Wilson from Joseph Tumulty's 1921 *Woodrow Wilson As I Knew Him* (p. 425) to Bernard Baruch's 1960 *The Public Years* (p. 133). What is more surprising is the degree to which scholars have been willing to perpetuate such a partisan and self-serving interpretation. It is still echoed, for example, in such otherwise useful works as Elletson's *Roosevelt and Wilson*, pp. 189–91; and Smith's *The Great Departure: The U.S. and World War I*, p. 185. Even Lodge's biographer, John Garraty, though recognizing that Lodge's position was "compounded of principles, politics, and prejudices," comes ultimately to the conclusion that "the fact that the league was Wilson's league was of unquestionable significance in explaining Lodge's resistance to it" (*Lodge*, pp. 354–55).

A variation of the "Wilsonian" interpretation is to be found in the writings of Arno Mayer, who claims that "it goes without saying that Henry Cabot Lodge and his cabal were more concerned with keeping progressivism in check at home than they were with the defeat of the Covenant as such" ("Historical Thought and American Foreign Policy in the Era of the First World War," in Francis L. Loewenheim, ed., *The Historian and the Diplomat* [New York, 1967], pp. 81–82). Also representing this view is James Oliver Robertson's "The Progressives in National Republican Politics, 1916 to 1921," diss. Harvard, 1964. Mayer is more persuasive when he demonstrates that Lodge was sensitive to the relationship between domestic politics and the nature of the international settlement than when he tries to make Lodge's domestic views the sole factor in his foreign policy stance. It is, after all, a two-way street and one's views as to the best way of assuring international peace can just as easily affect one's domestic political stance as vice versa. The point is that there is often interaction between the two and, indeed, Mayer demonstrates an understanding of this process in his treatment of almost everyone *except* Lodge.

10. Key Pittman of Nevada rose in the Senate to depict the 1918 Congressional contest as one "between the policies of Woodrow Wilson and those of Henry Cabot Lodge" (quoted in Arno Mayer, *Politics and Diplomacy of Peacemaking: Containment and Counterrevolution at Versailles, 1918–1919* [New York, 1967], p. 57). Wilson's 1918 call for the election of a Democratic Congress was, as delivered, markedly partisan in the context of his frequent appeals for wartime unity, and may well have backfired, but his initial draft was even more partisan and contained bitter references to Lodge and other prominent Republicans. See Bailey, *Woodrow Wilson and the Lost Peace*, p. 58.

dress"; even when "really large and constructive in his purposes, he . . . managed to impress people as a rather cynical opportunist at best."[11] It was Lodge's misfortune that his demeanor presented a standing invitation to opponents to disregard the issues he wanted to stress, but it would not seem unreasonable to expect historians to endeavor to surmount that obstacle.

Implicit in all "Wilsonian" interpretations is the assumption that Lodge would have supported a league such as Wilson advocated if a Republican had proposed it. Certainly Lodge hated Wilson and was intent on effecting his political demise, but that does not mean that his animosity was solely a function of personal or partisan feelings. He also hated what Wilson stood for and the way he did things, not least the manner in which he conducted the nation's foreign policy. It is one thing to claim that Lodge had a political and even personal interest in the defeat of the League, which is obvious, and yet quite another to say that interest so dominated his thinking that he would have supported a league such as Wilson fashioned if only its sponsorship had been different. That goes in the face of Lodge's course with respect to the Taft arbitration treaties and of everything which I have been able to discover about his foreign policy views. Lodge's views on Wilson's league were not only compatible with, but flowed directly out of, his perception of the type of foreign policy most appropriate under American conditions.

II

Because Lodge was committed to an Allied victory at a time when Wilson still hoped to arrange a "peace without victory," their conceptions of the role and structure of a league of nations were in conflict from the beginning. American entry into the war changed that very little. Differences of opinion respecting the origins of the war in Europe and its implications for the United States led easily to different theories about the cause of American participation and these in turn to divergent war aims and to contrasting conceptions of what was necessary to prevent the recurrence of such a catastrophe. The contrast between the views of those in Lodge's camp and those who followed Wilson was

11. Wendell to R. W. Curtis, Jan. 18, 1920, in Howe, *Barrett Wendell and His Letters*, p. 321.

most sharply delineated in late 1916 and early 1917 and again at the close of the war when the precise nature of the peace settlement once more became a concrete issue. As Edward Buehrig once observed, "the deeply divided opinion of the neutrality period . . . reappeared at the moment of victory" and this "earlier disunity proved in the end insurmountable."[12]

The peace, as Lodge understood, was really a part of the war.[13] One's conception of what was necessary to reestablish peace flowed directly out of the manner in which three basic questions were answered: (1) what had started the war in the first place? (2) what had prompted American entry? and (3) what were the purposes for which the country fought? Merely to state the various responses to the first question (the French theory that the war was all Germany's fault, the British theory that it was the result of the breakdown of the Concert of Europe, and Wilson's belief that it was a function of the political and social structure of the conservative regimes) is to understand the issue's implications for one's views on the kind of settlement necessary for a lasting peace.[14]

The American people were deeply divided not only with respect to what the national interest required, but even as to what their much vaunted idealism commanded them to do. These conflicts were never

12. "Woodrow Wilson and Collective Security," in Edward H. Buehrig, ed., *Wilson's Foreign Policy in Perspective* (Bloomington, 1957), p. 54.

13. Lodge to Henry White, Feb. 1, 1919, Lodge MSS. The point Lodge was making is the responsible one that we "have got to take our share in carrying out the peace which is really part of the war." However, he can be criticized for failing to recognize the extent to which war aims were a function of the dynamics of the war itself, and oscillated accordingly. His attention was focused rather rigidly on responsibility for the outbreak of war.

14. What emerged at Versailles was an inconsistent conglomeration of these various notions, a victor's peace shrouded in the rhetoric of a peace of accommodation and therefore neither politically nor philosophically sound. It is not difficult to believe, as Richard Rosecrance puts it (*Action and Reaction in World Politics* [Boston, 1963], pp. 180–82), that any of the three notions consistently acted upon might have better served to prevent World War II, or as Harold Nicolson wrote (*Diplomacy* [New York, 1939], p. 59), "if the treaties of peace had been wholly Wilson or wholly Clemenceau [for our purposes we can read Lodge] they might . . . have stood some chance of survival. . . ." Most historians have contended that it was the severity of the peace terms that created a climate of opinion in Germany conducive to the rise of Nazism. But a good argument can also be made for the case that the treaty's hypocrisies and inconsistencies contributed much to its demise, instilling in the Germans the belief that they were being judged by standards that did not apply to other nations and undermining in the minds of the Allies the idea that this was a legitimate and moral peace, deserving of respect and of being forcefully upheld.

effectively resolved, only overtaken by events and in a way that added to the confusion. Taking the rules of maritime warfare as a basis for American policy had made some sense during the neutrality period, but the violation of those rules left much to be desired when it came to mobilizing the people for war. There was little agreement about why the United States entered the war, and even less about the nation's stake in the peace settlement.[15]

Nothing is as revealing of the philosophical and psychological differences which beset the human race as the theories expounded on the origins of war and the rationales proffered for resorting to combat. Because such matters cut so deeply, there was something almost predictable about the reactions of our protagonists. Just as in England two and a half years earlier, those of Roosevelt and Lodge's persuasion had no difficulty in going to war.[16] It was more their war than Wilson's. They accepted war as a necessary risk in international affairs and based their advocacy of war on the threat posed to the national interest by the possibility of German hegemony. If they had been in power they would have endeavored to present the war to the American people as one in the self-interest of the United States. They tried repeatedly to make that point. Roosevelt claimed that "this is our war, America's war." Lodge congratulated Secretary of State Lansing for pointing out that America fought not for world liberty but for its own security, and in his speeches emphasized that America was fighting for its own independence and security, that if Germany were to prevail in Europe the United States would be the next victim.[17]

However, like their English counterparts, most American liberals and progressives had long since rejected the validity of such arguments. Wilson in opposing American entry into the war had denied not only the fact of a threat to the national interest but even the primacy of considerations of national interest. His America would contend only

15. Smith, *The Great Departure: The U.S. and World War I*, p. x.
16. See Laurence W. Martin, *Peace Without Victory: Woodrow Wilson and the British Liberals* (New Haven, 1958), especially pp. 51–53.
17. Arno Mayer, *Political Origins of the New Diplomacy*, pp. 344, 349; Lodge to Secretary Lansing, July 30, 1917, Robert Lansing Papers, Library of Congress; Lodge, "Recent Congressional Legislation," *Proceedings of the Massachusetts Historical Society* 51 (Oct. 1917): 17; Lodge, "Speech at the Republican State Convention, Springfield, Oct. 6, 1917," Lodge MSS; Lodge, "Address at the Nineteenth Annual Dinner of the Pennsylvania Society," Dec. 8, 1917, Lodge MSS.

for moral principle.[18] When finally forced into the war by a complicated set of circumstances, forced to make a rapid *volte face*, and in Wilson's case forced both to justify the decision to himself and to rally his bewildered supporters (who had only recently returned him to the Presidency on the basis of his having kept the country out of the war), the enunciation of war aims of a particular type became a political and psychological necessity.[19] Again in keeping with the experience of their English Liberal counterparts, the only kind of war he and his followers could support was one to end war and create a better world, and so it came to be depicted.[20]

Such differences were basic and the more insurmountable because they had crystallized in, and were the consequences of stands taken in, a period when deep divisions beset the American body politic and animosities flourished. On both sides there was a tendency to emphasize the very reasons for intervention the other side found most unsatisfactory.[21] Lodge and Roosevelt continued to be haunted by the fears that had come to dominate their perception of Wilson's foreign policy in the years of neutrality. Their personal feelings were but little affected by Wilson's acquiescence in the war.[22] Roosevelt likened going to war under Wilson's leadership to "fighting the Civil War under Buchanan" and neither he nor Lodge ever lost the fear that Wilson would revert to the idea of peace without victory at the first opportune moment.[23] Lodge also feared that Wilson might try to make it a "little war," and coun-

18. Blum, *Woodrow Wilson and the Politics of Morality*, p. 84.
19. Osgood, *Ideals and Self-Interest*, p. 275.
20. Martin, *Peace Without Victory*, pp. 51-53.
21. Osgood, *Ideals and Self-Interest*, p. 273, points to TR's proclivities in this direction.
22. If anything their personal relations grew even worse in this period. Wilson's refusal to allow Roosevelt to raise a volunteer brigade and his passing over of General Leonard Wood incited from Lodge the comment that Wilson's course was "not only despicable but a pure sacrifice of the country's interest to his own malignant hatred" (Lodge to Roosevelt, May 28, 1917, Lodge MSS). Another bone of contention with personal overtones was the recall to active duty of Lodge's son-in-law, Augustus P. Gardner, best known for his clashes with Wilson over the preparedness issue. Gardner had a bad heart, was recalled without a physical examination, and soon succumbed to pneumonia in a Southern camp. Lodge may not have blamed Wilson personally, but did excoriate the "petty spite" of the War Department, and did believe its actions were designed to please Wilson. See Garraty, *Lodge*, pp. 339-40.
23. Anna Roosevelt Cowles, ed., *Letters of Theodore Roosevelt to Anna Roosevelt Cowles*, p. 312; Morison, ed., *Letters of Theodore Roosevelt*, VIII, p. 1224; *Correspondence of Roosevelt and Lodge*, II, p. 540 (Oct. 7, 1918).

tered with the suggestion that the most merciful war was the one "most vigorously waged and which comes most quickly to an end." Lodge was also the first to urge that American troops be sent to France.[24]

Lodge and Roosevelt's program for the war and for America's future was an extension of their concerns in the neutrality period. Not too surprisingly Roosevelt was determined to commit the country to a "policy of permanent preparation."[25] Believing that the war had been brought on by German militarism and American pacifism working in tandem, he could not but feel that "to let either or both of them dictate the peace that is to end it would be an immeasurable disaster."[26] Lodge also opted for a policy of preparedness and temporary alliance as prescribed in Washington's Farewell Address and took pains to make the point that "the cause of the other nations who are fighting Germany has become our cause."[27] From this it followed that "to desert them now or at any time hereafter would be to place an indelible stain upon our honor, . . . to betray the principles on which the whole system of the United States rests, without which it will fall."[28] This, however, was as far as they dared go. Like many Eastern Republicans they looked to at least a working alliance with England and France in the postwar period but were not too explicit about that in April 1917.[29] This has led to the charge that neither then nor during the fight over the League did Lodge identify American interests "with any precise conformation in European or world politics."[30] The Rooseveltian solution had, however, never rested on more than a tacit alliance with England and France, and

24. Lodge, *War Addresses*, p. 301; *Cong. Record*, 65th Cong., 1st sess., 1917, pp. 1439–40; Lodge, *The Senate and the League*, pp. 78–79; Lodge to Corinne Roosevelt Robinson, April 5, 1917, Houghton Library, Harvard University; Lodge to Henry Higginson, April 5, 1917, and to Trevelyan, Sept. 1, 1917, Lodge MSS; Lodge to John T. Morse, Jr., May 16, 1918, Morse MSS.

25. "Broomstick Preparedness" in Ralph Stout, ed., *Roosevelt in the Kansas City Star* (Boston, 1921), p. 10.

26. Roosevelt, *National Strength and International Duty* (Princeton, 1917), p. 84.

27. Lodge, *War Addresses*, p. 299.

28. *Cong. Record*, 65th Cong., 1st sess., 1917, p. 1440.

29. Richard W. Leopold, "The Emergence of America as a World Power," in Braeman et al., eds., *Change and Continuity in Twentieth Century America*, p. 23. Something of the feeling of this group is captured in Henry Adams's observation on finding the U.S. and Britain fighting side by side: "I find the great object of my life accomplished in the building up of the great community of Atlantic Powers which I hope will at last make a precedent that can never be forgotten." See W. C. Ford, ed., *Letters of Henry Adams*, II, p. 642.

30. Norman Graebner, ed., *Ideas and Diplomacy*, p. 464.

moving the country to accept even that again was a considerable task, what with Borah declaring "I seek or accept no alliances; I obligate this Government to no other power," and Wilson intent on identifying England and France as "associates" rather than as allies.[31] An opportunity to build public support for postwar cooperation with other countries was clearly lost in the process, but that opportunity was at least as available to Wilson as it was to Roosevelt or Lodge.[32]

Occupying as prominent a place in Lodge's program as "no peace without the Allies" were a number of closely related propositions which had also taken root in the neutrality period. The obvious counter to Wilson's efforts to secure a "peace without victory" was the conviction that a worthwhile peace could only emerge from an Allied victory. Having long argued that the United States had both a moral and a security interest in such a victory, nothing came more easily to Lodge once the U.S. entered the conflict than the insistence that the war could only be justified by a victorious peace, that there was "no hope for a final settlement except in physical guarantees won on the field of battle."[33] From the outset Lodge had enjoined against any peace that meant a reestablishment of old conditions. Believing that "to restore the status quo ante bellum would simply be to give Germany a breathing space in which she may prepare to renew the war," he maintained, once America entered the war, that if peace were ever established on the basis of the status quo ante bellum, the President and all who voted for the war would be guilty of a criminal act.[34]

Consequently what Lodge most wanted to hear from Wilson was a statement of intention to pursue the war until victory was achieved. When it was given he felt a deep sense of satisfaction and accomplishment.[35] Wilson was ultimately forced to accept the fact that there was

31. Borah quoted in Leopold, "The Emergence of America as a World Power," p. 23.

32. Wilson opposed a wartime visit by Taft to England because the two nations had divergent aims. Consequently, he did not want the U.S. involved in British policy or the two nations drawn too closely together (Pringle, *Taft*, I, p. 935).

33. Roosevelt, "The Peace of Victory For Which We Strive," *Metropolitan* 46 (July 1917): 24; Lodge, "Address at the Nineteenth Annual Dinner of the Pennsylvania Society," Dec. 8, 1917, Lodge MSS.

34. Lodge, "Speech at the Republican State Convention," Springfield, Oct. 6, 1917, and "Address at the Nineteenth Annual Dinner of the Pennsylvania Society," Dec. 8, 1917, Lodge MSS; *Cong. Record*, 65th Cong., 1st sess., 1917, p. 5419.

35. Lodge, *The Senate and the League*, p. 82.

an almost inescapable logic (both political and psychological) to the manner in which the American democracy committed itself to war. This Lodge not only understood but found reassuring. What Lodge did not realize was that he too was a captive of the American historical experience, especially of the Civil War paradigm. He never once considered the possibility of a war of limited objectives to which, under other circumstances, his conservatism and pursuit of the national interest might have led him. Americans went to war for a variety of reasons, but restoration of the balance of power in Europe was a reason appealing to very few. Under American conditions such a war was as impossible as a diplomacy of *Realpolitik*.[36] The American democracy, whether from self-deception or true commitment, fought only "holy" wars. In no other way could its sacrifices be justified.

Both Lodge and Wilson portrayed the war in a manner consistent with their political past and respective value systems, but neither had an interest in this period in pushing their different conceptions to a point where the nation would have to choose between them. The nation was at war, and at first a considerable number of its citizens did not support that war. A much larger number took a narrow, parochial view of the causes and purposes of the conflict. Borah not only rejected all alliances, but refused to join any sort of crusade and made "war alone for my countrymen and their rights, for my country and its honor."[37] Bryan insisted America would not have entered but for the invasion of its rights.[38] Initially there was considerable sentiment for a war of limited liability, a war from which America might withdraw as soon as its rights were acknowledged.[39] This position collapsed rapidly, but

36. A self-styled "realist" like Hans Morgenthau (*In Defense of the National Interest*, p. 26) describes Wilson as pursuing the right policy in going to war, but for the wrong reason, and then criticizes him severely for being "morally unable to permit the restoration of the European balance of power, the traditional guarantor of American security." In rejoinder one might ask if there was ever any public support for such a course. Both Lodge and Wilson would have told him that American foreign policy had to have an ideological component; the struggle was over the nature of that component.

37. Quoted in Leopold, "The Emergence of America as a World Power," p. 23.

38. *World Peace: A Written Debate Between William Howard Taft and William Jennings Bryan* (New York, 1917), p. 54.

39. Thomas A. Bailey, *Woodrow Wilson and the Lost Peace*, p. 14. Here were people who did not conceive of the war in ideological terms (at least not supranational ones) and who might logically have later contended for the restoration of the balance of power in Europe à la Morgenthau. But these people were so isolationist in their outlook that they didn't much care what happened in Europe.

it was symptomatic of the isolationist prejudice that continued to pose a threat to the internationalist conceptions (however different) of both Lodge and Wilson. Most Congressmen concentrated on the U-boat issue. They tended to ignore Wilson's reference to a league as a goal of the war, and were also reluctant to endorse Lodge's claim that in aligning itself with England and France the United States was joining in a great struggle for "freedom, democracy and modern civilization."[40] The majority of the American people fought only for their own rights and in the process enlarged their commitment to the community of nations very little.[41]

Wilson, by the amorphous nature of his war aims, contributed to this situation. To the eve of the peace negotiations he kept his distance from all detailed plans for international organization and seemed content with generalities, with proclaiming the necessity of making "the world safe for democracy" and the need for some sort of an international organization to maintain peace. Given the deep divisions which developed in the American body politic during the period of neutrality, divisions which carried over to the question of war aims, it would have been politically disadvantageous for him to have done otherwise.

Lodge and Roosevelt were governed by much the same considerations. For almost a year and a half after American entry into the war they acquiesced in Wilson's war aims. In the context of "wartime unity" it was not good politics to come down on the President too hard. Probably even more important were the divisions which beset the Republican party; Wilson's vagueness served as a means of postponing trouble between its "isolationist" and "internationalist" wings.[42] Yet another reason is that Lodge and Roosevelt were interested in securing a nation united in behalf of the war effort. Lodge fully appreciated the effective-

40. Smith, *The Great Departure: The U.S. and World War I*, p. 79; Leopold, "The Emergence of America as a World Power," p. 22; Lodge, *War Addresses*, p. 302.

41. Leopold, "The Emergence of America as a World Power," p. 22.

42. George Mayer, *The Republican Party, 1854–1964* (New York, 1964), p. 349. Admittedly, the terms "isolationist" and "internationalist" are imprecise and unsatisfactory, but in this period and within the Republican party they can be given a fairly definite meaning. The "internationalists" were those who were pro-Ally before the events of early 1917, while the "isolationists" were those who until then had insisted on an absolute neutrality and recognized neither a security nor a moral interest in the outcome of the conflict. It was from the ranks of the latter that all those who subsequently became "irreconcilables" on the League issue were drawn. See Ralph Stone, *The Irreconcilables* (Lexington, Ky., 1970), p. 13.

ness in this regard of Wilson's War Address to Congress.[43] Then, too, Wilson, once in the war, was having to accommodate himself to their point of view. Particularly important in this respect were his August statement of intention to pursue the war until victory was achieved and the declaration in his Fourteen Points Address that Alsace-Lorraine should be returned to France. Lodge thought the latter precluded all possibility of a negotiated settlement. It was such a milestone that Lodge even allowed that the Fourteen Points speech was "a good speech . . . as to terms."[44] Lodge probably also appreciated that the Fourteen Points were excellent wartime propaganda and had in that sense a quite "realistic" character.[45]

There were a number of points among the fourteen which were soon to cause trouble (particularly those that affected the United States and involved possible American sacrifice or commitment), but Americans were practically of one mind with respect to what the future map of Europe should look like. The guiding principle, as first stated by Roosevelt, was "the right of each people to govern itself and to control its own destinies. . . ."[46] This became the cornerstone first of Wilson's Fourteen Points Address and then eventually of the peace settlement itself. Unanimity of opinion on this subject and the exigencies of wartime politics served to obscure the basic differences respecting the conduct of international relations and the creation of conditions conducive to peace which had briefly become so evident in January of 1917, but as the war neared its conclusion it became increasingly apparent that those differences had not been resolved.

At no point during the war were politics actually adjourned.[47] The

43. Lodge to Roosevelt, April 23, 1917, Roosevelt MSS.
44. Lodge to William Sturgis Bigelow, Jan. 10, 1918, Lodge MSS. He appears to have missed (perhaps deliberately) the fine distinction Wilson drew between Belgium which "must" be evacuated and restored and Alsace-Lorraine where the wrong of 1871 "should" be righted. Despite what he said on January 8, in private Wilson continued to reserve his position. Shortly thereafter he told Taft that he did "not believe that either the British people or our own would insist on fighting the war merely to restore Alsace-Lorraine to France and if that was all that stood between peace and continued war, Germany would be allowed to retain them" (Pringle, *Taft*, I, pp. 938–39).
45. For the "realism of idealism" in the context of the war see Arno Mayer, *Political Origins of the New Diplomacy*, p. 352; and also Sondra R. Herman, *Eleven Against War: Studies in American Internationalist Thought, 1898–1921* (Stanford, 1969), pp. 203–04.
46. "The Peace of Victory For Which We Strive," p. 24.
47. I have relied heavily on Seward W. Livermore's thorough study, *Politics Is*

situation can best be described as an uneasy truce regularly broken by forays emanating from both sides. Wilson had always emphasized that his was a party government, and American entry into the war did not change that.[48] He seems never to have considered taking prominent Republicans into his Cabinet, let alone a government of national unity such as was common in Europe. As a result there was bad feeling from the start. It took only a couple of weeks to convince Lodge that Wilson was trying to make it "a party war."[49] Wilson, for his part, would never allow Lansing to take the Republican members of the Senate Foreign Relations Committee into his confidence because he thought *they* were playing politics with the war.[50]

There were constraints. Though Lodge felt the Military Affairs Committee had given the public enough information to defeat a dozen administrations, he cautioned that "we should run the risk of defeating our own ends if we made the attacks on Wilson that we all want to make; we must give no opening for the charge that we are drawing the party line and the cry that we are not loyal to the war."[51] But those were excellent grounds on which to attack one's opponents. Lodge accused Senator Stone (Democrat from Missouri) of making the first political speech in the Senate since the war began, and Wilson intervened in a spate of local elections, applying the "acid test" of loyalty to his opponents and invariably finding them wanting.[52] There were new ground rules and new concerns, but it was politics as usual. Lodge feared that the Republican party risked submersion in the wake of the

---

Adjourned: Woodrow Wilson and the War Congress, 1916–1918 (Middletown, Conn., 1966).

48. E. David Cronon, ed., *The Political Thought of Woodrow Wilson* (Indianapolis, 1965), p. lxxv.

49. Lodge to Roosevelt, April 23, 1917, Roosevelt MSS. A not atypical Republican view of Wilson's conduct of the war was the summary Henry Stimson confided to his diary in early 1919: "When the war came he conducted it on a wholly partisan basis unlike any government of the other large allied nations. He conducted it with an incompetent cabinet, the two most conspicuously unfit members being the Secretary of the Navy and the Secretary of War. He excluded from service the most efficient general officer which the Army had for reasons of personal dislike, and he rubbed these actions in by personally appealing for a partisan Congress to carry on the work of reconstruction after the war" (Henry Stimson Diary, Vol. III, p. 63, Sterling Library, Yale University).

50. Robert Lansing, "Memo on Conference With Committees on Foreign Relations on Declaring War on Turkey and Bulgaria, May 2, 1918," Lansing MSS.

51. Lodge to William Sturgis Bigelow, Jan. 10 and Feb. 21, 1918, Lodge MSS.

52. *Cong. Record*, 65th Cong., 2nd sess., 1918, pp. 1087–88; Livermore, *Politics Is Adjourned*, Chapter XI, "The Acid Test," pp. 153–68.

Administration's appeals for national unity. Good political strategy therefore dictated a policy of broad attacks on the Administration lest the Democrats reap credit for the war effort.[53] To prevent that the Republicans launched a series of Congressional investigations of the Administration's inefficiency and sought (unsuccessfully as it turned out) to saddle Wilson with a "Committee on the Conduct of the War" based on the Civil War prototype.[54] Wilson did not declare his famous moratorium on politics until after he had intervened, with disastrous effect, in a Senatorial election in Wisconsin and, according to Lodge, that moratorium lasted not two months before Wilson, completely ignoring his "acid test" qualification as to loyalty and patriotism, made "one of the lowest political deals to steal a Republican seat in Michigan with a Pacifist of the worst stripe."[55]

Another aspect of the continuing political struggle with important ramifications for the future was the contest for dominance between the Executive and Congress.[56] In order to cope with the war emergency Wilson demanded and received vast powers. Lodge cautioned that "we shall not expedite the war by destroying the legislative powers of this Government," but there was no stopping the accumulation of power in the White House.[57] Lodge began, as a result, to worry whether it would be possible to return to the old constitutional limits.[58] As the war

53. Lodge to Roosevelt, May 18, 1917, Lodge MSS.

54. My interest is in the political aspect of this, but I do not mean to imply that the Administration's conduct of the war (both as regards efficiency and corruption) did not warrant investigation. My point is that such investigations cannot by the very nature of the American political system ever be completely nonpartisan.

55. George Mayer, *The Republican Party*, p. 351; Lodge to Roosevelt, July 2, 1918, Roosevelt MSS. The reference is to Henry Ford. Lodge found about this "a cynical hypocrisy and immorality . . . beyond words." Others have also commented on Wilson's ill fated effort to play what were really two basically incompatible roles at the same time, that of the great idealist and that of the caucus politician. See, for example, the observation of Winston Churchill quoted in Herbert Hoover, *The Ordeal of Woodrow Wilson* (New York, 1958), p. 257.

56. It is a contest which seems to invite hypocrisy. American political figures have demonstrated remarkable agility in moving from a pro-Executive to a pro-Congressional position, or vice versa, on the rather practical basis of which party controls which branch, while never ceasing to base their arguments on the supposedly great constitutional principles involved.

57. *Cong. Record*, 65th Cong., 1st sess., 1917, p. 2383.

58. Lodge to Lord Bryce, Aug. 2, 1918, Lodge MSS. Spring Rice, with experience not only in Germany and Russia but also in Turkey and Persia, thought Wilson's the most autocratic government to which he had ever been accredited. See Gwynn, ed., *Letters of Spring Rice*, II, p. 372.

drew to a close and the emergency passed, it was natural that Congress would seek to regain its former prerogatives.[59] Lodge fired one of the opening salvos of that struggle when, even before the war was over, he warned that "the responsibility of a Senator in dealing with any question of peace is as great in his sphere as that of the President in his."[60]

Politics could not be adjourned for the simple fact that elections could not be postponed, and as the Congressional elections of 1918 approached the pace inevitably quickened. It was generally recognized, as Lodge put it, that the nation was "facing the world's greatest issues."[61] Perhaps it was this that made the Congressional campaign so bitter and the most expensive to date.[62] With the war nearing its conclusion it was a campaign destined to bring again into focus the different philosophies which underlay our protagonists' conceptions of a just and workable peace settlement.[63] This was the more likely because Wilson, in response to German and Austrian initiatives in early October, had again raised the spectre of a negotiated settlement and because Lodge and Roosevelt saw in the campaign a means of pushing Wilson toward a settlement more in line with their views. There was a significant political component in the war aims debate in all the countries involved in the war, but only in the United States was there an election at this crucial juncture. With the issue so close at hand the restraints imposed by the demands of wartime unity became increasingly inoperative and Wilsonian generalities less satisfying. For Lodge and Roosevelt, just as in early 1917 when they had moved to thwart an earlier "Wilsonian" settlement of the war, it was a moment of truth. Their ideas of a proper settlement had changed little, but the election campaign added a political dimension to what had originally been primarily a philosophical argument. Attitudes hardened accordingly. Republican hostility to Wilson's conception of a just and workable peace settlement went back to his efforts to end the war on the basis of "peace without victory," but the decision to launch a full-scale attack on Wilson on that

59. Bailey, *Woodrow Wilson and the Great Betrayal*, p. 49.
60. *Cong. Record*, 65th Cong., 2nd sess., 1918, p. 11170.
61. Boston *Herald*, Oct. 31, 1918, p. 1.
62. Livermore, *Politics Is Adjourned*, p. 113.
63. Livermore presents persuasive evidence that the election actually turned, particularly in the Mid-West, on domestic, bread and butter issues. It is a measure of Lodge's preoccupation with the war and foreign policy that he wanted the Republican party "to go to the country on unconditional surrender and nothing else." See Lodge to Roosevelt, Oct. 14, 1918, Roosevelt MSS.

score grew out of those earlier differences *and* out of the political exigencies of the 1918 Congressional campaign.[64]

Continued flexibility would have served Wilson's purposes, but Lodge and Roosevelt saw the campaign as an opportunity to smoke him out and force him to accept at least a modicum of their views. Given the mood of the country, with war fever and xenophobic feeling at their height, theirs was not an idle hope. The public was finally ripe for a program which involved a complete Allied victory and a peace resting on a policy of permanent preparedness and continued Allied military predominance. The keynote to Roosevelt's attitude in this period was neither isolationism nor internationalism, but "nationalism"; that was the issue they could use against Wilson.[65] It seemed the most likely way of channeling the national mood toward support for their kind of peace settlement.

Wilson's problem was that he had long been carrying water on both shoulders. Even as late as September and October of 1918 he had spoken of a peace based on impartial justice, and this naturally had revived fears that he was again about to assume the role of mediator between the Allies and the Central Powers.[66] Apparently committed to victory, but still wanting a peace that would be recognized as a "liberal" settlement, Wilson in his negotiations with the Germans and Austrians seemed to be trying to put together such a combination of the two as

64. Livermore, *Politics Is Adjourned*, p. 210. As Livermore puts it, this should be sufficient to put an end once and for all to the nonsense written about a Republican plot, hatched on Roosevelt's deathbed, to defeat Wilson on the League issue for solely personal and narrow partisan motives. See, for example, Schriftgiesser, *The Gentleman from Massachusetts*, p. 300; and Gene Smith, *When the Cheering Stopped* (New York, 1964), p. 56.

65. Morison, ed., *Letters of Theodore Roosevelt*, VIII, pp. 1352–53. Rather damaging to his reputation for "internationalism" is a letter to Beveridge (Morison, ed., *Letters of Theodore Roosevelt*, VIII, p. 1385), in which he labeled his internationalism "merely a platonic expression, designed to let Taft and his followers get over without too much trouble, and also to prevent any accusation that we are ourselves merely Prussian militarists." It should be remembered, however, that in Roosevelt's conception "sound nationalism" and "sound internationalism" went hand in hand. What he told Beveridge (who probably misunderstood and took it for a commitment to isolationism) did not preclude his being "more convinced than ever that there should be the closest alliance between the British Empire and the United States. . . ." (Morison, ed., *Letters of Theodore Roosevelt*, VIII, p. 1398).

66. Garraty, *Lodge*, p. 340; Morison, ed., *Letters of Theodore Roosevelt*, VIII, p. 1397. The Republican response was to point out how difficult it was to be a belligerent and an umpire at the same time. See, for example, "The Resolutions of the Middlesex [Mass.] Club, Oct. 19, 1918," Lodge MSS.

might still be politically digestible.[67] It was a tight stretch even for someone of Wilson's semantic ability. There was something basically incompatible about trying to distinguish between the German people and their rulers,[68] while at the same time calling for a continuation of the struggle until full victory was achieved.[69] Perhaps only Wilson could in the same speech have declared that "we wish her [Germany] only to accept a place of equality among the peoples of the world" and yet have depicted the struggle against that country as "the culminating and final war for human liberty."[70] American idealism once unleashed seemed to generate the kind of expectations reflected in the latter part of Wilson's statement.

If Wilson had a serious problem and sought refuge in generalities, that only made Lodge the more determined to pin him down. The President's vagueness nourished the Senator's worst fears. Lodge seized on the war aims issue in order to prevent Wilson from making a negotiated, compromise, and pro-German peace, in order to tie him down and "help him to be definite."[71] Uncharitably and unfairly, Lodge usually attributed Wilson's attraction to a compromise peace to his interest in capturing the German vote. Like the Wilsonians, he too found it convenient to substitute the political for the philosophical argument. Lodge had the distinct advantage over Wilson of knowing precisely what he wanted. There was in the country probably no more outspoken advocate of the on-to-Berlin school than Lodge.[72] He regarded an armistice as tantamount to losing the war, believed the right kind of peace could not be obtained by stopping short of Berlin, and

---

67. Such efforts occasioned in Lodge the feeling that the suspicions he had long entertained were completely justified. See Lodge to Roosevelt, Oct. 7, 1918, Roosevelt MSS. Such suspicions were widespread among those Republicans who were pronouncedly pro-Ally in their sentiments. Root wrote to Roosevelt as early as March 11, 1918 expressing the fear that "he [Wilson] is veering toward the attitude of the New Republic and a pacifism that will be content with a treaty with the Potsdam gang" (Root MSS).

68. This was a distinction which Lodge could never accept. He insisted that we *are* fighting the German people and that "this war would not exist if they did not fully sustain it" (Lodge to Desha Breckinridge, Aug. 31, 1918, Lodge MSS).

69. Smith, *The Great Departure: The U.S. and World War I*, p. 89.

70. Woodrow Wilson, *State Papers and Addresses* (New York, 1918), pp. 471–72.

71. Lodge to J. D. H. Luce, Aug. 19, 1918; to Joseph Buckley Bishop and Henry Higginson, Aug. 31, 1918; and to George Harvey, Sept. 3, 1918, Lodge MSS; *Correspondence of Roosevelt and Lodge*, II, p. 536 (Sept. 3, 1918).

72. Schriftgiesser, *The Gentleman from Massachusetts*, p. 296.

thought how the war ended more important than when it ended.[73] By his own proclamation the Republican party stood "for unconditional surrender and complete victory just as Grant stood."[74]

The 1918 Congressional campaign was a "khaki election."[75] Having for years chafed under the first half of Tocqueville's dictum ("There are two things that will always be very difficult for a democratic nation: to start a war and to end it") Lodge now found satisfaction and political opportunity in the second half.[76] In this sense Arno Mayer's comparison of Lodge's broadsides with those of the most ardent bitter-enders in Europe is apt.[77] But such an insight obscures at the same time that it enlightens. Even in Mayer's own terms, "the forces of movement" in America were not as war weary, nor "the forces of order" so apprehensive about the political consequences of defeat as in Europe. To understand the moral fervor with which Lodge and Roosevelt approached the peace-settlement problem and the nature of the groundswell of public opinion they tapped, it is necessary to look at these phenomena in the context of the American historical experience. It was easy for Americans, and especially for those of Lodge's background, to believe that they were fighting a "Second Holy War," that this was no ordinary war, but rather a fundamental clash of ideals and philosophies in which they were arrayed on the side of moral progress.[78] The Civil War parallel was never far from their minds.[79] The manner in which that war

73. This led inevitably to the view that the armistice which concluded the war was a mistake. Roosevelt felt that it would have been better, from the standpoint of the future, if Germany's army had to return home fully defeated and if the Allies had entered Berlin as victors. See Corinne Roosevelt Robinson, *My Brother Theodore Roosevelt*, p. 360. It is a point of view which has always found more favor with students of German history than with those of American history.

74. *New York Times*, Oct. 8 and 14, 1918; *Cong. Record*, 65th Cong., 2nd sess., 1918, pp. 11170–71; *Boston Herald*, Oct. 31, 1918; Lodge, "The Necessary Guarantees of Peace," *Scribner's Magazine* 64 (Nov. 1918): 471–72; Lodge to John T. Morse, Jr., Sept. 11, 1918, Lodge MSS.

75. Mayer, *Politics and Diplomacy of Peacemaking*, p. 119.

76. *Democracy in America*, II, pp. 622–23.

77. Mayer, *Politics and Diplomacy of Peacemaking*, p. 55.

78. As Lodge told Roosevelt (*Correspondence of Roosevelt and Lodge*, II, p. 539 [Oct. 2, 1918]), he saw the underlying struggle as one "between materialism and idealism, between the pure materialism of Germany and [the] ideals of the other nations. The first battle in England, France and the United States is with our [own] materialism, and the victory of the ideals achieved really made those nations great, and the second is the struggle with the pure materialism of Germany."

79. Roosevelt likened peace talk in September of 1918 to that of the anti-Lincoln men in 1864 (Morison, ed., *Letters of Theodore Roosevelt*, VIII, pp. 1368–

had ended served as their model. Lodge dreaded making a peace in the "old-fashioned" European manner.[80] His principal objection to Lord Lansdowne's Five Points was that they contemplated a settlement like that of 1815, when he was convinced that the war "must end substantially as our civil war ended." "Right" had obviously to triumph. Germany had to be beaten to the ground so that it could never again repeat its performance. After such a war and such sacrifices a compromise peace was out of the question.[81] Europeans may have been attuned to the differences between a "conservative" and a "liberal" peace, but in the American experience the distinction was easily blurred.

Wilson's vision of a peace settlement was no less idealistic. He too could probably have subscribed to Lodge's formulation that "we have no territory to gain and seek no conquests, but I think the American people are determined on placing Germany in a position where she can never again menace the peace, liberty and civilization of the world or the independence of other nations."[82] They differed primarily as to means. Fearing a renewed German peace initiative and Wilson's susceptibility thereto, Lodge rose in the Senate on August 23, 1918 to insist that it was "of the last importance to know exactly what we mean by peace," and to stress that "the details are really far more important than the general propositions, in which we all agree."[83] He conceded nothing to Wilson by way of interest in a "just and righteous" peace, but shunned aspirations at a universal beneficence. To Lodge democracy was a concrete proposition to be found only in national states such as England, France, Belgium, and the United States and to be defended only by due concern for the interests of those states. Fearing that aiming too high would result in hypocrisy and moral debilitation, his plea

---

69) and Lodge thought it inevitable (and not particularly distressing) that the military, as after the Civil War, would again become the dominant factor in the country (Lodge to John T. Morse, Jr., Sept. 11, 1918, Lodge MSS).

80. Lodge to Trevelyan, Oct. 14, 1918, Lodge MSS.

81. Lodge to Lord Bryce, Aug. 2, 1918, Lodge MSS.

82. *Ibid.*

83. Privately he complained about the Fourteen Points being "mere words and general bleat about virtue being better than vice"—so vague that "almost anything in the way of details can be built up under them" (Lodge to W. R. Thayer, Oct. 14, 1918, and to Hampton L. Carson, Nov. 28, 1918, Lodge MSS), but in public he was more circumspect. However, Roosevelt in articles in the *Kansas City Star* became increasingly less so. See especially his "Further Consideration of the Fourteen Points," Oct. 30, 1918, in Ralph Stout, ed., *Roosevelt in the Kansas City Star*, pp. 243–48.

was "let us be true to ourselves, and we shall not then be false to any man."[84] His object, as he described it, was to put "in the most simple and practical form so that he who runs might read a series of conditions which would act upon Germany like handcuffs and fetters. . . ."[85]

Physical guarantees for the Allies became Lodge's preoccupation. He regarded the erection of independent Slav and Polish states "as of a greater importance for the future peace of the world than anything else."[86] The erection of such national states was not just the concomitant of a "liberal" peace. It was also in the security interest of the Democracies. Similarly, he declared that Alsace and Lorraine *must* be returned to France "not merely because sentiment and eternal justice demand it, but because the iron and coal of Lorraine must be forever taken from Germany."[87] Lodge proposed to base the peace settlement on a different philosophical foundation, on grounds most Wilsonians could not accept. Present positions were but extensions of those previously taken up; so much depended on one's answer to the question why the United States had entered the war. *The New Republic* noticed that Lodge had made no reference to international organization nor suggested any way of alleviating the problems caused by economic nationalism.[88] *The Public*, while finding his war aims "in form unexceptionable," vehemently objected to his "strange" reasoning and declared that "so complete a repudiation of what has hitherto given us the will to fight, so frank an acceptance of an outlook dominated by force, must cause astonishment wherever Americanism has meant a liberalizing and unselfish spirit." America, according to *The Public*, was fighting to create a new world order in which there could be no place for considerations such as Lodge raised.[89] Lodge found himself having to combat not a precise set of proposals, but rather a whole mentality.

It was not just a matter of his wanting to see the peace established on a different philosophical basis. In the process of outlining his war and peace settlement aims, the Senator was also constructing a party platform. With both the end of the war and elections imminent, war aims and party politics could no longer be separated. Lodge was convinced

---

84. Lodge, "America's War Aims," *Current History* 9 (Oct. 1918): 141–43.
85. Lodge to James Beck, Oct. 5, 1918, Lodge MSS.
86. Lodge to James Ford Rhodes, Sept. 11, 1918, Lodge MSS.
87. Lodge, "America's War Aims," p. 141.
88. "War Aims and Party Politics," *The New Republic* 16 (Aug. 31, 1918): 122.
89. "The Irreducible Minimum," *The Public* 21 (Sept. 7, 1918): 1134–35.

that his speech of August 23 would make "good standing ground for the Republican party."[90] Wilson in turn, fearing that his plans for peace were being undermined, launched an appeal for the election of a Democratic Congress so that he might serve as the American people's "unembarrassed spokesman in affairs at home and abroad."[91]

A nonpartisan issue is a rarity in American politics, and the remote possibility that the peace settlement would so qualify was lost in the fall of 1918. The election settled nothing, but the campaign gave life to a pattern of opposition. The result may actually have turned on domestic issues, but it was a result that gave encouragement to those who believed in the necessity of a peace settlement founded on a basis different from that envisaged by Wilson. The verdict rendered Wilson vulnerable to the charge that his personal leadership had been repudiated and for the first time in his Presidency required him to face a Congress controlled by the opposition party.[92]

Hard on the heels of Wilson's electoral setback came the end of hostilities. There was an armistice, but what ensued can scarcely be termed a negotiated settlement. Thwarted in some respects (there were never to be Allied troops in Berlin nor an unconditional surrender), Lodge could nevertheless take satisfaction in the fact that the peace was far different from that originally contemplated by Wilson.[93] To reconcile such a peace with the extravagant promises of future world harmony he had made, and with a peace program conceived in pacifist abstention from the war, and probably much better suited to a "peace without victory," was now Wilson's task. It was a formidable one.

III

As the war ended and the world turned its attention to the peace settlement, it would have been hazardous to predict the precise nature of that settlement. The armistice arrangement left considerable doubt

90. Lodge to Roosevelt, Aug. 31, 1918, Lodge MSS.
91. Quoted in Garraty, *Lodge*, p. 342.
92. Lodge lost no time in impressing on the British the magnitude of Wilson's setback, emphasizing that it was one of the worst mid-term defeats suffered by any President and that such a defeat had never before occurred in time of war (Lodge to Lord Bryce, Nov. 16, 1918, and to Arthur Balfour, Nov. 25, 1918, Lodge MSS).
93. Charles Washburn to Lodge, Nov. 23, 1918, Roosevelt MSS. Lodge was so taken with Washburn's perception of the character of the peace that he sent his letter on to Roosevelt.

as to whether the peace would be imposed or negotiated. Even more questionable was the part to be played by the proposal to establish a league of nations. Wilson's fourteenth point proclaimed that "a general association of nations must be formed under specific covenants for the purpose of affording mutual guarantees of political independence and territorial integrity to great and small states alike."[94] But, to focus on perhaps the most basic issue, the President had never made it clear whether he contemplated an international army of enforcement or merely a self-denying ordinance. We have always known that he isolated himself from those who opposed his league, but what has only more recently come to light is the extent to which he isolated himself from those who had long worked for the creation of an international league.[95] As a result public discussion had not moved much beyond the point reached in the winter of 1916–17 when Lodge first asked some pointed questions about Wilson's plans. Wilson had then refused to allow himself to be pinned down and throughout the war he kept his distance from those who advanced specific proposals. "Taft and his colleagues were never to know precisely where they stood with Wilson or to what degree he really believed in their League to Enforce Peace."[96] Wilson scotched a plan whereby the League to Enforce Peace would have worked closely with the British League of Nations Society, and he refused to allow the Taft plan even to be submitted to Congress. Moreover, he told Taft that the Senate "would be unwilling to enter into an agreement by which a majority of the other nations could tell the United States when they must go to war," and gave both Taft and Lowell the impression that he was turning against the use of force and of a mind to throw over the whole league idea.[97]

One can only believe that Wilson either had given the matter little thought or was deliberately choosing to be vague. The problems involved in constructing a league which would be both workable and in sufficient conformity with American experience to make it feasible in terms of domestic politics were manifest from the outset. There was

94. *President Wilson's State Papers and Addresses*, p. 470.

95. See especially Warren Kuehl, *Seeking World Order*. Charles Seymour was also aware of this Wilsonian proclivity. See Charles Seymour, ed., *The Intimate Papers of Colonel House* (Boston, 1926–28), IV, pp. 4–5.

96. Pringle, *Taft*, I, p. 932.

97. *Ibid.*, pp. 936–37; Vinson, *Referendum for Isolation*, p. 32; Lowell to Taft, March 30, 1918, League to Enforce Peace MSS.

no dearth of comment on the difficulties likely to be encountered. Some tough decisions were involved, and while it may have been politic to avoid them as long as possible, to do so was to miss an opportunity to secure public and Congressional support for something more tangible than the mere idea of a league and to invite their reappearance at a later and less opportune time. One of the more thoughtful commentaries on the league idea was that of "Cosmos," who in 1917 published a prescient little book entitled *The Basis of a Durable Peace*. "Cosmos" (actually Nicholas Murray Butler) stressed the need for building on the foundations laid at The Hague, and the importance Americans had always attached to establishing international organization on a juridical basis. He warned that the Monroe Doctrine would have to be "accepted as an elementary fact in attempting to arrive at any practical conclusion as to the participation of the United States in the administration of a new international order," and therefore proposed the formal erection of two separate jurisdictions, one American and one European (an interesting transitional type of proposal). Above all, he insisted that Congress's power to declare war was an insuperable obstacle to American participation in an organization dependent on automatic sanctions.[98]

Even more revealing of the difficulties inherent in American participation in a league to enforce peace was a written debate, "World Peace," between William Howard Taft and William Jennings Bryan. There had always been a certain ambiguity in Taft's conception; he could at one and the same time talk about a universal league and yet refer to the Allied effort against Germany as a prototype. Bryan pressed him on the practicability of a universal league in view of the prevalent war psychology, and Taft had no reply but to suggest that American leadership might reconcile the contending nations. But even as Taft and Bryan were still arguing, the United States entered the war, and the stock image of a league began slowly but inexorably, under the logic of wartime conditions, to change from that of a universal league to a league of victors. For Taft this presented few problems; American entry into the war led him to proclaim that a World League to Enforce Peace had been formed.[99] The watchword of the League to Enforce Peace

98. Cosmos [Nicholas Murray Butler], *The Basis of a Durable Peace* (New York, 1917), pp. 91–93, 99–101, 103, 109.
99. *World Peace: A Written Debate Between William Howard Taft and William Jennings Bryan*, pp. 23, 31, 42–43, 52–53, 93, 147.

readily became: "We are engaged with our Allies in precisely the kind of war the League's program holds to be both justifiable and necessary."[100] But Bryan's constituency was also Wilson's and this made the subject a ticklish one for the President. He could never quite accept the association the League to Enforce Peace found so compelling and as late as his Fourteen Points address looked to the inclusion of Germany in his "covenants of justice and law and fair dealing."[101] The possibility of forming a universal league along the lines Wilson originally envisaged (if it had ever existed) was destroyed by American entry into the war. Yet its attraction remained so strong as to invite the development of a league which was neither quite a league of victors nor yet a universal league, but rather a hypocritical blend of the two.

Wilson preferred as in May of 1916 and January of 1917 to let the league be all things to all men. He made no attempt to educate public opinion on what Lodge considered the all important details of prospective world organization. Both personally and politically he found it convenient to ignore the problems inherent in the relationship between force and peace. The league as depicted in his Fourteen Points Address seemed to rest on an implied threat to use force against would-be violators of the new international order, and yet the pacifist impulse in his thinking and in that of many of his followers was so strong that it was tempting to picture a league so morally ascendant that force would never have to be employed.[102] It was this particularly Wilsonian straddle that caused Roosevelt to focus on the problem of credibility, and to fear that Wilson would inevitably make the league a thing of words and do his best to substitute "some fake policy of permanent pacifism" for one based on permanent preparation.[103]

While the war was in progress Lodge also had little to say on the

100. Lawrence Lowell, "Win the War," (A Reference for Speakers on Behalf of the League to Enforce Peace), League to Enforce Peace MSS.

101. *President Wilson's State Papers and Addresses*, p. 471.

102. As Roosevelt liked to point out, there were some basic incongruities in the Fourteen Points. Coupled with the undertaking of vast commitments (Point 11) to guarantee the political and economic independence and territorial integrity of the Balkan states (a particularly volatile area where the populations were so mixed that the invocation of the nationality principle did not automatically create viable states) was the declaration (Point 4) that "national armaments will be reduced to the lowest point consistent with domestic safety." See Roosevelt, "Further Consideration of the Fourteen Points," in Stout, ed., *Roosevelt in the Kansas City Star*, pp. 244–45.

103. Hagedorn, *The Bugle That Woke America*, p. 108; Roosevelt, *National Strength and International Duty* (Princeton, 1917), p. 52.

subject of a league. To him all talk of a league still carried the connotation of a desire for a negotiated settlement, and he saw no reason to change the position detailed in his February 1, 1917 speech on "The President's Plan For World Peace." When the subject of the league again came to the fore he had only to reach back to that speech for his arguments. It continued to serve his purposes. He had emphasized the practical and political difficulties involved in the construction of a system to actually enforce peace, had warned against entangling the question of how to make peace permanent with the peace to end the present war, and had insisted that "a treaty which cannot or will not be scrupulously fulfilled is infinitely worse than no treaty at all."[104] He recurred to the latter point during the war, characterizing the maintenance of the sanctity of treaties as "one of the war's great features and objects."[105] But like most Congressmen he focused his attention on more immediate issues and left it to Roosevelt, the publicist in the partnership of parliamentarian and publicist, to carry on discussion of the league proposal.

To Roosevelt the spirit behind a league remained of more significance than its institutional arrangements. He thought it might be possible to limit future wars, but only "by wise action, based equally on observed good faith and on thoroughly prepared strength" and those, he insisted, were the precise characteristics in which his countrymen were wanting.[106] Hence, he accorded a higher priority to the cultivation of those characteristics than to the formation of a league. "Sound nationalism" was still a necessary antecedent to "sound internationalism." Roosevelt was ready to see the United States join a league to enforce peace, but only on condition that "we do not promise what will not or ought not to be performed" and "do not surrender our right and duty to prepare our own strength for our own defense." Above all he wanted the coun-

104. Lodge, *War Addresses*, pp. 247–79, especially pp. 264–65. This is much the same warning Elihu Root gave to Colonel House in response to a solicitation of his views on the subject of a league in August 1918: "Nothing can be worse in international affairs than to make agreements and break them. It would be folly, therefore, for the United States in order to preserve or enforce peace after this War is over to enter into an agreement which the people of the United States would not regard as binding upon them. I think that observation applies to making a hard and fast agreement to go to war upon the happening of some future international event beyond the control of the United States" (Jessup, *Elihu Root*, II, p. 378).

105. *Cong. Record*, 65th Cong., 1st sess., 1917, p. 6999.

106. William H. Harbaugh, ed., *Writings of Theodore Roosevelt* (Indianapolis, 1967), p. 385.

try to be wary of those who thought it possible "to secure peace without effort and safety without service and sacrifice. . . ." His greatest problem with Wilson's version of a league was that the President seemed to be telling the American people that a league and preparedness need not go hand in hand, that if they accepted the league they could safely reject preparedness. Roosevelt, on the contrary, felt that only on the basis of the adoption of a policy of permanent national preparedness could the U.S. afford to try the league experiment.[107] He and Taft were eventually able to get together on the league issue because Taft came out for universal military training, and this allowed Roosevelt to say that he backed the League to Enforce Peace as an addition to, and not as a substitute for, national preparation.[108]

The battle lines, drawn since the winter of 1916–17, became ever more taut as the war neared its conclusion. "Unanimity in approving a world organization," as Lansing later so aptly put it, "did not mean that opinion might not differ radically in working out its forms and functions."[109] Just under the surface of support for the principle lay a plethora of qualifications. Roosevelt in conditioning his support for league membership on a prior commitment to national preparedness was engaged in something of a personal crusade, but there was also a widespread feeling (at least in Republican ranks) that the league was already a reality, that the Allies constituted a de facto league. Lodge thought the Allies a "good enough league for the present at least," and even Taft and Lowell felt the league might initially consist of only the major Allied powers—England, France, Italy, Japan, and the U.S.[110] Other and predictable Republican concerns were the preservation of the Monroe Doctrine (with Roosevelt taking up Cosmos's idea and suggesting the reservation of specific spheres of influence under any league arrangement) and the revitalization of the Hague Tribunal, a way of expressing their continued interest in a juridically based internationalism.[111] Most people were still talking about a league in general

107. Stout, ed., *Roosevelt in the Kansas City Star*, pp. 195, 229–31.

108. Pringle, *Taft*, I, p. 932; Morison, ed., *Letters of Theodore Roosevelt*, VIII, p. 1362.

109. Lansing, *The Peace Negotiations*, p. 34.

110. Boston *Herald*, Oct. 31, 1918; Theodore Marburg, ed., *Taft Papers on the League of Nations* (New York, 1920), pp. 160–61; Lowell to Lodge, Nov. 27, 1918, Lodge MSS.

111. See, for example, Stout, ed., *Roosevelt in the Kansas City Star*, p. 262; and "The Resolutions of the Middlesex [Mass.] Club, Oct. 29, 1918," Lodge MSS.

terms, but the magic phrase "league for peace" already masked many different and even contradictory ideas about how it ought to be constituted. Many people had already formulated distinct reservations with respect to a league.

Insufficient attention has been given to the extent of Lodge's own reservations in regard to a league at this time.[112] True, he did not mount a full scale attack on the league idea. To have done so would have been impolitic and counter to the advice of close English associates. It might also have played into the hands of the "isolationists," and Lodge was "internationalist" enough to be searching for a means of continuing to cooperate with the Allies. Lord Charnwood warned him against any merely negative criticism of a league, and they easily reached agreement on a league based on recurrent conferences of the "civilized" powers, conferences which would deal with problems as they arose and not try to anticipate all possible points. That came closest to "what we English-speaking people mean by a league."[113]

The idea (which could cover so much ground) was, Lodge told Beveridge, "all right—fine—but the details are vital."[114] Lodge did not

112. For Lodge to have had serious reservations about a league at this point in time ill accords with the theory that he opposed the league primarily because it was Wilson's league. Actually his thinking at this stage was considerably more incisive than would appear from Garraty's summary which depicts him as "expressing a lack of faith in the possibility of successful international organization without rejecting the idea of a league" and which attributes this position to his general pessimism (Garraty, *Lodge*, p. 347). Lodge had long since come to the conclusion that the only way to make a league effective was to put automatic force behind it, but he did not believe that conditions had yet evolved to a point where the American people either would or ought to support such an arrangement.

113. Lord Charnwood to Lodge, Nov. 26, 1918; and Lodge to Lord Charnwood, Nov. 28, 1918, Lodge MSS. The same idea was conveyed to Lowell: "I think we shall find that we can do more by periodic meetings dealing with specific questions than by attempting to draft a treaty which shall cover all possible questions" (Lodge to Lowell, Nov. 29, 1918, League to Enforce Peace MSS). For the development of British thinking on the subject of a league see Henry Winkler, *The League of Nations Movement in Great Britain*; Sterling J. Kernek, "Distractions of Peace During War: The Lloyd George Government's Reactions to Woodrow Wilson, Dec. 1916–Nov. 1918," *Transactions of the American Philosophical Society* 65 (n.s.), pt. 2 (1975); George W. Egerton, "The Lloyd George Government and the Creation of the League of Nations," *American Historical Review* 79 (April 1974): 419–37; and George W. Egerton, *Great Britain and the Creation of the League of Nations: Strategy, Politics, and International Organization* (Chapel Hill, 1978).

114. Lodge to Albert J. Beveridge, Nov. 23, 1918, Lodge MSS. Again he told Lowell essentially the same thing: "I have no intention of attacking the League of Peace . . . simply as a general proposition; I am waiting to come down to details, which are absolutely vital" (Lodge to Lowell, Nov. 29, 1918, League to Enforce Peace MSS).

believe that either world conditions or the nature of the American political system were conducive to the formation of an effective league. He hedged his bets even before the war was over, telling James Beck that "The League to Enforce Peace is all right after the war is won, but the main thing to do is to put Germany under such physical bonds . . . that it does not make any matter who signs the peace for her or whether there is a league of nations or not. . . ."[115] He was still waiting for somebody to explain to him "the condition of the League of Nations which shall make it a working body."[116] The more he studied it, "the greater the difficulties appeared. . . ."[117] The whole idea seemed fraught with peril.

One very dangerous thing is the League for Peace. It is easy to state the name. Everybody wants peace preserved; but the details are vital, and I do not believe the United States will consent or ought to consent to join any international body which would arrange our immigration laws or our tariff laws, or control the Monroe Doctrine or our actions in our own hemisphere, or have power to order our army or navy. It is being used by Wilson as a phrase, with perhaps an ultimate idea that he will be the head of the league. I think the practical difficulties are so great that it will be a long day before they really do anything about it. One thing is certain—it ought not to be attached to the treaty of peace. It would only lead to delays and disagreements. We should deal with the treaty of peace first by itself; it will be difficult enough to get a decent treaty, with Germany in a position where she cannot break out upon the world again.[118]

Believing in the necessity of enforcing the peace with Germany, Lodge feared that Wilson and those who had not been with the Allies from the beginning would seek to substitute the league proposal for the exaction of physical guarantees against the resurrection of German military power. This fear was the greater because he did not believe the league could perform such a function. In fact, he never believed it possible to form an effective league. He felt the whole thing would break down in conference: "there may be some vague declarations of the beauties of peace, but any practical league I do not think they can form."[119] The terms, the actual working arrangements, would be

115. Lodge to James M. Beck, Sept. 18, 1918, Lodge MSS.
116. Lodge to Mrs. August Belmont, Dec. 24, 1918, Houghton Library, Harvard University.
117. Lodge to Lowell, Nov. 29, 1918, League to Enforce Peace MSS.
118. *Correspondence of Roosevelt and Lodge*, II, p. 547 (Nov. 26, 1918).
119. Lodge to Albert J. Beveridge, Dec. 3, 1918, Lodge MSS. See also his letters

fatal to the scheme.[120] Stressing the enormous difficulty involved in converting human aspiration into law and the extraordinary permanence of human nature, he counselled the necessity of dealing with human nature "as it is and not as it ought to be . . . if we are to convert ideals into realities."[121] But at the heart of his position was a conclusion drawn after much rumination on the relationship between "Force and Peace." There was, Lodge was convinced, no half-way house, no way of constructing an effective League without putting an international military force behind it. As he told the Senate on December 21, 1918:

If, however, there is to be a league of nations in order to enforce peace, one thing is clear. It must be either a mere assemblage of words, an exposition of vague ideals and encouraging hopes, or it must be a practical system. If such a league is to be practical and effective, it can not possibly be either unless it has authority to issue decrees and force to sustain them. It is at this point that the questions of great moment arise.[122]

It was "easy to talk about a league of nations and the beauty and necessity of peace," he said, "but the hard practical demand is, are you ready to put your soldiers and your sailors at the disposition of other nations?"[123] In public he left the answer open, but, aware of the strength

---

to Beveridge of Nov. 23, Dec. 14 and 30, 1918, Beveridge MSS. His perception was not unique. Henry White, perhaps as experienced a diplomatist as the United States then possessed, allegedly comforted Alice Roosevelt Longworth by the observation "A League of Nations perhaps, en principe, my dear, but nothing that we should really have to worry about" (*Crowded Hours*, p. 277).

120. Lodge to Louis A. Coolidge, Dec. 3, 1918, Lodge MSS. See also Lodge to William Sturgis Bigelow, Nov. 29 and Dec. 23, 1918, Lodge MSS.

121. *Cong. Record*, 65th Cong., 3rd sess., 1918, p. 724; Lodge to Trevelyan, Dec. 7, 1918 and to John T. Morse, Jr., Dec. 25, 1918, Lodge MSS. As Roosevelt put it "there is so little that really can be done by any form of treaty to prevent war. . . . Any treaty adopted under the influence of war emotions would be like the good resolutions adopted at a mass meeting. We have an anti-vice crusade. Everybody is aroused. The movement culminates in a big meeting and we adopt resolutions abolishing vice. But vice isn't abolished that way" (*Roosevelt in the Kansas City Star*, p. xlvi).

122. *Cong. Record*, 65th Cong., 3rd sess., 1918, p. 727.

123. *Ibid.*, p. 728. In the last weeks of his life Roosevelt addressed himself more frequently to this issue than to any other. He stressed the difference between what he, personally, would be willing to do and what the nation might do, and his advice was "let us with deep seriousness ponder every promise we make *so as to be sure our people will fulfill it.*" Believing that the league would inevitably rest on the "willingness of each nation to fight for the right in some quarrel in which at the moment it seems to have no material concern," his experience told him that "the American people do not wish to go into an overseas war unless for a very great cause or where the issue is absolutely plain." See Hagedorn, *The Bugle That Woke America*, p. 205; Stout, ed., *Roosevelt in the Kansas City Star*, p. 294; Roosevelt, "The League of Nations," *Metropolitan* 44 (Jan. 1919): 9, 70.

of the pacifist and isolationist blocs in Congress, he never for a moment thought a plan for an international army could get through the Senate.[124] There was an insuperable obstacle to the formation of an effective league. That obstacle lay deep in the American character and in the nature of the American political system. Hence Lodge could confidently state that "the strength of our position is to show up the impossibility of any of the methods proposed and invite them, when they desire our support, to produce their terms; they cannot do it."[125] What was required for the construction of an effective collective security organization was never politically feasible at home. It was a dilemma from which Lodge determined that Wilson should not be permitted to escape.

Though he was already in close contact with people like Beveridge who were reassuming the traditional "isolationist" posture, Lodge's concerns were never theirs. True, their arguments were often the same and Lodge was as opposed as anyone to any derogation of national sovereignty. But Lodge cared about the peace settlement in Europe in a way that the "isolationists" never did (was concerned not only about its morality but about its viability), and many of the considerations which impelled him to oppose a league of Wilsonian design were "internationalist" reasons. During the war he often made the "internationalist" point that, the Monroe Doctrine notwithstanding, we *were* interfering in Europe and there was no longer any place for talk about the war being three thousand miles away and of no concern.[126] Naturally, he still believed in Washington's injunction against permanent alliances, but, as he expressed it, "we must make up our minds that as we have shared in the war we must share in the settlement of peace."[127] He also had a concern for the preservation of close relations with the Allies unknown among those who became isolationists. Though technically the U.S. had no treaty of alliance with those on whose side it fought, technicalities, he maintained, were of no consequence in the presence of facts. "To encourage or even to permit any serious differences to arise between the United States and Great Britain, or with France, or Italy, or Belgium, would be a world calamity of the

124. Lodge to William Sturgis Bigelow, Nov. 29, 1918, Lodge MSS.
125. Lodge to Albert J. Beveridge, Dec. 3, 1918, Lodge MSS.
126. Clipping from the Boston *Herald* of July 15, 1918, giving an account of Lodge's speech at a Bastille Day celebration in Symphony Hall, Boston, Lodge MSS.
127. Lodge to Charles G. Washburn, Nov. 26, 1918, Lodge MSS.

worst kind." Carrying out the peace with Germany would be the work of a generation and would necessitate the closest cooperation among the Allies.[128]

Another measure of Lodge's internationalism can be derived from the fact that on the eve of the Peace Conference he seemed willing to go considerably further than Wilson in making the United States a guarantor of the European settlement.[129] He considered it imperative that the Slavic nationalities be helped in establishing themselves as independent states, and privately he even suggested the possibility of the United States becoming a mandatory for such trouble spots as Constantinople.[130] At a time when Wilson was trying to distance himself from the Allied governments, Lodge wanted to tie the United States more closely to them.

We cannot halt or turn back now. We must do our share to carry out the peace as we have done our share to win the war, of which the peace is an integral part. We must do our share in the occupation of German territory. ... We can not escape doing our part in aiding the peoples to whom we have helped to give freedom and independence in establishing themselves with ordered governments, for in no other way can we erect the barriers which are essential to prevent another outbreak by Germany upon the world. ... .[131]

Lodge's outlook, in short, was no more isolationist than Wilson's and, in its emphasis on sacrifice and on the responsibilities of the United States, perhaps less so. Even Taft was prompted to remark in response to Lodge's Senate speech on the 21st of December that it "was the best yet made on the aims of the Allies and the elements of a satisfactory

128. *Cong. Record*, 65th Cong., 3rd sess., 1918, p. 727. A measure of the intensity of Lodge's feeling on this point is that he, by his own confession "always an extremist in regard to the navy," wanted absolutely no part of the Administration's plans for building a navy equal to that of England, believing that such a navy could only be directed at England and fearing its effect on Anglo-American relations. See the *Cong. Record*, same reference, and Lodge to Dudley L. Pickman, Dec. 30, 1918, Lodge MSS.

129. Bailey, *Woodrow Wilson and the Great Betrayal*, pp. 66–67.

130. Lodge to Lord Bryce, Dec. 14, 1918, and to Moreton Frewen, Dec. 4, 1918, Lodge MSS.

131. *Cong. Record*, 65th Cong., 3rd sess., 1918, p. 725. With respect to the Czecho-Slovaks he was particularly forthcoming, declaring that their independence "must be made secure and sustained by the Allies and the United States in every possible way." In support of this position he noted that Bismarck had said that whoever controlled Bohemia controlled Central Europe. See the Memorandum (prepared by Lodge and intended to be shown to Balfour, Clemenceau, and Nitti) attached to Lodge to Henry White, Dec. 2, 1918, Lodge MSS.

treaty of peace. . . . Its great merit is in its broad vision of the real purposes of the United States and her present obligation. . . . He [Lodge]
is not a little American."[132]

Both Lodge and Wilson were internationalists interested in making
the peace secure, but there the similarity ended. Their respective priorities were quite different. The President's mind, as Lodge suggested, was
"fixed on general questions lying outside the making of a peace with
Germany." Lodge could not have been too surprised that immediately
upon reaching Paris Wilson announced that the foundation of a League
of Nations would be the first and foremost task of the conference.[133]
The Senator believed, on the other hand, that "the first and controlling
purpose of the peace must be to put Germany in such a position that
it will be physically impossible for her to break out again upon other
nations with a war for world conquest."[134] Lodge saw no alternative.
Only by building on present conditions, only by the "existing and most
efficient league" [the Allies], could the peace be effectively implemented.
"The attempt to form now a league of nations—and I mean an effective league, with power to enforce its decrees—no other is worth discussing—can tend at this moment only to embarrass the peace that we
ought to make at once with Germany."[135] Both privately in a memorandum prepared to be shown to Balfour, Clemenceau, and Nitti, and
publicly in the Senate he warned that the consequences of Wilson's
persistence could be dire:

. . . under no circumstances must provisions for such a league be made a
part of the peace treaty which concludes the war with Germany. Any attempt
to do this would not only long delay the signature of the treaty of peace,
which should not be unduly postponed, but it would make the adoption of
the treaty, unamended, by the Senate of the United States and other ratify-
ing bodies, extremely doubtful.[136]

132. Marburg, ed., *Taft Papers on the League of Nations*, p. 174.
133. Lodge to Lord Bryce, Dec. 14, 1918, Lodge MSS.
134. Memorandum enclosed with Lodge to Henry White, Dec. 2, 1918, Lodge
MSS. Lodge's attitude was extremely close to that of Clemenceau, and he came to
admire the French greatly for their forthrightness, for knowing what they wanted
and understanding what their security demanded. See Nevins, *Henry White*, p.
374.
135. *Cong. Record*, 65th Cong., 3rd sess., 1918, p. 728.
136. The quotation is from the memorandum enclosed with Lodge to Henry
White, Dec. 2, 1918 (Lodge MSS), but the same message is conveyed in Lodge to
Arthur Balfour, Nov. 25, 1918 (Lodge MSS) and in his speech in the Senate on
Dec. 21, 1918 (*Cong. Record*, 65th Cong., 3rd sess., 1918, p. 728).

There developed out of this what Arno Mayer has described as a "transnational political confrontation."[137] The patterns of allegiance and mistrust formed in the years of America's neutrality were too strong to be overcome. Lodge so distrusted the President that he was quite willing to undermine his position at the Peace Conference. In his affinity for the British Lodge was prepared to undercut Wilson as Hamilton had once undercut John Jay. His views had long been more in accord with those of the leaders of the Allies, and now he sought to encourage them to stand up to Wilson, particularly on the league issue and the exaction of physical guarantees. The memorandum he gave to Henry White might "in certain contingencies be very important to them [Balfour, Clemenceau, and Nitti] in strengthening their position." His December 21 Senate speech was "intended chiefly for the benefit of the Allies."[138]

Wilson for his part distrusted not only Lodge but also the Allied leaders and told his advisers that the men with whom they were about to deal did not really represent their respective nations.[139] Tragically, events had long since precluded even the possibility of Lodge and Wilson listening to one another.[140] Lodge's warnings probably only increased Wilson's determination to put his own stamp on the Peace Conference. Perhaps even more unfortunate, their disdain for each other also precluded an appreciation of their respective abilities and strengths. As a result Wilson began to think in terms of arranging things so that the Senate would be forced to accept a league and Lodge, having confidence only in the sense of the Allies, determined to "force Wilson, as we forced him before, to do what ought to be done but which he is not planning to do."[141] Thus did they underestimate one another and thus did a historic and (if there be any logic in history) well-nigh inevitable struggle begin.

137. *Politics and Diplomacy of Peacemaking*, p. 19.
138. Lodge to Henry White, Dec. 2, 1918, Lodge MSS; and *Correspondence of Roosevelt and Lodge*, II, p. 550 (Dec. 23, 1918).
139. Elletson, *Roosevelt and Wilson*, p. 154.
140. Alice Roosevelt Longworth (*Crowded Hours*, pp. 276–77) recalls Lodge quoting from *Richard III* to describe Wilson's aloofness: "I will converse with iron-witted fools, and unrespective boys: None are for me, that look into me with considerate eyes."
141. Lodge to John T. Morse, Jr., Dec. 25, 1918, Lodge MSS.

Chapter Eight

Wilson and the Fourteen Reservations, or the Struggle over the Nature of American Internationalism

December and January were anxious months. Uncertainty over Wilson's intentions stirred Lodge's old fears.

I know nothing about what the President is trying to do in Europe. I doubt if he knows himself. I read his speeches and they are all in the clouds and all fine sentiments that lead nowhere. What I am afraid of is that he will manage to get himself into difficulty with some of the Allies.[1]

In the dark as to Wilson's intentions, Lodge prudently began to erect barriers which would ensure a remedy against a settlement that did not take his and Roosevelt's views on the proper scope of American internationalism into account.[2]

The Administration's foreign policy had figured prominently in the recent Congressional elections and, as Thomas Bailey once wrote, it was "as inescapable as the law of gravitation" that calculations of political advantage would enter into consideration of the Versailles

1. Lodge to Elihu Root, Jan. 3, 1919, Root MSS. Lodge, always sensitive to the domestic political advantage available to those who put the British in their place, was "very much afraid of trouble with the Allies" and thought "it may be deliberately entered upon" (Lodge to William Sturgis Bigelow, Nov. 26, 1918, Lodge MSS).
2. *Internationalism* is not altogether a satisfactory word. The standard dictionary definition, "the principle of international cooperation for the common good," is vague and inclusive. It really only acquires meaning in historical context, in the context of the pervasive American feeling that the quarrels of Europe were of no concern to the United States. Those who thought differently, no matter how disparate their plans, were all "internationalists" of a sort.

Treaty.[3] Bailey explained that the nature of the American political system precluded its being considered on a nonpartisan basis; just as the Democrats had benefitted from having won the war, so too did they stand to profit from the formation of a league for peace.[4] The Lodge who was astute enough to see political opportunity in the interest in the peace settlement (particularly as it pertained to their country of origin) being manifested among so many of America's ethnic communities,[5] scarcely needed Albert Beveridge to remind him that "the future of the party is in your hands more than in those of any other man," that Republican prospects would suffer greatly if the Democrats could claim that Wilson had brought about "the greatest constructive world reform in history."[6]

Beveridge, whose isolationism was nurtured on an antipathy for the British, was early convinced that "besides the solid argument on the merits, we have in it [the League] a real, a great and a winning political issue."[7] Lodge and Roosevelt, however, were not so sure; as they saw it, that opportunity was at least initially more available to the Democrats. As Roosevelt put it just before his death, the problem was primarily political:

. . . in forming the league the chief danger will come from the enthusiastic persons who in their desire to realize the millennium at once, right off, play

3. Bailey, *Woodrow Wilson and the Great Betrayal*, p. 38.

4. Bailey, *Woodrow Wilson and the Lost Peace*, pp. 200–01. Arno Mayer, on the other hand, insists that Wilson "in his dual capacity as Chief Executive and World Statesman" was "less concerned with turning his diplomacy to political account than with maintaining sufficient domestic support to implement it" (*Politics and Diplomacy of Peacemaking*, pp. 59–60). "Less concerned" perhaps, but not oblivious to the possibilities as we shall see. With that qualification Mayer's assertion is probably acceptable, but he goes on to claim that only the Republicans were in a position to play politics with foreign policy. That is like saying the possibility only presents itself to the opposition party that has a Congressional majority and never to the party that controls the Executive branch. Our recent history has shown that not to be the case. For the contrasting view that Wilson sought to make the League a vehicle for a Democratic victory, and even perhaps for his election to a third term, see Wesley M. Bagby, "Woodrow Wilson, A Third Term and the Solemn Referendum," *American Historical Review* 60 (April 1955): 567–75.

5. On December 20, 1918 Lodge wrote to Republican National Chairman Will Hays saying "I am going to send you some resolutions I introduced for the Poles, the Lithuanians and the Armenians. I have had a great response to them from all over the country for we have many people of those races who are voters and American citizens, and I know that they can be used in certain quarters effectively" (Lodge MSS).

6. Albert J. Beveridge to Lodge, Jan. 28, 1919, Beveridge MSS.

7. Beveridge to Lodge, Nov. 14, 1918, Lodge MSS.

into the hands of the slippery politicians who are equally ready to make any promise when the time for keeping it is far distant. . . .[8]

To counteract this possibility they devised a strategy of their own. Their only chance seemed to be that of bringing the people gradually to the practical details.[9] Lodge had as yet no intention of directly attacking the League, but thought it well that "they should begin to know what the practical difficulties and dangers are."[10] Though they still hoped to exercise some influence over Wilson's decision, it was time to begin an educational campaign.

Lodge also prepared to do battle on the constitutional ground of the Senate's proper role in the formulation of the nation's foreign policy. Here he also laid his defenses carefully. Always sensitive and outspoken on that score, Lodge seized upon the first indication that the Administration believed that the country could be committed to an abandonment of isolation without Senate action.[11] If he had known that Wilson seriously entertained the idea of including the Covenant in a preliminary treaty not to be submitted to the Senate, he would have been even more adamant on the subject of the Senate's prerogatives.[12] As it was he made it clear that he considered the present situation unparalleled ("the most important diplomatic negotiation ever entered upon" by the United States). Therefore the normal right of the Senate to advise was now a duty.[13] Taking full advantage of the growing feeling, inevitable after a war under the American system of government, that the time had come for Congress to reassert itself, he stimulated that feeling by warning:

8. Roosevelt, "The League of Nations," *Metropolitan* 49 (Jan. 1919): 9.

9. Lodge to Brooks Adams, Dec. 28, 1918, Lodge MSS. Lodge informed Adams that Roosevelt "feels that the only way to meet it is by bringing them gradually to the practical details which are vital."

10. Lodge to Trevelyan, Dec. 27, 1918, Lodge MSS.

11. Lodge, "The Peace Note of the President," *War Addresses*, pp. 212–13. During the debate on the Taft arbitration treaties in 1912, for example, he claimed that "in the last resort a complete control over them" [the nation's foreign relations] had been given to the Senate. See the *Cong. Record*, 62nd Cong., 2nd sess., 1912, p. 2597.

12. See Robert Lansing, *The Peace Negotiations*, pp. 206–07; and Kurt Wimer, "Woodrow Wilson's Plans to Enter the League of Nations Through an Executive Agreement," *Western Political Quarterly* 11 (Dec. 1958): 800–12. Wilson's attitude provides an interesting contrast to events in Europe where, in the wake of war, legislatures were everywhere securing more control over foreign policy decisions.

13. *Cong. Record*, 65th Cong., 3rd sess., 1918, p. 724.

The plan seems to be to project upon the Senate the most momentous treaty ever made without any information as to the steps which led to it or as to the arguments and conditions which brought about its adoption. This scheme, which is indicated by all the facts known to us, rests on the theory that the Senate, although possessing the power, would not and could not dare to reject a treaty of peace.[14]

With such an important settlement in the offing and with the United States seemingly destined to play a major role in the formulation of its terms, the issue of control over the nation's foreign policy was bound to arise. As Edwin S. Corwin once observed, the Constitution virtually invited such a struggle.[15] In the context of the times and of Wilson's proclivity for gathering power in the Executive branch it was neither a minor nor a contrived issue. Lodge first raised it as a means of influencing the terms of the peace settlement. The war had barely ended when he introduced a resolution in the Senate attempting to tie Wilson irrevocably to his Fourteen Points statement on Poland.[16] The same determination to "advise" the President can be seen in the resolution introduced by Senator Philander Knox of Pennsylvania calling for the limitation of American aims at the peace conference to "restitution, reparation, and guarantees against the German menace," and for the postponement until some future date of any project for a general league of nations. This resolution reflected Lodge's views (ideas which went back to the winter of 1916–17) and he may even have had a hand in its drafting.[17] These resolutions were not intended for immediate adoption,

14. *Ibid.* Senator La Follette interrupted Lodge's speech to drive home the same point even more forcefully by quoting from his *Constitutional Government* Wilson's opinion that "to guide diplomacy is to determine what treaties must be made if the faith and prestige of the Government are to be maintained. He [the President] need disclose no step of negotiation until it is complete, and when in any critical matter it is completed the Government is virtually committed. Whatever its disinclination, the Senate may feel itself committed also."
15. *The President: Office and Powers* (New York, 1957), p. 171.
16. The resolution (S. Res. 338) followed the wording of Wilson's 13th point: "Resolved, That in the opinion of the Senate an independent Polish State should be erected which should include the territories inhabited by indisputably Polish populations which should be assured a free and secure access to the sea [Lodge made it clear that to him that meant Danzig] and whose political and economic independence and territorial integrity should be guaranteed by international covenant." See the *Cong. Record*, 65th Cong., 2nd sess., 1918, p. 11579.
17. *Cong. Record*, 65th Cong., 3rd sess., 1918, p. 23; Jack E. Kendrick, "The League of Nations and the Republican Senate, 1918–1921," diss. North Carolina, 1952, pp. 57–58.

but as a warning to the President that the Senate's views would have to be taken into account. A sparring match had begun.

Lodge made it clear that he was not prepared to accept a league on faith alone and that he expected full consideration of "the enormous difficulties involved. . . ." He was carefully laying the basis for making the League a fundamental constitutional issue and a major issue in domestic politics. That was implicit in his claim and warning of January 3:

the ambitions or the fate of Presidents or presidential candidates, the fate of political parties, are infinitely small compared to what is before the Senate as part of the treaty making power; . . . we are concerned here with the settlement of questions which involve the peace of the world.[18]

But this was merely preliminary and precautionary skirmishing. The Congressional posture was defensive and the situation still in flux. The League and the peace settlement were likely to raise both a political and a constitutional issue. But such issues could not be fabricated; to make them artificially would be to risk the charge of unnecessary partisanship and of Congressional usurpation and serve only to create sympathy for the President. The extent to which these issues would and could be raised and whether the League would become an issue in its own right were still dependent on the nature of the arrangements Wilson would fashion in Paris.

Though Lodge prepared himself for the worst and laid his defenses carefully, these were only contingency plans that he did not really expect to have to employ. His preoccupation remained that of "putting Germany where she could not again break out upon the world." Lodge never once contemplated an isolated America. Rather, he was convinced that if there were to be a peaceful world "a good understanding of all English-speaking peoples" would lie at its foundations.[19] Moreover, he endorsed Knox's "new American doctrine," declaring that the domination of Europe by an aggressive military power was also a menace to the safety of the United States, and sincerely believed that such a league as the present one (the Allies) could "be brought together at any time should the world again be in danger."[20]

Lodge's information (however erroneous) was that Wilson contem-

18. *Cong. Record*, 65th Cong., 3rd sess., 1919, p. 974.
19. Lodge to Charles G. Washburn, Feb. 10, 1919, and to William Sturgis Bigelow, Feb. 13, 1919, Lodge MSS.
20. Lodge to Trevelyan, Jan. 20, 1919, Lodge MSS.

plated only a "very slender organization" at the start and was not even considering an organization that would involve placing U.S. military forces under international command.[21] Moreover, the Senator noted with considerable anxiety the growth of the feeling among the American populace that "the boys" should be brought home immediately, fearing that this feeling might become controlling and prevent the United States from playing its part in carrying out the peace. Without sacrificing fundamentals he was willing to trim his own sails a little. He began to retreat, for instance, from his earlier enthusiasm for mandates, coming to believe that the people would not stand for mandates that required the use of troops. Lodge probably thought Wilson would respond to changing public sentiment in a similar fashion. Convinced that a league with force behind it could never get through the Senate, it was clear to him that the league would have to be voluntary.[22] Nor was that just an opinion meant for Wilson's ears. Lodge was convinced that the problems involved in creating a league acceptable to all the powers were so great that the league would have to be "purely voluntary," that "we shall remain on the old voluntary system with improvements perhaps in statement of the Hague conventions."[23] He both underestimated Wilson and gave him credit for a better understanding of domestic political trends than the President in fact possessed.

As a result Lodge must have been surprised when on February 14 Wilson presented the completed Covenant of a League of Nations to the Peace Conference. The next day Wilson departed for the United States and cabled an invitation to the Senate Foreign Relations Committee to dine with him on his return. He also asked them to hold off all discussion until he had an opportunity to explain the Covenant's provisions to them. Not all Senators complied, but Lodge did, and his surprise soon turned to anger when he discovered that Wilson, having secured his silence, was going to land in Boston and address a mass meeting.[24]

Wilson had also devised a political strategy. It flowed directly from

21. Henry White to Lodge, Dec. 24, 1918, Lodge MSS. White was a member of the U.S. delegation to the Paris Peace Conference and had talked with Wilson.
22. Lodge to Henry White, Feb. 1, 1919, and to Russell Gray, Feb. 4, 1919, Lodge MSS.
23. Lodge to Trevelyan, Jan. 20, 1919, and to William Sturgis Bigelow, Feb. 13, 1919, Lodge MSS.
24. Lodge to William Thayer and to Henry White, Feb. 21, 1919, Lodge MSS.

the fact that the Covenant he brought home was an uneasy compromise. It was not quite the "definite guarantee of peace" that Wilsonians, then and later, pictured it to be.[25] Rather it was an instrument fraught with ambiguity and requiring the full explication that Wilson initially proposed to give it. It begged the most basic questions. It was not even clear whether it was meant to be an instrument of reconciliation or a means of giving permanence to the Allied victory, whether it was to be a universal association or only an organization of "free" nations.[26] The fault was not really Wilson's but lay in the nature of things. He faced virtually insoluble problems. As Brooks Adams trenchantly observed: "to attain to a relation among its parts in which physical force could be used by a League, would imply an effort of collective thought of which we have no adequate notion."[27] On the all-important question of the nature of the obligation incurred under Article X (which pledged all members not only "to respect" but to "preserve as against external aggression the territorial integrity and existing political independence of all Members of the League") the Covenant was equivocal. This confusion was but the inevitable consequence of the effort (however politically and diplomatically unavoidable) to "preserve national sovereignty while suppressing its consequences."[28] This, the classical problem in the construction of a viable universal collective security organization, was only compounded by the fact that Wilson had to appeal to two constituencies at home, one which expected that the League would on occasion have to employ military force and another, much the larger of the two, which conceived of a league invested with such moral force that the occasion for, and critical problems inherent in, the employment of force would never arise.[29] Under such circumstances Wilson saw that

25. See, for example, Fleming, *The United States and the League of Nations*, p. 114.

26. Herman, *Eleven Against War: Studies in American Internationalist Thought*, p. 206.

27. Quoted in Anderson, *Brooks Adams: Constructive Conservative*, p. 171. Adams was in frequent contact with Lodge throughout the League struggle and was always urging him to stiffen his opposition.

28. Stromberg, "The Riddle of Collective Security," p. 161.

29. Wilson was never particularly lucid or forthright on this matter. The best he ever did was in presenting the Covenant to the Peace Conference, when he said: "Armed force is in the background of this programme, but it is in the background, and if the moral force of the world will not suffice, the physical force of the world shall. But that is the last resort, because this is intended as a constitution of peace, not as a League of War" (quoted in Fleming, *The United States and the League of Nations*, p. 114). Even this was considerably weakened when in the

his hope lay not in gradually leading the people to accept new international responsibilities, not in teaching them that their vital interests were involved in the maintenance of peace in Europe, but rather in presenting them with a *fait accompli*—lay not in detailed discussion of the multifarious provisions of the Covenant, but rather in firing in the people a sense of moral urgency that would overwhelm all specific criticism.[30] As a result Wilson never attempted to explain his program in detail until his fateful Western tour in September (and then only after his hand had been forced by the Senate). In Boston and then two weeks later in his New York Opera speech, he avoided discussing the specific League arrangements, made no attempt to answer his opponents' arguments, and spoke only in exalted tones.[31]

This strategy, geared as it was toward creating an irresistible public demand for immediate ratification, had an important ancillary aspect which has often been overlooked. It was developed in a cablegram from Joseph Tumulty to Wilson dated January 6, 1919. Tumulty, arguing that Wilson's personal contact with the peoples of Europe had done much to advance his program, thought the President should use the occasion of his return "to strike in favor of [the] League of Nations." Specifically he suggested: "Could you not consider stopping upon your return at port of Boston instead of New York. The announcement of your stopping at Boston would make ovation inevitable throughout New England and would centre attack on Lodge."[32] Neither side ever

---

same speech he declared that "throughout this instrument we are depending primarily and directly upon one great force, and that is the moral force of the public opinion of the world, the cleansing and clarifying influences of publicity" (David Hunter Miller, *The Drafting of the Covenant* (New York, 1928), II, p. 562). At home he avoided all mention of the possibility of having to employ physical force. During his Western tour he even came to picture the League as the one alternative to the use of force, claiming that if the American people did not accept the treaty and opted to play a lone hand, "the hand that you play must be upon the handle of the sword" (Cronon, ed., *The Political Thought of Woodrow Wilson*, p. 508).

30. Vinson, *Referendum for Isolation*, p. 36.

31. *Ibid.*; Bailey, *Woodrow Wilson and the Great Betrayal*, p. 2; Kendrick, "The League of Nations and the Republican Senate, 1918–1921," p. 88.

32. Tumulty, *Woodrow Wilson As I Knew Him*, p. 517. Practically all those historians who have emphasized the political rather than the substantive nature of Lodge's opposition to the League have ignored this aspect of the situation. Even Lodge's biographer, Garraty, fails to mention it. Colonel House was alarmed by this blatantly political stratagem and sent a message urging the President to "compliment" the Foreign Relations Committee by making his first explanation of the Covenant to them. See Alexander and Juliette George, *Woodrow Wilson and Colonel House, A Personality Study* (New York, 1964), p. 235.

operated on the assumption that the League would not become entwined with domestic political considerations.

Wilson's strategy was not ill-conceived. It produced a considerable amount of pressure on Lodge to soften his opposition to the league idea. It also set the framework within which Lodge had to respond. The league idea was popular in Massachusetts and Wilson was well received in Boston. Even before Wilson's speech on the 23rd, Governor Coolidge wrote to Lodge suggesting the political wisdom of soft-pedalling his opposition to the League and reminding him that "Massachusetts is a pacifist state in a way."[33] Such advice was unneeded. Lodge was aware of his tactical disadvantage and had adjusted his horizons accordingly. He warned Beveridge that the situation required careful handling and that he did "not think it would be wise for us at this stage to make it a party issue, nor to confront it with a blank negative."[34] He allegedly told Borah that it could not be defeated outright, that "the best we can do is to get changes that will emasculate it as much as possible."[35]

Lodge was a man accustomed to accommodating himself to political realities, but in response to Coolidge's unsolicited advice he got up on his high horse. There were, he hastened to remind Coolidge, speaking as the aristocrat he was to a man he considered little more than a parochial politician, some things more important than consideration of political advantage. The League, he emphasized, was "a matter so momentous for the future of my country that I am unable to consider either personal or party interests." He promised to be circumspect, but also declared that he could never lend his support "to things which I believe will not make for the peace of the world. . . ."[36]

Did Lodge feel so strongly about the League issue that he was oblivious to the political considerations to which Coolidge alluded? Or was his a national political game for which he was prepared to neglect temporarily the drift of sentiment in Massachusetts? The argument has been taken to extremes on both sides. Lodge's defenders would have us believe that he opposed the League totally as a matter of principle, that "the views held by Mr. Lodge and expressed by him throughout this

33. Calvin Coolidge to Lodge, Feb. 22, 1919, Lodge MSS.
34. Lodge to Albert J. Beveridge, Feb. 18, 1919, Beveridge MSS.
35. John McCook Roots, "The Treaty of Versailles in the U.S. Senate," p. 86, Widener Library, Harvard University.
36. Lodge to Calvin Coolidge, Feb. 24, 1919, Lodge MSS.

contest were the views he had always expressed upon the great principles involved."[37] On the other hand his detractors to this day insist that he had no strong convictions on the League issue, that his "position or positions on the League of Nations derived not from grand principles but from considerations of tactical advantage in the twin battles of constitutionalism and party politics."[38] Both points of view are simplistic. One assumes that Lodge took positions on foreign policy matters without regard to their domestic political impact, while the other assumes that he would have made the League an issue in domestic politics without regard for the foreign policy consequences of his action. To take either position is to neglect the fact that Lodge was acutely aware of the interaction between domestic and foreign politics and that the Rooseveltian approach to the conduct of foreign policy to which he was so partial had been dependent on an ability to look both ways at once.

Lodge had two preoccupations in early 1919: one was a matter of foreign policy, the other of domestic politics. He was determined that Germany be placed under constraints and he was also determined to unify the Republicans so that "the Wilsonian party" might be driven from power.[39] Others, while defining Lodge's foreign policy interest somewhat differently (as, for example, the protection of American interests, which to my mind does not exclude but also does not place sufficient emphasis on his desire to have the European settlement rest on a firm basis), have commented on Lodge's facility in merging these twin goals.[40]

There is some indication that the second object gradually became predominant. If Wilson had been able to maneuver Lodge into a position where he were forced to choose, then things might have gotten interesting, though we may reasonably assume that Lodge would have swallowed the League had he seen therein the means of securing a Republi-

37. See, for example, Washburn, "Memoir of Henry Cabot Lodge," pp. 361–62. David Andelman in an interesting study, "Senators and the Public; A Case Study —1919: Massachusetts Public Opinion and the Ratification of the Treaty of Versailles," Harvard honors thesis, 1965, pp. 44 and 57, concludes that Lodge was seldom influenced by his constituents' views, that "he seemed to consider his office virtually a civil service position, and that he belonged not to any particular state but to the country and to history."

38. Mervin, "Henry Cabot Lodge and the League of Nations," pp. 211, 214.

39. Lodge to Charles G. Washburn, Feb. 10, 1919, Lodge MSS.

40. Robert James Fischer, "Henry Cabot Lodge's Concept of Foreign Policy and the League of Nations," diss. Georgia, 1971, p. 193.

can victory. From his point of view only a Republican victory could ensure a return to a proper and appropriate foreign policy.[41] But Wilson was never sufficiently master of the situation to force Lodge to choose between his twin goals. The Senator and the President battled on two fronts; they struggled over the substance of American foreign policy and for partisan advantage. It is a measure of Lodge's success that the one struggle gradually became indistinguishable from the other. Lodge in declaring his "first duty" to be that of uniting the Republicans in the Senate on the League issue was serving more than a partisan interest;[42] he was also enlisting the party in support of his foreign policy position.[43]

To argue that Lodge did not feel strongly about the League issue is to neglect the fact that he and Roosevelt had their own conception of how the nation's foreign policy ought to be conducted and that Lodge, after Roosevelt's death, saw himself as custodian of that legacy. In his circles it was taken for granted that Roosevelt would be the Republican presidential candidate in 1920, and when death snatched from him this opportunity of effecting his twin goals in one sure stroke, Lodge was disconsolate.[44] He felt "chilly and grown old"; the deaths of Gus Gardner,

41. Lodge made a point of claiming that Roosevelt had come to recognize that the Republican party was the only instrument through which he could attain his goals. See Lodge, "Theodore Roosevelt," *The Senate of the United States,* p. 131.

42. This he did over and over again. See, for example, Lodge to Beveridge, March 21, 1919, Lodge MSS. It should be noted, however, that this tack was taken with the party's irreconcilables more often than with its internationalists. It was a means of keeping potentially troublesome individuals in line. It is well to keep this aspect of the situation in mind when interpreting such Lodgian statements as his claim in a letter to George Harvey, April 18, 1919 (Lodge MSS), that "if the Republican party as an organization fails us, there is nothing else. Therefore my one desire is to give the Republican party control in the Senate and maintain its unity on the great issues so far as possible."

43. A number of commentators have pictured a Republican party still deeply divided between its progressive and stand-pat wings and have concluded that Lodge saw in opposition to Wilson's foreign policy a means of bridging that gap. See Selig Adler, *The Isolationist Impulse* (New York, 1957), p. 68; George F. Sparks, ed., *A Many-Colored Toga: The Diary of Henry Fountain Ashurst* (Tucson, 1962), p. 96; and particularly James Oliver Robertson ("The Progressives in National Republican Politics, 1916 to 1921," diss. Harvard, 1964, pp. 27, 146, 166, 252), who sees in Lodge's use of the League issue a conspiracy to thwart the Democratic reconstruction program and render the Progressives politically impotent. Actually the Republican party was in 1919, as a result of the long struggle over the nature of American neutrality and then over the country's war aims, as divided on foreign policy as on everything else. A good indication of this is that Lodge never dared to bring the Knox resolution (which he favored) to a vote for fear of revealing how deep those divisions went.

44. See, for example, Washburn, "Memoir of Henry Cabot Lodge," p. 350, and Hays, *Memoirs*, p. 189.

Spring Rice, Henry Adams, and Theodore, all within a year, he confessed, had left him feeling quite alone.[45] Roosevelt's passing left a great void in Lodge's life, a void which he was partially able to fill by making sure that Roosevelt's views were heard. This aspect of the fight over the League has been too long neglected. We have been too ready to see in Lodge's claim that he was in "entire agreement" with Roosevelt on the League issue, that the line he "followed in the Senate and elsewhere was the one which he [Roosevelt] wished to have followed," only a politically motivated attempt to enlist the support of Roosevelt's many partisans.[46] Of course, the frequent invocation of the Rooseveltian legacy served a political purpose, but in the face of Lodge's deep attachment to Roosevelt it seems unreasonable to assume that Lodge was just posturing. He may, in fact, have been remarkably forthright when he declared that the spirit of Roosevelt inspired his fight against the treaty, that he had simply followed in the path blazed by the man who "had a most distinct and clear conception of how foreign questions should be handled by a President."[47]

Even Lodge's tactics—bringing the people gradually to the practical details of the League—were in a measure Roosevelt's. Moreover, they were the same piecemeal tactics they had employed on previous occasions when they found that they were in a minority position. Lodge had long traded on the virtue of patience and his ability to anticipate the public's response. Theirs were tactics that developed naturally out of their understanding of the role of public opinion in the determination of the nation's foreign policy, and of the nature and depth of the American public's interest in such matters. They fully appreciated the limitations inherent in the American approach to foreign policy—appreciated what Harold Nicolson once portrayed as a salient vice of the democra-

45. Lodge to Charles G. Washburn, Feb. 14, 1919, Lodge MSS.
46. *Cong. Record*, 66th Cong., 2nd sess., 1920, p. 4458.
47. Boston *Herald*, Oct. 28, 1920, pp. 1, 10. He invoked Roosevelt's name, for example, to try to win Henry White over to his position, telling him that "Theodore and I discussed the whole question with the greatest thoroughness and we were in full agreement; I am following precisely the line that he wished me to follow and that he mapped out as the true line to be followed in dealing with the League whenever it came before us" (Lodge to Henry White, April 8, 1919, White MSS). This was also a prominent feature of his public discussions of the League issue. He seldom missed an opportunity to claim that his position was identical with that Roosevelt had assumed before his death. See, for example, the *Cong. Record*, 66th Cong., 1st sess., 1919, pp. 5502–03, and Lodge's "Joint Debate on the Covenant of Paris" with Lawrence Lowell reprinted in the World Peace Foundation's *League of Nations* (Boston, 1919), II, p. 52.

cies' foreign policy (namely their irresponsible attitude toward obligations and their preference for vague, comforting formulas as opposed
to precise and binding definitions) and what Louis Halle has more recently described as the public's proclivity for separating enthusiasm
for a cause from sacrifice for that cause.[48] That was the lesson Lodge
and Roosevelt had drawn from the public's dwindling support for imperialism and unwillingness to defend the Open Door in practice. They
devised their tactics accordingly.

The lesson of Lodge's experience was that in matters pertaining
to the country's foreign policy it was wise "to commit the Government only so far as the Government could redeem its pledges."[49] For
this reason he felt that in the Covenant the United States was "running
into grave dangers, the chief of which is being entangled in an agreement which at certain points would be broken by this country if in a
moment of stress or excitement. . . ."[50] The American delegation's principal shortcoming, Lodge quipped, was that they "considered feeling
and opinion in every country but their own."[51] To his way of thinking
the sanctity of treaties was so basic to peaceful international relations
that if the United States ever gave a guarantee such as that envisaged
under Article X, then it would have to be sustained.[52] Consequently, it
was to him of signal importance to have the American people under-

48. Nicolson, *Diplomacy*, p. 96; Halle, *Dream and Reality: Aspects of American Foreign Policy*, p. 144.

49. William Lawrence, *Henry Cabot Lodge*, p. 60.

50. Lodge to Elihu Root, March 14, 1919, Root MSS. Root often made the same point, claiming that "making war nowadays depends upon the genuine sympathy of the people of the country at the time when the war has to be carried on" (Root to Lodge, June 19, 1919, Lodge MSS). The easy answer to this very American prob-lem was what the Republican platform advocated in 1920, namely a kind of inter-national association which did not deprive the people of the United States in ad-vance "of the right to determine for themselves what is just and fair when the occasion arises" (Porter and Johnson, eds., *National Party Platforms*, p. 231). But that, of course, was to remove the basis for any kind of international commitment.

51. Lodge to Henry White, Aug. 19, 1919, quoted in Nevins, *Henry White*, p. 466.

52. "Joint Debate on the Covenant of Paris," pp. 56, 62. He believed that even the "suggestion that we can safely sign because we can always violate or abrogate is fatal not only to any league but to peace itself." See the *Cong. Record*, 65th Cong., 3rd sess., 1919, p. 4521. Here we see the thinking of a man who voted against Prohibition, but for its enforcement in the Volstead Act once it had become part of the Constitution, and who argued in 1890 for the "Force Bill" to protect Negro voting rights on the ground that "no people can afford to write anything into their Constitution and not sustain it." See the *Cong. Record*, 51st Cong., 1st sess., 1890, p. 6543, and 65th Cong., 1st sess., 1917, pp. 5586–87.

stand the road they were traveling, that they be prepared for and deliberately undertake such obligations.[53] He early came to the conclusion that once they understood, the American people would not be willing to give such a guarantee and that therefore, as he told Beveridge, "the second thought is going to be with us. . . ." But meanwhile the first thought, Lodge conceded, was "probably against us," and this called for special tactics.

I have no doubt that a large majority of the people of the country are very naturally fascinated by the idea of eternal preservation of the world's peace and that there shall be no more war. They are told that that is what this league means. They have not examined it; they have not begun to think about it. Now I do not think it would be wise for us at this stage to make it a party issue, nor to confront it with a blank negative. I think what is necessary for us to do is to begin to discuss it and try to get what it involves and what it means before the American people. That will be done.[54]

Lodge, the intellectual heir of the Federalists, did not trust the community's first thought on an issue involving perhaps "the most momentous decision that this country has ever been called upon to make."[55] Like the Federalists he viewed the Constitution as a means of ensuring that "the operation of the popular will depend for its final expression upon the calm second thought of the community and not be governed by the passions of the moment."[56] Democracy in order to function on a large scale had to be limited. In the realm of foreign policy the Constitution had provided the appropriate limitation, the requirement that treaties have the consent of two-thirds of the Senate.[57] Believing that to give a decision on the Covenant "hastily and without complete knowledge of what we are to agree to would be almost criminal," he determined to await the community's "calm second thought" and found therein a justification for adopting delaying tactics and assuming a position on the League that was less than forthright.[58]

53. "Joint Debate on the Covenant of Paris," pp. 62, 96–97.
54. Lodge to Beveridge, Feb. 18, 1919, Beveridge MSS.
55. Lodge to Charles G. Washburn, Feb. 22, 1919, Lodge MSS; *Cong. Record*, 66th Cong., 1st sess., 1919, p. 6128.
56. Lodge, *The Senate of the United States*, p. 16.
57. See James Polk Morris, "Henry Cabot Lodge and Congressional Control of Foreign Policy," Master's thesis, LSU, New Orleans, 1969, p. 56, for an interesting discussion of Lodge's belief that Wilson was threatening "the limited democracy of the Constitution."
58. Lodge to Charles G. Washburn, Feb. 22, 1919, Lodge MSS. John Garraty (*Lodge*, pp. 366–67), reflecting the then dominant view that Congress had best leave

Lodge's tactics may be described either as an effort to allow the people to make up their own minds (his own description), or as a cynical effort to defeat the league by devious methods. But if a case can be made that the public was uninformed on the league issue, then Lodge's tactics become less reprehensible.[59] John Garraty found Lodge's explanation (as in the letter to Beveridge above) of the popularity of the League "peculiar," and other critics have insisted that "all surveys of opinion in 1918 and 1919, even in 1920, showed that the American people wanted to join a world organization to preserve peace."[60] The choice of words is revealing. Putting it that way would undoubtedly have elicited just such a favorable response, but it is a response which tells us next to nothing. More recent analyses and any dispassionate examination of Wilson's speeches on the League suggest that Lodge's judgment that the public was uninformed had considerable basis in fact. Even men who might normally have been expected to exercise their critical faculties were caught up in the general enthusiasm. Henry Higginson wanted to "vote it through and get it going and get the world going," and Moorfield Storey was determined "to support the League of Nations in whatever form it is finally adopted."[61] But whatever one's assessment of public opinion in the early spring of 1919, it is difficult to deny that the more the public learned about the league the more they became

foreign policy to the Executive, wrote that "the tactics he [Lodge] displayed in the hearings make up the most discreditable portion of his role in the League fight" and complained of the Committee's constantly "badgering" the President with demands for papers and documents. All this sounds rather strange twenty-five years later. Now we can more readily sympathize with Lodge's frequent complaint that the President "would give us literally no information" which was "not the way that a Committee of Foreign Relations of the Senate should be forced to proceed." See, for example, Howe, *Barrett Wendell and His Letters*, pp. 316–17.

59. Lodge to Charles G. Washburn, Feb. 22, 1919, Lodge MSS. This point of view is nourished by the possibly apocryphal story related by James E. Watson in *As I Knew Them* (Indianapolis, 1936), p. 190. Watson alleged to have told Lodge that 80 percent of the people were for the League and that he didn't see how it could be defeated. Lodge was supposed to have replied: "Ah, my dear James, I do not propose to try to beat it by direct frontal attack, but by the indirect method of reservations."

60. Garraty, *Lodge*, p. 362; Alan Cranston, *The Killing of the Peace*, p. ix. Ruhl Bartlett (*The League to Enforce Peace*, p. 130) was even more categorical, claiming that "it is as certain as anything in the realm of public opinion can be that in May, 1919, the majority of the American people favored ratification . . . with the Covenant as it was."

61. Perry, *Life and Letters of Henry Lee Higginson*, p. 526; Howe, *Portrait of an Independent*, p. 324.

disenchanted with it. Public opinion somersaulted from pro- to anti-League as the vague Wilsonian ideal became a concrete reality demanding specific American pledges and sacrifices.[62]

Lodge lost little time in implementing his strategy. He went before the Senate on February 28 and delivered what Denna Frank Fleming once termed a "wholly reasonable," if "cold-blooded," speech.[63] His plea was for "consideration, time and thought." He wanted "facts, details and sharp, clear-cut definitions" that the American people might look into it "with considerate eyes." Democracy's customary foibles in the conduct of its foreign policy were much in his mind. He worried about the vagueness of the Covenant and warned that it would lead to misunderstandings and thence to conflict. Specifically, he demanded that the constitution of the League contain a definite statement as to whether the League would have a military force of its own or the power to summon the forces of its members. Here he put his finger on what was perhaps the League's greatest shortcoming as a collective security organization, the lack of an explicit agreement in this most vital of areas. Imploring his countrymen to be honest with themselves, he wondered whether they were now prepared to do in peace, "deliberately, coolly, and with no war exigency" what they had refused to do in war, whether "now in the twinkling of an eye, while passion and emotion reign, the Washington policy is to be entirely laid aside and we are to enter upon a permanent and indissoluble alliance."[64]

Four days later he introduced the famous "Round Robin," a letter in the form of a resolution which had been signed by more than a third of the Senate. It declared that the "constitution of the league of nations in the form now proposed to the peace conference should not be accepted by the United States" and suggested that the League be given serious consideration only after the conclusion of peace with Germany.[65] Lodge had been seeking to separate the two since the winter of 1916–17. Now he was fighting for time and influence in the deliberations of the Allies in Paris. The Round Robin was meant to "strengthen our friends abroad" and to let the Peace Conference know that "the President was not the only part of the government necessary to the making of

62. Stromberg, "The Riddle of Collective Security," p. 156.
63. *The United States and the League of Nations*, p. 136.
64 *Cong. Record*, 65th Cong., 3rd sess., 1919, pp. 4520–28.
65. *Ibid.*, p. 4974.

a treaty. . . ."[66] Wilson replied by boasting on the eve of his departure for Paris that he had so tied the treaty and the Covenant together that they were inseparable. In neither case were these the actions of men who did not care deeply about the nature of the peace settlement.

II

Criticism of the Covenant surfaced immediately, and Lodge found that more than half the Senate thought the original draft objectionable.[67] Unwilling yet to talk in terms of amendments or reservations, Lodge voiced his opposition to any provisions that would weaken the Monroe Doctrine, derogate from the Congress's constitutional power to declare war, or permit international control over such matters as immigration. With respect to Article X he declared:

I do not now say that the time has not come when, in the interest of future peace, the American people may not decide that we ought to guarantee the territorial integrity of the far-flung British Empire, including her self-governing dominions and colonies, of the Balkan States, of China or Japan, or of the French, Italian and Portuguese colonies in Africa; but I do suggest that it is a very grave, a very perilous promise to make, because there is but one way by which such guarantees, if ever invoked, can be maintained, and that way is the way of force—whether military or economic force, it matters not. If we guarantee any country on earth, . . . that guarantee we must maintain at any cost when our word is once given, and we must be in constant possession of fleets and armies capable of enforcing these guarantees at a moment's notice. There is no need of arguing whether there is to be compulsive force behind this league. It is there in article 10 absolutely and entirely by the mere fact of these guarantees.[68]

He was not entirely negative. He made one particularly interesting suggestion, an idea with which Roosevelt and Nicholas Murray Butler had also toyed.[69] In line with the thinking behind the Knox Resolution, he suggested "the possibility of arranging for two Leagues,—one in Europe, and the other American with the United States in control under

66. Lodge to James M. Beck, March 4, 1919, Lodge MSS; Lodge to Henry White, March 5, 1919, quoted in Nevins, *Henry White*, p. 391.
67. Lodge to Henry White, April 8, 1919, White MSS.
68. *Cong. Record*, 65th Cong., 3rd sess., 1919, p. 4522.
69. See above, pp. 289 and 292.

the Monroe Doctrine, the two Leagues to cooperate if the need arose."[70] This would have catered to American traditions and prejudices and, yet, in the hands of a leader like Roosevelt might also have become a means of moving the American people closer to an acceptance of an internationalist viewpoint. Wilson, however, was not interested in halfway measures, but rather in a final solution, and closed his mind to such suggestions.[71]

Certain passages in Lodge's February 28 speech raise the question whether he might not already have given up on the idea of forming even a rudimentary league. He claimed, *inter alia*, that we were being asked "in a large and important degree to substitute internationalism for nationalism and an international state for pure Americanism," being "invited to move away from George Washington toward the other end of the line at which stands the sinister figure of Trotsky the champion of internationalism."[72] Such rhetoric came easily to as ardent an American nationalist as Lodge, and found perhaps its culminating expression in his August 12, 1919, speech:

I can never be anything else but an American, and I must think of the United States first, and when I think of the United States first in an arrangement like this I am thinking of what is best for the world, for if the United States fails the best hopes of mankind fail with it.[73]

In this crucial area his thinking was much like Wilson's; he believed in an American mission and in American moral superiority. He wanted, as had Washington, "an American character" in foreign affairs, a character which could exist only on the basis of differentiation from Europe.[74] Yet surprisingly it is also not far from the mark to say that Lodge had an "essentially rational, realistic and European outlook on world politics."[75] He knew the United States was of this world and that it had enjoyed and needed working alliances with other states. He may like

70. Lodge to John Jay Chapman, March 7, 1919, Lodge MSS; *Cong. Record,* 65th Cong., 3rd sess., 1919, p. 4527.

71. See Alexander and Juliette George, *Woodrow Wilson and Colonel House,* especially p. 291, for a provocative, but not entirely convincing, interpretation of Wilson's inability to compromise. Wilson, just as did Lodge, cared deeply about the issues involved and believed some of them were not subject to reasonable compromise.

72. *Cong Record,* 65th Cong., 3rd sess., pp. 4522, 4528.

73. Daniel Boorstin, ed., *An American Primer* (Chicago, 1966), p. 790.

74. Clipping from the Boston *Evening Transcript,* Oct. 14, 1920, Scrapbooks, Lodge MSS.

75. Hewes, "Henry Cabot Lodge and the League of Nations," p. 255.

Elihu Root (though he could never bring himself to use the word "alliance") even have wanted to form an alliance with England and France for the purpose of containing Germany and preserving the Allied victory.[76] This rather schizophrenic attitude was also reflected in the type of league that Lodge wanted to see develop.

Lodge favored a limited league, a noncoercive, intermediate type of organization which might serve as a substitute for the alliance that was not politically feasible, a league that might secure the benefits of close association with the Allies and hold Germany in check, and yet at the same time not derogate from "the American character" in foreign affairs. Not a true internationalist, but never an isolationist, Lodge wanted the best of both worlds; he "would keep America as she has been—not isolated, not prevent her from joining other nations for these great purposes—but . . . master of her fate."[77] However objectionable this may have been in logic, it was not politically unsound. Lodge favored *a* league, but that old argument is probably irrelevant. The point is (and it is a point which escaped the vast majority of his contemporaries, unused as they were to the subtleties of international organization) that Lodge's conception of a league was so far removed from Wilson's formulation that to emphasize the fact that they both favored a league is to say almost nothing.

Lodge's qualifications speak volumes. Claiming that he was not against *a* League of Nations, he told the huge audience assembled in Symphony Hall in Boston on March 19 to hear his and Lowell's "Joint Debate on the Covenant of Paris" that he was "anxious to have the nations, the *free* nations of the world, united in *a* league . . . to do *all that can be done* to secure the future peace of the world and to bring about a general disarmament." If it could be made to promote peace instead of breeding dissension and quarrels—if it could be put "in such shape that it will bring *no injury or injustice to the United States*" then he would support it.[78] To Beveridge, who opposed any league, he wrote his disagreement with that position, saying that he could "conceive of *a* League that would do great good, *if properly guarded and in exact accord with our feelings*."[79] In writing to Henry White he employed the following careful formulation:

76. Diary of Henry L. Stimson, III, p. 71, Stimson MSS.
77. "Joint Debate on the Covenant of Paris," pp. 96–97.
78. *Ibid.*, pp. 90, 96–97. Italics mine.
79. Lodge to Beveridge, March 8, 1919, Lodge MSS. Italics mine.

I am not opposed to any League; on the contrary, I should like to see *a League among the Nations with whom we have been associated in the war* which would tend to promote and secure the future peace of the world, *without impairing certain rights and policies of the United States which do not in the least concern or trouble Europe.*[80]

As these passages indicate Lodge's problem, in addition to being forced to give lip-service to an idea in which he did not really believe, was that of getting the American public to understand that the differences between his conception and the President's could not be readily compromised. Both Lodge and Wilson appear to have understood the situation. The American people, hearing only the word *league*, remained to be convinced.

The initiative was entirely Wilson's. It was his League that was before the Peace Conference and his League that would eventually come before the Senate. Only if Lodge, Root, or Roosevelt had been in actual control of American foreign policy could they have constructed an alternative to the Wilsonian settlement. As it was, their ideas were little more than hypotheses. The time *was* opportune; the United States *was* ripe for an abandonment of the isolation against which Lodge had long, and Wilson more recently, contended. But there remained the question of what kind of internationalism would take its place. Root was convinced that Wilson was on the wrong track and told Lodge that if his proposal is not materially amended "the world will before very long wake up to realize that a great opportunity has been wasted in the doing of a futile thing."[81] Lodge also felt that a great opportunity was being wasted and urged Root to "show the public what ought to be done to accomplish as much as can practically be accomplished by a union of the nations to promote general peace and disarmament."[82] This Root soon did in a March 29 letter to Republican National Chairman Will Hays, a letter which culminated in six far-reaching amendments to Wilson's draft. But their position was defensive by definition; they could try to amend Wilson's proposal but they had no power to put anything in its place. The President was in a position to force them to

80. Lodge to Henry White, April 8, 1919, White MSS. Italics mine.
81. Elihu Root to Lodge, March 13, 1919, Root MSS.
82. Lodge to Elihu Root, March 14, 1919, Root MSS. These were scarcely the words of a man opposed to any league whatsoever. Lodge carried this same theme over into *The Senate and the League*, which ended (p. 226) with the charge that Wilson "was given the greatest opportunity ever given to any public man in modern times. . . ."

adopt a narrow, insular nationalism in order to prevent the construction of what they regarded as a dangerous, unstable form of internationalism. "In trying to do too much," Lodge feared (prophetically as it turned out) that "we might lose all."[83] It might have been otherwise. As Root recounted, when the proposal had been laid before the Paris Conference, the French representative, Leon Bourgeois, emphasized that "we do not present it as something that is final, but only as the result of an honest effort to be discussed and to be examined not only by this conference but the public opinion of the world."[84]

But this was not the manner in which Wilson presented the League to the American people. He offered a finished product, a *fait accompli*. On his return to Paris Wilson did try to meet some of Taft's suggestions for amendments, did try, for example, to secure some recognition of the Monroe Doctrine and establish a category of domestic issues over which the League would have no jurisdiction, but one would be hard pressed to argue that the Covenant underwent any substantial revision between February 15 and April 28, 1919, when the final draft was published. Lodge called Root that night to say that he found the amendments unsatisfactory and thought the League in its new form "but slight improvement over the first draft."[85] His complaints were essentially the same as in February. Still he was probably not too surprised. At the time of the Round Robin he still hoped to jolt the Peace Conference into a full reconsideration of the Covenant, but only two weeks later (after Wilson's uncompromising New York Opera speech) he had despaired of this happening and had suggested that it would have to be done elsewhere—plainly in the Senate.[86]

That made it a problem in domestic politics and served to increase the importance of Lodge's gauging the public attitude correctly. The American people never came as completely around to Lodge's way of thinking as he hoped. As he told a constituent in October of 1919: "If everyone in this country would study the League as you have studied it, I am convinced that 99 percent of our people would be heartily against it; but the great mass have not studied it and cannot." Consequently, he continued, "we are left to do the best we can and I think we shall

83. "Joint Debate on the Covenant of Paris," p. 50.
84. Elihu Root to Will Hays, March 29, 1919, Root MSS.
85. Vinson, *Referendum for Isolation*, p. 73; Lodge to Elihu Root, April 29, 1919, Root MSS.
86. "Joint Debate on the Covenant of Paris," p. 91.

attain at least to safety for the United States. . . ."[87] He slowly adjusted his horizons to the point where his "one desire" was "to get the United States out of dangerous complications."[88] Yet in making that adjustment he never surrendered the essence of his position. This is apparent from an examination of what, from his point of view, was entailed in making the League safe for the United States. That was a twofold proposition that reflected both domestic and foreign policy concerns; he meant to "release us from obligations which might not be kept and preserve rights which ought not to be infringed."[89] To accomplish that, given the disparity of opinion within his own party, was no easy task. He had no illusions about that. As he told Root, the situation was "not an easy one for anybody who is forced as I am to be the leader and in a sense manager. Forty-nine men, . . . ranging from Borah to Colt, presents [sic] a variety of subjects to deal with and one not always easy to grasp."[90] For consensus within the Senate and among the public at large he had to substitute political and manipulative skills, talents with which he was particularly blest.

He liked to pose, especially in his correspondence with those more "irreconcilable" than himself, as a man devoted principally "to watching the votes," as one whose chief business was to unite Republicans on what he called "strong and effective reservations."[91] Implicit in this pose was a warning which occasionally became explicit. He once had to admonish Beveridge not to rock the boat because there was no alternative to the situation he had been able to bring about: "beyond that a majority in the Senate is not to be found able to control."[92] The key word is "control." Lodge managed to secure control of the situation in the Senate at the outset and never relinquished it.

This was possible because he held the command posts. He was both Chairman of the Senate Foreign Relations Committee and Senate Majority Leader. But it also took circumspection, many compromises, and

87. Lodge to P. F. Hall, Oct. 18, 1919, Lodge MSS.
88. Lodge to Elihu Root, Sept. 3, 1919, Root MSS.
89. Lodge to John T. Morse, Jr., Aug. 19, 1919, Lodge MSS.
90. Lodge to Elihu Root, Aug. 15, 1919, Lodge MSS. This was a familiar and continuing complaint. Even after the second vote he told George Harvey that "in regard to the League no one knows better than you what a narrow channel I have to navigate in, with rocks on both sides" (quoted in Fleming, *The U.S. and the League of Nations*, p. 486).
91. Lodge to Louis A. Coolidge, Aug. 7, 1919, Lodge MSS.
92. Lodge to Albert J. Beveridge, Aug. 4, 1919, Beveridge MSS.

considerable agility to maintain that control and, even in the first instance, to achieve Republican organization of the Senate. Lodge readily
identified with the role of party leader under difficult circumstances. It
suited his temperament perfectly; he was an intense partisan and ever
appreciative of the trials of those striving to hold "great conservative
parties" together.[93] To stay in control of the situation he had to be less
than forthright in expressing his own views, had often to be all things
to all men, and had frequently to appear in the role of mediator. His
success can be measured by the fact that in April of 1919 he was simultaneously "heralded by Root as a 'real friend' of the League of Nations
and by Beveridge as a man who would lead an outright assault on the
League."[94]

Beveridge, while acknowledging Lodge's "delicate position," thought
that once the Republicans organized the Senate Lodge would be more
forthright.[95] Albeit somewhat encouraged by Lodge, he misread the situation. The organization of the Senate was only an important battle in
Lodge's campaign to effect his twin goals—the preservation of unity
among Republicans so that the "Wilsonian" party might be driven
from office and the rejection of the Wilsonian version of the peace settlement and its replacement by the Lodgian version.[96] The two were
ultimately connected, as we have seen, by Lodge's opinion that only
the Republican party understood how to conduct the nation's foreign
policy. But there was also an important foreign policy dimension to the
initial political skirmishing. Lodge wanted the Republicans to organize
the Senate not just for partisan reasons, but also as a means of ensuring

93. He commiserated with Arthur Balfour in a letter of Jan. 28, 1906 (Lodge
MSS) saying that "to the man or men who are trying to hold the great body of a
party together because they feel it to be their duty and because they do not wish
to shatter a great instrument of good government the resistance of extremists
at either end is very trying. . . ." The full extent of his admiration for Balfour can
be seen in an earlier letter to his daughter Constance; from London he wrote: "I
feel great sympathy for Balfour, who is in a most trying place. Chamberlain has
cut loose, has a free hand, and can fight as he likes, but Balfour has had to stay
behind, hold the fort and engage in the difficult and ungrateful task of keeping the
party together. Thus he is fettered and laid open to the meanest sort of attacks.
I appreciate his difficulties and sympathize with him, especially as he is so cool
and calm under it all" (quoted in John A. Garraty, "Henry Cabot Lodge and the
Alaskan Boundary Tribunal," *New England Quarterly* 24 [Dec. 1951]: 489).
94. Kendrick, "The League of Nations and the Republican Senate," p. 131.
Kendrick's observation is based on Beveridge to William E. Borah, April 27, 1919,
Borah Papers, Library of Congress, and Root to Lodge, April 4, 1919, Lodge MSS.
95. Beveridge to Borah, April 27, 1919, Borah MSS.
96. Garraty, *Lodge*, p. 390.

an "intelligent resistance to the League."[97] The "essential point," he told Root, was to put the reins of control in the right hands, "to have a majority in the Senate for necessary amendments and for handling the treaty when it is before us."[98]

There were a number of keys to this sort of control. One, as Lodge readily acknowledged, was Root's position and their ability to accommodate one another's views. This they were soon able to do. Their agreement took the form of a letter from Root to Lodge on June 19, 1919. It was sent at Lodge's request and only after Lodge had approved the text, and, as Will Hays later explained, it was "designed to do two things: to set forth a sound, constructive policy on the merits of the League issue, and to present that policy in such a way as to unite the two wings of the Republican party."[99] Another key was the weapon afforded by the existence of those who felt so strongly that they would vote to kill the treaty unless they got effective reservations, a group which naturally coalesced around Lodge.[100] A final key stemmed from the control of the Senate Foreign Relations Committee guaranteed by Republican organization of the Senate, by Lodge's chairmanship, and by his say in the committee's composition. As a consequence of Republican organization of the Senate Lodge was able to persuade the Senate to authorize a 10–7 Republican–Democratic ratio on that crucial committee.[101] He appears to have sounded out the new appointees and extracted pledges to support him in handling the Covenant.[102] Under the old 9–8 ratio the vote of Porter McCumber (Republican from North Dakota) would probably have been decisive, and he and Lodge subscribed to quite different philosophies of international relations. By securing the 10–7 ratio Lodge neutralized McCumber and greatly strengthened his own position.[103]

97. Lodge to James T. Williams, Jr., May 13, 1919, Lodge MSS.
98. Lodge to Elihu Root, April 29, 1919, Root MSS.
99. Lodge to William Sturgis Bigelow, June 23, 1919, Lodge MSS; Hays, *Memoirs*, p. 203.
100. Lodge to James T. Williams, Jr., Aug. 20, 1919, Lodge MSS.
101. Whether he agreed to appoint "irreconcilables" to the new positions as a *quid pro quo* for Borah's acquiescence in Republican organization and having crucial committee chairmanships pass to such standpatters as Penrose and Warren is still an open question. See Kendrick, "The League of Nations and the Republican Senate," p. 143.
102. See, for example, Lodge to Frank Kellogg, May 28, 1919, and Kellogg's reply of May 31, Lodge MSS. Kellogg was not appointed.
103. Mayer, *The Republican Party, 1854–1964*, p. 360. This is the answer to

As party leader Lodge often subordinated his personal convictions to the dictates of party advantage, and this has occasioned comment on the difficulty of clarifying his true attitude.[104] It has even led to speculation that he may have harbored no strong feelings on the League issue.[105] However, his political maneuverings seem to have been directed as much toward seeing that he had some control over the future direction of American foreign policy as towards advancing the interests of his party. For all his temporizing his views on the League issue were much the same as they had been in the winter of 1916–17.[106]

It has also been charged that he deliberately interjected foreign policy matters, such as the disposition of Fiume, into the domestic political arena in order to secure partisan advantage and with little concern for their policy ramifications.[107] It has even been suggested that he raised issues like the fate of Shantung chiefly to make points against Wilson, to show up the flaws in the armor of the "great moralist."[108] No doubt he enjoyed doing so and was acutely conscious of the domestic political impact of such issues, but he was also trying to make some legitimate points about the dangers inherent in the Wilsonian approach to foreign policy. Here too it is no easy matter to distinguish between his domestic and his foreign policy goals.

True, he publicly declared in a telegram to leading figures in the Italian-American community that he thought Italy should control the Adriatic and be allowed to keep Fiume.[109] But to say that *he* made Fiume an issue in domestic politics is to show little appreciation of the political consciousness of the Italian-American community. It is difficult to believe that Lodge alone was responsible for the fact that the Massachusetts legislature, with but one dissenting vote, adopted a resolution calling on Wilson to support Italy's position on Fiume.[110] If the general public had little or no interest in such matters there were com-

---

Thomas Bailey's question (*Woodrow Wilson and the Great Betrayal*, p. 73) as to why the Lodge who professed to favor the treaty packed his committee with irreconcilables.

104. See, for example, Vinson, *Referendum for Isolation*, pp. 81–82.
105. Kendrick, "The League of Nations and the Republican Senate," p. 135.
106. Vinson, *Referendum for Isolation*, pp. 81–82.
107. See, for example, Mayer, *Politics and Diplomacy of Peacemaking*, p. 714.
108. Garraty, *Lodge*, pp. 373–74.
109. *New York Times*, April 30, 1919, p. 1.
110. J. Joseph Huthmacher, *Massachusetts People and Politics, 1919–1933* (Cambridge, Mass., 1959), p. 21.

munities within the American body politic who cared deeply. In each case, Fiume, Danzig, and Shantung, Lodge did not shy from raising the simple and popular issue of moral right. But those decisions also raised a number of issues that went to the heart of his quarrel with Wilson over the philosophical bases of American foreign policy.

Lodge, the vocal advocate of immigration restriction, deplored even the existence of such feelings as were aroused by Fiume, but could rationalize playing on them by believing that attention had to be drawn to the problem. Here was another aspect of the American situation that ought to impose a sense of limitations on policy-makers. It raised both a domestic and a foreign policy problem. As Root asked: "How can we prevent dissension, and hatred among our own inhabitants of foreign origin when the country interferes on foreign grounds between the races from which they spring?"[111] To him Washington's advice still had its point. Lodge made this concern a major part of his critique of the League. He strongly objected "to having the politics of the United States turn upon disputes where deep feeling is involved but in which we have no direct interest." Looking both ways as the Rooseveltian solution had required, he believed that the end result would be a distorted policy. He was forced to conclude that "the less we undertake to play the part of umpire and thrust ourselves into European conflicts the better for the United States and for the world."[112]

Lodge also believed that Germany was certain to plan a war of revenge and was therefore concerned to erect a string of strong barrier-states around her. He feared, not without reason, that taking Fiume from Italy might throw her back into the arms of Germany.[113] The United States had no reason to be involved, and Wilson's problems with the Italians were but "an illustration of the mistakes and troubles which are likely to arise from the United States undertaking to meddle with purely European questions in which they have no direct interest."[114] Policy divorced from interest was to Lodge no policy at all.

Never a universalist, Lodge early sought to differentiate between a "general, indefinite, unlimited scheme of always being called upon to

111. Root to Lodge, June 19, 1919, Lodge MSS.
112. Boorstin, ed., *An American Primer*, p. 788.
113. Lodge to John T. Morse, Jr., May 2, 1919, and to Lord Charnwood, July 2, 1919, Lodge MSS.
114. Lodge to Trevelyan, April 30, 1919, and to Henry White, May 20, 1919, Lodge MSS.

meddle in European, Asian and African questions" and a policy designed to ensure that the strong barrier-states necessary to fetter Germany were erected.[115] As he saw it, the future peace of the world depended, not on the universal prevalence of American ideals, but rather on the strength of France, a fact which Wilson seemed not to appreciate.[116]

Lodge's conception of America's world role was as idealistic as Wilson's, but there was a crucial difference. Lodge believed that America had evolved a special, historical individuality and a unique system of values which were as much the product of propitious circumstance as anything else. Though he was prepared to go to great lengths to defend and preserve that individuality, he did not, like Wilson, seek its preservation in an attempt to secure its universal acceptance. The United States, at least toward Europe, served best as an example; it would remain mankind's best hope only so long as it did not destroy itself by becoming involved in every broil that desolated the earth.[117] Conservative in his assessment of the human condition and too particularist to believe it possible to universalize American values, he readily conceded that Europe had different interests and priorities and understood its own needs better than could any American. The United States, in his view, did have an interest in the European settlement, but he was quick to emphasize that "there is a wide difference between taking a suitable part and bearing due responsibility in world affairs and plunging the United States into every controversy and conflict on the face of the globe."[118]

Lodge and Root would have done it differently:

It seemed to me at the time and has seemed to me ever since so clear what the President ought to have done; that he should have said to the Powers associated with us in the war: "We want the world made safe against Germany and as long as that is done we are content. So far as European matters are concerned, you are the people to settle them. Settle them all among yourselves and we will back you up. When it comes to Asia and Africa, of course we expect to have a voice; and we ask to be let alone in our own hemisphere." If that had been done the situation today would have been wholly different. But Mr. Wilson has undertaken to be the final umpire in every European question, incurring hostility both for himself and for his country,

115. Lodge to Beveridge, Jan. 30, 1919, Lodge MSS.
116. *Cong. Record*, 65th Cong., 3rd sess., 1919, p. 4527.
117. *Ibid.*, 66th Cong., 1st sess., 1919, p. 5504.
118. Boorstin, ed., *An American Primer*, p. 786.

and meddling with things in which the United States has no interest whatsoever.[119]

But Wilson, having less appreciation of the factors that circumscribed the nation's ability to act wisely in foreign affairs, so influenced the Peace Conference that they "made omnipotence their province and occupied the entire sphere on national and international relations the world over."[120] Policy divorced from the reality of interest produced such aberrations as the Conference's decisions respecting Fiume, Danzig, and Shantung. It probably would have turned out better, Lodge felt, had it all been in Clemenceau's hands. At any rate, the sooner a country that so mismanaged things got out of the business of meddling in other nations' affairs the better.[121]

Shantung, like Fiume, had an importance which transcended the significance of the territory involved or the alleged "immorality" of the Conference's disposition of it. Lodge seems actually to have believed that "the taking of Shantung . . . from an ally and handing it over to another ally as the price of a signature to the League is one of the blackest things in the history of diplomacy," equalling even the partition of Poland.[122] This was probably not so much because he was a staunch defender of China as because he was suspicious of "the Prussia of the

119. Lodge to Lord Charnwood, July 2, 1919, Lodge MSS. This closely paralleled the opinion Root had expressed in his June 19 letter to Lodge. Root was particularly concerned to dissipate the impression that the U.S. had a wish "to dictate to European states and control European affairs, thus assuming responsibility for those affairs." In his always careful language he went on to suggest that "such interposition in the affairs of Europe as our representatives have been engaged in, was properly but a temporary incident to the fact we had engaged in the war, and had therefore to discuss the terms of peace; and we should make it clear that we neither assume responsibility for nor intend interference in, the affairs of Europe beyond that necessary participation under the organization of the League of Peace which we enter upon by the request of the European nations themselves" (Lodge MSS).

120. *Cong. Record*, 66th Cong., 1st sess., 1919, p. 729. Lodge was bothered by the fact that the Peace Conference had gotten into the matter of the Monroe Doctrine and apparently also by the fact that "the Irish question" had been raised. Though the latter was to redound to the Republicans' political benefit and though he was soon gloating over the fact that the Irish were opposed to the League and that "the fate of the Democratic party in the Northern states is in their hands," he appears also to have been genuinely worried about the effect this would have on Anglo-American relations. See Nevins, *Henry White*, p. 455.

121. Lodge to Henry White, Oct. 2, 1919, Lodge MSS; *Cong. Record*, 66th Cong., 1st sess., 1919, p. 8296.

122. Lodge to Henry White, May 20, 1919, and to William Astor Chanler, Aug. 19, 1919, Lodge MSS. See also Lodge to W. Cameron Forbes, Aug. 9, 1919, Lodge MSS, wherein he refers to Japan as "the coming danger of the world."

East." It was the Shantung question that triggered massive attrition on the left flank of Wilson's support, and Lodge used the issue to the hilt in the struggle for domestic political advantage. But perhaps of even more significance to Lodge and Root was the fact that Article X of the Covenant appeared to bind the United States to defend the Shantung settlement, to sustain Japan against China should the latter rise up and attack Japan in an effort to undo "the great wrong" of the cession of control over Shantung.[123] Public reaction to the Shantung arrangement convinced them that this was something the United States would never do, and this in turn made them regard Article X with even greater suspicion. What had a telling effect on public opinion in the short run, and put Wilson at a political disadvantage, was also predictive of the form American public opinion would take were the United States ever asked to support its pledge under Article X. Therein lay a justification for exploiting the Shantung issue and also proof that one can not readily draw a line between "political" and "principled" opposition to the League.

III

The nature and extent of Lodge's internationalism can also be gleaned from an analysis of his relationship with Root and the "mild reservationists" (generally regarded as "sincere" internationalists) and from an examination of his position on the French Guarantee Treaty. Unable to unify the Senate Republicans behind the Knox Resolution, Lodge turned to Root, whose position, he acknowledged, was "essential to our holding control of the Senate and of the vote in regard to the treaty."[124] From that point on Root formulated Republican policy.[125] That policy was established in Root's June 19 letter to Lodge and in the announcement that the Republican party officially favored "a League

123. See Root to Lodge, July 24, 1919, Lodge MSS; and Lodge's August 12, 1919 Senate speech, in Boorstin, ed., *An American Primer*, p. 784.
124. Lodge to Root, April 29, 1919, Root MSS.
125. Jack E. Kendrick ("The League of Nations and the Republican Senate," pp. 159, 389) argues this point persuasively. Ruhl Bartlett (*The League to Enforce Peace*, pp. 136, 139) also emphasizes the importance of Root's role and the fact that he chose the reservations Wilson could not accept.

of Nations."[126] Lodge and Will Hays decided to base the party's program on Root's proposals for reservations.[127] Those proposals issued, it
should be emphasized, from a feeling that despite its shortcomings
there remained in the Covenant "a great deal of very high value which
the world ought not to lose."[128] There is nothing in the correspondence
of Lodge and Root to support the contention that Lodge never favored
ratification of the Covenant in at least some form.[129] Moreover, Lodge
appears to have readily acquiesced in handing over to Root control of
Republican party policy on the League. Root "never for a moment
wavered in his position that the treaty should be ratified" and in his
June 19 letter made it clear that Republican policy would be ratification
together with "an expression of such reservations and understandings
as will cure so far as possible the defects which I [Root] have pointed
out."[130]

A reservations as opposed to an amendments policy reflected a concern for conditions in Europe; it meant that the treaty would not have to
be renegotiated and that the League could be set up without delay. Lodge
put it negatively, blustering that he was "not interested in rescuing
Europe from Article 10," but only in protecting the United States,
and that he did "not care a straw whether Europe has the League or
not."[131] But this actually meant that he had acquiesced in Root's reservations policy. Lodge continued to support a few amendments (on
Shantung, for example) but used them primarily as a means of appeas-
ing the irreconcilables and of forcing the mild reservationists toward a
middle ground. He appears not to have expected such amendments to
pass.[132]

Thomas A. Bailey once speculated on what might have been the
result if the Democrats had opened their arms to the Republican mild

126. *New York Times*, June 27, 1919.
127. An indication of the extent to which Lodge adhered to the line set forth in
Root's June 19 letter may be obtained by comparing that letter with Lodge's first
full-dress statement on the Treaty, his Senate speech of August 12, 1919. In argument they differ scarcely at all.
128. Root to Lodge, June 19, 1919, Lodge MSS.
129. Jessup, *Elihu Root*, II, pp. 402–03.
130. *Ibid.*, II, p. 397; Root to Lodge, June 19, 1919, Lodge MSS.
131. Garraty, *Lodge*, p. 366; Lodge to Root, July 7, 1919, and to Louis A. Coolidge, Aug. 7, 1919, Lodge MSS.
132. Kuehl, *Seeking World Order*, pp. 318–19; Diary of Henry L. Stimson, III,
p. 100, Stimson MSS.

reservationists, but as it was they made no move in that direction until October 2, 1919. Then they found they were too late. The mild reservationists were already committed.[133] Lodge *had* opened his arms to them; the reservations that bore his name were not so much his as they were the work of Root and the mild reservationists, especially Senator Lenroot.[134] In fact considerable truth underlay Senator Kellogg's assertion that they had "not been drawn by the enemies of the treaty" but rather "by its friends, who want to save it. . . ."[135] This helps to explain why the mild reservationists stood so strongly behind the Lodge reservations and were so unreceptive to Democratic overtures. Thus, by early September Lodge could report that "our people" were united on his four central points, including a reservation to Article X declaring that no American troops could be despatched without Congressional authorization.[136] Even Senator McCumber admitted that "the reservations proposed by the chairman [Lodge] agreed in the main with those he had drawn in co-operation with other Senators."[137] McCumber, however, still objected to the phrasing of the reservation to Article X, and it is an indication of Lodge's ability to work with those who favored the treaty that he and McCumber were able to come to an agreement. Lodge "personally went over this reservation to Article 10 again and again with groups of Senators and with individual members" and "finally" asked McCumber to lunch. After much discussion they were able to agree upon the reservation in the form later presented to the Senate. McCumber even introduced it in his own name.[138]

133. Bailey, *Woodrow Wilson and the Great Betrayal*, pp. 58, 171–72; Kendrick, "The League of Nations and the Republican Senate," p. 233. James E. Hewes ("Henry Cabot Lodge and the League of Nations," p. 251) observes that "in rejecting the principle of reservations the President forfeited the opportunity to control a Senate majority in favor of the treaty." Jack E. Kendrick ("The League of Nations and the Republican Senate," p. 83) attributes Wilson's failure to work with the Republican mild reservationists to his personal and partisan approach to the league issue. Much of Warren Kuehl's *Seeking World Order* goes to the same point.

134. Kendrick, "The League of Nations and the Republican Senate," pp. 211, 254; Herbert F. Margulies, *Senator Lenroot of Wisconsin: A Political Biography, 1900–1929* (Columbia, Mo., 1977), pp. 276–77.

135. *Cong. Record*, 66th Cong., 1st sess., 1919, pp. 8778–80.

136. Lodge to Root, Sept. 3, 1919, Root MSS; Lodge to George Harvey, Sept. 5, 1919, Lodge MSS. See Senate Report No. 176 in the *Cong. Record*, 66th Cong., 1st sess., pp. 5113–14, for the text of those reservations.

137. *Proceedings of the Committee on Foreign Relations, 63rd to 67th Congresses Inclusive*, p. 171.

138. Lodge, *The Senate and the League*, pp. 183–84; Hewes, "Lodge and the League of Nations," p. 252.

If Wilson's main concern at Paris was the construction of a League of Nations, that of the French delegation was markedly different. They sought military security against Germany and conceived of the League as an alliance of victors endowed with a general staff and an army sufficient to compel obedience to the League's decrees. Another uneasy compromise was the result. The French gave up their demands for an international force and weakened their own military defenses against Germany in exchange for an agreement whereby Wilson and Lloyd George pledged to recommend to their respective legislatures at the same time that they submitted the Versailles Treaty (a pledge Wilson failed to keep) another treaty providing for military assistance to France in case of a German attack. This came close to an admission that the League itself was not sufficient protection, and Wilson never liked the Treaties of Guarantee. However, he was able to paper over the logical inconsistency by inserting a provision requiring action by the League Council before the implementation of the Guarantees. Still, most of the American delegation thought the Guarantee Treaty "preposterous," and Henry White was convinced that Wilson had no faith in it.[139]

Lodge, however, quickly informed White that he had no objection to a special treaty pledging American military aid to France in the event of a German attack.[140] This issue reveals more sharply than any other how far apart Wilsonians and conservative internationalists like Lodge and Root were on the question of the proper scope of American commitments. Lodge and Root were concerned that the American people understand precisely what they were undertaking to do and why they were doing so. As Root expressed it in his June 19 statement of Republican policy:

If it is necessary for the security of western Europe that we should agree to go to the support say of France if attacked, let us agree to do that particular thing plainly, so that every man and woman in the country will understand that. But let us not wrap up such a purpose in a vague universal obligation, under the impression that it really does not mean anything [is] likely to happen.[141]

139. Louis A. R. Yates, *The United States and French Security, 1917–1921* (New York, 1957), pp. 15–18, 73; Nevins, *Henry White*, p. 441.

140. Nevins, *Henry White*, p. 438.

141. Root to Lodge, June 19, 1919, Lodge MSS. The same underlying philosophy is also apparent in Root to Lodge, Nov. 1, 1919, Root MSS. Root emphasized that "it is desirable to accompany the opposition which you are making to the vague and indefinite commitments of the League Covenant with an exhibition of will-

Lodge used the same arguments in a letter to Beveridge. He declared his strong support for "a simple proposition that it would be our intention to aid France, which is our barrier and outpost, when attacked without provocation by Germany. . . ." He objected, however, to the French treaty having been made subject to the League's authority. That provision, he felt, would "probably make it impossible to do anything for France as Root recommends and as many of our Senators desire." The French Guarantee Treaty was a "distinct and separate thing which we could well afford to do," and were it not for Article X and the League (that is, for the Wilsonian version of internationalism) Lodge felt it "unquestionably" would have been approved.[142] Later his "unquestionably" became "might have been possible," and finally "not the slightest chance that the Senate would ever have voted to accept it."[143] But his developing pessimism regarding the prospects for ratification of the French treaty should not be allowed to obscure his support for it. He hoped it would pass and never hedged his willingness to vote for it.[144] But he could never even get it out of committee with a favorable report. He always felt that it could have been ratified had it had the real support of the Administration and of those Democrats who ought to have favored it, but he was blocked by the same coalition of irreconcilables and loyal Wilsonian Democrats who refused to vote for the Covenant with the Lodge reservations attached.[145]

Another measure of the nature and extent of Lodge's internationalism would follow if we could give a definite answer to Arthur Link's question whether Lodge was himself "an irreconcilable who desired the defeat of the treaty, or . . . merely a strong reservationist. . . ."[146] Another way of putting it would be to ask whether he sincerely advocated ratification with reservations and made a sincere effort to effect the compromises that would have made ratification possible. While

---

ingness to do the definite certain specific things which are a proper part of true American policy, and which are necessary to secure the results of the war. . . ."

142. Lodge to Henry White, June 23, 1919, Lodge MSS; Lodge to Beveridge, Aug. 11, 1919, Beveridge MSS. That he wrote so forthrightly on the matter to someone as unsympathetic as Beveridge is surely a measure of Lodge's feelings.

143. Lodge to Jules Cambon, July 6, 1921, Lodge MSS; Lodge, *The Senate and the League*, p. 156.

144. Lodge to William Astor Chanler, Oct. 14, 1919, Lodge MSS; Lodge to Root, Nov. 3, 1919, Root MSS.

145. Lodge to Richard W. Hale, Dec. 13, 1919, Lodge MSS; Hewes, "Lodge and the League of Nations," p. 253.

146. Arthur S. Link, *Wilson the Diplomatist* (Chicago, 1965), p. 139.

some evidence supports the claim that Lodge was just going through the motions and had no intention of compromising with the Democrats, those who have emphasized Lodge's "willingness to accept the treaty with reservations" and the fact that "he actually tried to get the treaty through with his reservations" have slightly the better of the argument.[147] Among the evidence they adduce is the negotiation Lodge undertook with Colonel House through Stephen Bonsal in an effort to work out compromise language, Lodge's allowing the treaty to come to a second vote, his willingness to enter into a bipartisan conference in January of 1920 which sought to devise reservations language acceptable to most Senators, and finally his support of changes in his own reservations that were designed to meet Wilson's objections (as when he vainly tried to secure a provision making American withdrawal dependent on a joint, rather than on a concurrent resolution of Congress).[148]

Of more than passing interest are Lodge's relationships with other principals in the struggle over the League and their opinion of him and his position. Revealing, both in its praise of Lodge and in its foreclosure of any other route to ratification, is a letter from Root to Lodge dated December 1, 1919, well after the vote in November. In Root's view Lodge's leadership in the Senate had been "extraordinarily able"; he termed it "one of the greatest examples of parliamentary leadership" he had ever known and expressed the wish that all the friends of the Treaty could understand that it was Lodge who had given the Treaty "its only chance for ratification. . . ."[149] Another important figure, Viscount Grey, sent by the British Government as its Ambassador to the United States with the special mission of composing American differences of opinion on the League, apparently came to the same conclusion as Root. He is said to have commented sympathetically on Lodge's handling of the treaty, and in a letter to the London *Times* he

147. David Mervin, "Henry Cabot Lodge and the League of Nations," pp. 201–14; Kendrick, "The League of Nations and the Republican Senate," p. 260; Bailey, *Woodrow Wilson and the Great Betrayal*, p. 279. A corollary of this point of view is that Lodge made more of an effort to compromise than did Wilson (Bailey, *Woodrow Wilson and the Great Betrayal*, p. 279) and that the Democrats were "the real non-compromisers" (Kendrick, "The League of Nations and the Republican Senate," p. 268).

148. See Bailey, *Woodrow Wilson and the Great Betrayal*, pp. 175–77, 255; and Stephen Bonsal, *Unfinished Business* (Garden City, N.Y., 1944), pp. 272–80. A "joint" resolution required the President's approval; a "concurrent" one would have been operative without it.

149. Root to Lodge, Dec. 1, 1919, Root MSS.

advocated British acceptance of the Lodge reservations as the best means of securing American participation.[150]

The relationship between Lodge and the irreconcilables also deserves attention. Senator Knox thought that only pressure from the irreconcilables had kept Lodge in line, that "on one occasion he was on the point of surrendering to the mild reservationists. . . ."[151] It is not an unreasonable construction of Borah's January 24, 1920, letter to Lodge (threatening to bolt the party unless Lodge dropped his backstage compromise negotiation with the Democrats) to say it demonstrated that Borah believed Lodge was doing his best to get the treaty ratified.[152] The irreconcilables forced him to break off those negotiations, but in the following weeks he reasserted his independence and continued to modify his reservations, their views notwithstanding.[153] He taunted the irreconcilables with the claim that his reservations had "acquired a sanctity with some of my friends which they did not have, I think, until after the 19th of November," announced his intention to support improvements in both substance and phraseology which might lead to securing a two-thirds vote for the treaty, and finally even suggested a substitute for that most sacrosanct of reservations, that to Article X.[154] In addition he wrote a letter to Beveridge on February 16, 1920, which seemed to anticipate a favorable vote on ratification and which had the evident purpose of consoling Beveridge by telling him, first, that the reservations made the League safe for the United States and, second, that no one would be able to say it was a victory for Wilson since the reservations were "too clearly ours to allow such a charge to have any effect."[155] Admittedly, the evidence cited here is selective. But it seems sufficient to make a fairly good case for the argument that Lodge was willing to acquiesce in ratification on the basis of strong and effective

150. E. L. Woodward and Rohan Butler, eds., *Documents on British Foreign Policy* (London, 1954), First Series, V ("The Grey Mission"), pp. 1059–60; Fleming, *The United States and the League of Nations*, pp. 411–13. Lodge had Grey's letter inserted in the *Cong. Record*, 66th Cong., 2nd sess., 1920, pp. 2335–37.

151. Diary of Chandler Anderson, entry for Dec. 16, 1920, Anderson MSS.

152. William E. Borah to Lodge, Jan. 24, 1920, Lodge MSS; Kendrick, "The League of Nations and the Republican Senate," p. 285.

153. Ralph Stone, *The Irreconcilables*, p. 160.

154. *Cong. Record*, 66th Cong., 2nd sess., p. 3238; Root to Lodge, March 11, 1920, and Lodge to Root, March 13, 1920, Root MSS.

155. Lodge to Beveridge, Feb. 16, 1920, Beveridge MSS. At about the same time he publicly stated that "if they let me alone we'll ratify the treaty, but it will have to be done on the basis of the majority reservations" (Boston *Herald*, Feb. 8, 1920, p. 7).

reservations. Nevertheless, that leaves much unsaid, for some of those reservations embodied principles which Lodge was not ready to compromise.

Many, however, have not been convinced of Lodge's willingness to accept ratification on the basis of his own reservations. A frequent charge has been that the reservations were a device to secure the treaty's defeat, and that if Wilson had shown any signs of accepting them Lodge would have come up with more drastic ones.[156] These charges apparently had their origin in a 1928 Council on Foreign Relations publication alleging that Lodge had "declared privately" that he "had proposed reservations which he was confident the President would reject, and that he was prepared to add to them if it were necessary, his purpose being to have the League rejected."[157] However, there is no hard evidence to support such an accusation. It has the markings of a rationalization employed by those seeking to defend Wilson's intransigence and is devoid of political logic.[158] The Lodge who knew within what tight limits he had to operate would never have risked such an affront to the mild reservationists.

A better case has been made in support of the view that Lodge was really an irreconcilable and opposed to any league whatsoever. Some historians have argued against Lodge's sincerity by citing remarks and publications from a later date. However, all their damaging evidence postdates the final vote on the treaty.[159] Lodge did gradually become more irreconcilable. Will Hays remarked on that and so did Root who, though he continued to believe that Lodge initially wanted to join the

156. See, for example, Ruhl Bartlett, *The League to Enforce Peace*, p. 146; and Royden J. Dangerfield, *In Defense of the Senate* (Norman, Oklahoma, 1933), p. 249.

157. Charles P. Howland, *Survey of American Foreign Relations 1928* (New Haven, 1928), p. 272. Howland did not identify his informants. According to his account (p. 279), the Republicans lent credence to this charge by adding a reservation demanding recognition of the independence of Ireland at the last moment. Actually the 15th reservation originated with Senator Gerry (Democrat from Rhode Island) and had the support of the irreconcilables and over half the Democrats present including Hitchcock. Those Republicans who were trying to secure a two-thirds vote for ratification opposed it. Lodge voted against it despite his large Irish constituency, declaring that he could not do otherwise "desiring as I do to ratify the treaty." See Bailey, *Woodrow Wilson and the Great Betrayal*, p. 264; and the *Cong. Record*, 66th Cong., 2nd sess., 1920, p. 4513.

158. See Kendrick, "The League of Nations and the Republican Senate," pp. 269–70.

159. See, for example, Bartlett, *The League to Enforce Peace*, pp. 161–62; and W. Stull Holt, *Treaties Defeated by the Senate*, p. 265.

League with reservations, recognized that he had gradually fallen under the influence of Brandegee and the other irreconcilables.[160] Lodge came eventually to feel that the Senate's rejection of the League had been "a fortunate result."[161] He may even have thought so shortly after the vote. There is considerable psychological resonance in Alice Longworth's observation that though he "at one time persuaded himself to believe that he was in favor of the League of Nations if amply safeguarded by reservations, my opinion is that in his heart he was really as opposed to it in any shape as an irreconcilable. . . ."[162] His views changed in response to the country's mood; as the country became more irreconcilable (not an unreasonable interpretation of the 1920 election results) he moved in the same direction, the more easily as the country's mood confirmed his view that America was not ready for such undertakings. But does that necessarily reflect on his sincerity in advocating ratification of the League before March 19, 1920, or on his willingness to compromise toward that end? It doesn't directly, but it seems to suggest that we may have been asking the wrong questions. Since Lodge appears to have abandoned his support for ratification rather readily after March 19, we might better ask whether he ever believed in the League and whether he thought the differences between his conception of a league and Wilson's—between his conception of the proper scope of American internationalism and the President's—could be compromised.

IV

Lodge was skeptical about the League from the outset and never entertained high hopes for it. In confidence he predicted its failure and to Lord Bryce he expressed the opinion that the League was "a mere ornament" since "the real force under the treaty with Germany is placed in the hands of the five great Powers." While sure that reservations would "do more for the chances of life to the League than anything else," he felt bound "to confess that this League is altogether too much like a political alliance to make me feel that it is likely to be either

160. Will Hays, *Memoirs*, p. 220; Henry L. Stimson Diary, VI, p. 83, Stimson MSS.
161. Lodge, *The Senate and the League*, pp. 211, 214.
162. *Crowded Hours*, p. 295.

enduring or successful."[163] Even worse from his point of view, the League arrangements sought to deny the power realities that underlay its existence and to that end made extravagant promises incapable of fulfillment. Lodge saw through to the heart of the dilemma confronting those trying to construct a workable universal collective security organization: "Really to fulfill the advertised intention of its framers, it would have been necessary to put force behind the League, . . ." and to have provided for an international army with an international command.[164]

That being politically unacceptable, the result was the murky compromise known as Article X under which Member States pledged to defend one another's territorial integrity and political independence, it being left to the League Council to "advise upon the means by which this obligation shall be fulfilled." This uneasy compromise caused Wilson considerable difficulty at home; it permitted his opponents to attack the League from both sides in the manner of Borah's famous question: "What will your league amount to if it does not contain powers that no one dreams of giving it."[165] This same uneasy compromise haunted the League throughout its history. Canada tried to have Article X suppressed in 1920, and the League Council could not in 1923 even decide whether its advice was binding.[166]

Wilson, as John Chalmers Vinson has observed, never gave a compelling interpretation of American responsibilities under Article Ten.[167] He was damned if he did and damned if he didn't. He could only equivocate. Though claiming that Article X was "the very backbone of the whole Covenant," he dared not claim that the Council's advice derogated from Congress's right "to exercise its independent judgment in all matters of peace and war." Consequently, he was left to resolve the contradictions inherent in American participation in the Covenant in the following unsatisfactory manner. The engagement under Article X, he claimed:

. . . constitutes a very grave and solemn moral obligation. But it is a moral, not a legal obligation, and leaves our Congress absolutely free to put its own

163. Lodge to John T. Morse, Jr., Aug. 19, 1919, and to Lord Bryce, Aug. 9 and Oct. 8, 1919, Lodge MSS.
164. Lodge, *The Senate and the League*, p. 211.
165. See above, p. 268.
166. See Hinsley, *Power and the Pursuit of Peace*, p. 319.
167. *Referendum for Isolation*, p. 92.

interpretation upon it in all cases that call for action. It is binding in conscience only, not in law.[168]

At first glance it would appear that Wilson and Lodge were not far apart; Lodge wanted only a reservation saying that the United States "assumes no obligation" under Article X "unless in any particular case the Congress . . . shall by act or joint resolution so provide."[169] But appearances were in this case particularly deceiving. To Wilson and his supporters the moral obligation was real (if only as a matter of faith), and their objection to Lodge's reservation to Article X was that it specifically removed that moral obligation.[170] This was not a minor point, but rather *the* obstacle to ratification; the nature of the obligation assumed by Member States would determine what kind of organization the League would be. To Lodge and Root it appeared as if Wilson and the Democrats wanted to accept an obligation which the United States might thereafter refuse, while their position has been characterized as one of wanting to refuse an obligation which might thereafter be accepted.[171] Believing that under American conditions it was important to make all commitments as definite as possible, they could never accept Wilson's attempt to distinguish between a moral and a legal obligation. It begged the question of whether the obligation was binding. Root denounced Wilson's "curious and childlike casuistry" and thought the attempted distinction "false, demoralizing and dishonest."[172] Lodge, believing that such an obligation could only be moral, wanted to prevent there arising a situation where Congress could not exert its Constitutional rights without breaking that moral obligation.[173] That was the purpose of his reservation to Article X; it "made us the judges of whether we should carry out the guarantees of Article 10 or not, and in case of our refusal this reservation prevented its being a breach of the treaty. . . ."[174]

168. Cronon, ed., *The Political Thought of Woodrow Wilson*, p. 505.
169. There is a convenient compendium of the Lodge reservations, showing the changes they underwent, in Bailey, *Woodrow Wilson and the Great Betrayal*, pp. 387–93.
170. Hewes, "Lodge and the League of Nations," p. 250; Bailey, *Woodrow Wilson and the Great Betrayal*, p. 157.
171. Stromberg, *Collective Security and American Foreign Policy*, p. 37.
172. Root to Lodge, Aug. 28, 1919, Lodge MSS; and Sept. 10, 1919, Root MSS.
173. "Article given to the Chicago *Daily News*, Sept. 8, 1920," Lodge MSS; Boston *Globe*, Sept. 10, 1920.
174. Boston *Herald*, Oct. 2, 1920, p. 2. As he put it in the report of the Senate

Since the success of a collective security organization would seem to rest on the absence of doubt as to the intentions of its members, that is, on the credibility of their commitments, Lodge's reservation stating that the United States assumed no obligation was a denial of the theory on which collective security was based.[175] His reservations, though leaving the League a useful instrument of collaboration (which was the way he had conceived it in the first place), "would have transformed the League into a non-coercive or an intermediate type of international organization."[176] That, of course, is essentially what it became.

But there remains the question of Lodge's intent and his understanding of what he was doing. Many of the irreconcilables were convinced that the reservations never amounted to anything, that once the League was set up they would influence its operation very little.[177] Some historians in their eagerness to criticize Wilson's handling of the matter have also come to regard the Lodge reservations as innocuous. They claim that Lodge hardly hoped for more than party unity and face-saving reservations, and that therefore a "reasonably sagacious political approach" by Wilson would have assured ratification.[178] Such arguments can, of course, be used to bolster either the case for Lodge's partisanship or the case for the "sincerity" of his internationalism, but they also carry the implication that Lodge was unfamiliar and unconcerned with the problems inherent in the application of force to ensure peace and neither appreciated Wilson's ploy nor understood how to meet it. Given what we now know about his thinking since the winter of 1916–17, that is difficult to accept. Despite the fact that he eventually became an irreconcilable, Lodge never wavered in the view that the

---

Foreign Relations Committee: "At this moment the United States is free from any entanglement or obligations which legally or in the name of honor would compel her to do anything contrary to the dictates of conscience or to the freedom and the interests of the American people. This is the hour when we can say precisely what we will do and . . . no man can ever question our good faith if we speak now." See the *Cong. Record*, 66th Cong., 1st sess., 1919, p. 5114.

175. Vinson, *Referendum for Isolation*, p. 108.

176. Leo Gross, "The Charter of the United Nations and the Lodge Reservations," *The American Journal of International Law* 41 (July 1947): 548, 551.

177. Fleming, *The United States and the League of Nations*, pp. 498–99.

178. Robert Ferrell, "Woodrow Wilson: Man and Statesman," *Review of Politics* 18 (April 1956): 136–37; Charles Seymour, "Woodrow Wilson in Perspective," in Earl Latham, ed., *The Philosophy and Policies of Woodrow Wilson* (Chicago, 1958), pp. 183–84.

reservations would have made the League safe for the United States.[179] And making it safe for the United States could not help but change its structure. Lodge took his reservations seriously and so did Wilson; they both knew they had profound implications. They were so far apart in their views on Article X that it is reasonable to assume there was virtually no prospect for compromise.[180] However, Americans have an abiding faith in their ability to compromise and that made Lodge's task more difficult. But Wilson at least would probably have understood and agreed with James Beck's observation that "the reservations would have driven a 'coach and four' through the League of Notions and made the obligations of the United States thereunder almost nominal. . . ."[181]

Lodge was unyielding on two crucial points. In October of 1919 he told the Senate that "this treaty will never be ratified unless the Monroe Doctrine is finally and absolutely reserved from the jurisdiction of the League." In February of 1920 he declared that he could "never assent to any change in principle in the two reservations relating to the Monroe Doctrine and article 10."[182] This could lead one to conclude that his efforts to reach a compromise in the context of the bipartisan committee were "an elaborate charade,"[183] but perhaps a fairer interpretation would be that, though he was convinced that compromise was impossible, he found it necessary to demonstrate that fact to others. Nothing short of an actual demonstration that nothing could be done by way of compromise would satisfy public opinion, he told Beveridge. Lodge attributed this to the press, which seemed "to overlook the fact that with the mass of the Senators this is not a question of personal fortune or party advantage but a great question of principle on which they cannot yield any essential point."[184] To the end he complained that "the differences between what Hitchcock offers and what we are willing to accept are much deeper and broader than people generally understand."[185] It was

179. Lodge, *The Senate and the League*, p. 209.
180. See Kuehl, *Seeking World Order*, pp. 329, 338.
181. James M. Beck to Lodge, Nov. 20, 1919, Lodge MSS. It is "Notions" in the original.
182. *Cong. Record*, 66th Cong., 1st sess., 1919, p. 6266; 66th Cong., 2nd sess., 1920, p. 3238.
183. Mervin, "Henry Cabot Lodge and the League of Nations," p. 209.
184. Lodge to Beveridge, Jan. 13, 1920, Beveridge MSS.
185. Lodge to W. Cameron Forbes, March 1, 1920, Houghton Library, Harvard University.

to counteract that situation that he agreed to the bipartisan conferences. "It was," he wrote to a confidant, "something we had to go through." It might also be described as the culmination of the educative process in which he had long been engaged. Viewed in that light the fact that he made up his mind "that if the conference was to break up without an agreement it should be on Article 10" appears less Machiavellian. Article 10 was "the crucial point throughout the contest over the covenant. . . ." What Lodge did was to arrange to break off the negotiations "on a question not only where I knew we could stand before the country but where, also, I could have my votes of more than one-third."[186]

This suggests not necessarily the sincere advocate of ratification with reservations, nor yet the reasonable compromiser, but a man strongly opposed to the Wilsonian conception of a League and determined to reveal its faults and prevent the United States from getting deeply involved in it. As Lodge saw it, the League was grievously flawed and would not work. Thomas Bailey once observed that Lodge was a failure if he really wanted the Treaty, but he could scarcely have "really wanted" something in which he did not believe.[187] Whether the United States joined the League was never of as much concern to him as were the conditions under which it joined. Those, as Wilson also understood, would determine the nature of the organization and involved "great principles." Lodge's detached view on the matter of American entry gave him a considerable tactical advantage and permitted him to maintain close working relations both with those who wanted and with those who did not want the United States in the League. He thereby maximized his control of the situation and ensured that no matter which way the final vote went his views would prevail. Though never absolutely sure how it would end, he knew, as he confided to Corinne Roosevelt Robinson, that it would end "not badly in any event for I have tried so to arrange it."[188]

It is possible to interpret this as evidence that he acted essentially as a mediator with no strong personal feelings on the issues involved, an interpretation suggested by his secretary's opinion that the role of medi-

186. Lodge to Louis A. Coolidge, Feb. 2, 1920, and to F. H. Gillett, July 26, 1920, Lodge MSS; Lodge, *The Senate and the League*, p. 194.

187. *Woodrow Wilson and the Great Betrayal*, p. 193.

188. Lodge to Corinne Roosevelt Robinson, Feb. 16, 1920, Houghton Library, Harvard University.

ator had become so habitual with him that near the end he didn't much care whether the treaty was ratified or not.[189] That's true enough, but care must be exercised in drawing sweeping conclusions therefrom. The letter to Roosevelt's sister Corinne suggests that he took a philosophical view not because he did not care deeply about the issues, but because he was in firm command of the situation.

By September of 1919 Lodge was so completely in control that Wilson's "swing around the circle" was an exercise in futility. The Senator was master of the parliamentary situation, having reached an agreement with the mild reservationists on what he regarded as strong and effective reservations. Moreover, Wilson's tepid reception served to demonstrate the fact that public opinion was finally taking the form Lodge had all along anticipated.[190] As a result Lodge began at this point to entertain the possibility of getting rid of the League entirely.[191] His concern for continued cooperation with the Allies diminished as the prospects of politically humiliating Wilson increased. As a first step Lodge began to assert his independence from Root and the mild reservationists. That was clearly the import of his late September declaration to Root that if he "were to go over and vote against the treaty because the reservations were not satisfactory it would be killed." He still looked to eventual ratification with "strong and efficient" reservations, but there began to develop in Lodge's mind a second, or alternative, scenario which begged or postponed the matter of ultimate ratification and envisioned a devas-

189. Kendrick, "The League of Nations and the Republican Senate," p. 135; John McCook Roots, "The Treaty of Versailles in the U.S. Senate," p. 88.

190. His own state, Massachusetts, was atypical in that opinion swung more sharply there than in any other state; whereas Wilson had been enthusiastically received in February and Gov. Coolidge had warned Lodge to soften his opposition because Massachusetts was "a pacifist state," just a few months later even the Democratic State Committee was denouncing the League. The Massachusetts American Federation of Labor also announced its "bitter opposition," the Democratic state platform plank was even more hostile than the Republican, and in the 1920 election Cox, the Democratic Presidential candidate, could poll only 28.9 percent of the vote. See Huthmacher, *Massachusetts People and Politics, 1919–1933,* pp. 26, 30, 42; and Charles Callan Tansill, *America and the Fight for Irish Freedom, 1866–1922* (New York, 1957), p. 331. This was due primarily to the opposition of the Irish who feared the League might become an instrument for perpetuating British control over Ireland. However much this attitude may have rested on a distortion of the provisions of the Covenant and on anti-British prejudice, it served to confirm Lodge in his opinion that the composition of the American population placed a severe limitation on the country's ability to pursue a consistent foreign policy.

191. Diary of Chandler Anderson, entry for Sept. 21, 1919, Anderson MSS.

tating political defeat for Wilsonianism. He could no longer resist confiding to correspondents that what he "should like best is to have him refuse to make the treaty and then come before the people next year as a candidate for the presidency."[192]

However, that was at best a possibility and despite its appeal Lodge was not about to depend upon a contingency over which he could exercise so little influence. The only safe assumption was that the League would be ratified in some form. Therefore the nature and scope of the reservations continued to be crucial. It followed that he derived great satisfaction from being able to report that "the reservations which I have particularly worked for all summer long have all been adopted by ample majorities and I can feel at last that I have achieved something, no matter what is to follow." With that under his belt, he could afford to permit "the experiment of the League" to be tried.[193]

Meanwhile, he would do nothing to jeopardize his reservations. He engaged in a holding operation. Publicly and to those who wanted the treaty he took the tack (designed to put pressure on Wilson) that the treaty would pass as soon as Wilson accepted the reservations. Lodge also made it clear that he would welcome an appeal to the electorate, a statement whose intent became more obvious when coupled with the prophecy that "from the way the country is voting at every election I have no doubt of the result and it might well take a form at the general election which would be fatal to the treaty."[194] He tried at the same time to prevent those who opposed the treaty from forcing his hand. With them he argued that he was totally dependent on the way the votes lined up in the Senate, that he had to do, not exactly what he wanted, but the best he could under the circumstances and that, as the votes stood, was to "compel them to accept a ratification with reservations that will protect fully the peace, independence and sovereignty of the United States, or force them to reject it."[195] To those who hoped for

192. Lodge to Root, Sept. 29, 1919, Root MSS. See also Lodge to Louis A. Coolidge, Aug. 5, 1919, Lodge MSS.

193. Lodge to R. M. Washburn, Nov. 15, 1919, and to Lord Bryce, Dec. 2, 1919, Lodge MSS.

194. *New York Times*, Nov. 27, 1919, p. 5, and Jan. 9, 1920, p. 8; Lodge to Root, Dec. 3, 1919, Root MSS.

195. Lodge to Louis A. Coolidge, Jan. 28 and Feb. 11, 1920, Lodge MSS. He clearly stated: "give me enough votes and I can stop the treaty; give me a majority and I can do anything," but was as pronounced in declaring that the votes simply were not there.

ratification he held out that possibility, telling Root, for example, that though he did not believe that Wilson would yield, many Democrats were getting restive.[196] To those who opposed ratification he emphasized his feeling that the President was "really immovable" and that ratification was "sure to fail."[197]

It was a delicate balancing act and it has naturally given rise to the view that Lodge was not sincere about wanting ratification and arranged things so that not only would the League be defeated but the Democratic party, and especially Wilson's friends, would be responsible for its defeat. Lodge lent credence to this interpretation by declaring in *The Senate and the League of Nations* that this was an "object which I had very much at heart," though he qualified this by saying that he wanted responsibility to rest there if the treaty were defeated. He further incriminated himself by saying he was convinced Wilson would prevent ratification if he possibly could (though he made it clear that he did not know whether Wilson could hold the majority of Democrats with him) and by claiming that "a correct analysis of Mr. Wilson's probable attitude was an element of vital moment to me in trying to solve the intricate problem which I . . . [was] compelled to face."[198] After the vote, when things had worked themselves out to his satisfaction, the temptation to give himself credit for such prescience was irresistible, but the only contemporary evidence seems to be a cryptic reference, in a letter to Corinne Roosevelt Robinson, to the irreconcilables coming to see "that I was worked [*sic*] on a well-settled plan. . . ."[199] That may have been just the impression he wanted to create among the irreconcilables, not his real plan. It is a matter that

196. Lodge to Root, March 6, 1920, Lodge MSS.

197. Lodge to Beveridge, Jan. 3, 1920, Beveridge MSS; Lodge to Louis A. Coolidge, March 13, 1920, Lodge MSS.

198. Lodge, *The Senate and the League*, pp. 164, 212, 219.

199. Lodge to Corinne Roosevelt Robinson, March 14, 1920, Houghton Library, Harvard University. See also Lodge to James M. Beck, Sept. 30, 1920, and to Robert Edwards Annin, April 4, 1924, Lodge MSS. His own account in *The Senate and the League of Nations* was probably the basis for the story recounted by James E. Watson in his 1936 memoir, *As I Knew Them*. Watson told the following story: "One evening at Senator Lodge's home, I said to him: 'Senator, suppose that the President accepts the Treaty with your reservations. Then we are in the League, and once in our reservations become purely fiction.' I shall never forget how he turned to me and said, with a smile that betokened his full confidence in the assertion that he was about to make: 'But, my dear James, you do not take into consideration the hatred that Woodrow Wilson has for me personally. Never under any set of circumstances in this world could he be induced to accept a treaty with Lodge reservations appended to it.' "

may never be conclusively resolved, but certainly the study of Wilson was not a new subject for Lodge. Several years before he *had* remarked on his ability to predict Wilson's course and *had* suggested that "a personal animosity is the only thing that will ever carry him against his interest."[200]

But even if he knew his Wilson well enough to predict his course, he could not have been sure of Wilson's ability to hold wavering Democrats in line. He never counted on Wilson's ability to do so and was equally prepared for the opposite. His surest defense against the Wilsonian version of the peace settlement was not to be found in Wilson's uncompromising attitude, but in the reservations for which he had been able to secure majority backing. They permitted him to take a detached attitude with respect to the final vote. There was the additional possibility that Wilson, in the face of a favorable Senate vote for ratification with the Lodge reservations, would simply withdraw the treaty as Taft, under similar circumstances, had withdrawn his arbitration treaties. Lodge would have been "very glad to see it end in that way," but thought that "too much to hope."[201] That would have been icing on the cake, but the important thing was having created a situation such that "they must either take it with my reservations or reject it." That was the true source of his ability to approach the *dénouement* "with a certain amount of philosophical calm."[202] One is reminded of his telling Roosevelt with respect to the Taft arbitration treaties in 1912 that "I am sure that I have got the situation now where nothing serious can happen and as for the rest I care very little."[203]

One way of maintaining that it was not Lodge's intention to completely close the door on internationalism is to point out that it was not the reservations but the spirit behind the treaty that mattered. If the

200. Lodge to Roosevelt, July 10, 1916, and May 18, 1917, Roosevelt MSS.

201. Lodge to Brooks Adams, March 12, 1920, Lodge MSS. Lawrence Lowell, whose perception of Lodge's position and motives was usually acute, put it this way: "At present I think he really sees the necessity for the Republican party of getting the Treaty out of the way so far as the Senate is concerned and really wants to get the Senate to ratify it, and he has constantly reduced his irreducible minimum. Perhaps, he would not be sorry, nevertheless, to have the President withdraw the Treaty after the Senate had acted upon it" (Lowell to F. F. Ayer, March 16, 1920, League to Enforce Peace MSS).

202. Lodge to Louis A. Coolidge, March 17, 1920, Lodge MSS.

203. See above p. 151. Warren Kuehl (*Seeking World Order*) has noted a number of other parallels between the struggle over the arbitration treaties in 1912 and that over the League Covenant.

American people were really willing to support the League, "the Lodge reservations did not prevent them from doing so."[204] This perception underlay Viscount Grey's famous letter to the London *Times* in which he made the point that international cooperation was more likely to blossom on the basis of America's entering the League "as a willing partner with limited obligations" than "if . . . she entered as a reluctant partner who felt that her hand had been forced."[205] Lodge had been in contact with Grey and thought his letter "splendid," and yet it is unlikely that Lodge ever accepted the idea that the League was an appropriate vehicle for an expression of the United States' interest in European peace.[206] He seems never to have given up on the idea of putting something else in its place, of even at this late date substituting for the Wilsonian version of the peace settlement something more compatible with his own views as to what would make for peace and yet engender lasting support among the American populace. There is at least a suggestion of what that might have been in the fact that he followed his insertion of Grey's letter in the *Congressional Record* with another item, an interview with "James" Bainville, a spokesman of the French Right. Bainville suggested a very limited league, one with the sole purpose of guaranteeing the execution of the treaty with Germany and one "which would not entail any nation alienating independence or finding itself forced against its will into vague far-away complications."[207]

Lodge never became an isolationist nor did he lose interest in the country's foreign relations. Though his premise was faulty and ethnocentric (he claimed that the world needed the United States too much) he adamantly excluded even the possibility of the United States being isolated.[208] His heart, he told Beveridge, remained "bound up in this matter of the League." All he had to ask of the President-to-be was a

204. Bailey, *Woodrow Wilson and the Great Betrayal*, p. 167.

205. *Cong. Record*, 66th Cong., 2nd sess., 1920, p. 2336. Sterling J. Kernek, "Distractions of Peace During War," provides insight into British thinking on the League. The British Government thought it their "best chance of involving the U.S. in European security arrangements on a long-standing basis" (p. 65).

206. Lodge to Louis A. Coolidge and James T. Williams, Jr., Feb. 2, 1920, Lodge MSS; Garraty, *Lodge*, p. 387.

207. *Cong. Record*, 66th Cong., 2nd sess., 1920, pp. 2336–37.

208. *Official Proceedings of the Seventeenth Republican National Convention* (New York, 1920), p. 32.

talk "before he makes up his mind as to his Secretary of State."[209] During the campaign of 1920 he suggested the possibility of putting aside this "ill-drawn, ill-conceived league" and taking up "under the auspices of the United States a new agreement, or association, or league—whatever you call it—with all the nations of Europe under the leadership of the United States itself."[210] This was not just a preelection sop to Republican internationalists. After the election Lodge suggested to President-elect Harding "a fresh start" involving passage of the Knox Resolution and an invitation to the signatories of the Versailles Treaty "to send representatives to Washington to consider an agreement which would take steps to codify international law and establish a world court, to deal so far as possible with non-justiciable questions and with the proposition of a general reduction of armaments. . . ."[211] As late as April of 1921 he was seeking a means of strengthening Poland and still looking toward "some separate agreement among the Powers for such things as we should be willing to join in," some "new treaty or agreement with our Allies."[212]

In this he was to be disappointed. In fact the hopelessness of these aspirations suggests that in his preoccupation with Wilson and his League Lodge may finally have lost his vaunted grasp of American political realities. He put up a good front, but the 1921 Washington Conference was in comparison to what Lodge originally had in mind only a gesture. Though he continued to blame Wilson for what happened, he came to realize that the result of the fight over the League "was not without its elements of tragedy."[213] In order to prevent the establishment of a type of internationalism which he considered dangerous and inappropriate under American conditions, Lodge was forced to adopt an insular nationalism. This proved an effective means of combating Wilsonianism, but could only be meaningfully defined as an alternative to internationalism. Lodge's call for the American people to "be now and ever for Americanism and Nationalism, and against In-

209. Lodge to Beveridge, May 14, 1920, and to Harry M. Daugherty, Oct. 21, 1920, Lodge MSS.

210. "Speech at Braves' Field, Boston, Aug. 28, 1920," pp. 11–12, Lodge MSS.

211. Lodge to Harding, Nov. 10 and Dec. 23, 1920, Lodge MSS.

212. Lodge to Ellis Loring Dresel (American Commissioner in Berlin), April 18, 1921, Lodge MSS.

213. Lodge to Robert Edwards Annin, April 4, 1924, Lodge MSS.

ternationalism" found all too much resonance, and as a result Wilson's referendum on the League became all too clearly a "Referendum for Isolation."[214] In the backwash of that election those who had a vision of an internationalism of another sort lost what remaining political leverage they had. Lodge, in that sense, was too successful for his own good.

Ultimately more tragic, the Wilsonians soon lapsed into their own emotional and rhetorical equivalent of the Republicans' "Americanism and Nationalism." They too had political interests to serve and they too developed a mythology to foster them. Wilson claimed not only that the United States had gone to war to establish a League of Nations, but that "the opinion of the whole world swung to our support and the support of the nations associated with us in the great struggle" because of that advocacy. Moreover, he insisted that any reservation to Article X would plunge the world back into imperialism and reaction, a clear invitation to the American people to attribute anything short of perfection in international relations to Lodge's reservations.[215] Never willing to admit that there were serious problems involved in the formation of a league to enforce peace, Wilson sought to limit such discussion by the introduction of yet another myth, namely that the Republican Senate "interposing partisan envy and personal hatred in the way of the peace and prosperity of the world" had refused to ratify the treaty "merely because it was the product of Democratic statesmanship."[216] Wilson knew something about lost causes and the manner in which they were romanticized. As a result, under the influence of another and even more horrible war, a new generation of Americans found it easy to believe that had the United States joined the League that war might not have occurred. In their devotion to atoning for the "mistake" of 1919–20 by constructing a new international organization for securing the world's peace, they were as blind to some of the other requisites of a lasting peace settlement as Wilson had been twenty-five years earlier. Instead of learning from their elders' mistakes, they only compounded their tragedy.

214. *Official Proceedings of the Seventeenth Republican National Convention*, p. 32; Vinson, *Referendum for Isolation.*
215. Wilson's letter of March 8, 1920, to Gilbert M. Hitchcock reprinted in the *Cong. Record*, 66th Cong., 2nd sess., 1920, pp. 4051–52.
216. Porter and Johnson, eds., *National Party Platforms*, p. 213.

Epilogue

In 1947 Walter Lippmann delivered the following indictment of American foreign policy:

. . . on the crucial issues our diplomacy has thus far always miscarried. It has been unable to prevent war. It has been unable to avoid war. It has not prepared us for war. It has not been able to settle the wars when they have been fought and won. Never has the country been able to achieve any of the principal objectives to which again and again it has been so solemnly and fervently committed. . . . the course of events during the American rise to pre-eminence is strewn with debris and wreckage of high and hopeful declarations of policy [here Lippmann began a long list beginning with Wilson's neutrality, Wilson's Fourteen Points and the Covenant of the League of Nations]. . . . When we reflect on this experience of repeated declarations and repeated disappointments, we must be struck by the contrast between our capacity as a people to develop national power and our ability to use it and to manage it successfully.[1]

The basic problem may be that we have expected too much of our diplomacy. Precisely because we so long sailed "upon a summer sea" and could be so free in criticizing European practice, when our turn came we were determined to do much better, to replace traditional diplomacy with a new order of things. We have as a result gone from one perfectionist scheme to another.

If American foreign policy has erred because it has often been di-

1. Merle Curti, Willard Thorp and Carlos Baker, eds., *American Issues: The Social Record* (Philadelphia, 1960), II, p. 1141.

rected toward impossible moral goals, that, as George E. Mowry once suggested, "was not the fault of Henry Cabot Lodge."[2] Meant to be even more caustic was the comment of Oswald Garrison Villard, who on the occasion of Lodge's death assessed his contribution this way:

Men will read his books, a few his speeches; they will find nowhere the divine afflatus and never will it be truthfully claimed for him that he broadened the range of American idealism, or brought the achievement of our ideals an hour nearer, or advanced in any way the brotherhood of man.[3]

Such criticism is not without foundation, but it is a mistake to use it, as so often has been the case, as a basis for dismissing Lodge altogether.

He was, like Lippmann, engaged by the problem of the conduct of foreign policy under American and democratic conditions. He wanted the United States to become a responsible world power and often in his later years despaired of its doing so. There is a suggestion of the role he wanted and imagined himself to be playing in a letter written shortly before his death. Though going to some length to point out that he was not yet as pessimistic as his Federalist ancestors, he recalled with sympathy the lines they were fond of quoting in their dark days: "Truths would you teach, or save a sinking land, All fear, none aid you, and few understand."[4]

Among these truths were the profound limitations that beset American foreign-policy makers. To Lodge's way of thinking the Federalists had understood this better than anyone else. Just as they had recognized that democracy had to be limited in certain ways in order to survive, so too had they recognized that the success of the American Democracy's foreign policy would be dependent on the recognition of limitations. Washington's foreign policy was successful because it was "firmly founded upon a profound knowledge of human nature." The Federalist approach was "just as sound at the beginning of the twentieth century." Human nature had scarcely changed at all.[5] No argument came more readily to Lodge's lips than antiutopianism based on an analysis of the human condition, on man's imperfections, and on his inhumanity to man. The proceedings at Versailles, Lodge felt, had once more exhibited

2. "Politicking in Acid," *Saturday Review* 36 (Oct. 3, 1953): 30.
3. "Henry Cabot Lodge—A Scholar in Politics," *The Nation* 119 (Nov. 19, 1924): 541.
4. Lodge to David Jayne Hill, Sept. 27, 1924, Lodge MSS.
5. Lodge's Preface to the 1920 edition of his *George Washington*.

in all its weakness "the beautiful scheme of making mankind suddenly virtuous by a statute or a written constitution."[6] Given the dark, barbaric side of human nature which the war had brought to the fore, that was the easy argument.

It was more difficult to get Americans to understand that they had some peculiar, indigenous problems which severely circumscribed their ability to conduct a foreign policy consonant with their aspirations. Those problems derived from the composition of the American population, from an ideology which encouraged the making of sweeping promises in the name of great universal principles and then facilitated their neglect when they proved to entail unwanted and impolitic sacrifices, and from the very nature of the American political process. These inevitably affected the determination and unity of the people when it came to the implementation of foreign policy. The Federalists had been aware of most of these weaknesses, and in this area Lodge was as fearful and pessimistic as they had been. All Lodge's experience bespoke the difficulty of conducting foreign policy under American and democratic conditions and caused him to "doubt whether under our form of government we ever can carry through a foreign policy anywhere for a long period of years to be sustained by one administration after another. . . ."[7] He saw only one solution and interestingly it did not involve compounding the problem of hypocrisy by removing foreign policy from the democratic process but rather patience; "he believed that national and international action must be built up from the people, their traditions and their intelligent assent, and not imposed from above."[8] If he had one overwhelming concern it was probably that of protecting the American people (and thereby also the rest of the world) from the dangers inherent in their peculiar proclivity for hypocrisy.

However, the dangers of hypocrisy which our idealists are so prone to incur are probably no greater than the dangers which emanate from the cynicism which infects our realists.[9] Cynicism was Lodge's personal cross. His "crime" in the fight over the League may only have been that of having had the prescience to foresee the attitude which his country-

---

6. Lodge, "After the Victory" (an address at the Harvard Commencement, June 19, 1919) in *The Senate of the United States*, p. 190.

7. Lodge to Dr. W. M. Collier, n.d., but presumably 1921, Lodge MSS.

8. William Lawrence, *Henry Cabot Lodge*, pp. 173–74.

9. Robert C. Good, "The National Interest and Political Realism: Niebuhr's 'Debate' With Morgenthau and Kennan," *Journal of Politics* 22 (Nov. 1960): 600.

men would eventually assume, but on the other hand he was seldom sanguine about that attitude and sometimes nurtured its more unattractive aspects.[10] It is easy to see, for example, in a speech such as the one he gave to the Republican National Convention in 1920 merely the uninspired utterances of "a weary and cynical politician."[11] The war had on Lodge, as on so many of his generation, a devastating and far-reaching impact. The world would simply never be the same again. As he confessed to Brooks Adams in September of 1919: ". . . we were all of us in our youth more or less under the spell of the 19th century doctrines that we were in continual evolution, always moving on to something better with perfection as the goal; . . . now it is all over."[12] Once the world, on the basis of the extended application of international arbitration and the conventions of Geneva and of The Hague, "made strong the hope that there could be no more wars," but now, "born of the great war and its legacies, the mental and emotional condition known as pessimism is rising up, looking us in the eye and calling upon us to face the hard facts of history and of the world about us."[13]

When asked to speak at Plymouth on the three hundredth anniversary of the landing of the Pilgrims he found himself confronted with this question: "What has the foundation of the new Plymouth, so full of the inspiration of hope to Webster and his time, to say to us as we look about us in this troubled and desolated world?"[14] The question appealed to him because it permitted him to draw the moral "that the Pilgrims whom we celebrated had no law of progress but managed to get on and do something in the world by adherence to some general principles, which are not regarded now quite as I should like to have them."[15] Their strength was in their character as was that of the nation they helped to bring into being. One is thereby reminded of the distinction Lodge, using Theodore Roosevelt as an example, often tried to draw between having ideals and being an idealist.[16] One demonstrated

10. *The Literary Digest* 83 (Nov. 29, 1924): 42.
11. Bailey, *Woodrow Wilson and the Great Betrayal*, p. 300.
12. Lodge to Brooks Adams, Sept. 19, 1919, Lodge MSS.
13. Lodge, "The Pilgrims of Plymouth" (an address at Plymouth, Mass. on the Three Hundredth Anniversary of the Landing of the Pilgrims, Dec. 21, 1920) in *The Senate of the United States*, pp. 233–35.
14. *Ibid.*, p. 238.
15. Lodge to William R. Thayer, Jan. 19, 1921, Lodge MSS.
16. Lodge to Leslie M. Shaw, Feb. 12, 1919, Lodge MSS; Lodge, *The Senate of the United States*, pp. 156–58.

possession of ideals primarily by example and not by moral conquest. Without a belief in the law of progress and with no hope of obtaining to perfection on earth—with an abiding sense of their own limitations —the Pilgrims "faced the world as they found it and did their best."[17] It was not much of a rallying cry, but then there did not seem to be occasion for anything else.

17. *The Senate of the United States*, p. 246.

Selected Bibliography

I. Manuscript Collections

Henry Adams Papers. Massachusetts Historical Society.
Correspondence of Brooks and Henry Adams. Houghton Library, Harvard University.
Chandler Anderson Papers. Library of Congress.
George Bancroft Papers. Massachusetts Historical Society.
Albert Beveridge Papers. Library of Congress.
William Borah Papers. Library of Congress.
Moreton Frewen Papers. Library of Congress.
John Hay Papers. Library of Congress.
Charles Evans Hughes Papers. Library of Congress.
Philander Knox Papers. Library of Congress.
Robert Lansing Papers. Library of Congress.
League to Enforce Peace Papers. Widener Library, Harvard University.
Henry Cabot Lodge Papers. Massachusetts Historical Society.
A. Lawrence Lowell Papers. Widener Library, Harvard University.
William McKinley Papers. Library of Congress.
Alfred Thayer Mahan Papers. Library of Congress.
John T. Morse, Jr., Papers. Massachusetts Historical Society.
James Ford Rhodes Papers. Massachusetts Historical Society.
Corinne Roosevelt Robinson Papers. Houghton Library, Harvard University.
Theodore Roosevelt Papers. Library of Congress.
Elihu Root Papers. Library of Congress.
Frederick Shattuck Papers. Massachusetts Historical Society.
Henry L. Stimson Papers. Sterling Library, Yale University.
William Howard Taft Papers. Library of Congress.
Henry White Papers. Library of Congress.

II. Dissertations, Theses, and Unpublished Papers

Andelman, David. "Senators and the Public, A Case Study—1919: Massachusetts Public Opinion and the Ratification of the Treaty of Versailles." Honors thesis, 1965, Widener Library, Harvard University.

Fischer, Robert James. "Henry Cabot Lodge's Concept of Foreign Policy and the League of Nations." Ph.D. dissertation, University of Georgia, 1971.

Forte, David F. "The Theory of International Relations of Henry Cabot Lodge." Honors thesis, 1963, Widener Library, Harvard University.

Greenlee, Howard Scott. "The Republican Party in Division and Reunion, 1913–1920." Ph.D. dissertation, University of Chicago, 1950.

Harbaugh, William Henry. "Wilson, Roosevelt, and Interventionism, 1914–1917: A Study of Domestic Influences on the Formulation of American Foreign Policy." Ph.D. dissertation, Northwestern University, 1954.

Harmond, Richard Peter. "Tradition and Change in the Gilded Age: A Political History of Massachusetts, 1878–1893." Ph.D. dissertation, Columbia University, 1966.

Hewes, James, Jr. "William E. Borah and the Image of Isolationism." Ph.D. dissertation, Yale University, 1959.

Hill, Thomas. "The Senate Leadership and International Policy from Lodge to Vandenberg." Ph.D. dissertation, Washington University (St. Louis), 1970.

Jamison, Alden. "Irish-Americans, the Irish Question and American Diplomacy, 1895–1921." Ph.D. dissertation, Harvard University, 1942.

Kendrick, Jack E. "The League of Nations and the Republican Senate, 1918–1921." Ph.D. dissertation, University of North Carolina, 1952.

Lowry, Philip H. "The Mexican Policy of Woodrow Wilson." Ph.D. dissertation, Yale University, 1949.

Meyerhuber, Carl Irving, Jr. "Henry Cabot Lodge, Massachusetts and the New Manifest Destiny." Ph.D. dissertation, University of California, San Diego, 1972.

Morris, James Polk. "Henry Cabot Lodge and Congressional Control of Foreign Policy." Master's thesis, Louisiana State University at New Orleans, 1969.

Myers, Newell. "The Influence of Henry Cabot Lodge on the Foreign Relations of the United States." Master's thesis, University of California, Berkeley, 1936.

Pearlman, Michael David. "To Make Democracy Safe for the World: A Social History of the Origins, Development and Aftermath of the World War I Military Preparedness Movement in America." Ph.D. dissertation, University of Illinois (Urbana), 1977.

Robertson, James Oliver. "The Progressives in National Republican Politics, 1916 to 1921." Ph.D. dissertation, Harvard University, 1964.

Roots, John McCook. "The Treaty of Versailles in the United States Senate." Honors thesis, 1925, Widener Library, Harvard University.

Seager, Robert. "The Progressives and American Foreign Policy, 1898–1917." Ph.D. dissertation, Ohio State University, 1955.

Stanley, Peter W. "Hoar and Lodge on the Philippine Question." Honors thesis, 1962, Widener Library, Harvard University.

Tinsley, William Waring. "The American Preparedness Movement, 1913–1916." Ph.D. dissertation, Stanford University, 1939.

III. Printed Material

A. PUBLISHED DOCUMENTS

Documents on British Foreign Policy (First Series [1919–1930]). Edited by E. L. Woodward and Rohan Butler. London, 1947–.

U.S. Congressional Record. 1887–1924.

U.S. Department of State. *Papers Relating to the Foreign Relations of the United States: The Lansing Papers, 1914–1920.* 2 vols. Washington, D.C., 1939.

U.S. Senate, Committee on Foreign Relations. *Report of the Committee on Foreign Relations Together with the Views of the Minority upon the General Arbitration Treaties with Great Britain and France.* Senate Document No. 98, 62nd Cong., 1st sess., 1911.

U.S. Senate. *Proceedings of the Committee on Foreign Relations, United States Senate, from the Sixty-Third Congress to the Sixty-Seventh Congress.* Washington, 1923.

U.S. Senate. *Treaty of Peace with Germany, Hearings before the Committee on Foreign Relations, United States Senate.* Senate Document No. 106, 66th Cong., 1st sess., 1919.

B. NEWSPAPERS

Boston Evening Transcript, 1874–1924.
Boston Globe, 1874–1924.
Boston Herald, 1874–1924.
Boston Journal, 1874–1903.
New York Times, 1884–1924.

C. ARTICLES BY LODGE (IN CHRONOLOGICAL ORDER)

"Rudolph Baxmann's *Die Politik der Paepste von Gregor I bis Gregor VII.*" *North American Review* 118 (April 1874): 398–401.

"*Découverte de l'Amérique par les Normands au Xe Siècle* par Gabriel Gravier." *North American Review* 119 (July 1874): 166–82.

"*The Life of Alexander Hamilton* by John T. Morse, Jr." *North American Review* 123 (July 1876): 113–44.

Review of Jacob H. Patton's *Concise History of the American People. The Nation* 23 (Aug. 31, 1876): 140.

"Critical Notice of Henry Dexter's *As To Roger Williams and His Banishment From Massachusetts.*" *North American Review* 123 (Oct. 1876): 474–77.

"Critical Review of Von Holst's *Constitutional and Political History of the United States.*" (With Henry Adams.) *North American Review* 123 (Oct. 1876): 328–61.

"Notice of George Shea's *Alexander Hamilton.*" *The Nation* 24 (May 10, 1877): 283–84.

"New England Federalism." *The Nation* 26 (Jan. 3, 1878): 11–12.

"May's Democracy in Europe." *The Literary World* 8 (April 1878): 188–89.

"Lecky's England." *The Literary World* 9 (June 1878): 3–4.

"A Whig Orator." *The Nation* 27 (Nov. 7, 1878): 287–88.

"Limited Sovereignty in the United States." *Atlantic Monthly* 43 (Feb. 1879): 184–92.

"Matthew Arnold's Mixed Essays." *International Review* 6 (June 1879): 695–99.

Review of *Every Man His Own Poet. International Review* 7 (August 1879): 216–17.

"Von Holst's *History of the United States.*" *International Review* 7 (Oct. 1879): 436–43.

Review of F. V. Greene's *Sketches of Army Life in Russia. International Review* 9 (Dec. 1880): 719–21.

"Naval Courts-Martial and the Pardoning Power." *Atlantic Monthly* 50 (July 1882): 43–50.

"The Fisheries Question." *North American Review* 146 (Feb. 1888): 121–30.

"International Copyright." *Atlantic Monthly* 66 (Aug. 1890): 264–70.

"The Federal Election Bill." *North American Review* 151 (Sept. 1890): 257–66.

"Horses and Riders." *Cosmopolitan* 9 (Oct. 1890): 694–701.

"Lynch Law and Unrestricted Immigration." *North American Review* 152 (May 1891): 602–12.

"The Political Issues of 1892." *The Forum* 12 (Sept. 1891): 98–105.

"Protection or Free Trade—Which?" *Arena* 4 (Nov. 1891): 652–69.

"Outlook and Duty of the Republican Party." *The Forum* 15 (April 1893): 250–58.

"The Census and Immigration." *Century* 24 (Sept. 1893): 737–39.

"The Opportunity of the Republican Party." *Harper's Weekly* 38 (Feb. 17, 1894): 150–51.

"The Results of Democratic Victory." *North American Review* 159 (Sept. 1894): 268–77.

"True Americanism." *Harvard Graduates' Magazine* 3 (Sept. 1894): 9–23.

"Our Blundering Foreign Policy." *The Forum* 19 (March 1895): 8–17.

"England, Venezuela and the Monroe Doctrine." *North American Review* 160 (June 1895): 651–58.

"Our Duty to Cuba." *The Forum* 21 (May 1896): 278–87.

"The Meaning of the Votes." *North American Review* 164 (Jan. 1897): 1–11.

"Alexander Hamilton." *McClure's* 8 (April 1897): 502–07.

"The American Policy of Territorial Expansion." *The Independent* 50 (Jan. 13, 1898).

"Shall We Retain the Philippines?" *Collier's Weekly*, Feb. 10, 1900, pp. 3–4.

"The Results of a Bryan Victory." *Harper's Weekly* 44 (Sept. 8, 1900): 837.

"The End of the Cuban Controversy." *Collier's Weekly*, June 29, 1901, p. 5.

"A Million Immigrants a Year." *Century* 67 (Jan. 1904): 466–69.

"Theodore Roosevelt: A Study of the Character and of the Opinions of the Man." *Critic* 44 (April 1904): 312–14.

"Why Theodore Roosevelt Should Be Elected President." *North American Review* 179 (Sept. 1904): 321–30.

"A Personal Tribute to Senator Hoar." *Harvard Graduates' Magazine* 13 (Dec. 1904): 213–18.

"What the People Endorsed." *Harper's Weekly* 49 (March 4, 1905): 306–08.

"Our Foreign Policy." *The Youth's Companion*, March 1, 1906, pp. 103–04.

"The Monroe Doctrine and Morocco." *Harper's Weekly* 50 (March 10, 1906): 332–33 and 352.

"Significance of the Results of the Election." *North American Review* 188 (Dec. 1908): 801–10.

"The Shipping Bill and March Fourth." *The Outlook* 109 (Feb. 24, 1915): 430–33.

"Force and Peace." *Annals of the American Academy of Political and Social Science* 60 (July 1915): 197–212.

"An Explanation of International Law." *The Youth's Companion* 90 (March 23, 1916): 155–56.

"Comments on Herbert Spencer's *The Coming Slavery*." *The Forum* 54 (Oct. 1915): 407–11.

"Recent Congressional Legislation." *Proceedings of the Massachusetts Historical Society* 51 (Oct. 1917): 5–20.

"The War Work of Congress." *The Forum* 59 (June 1918): 674–87.

"America's War Aims." *Current History* 9 (Oct. 1918): 141–43.

"The Necessary Guarantees of Peace." *Scribner's Magazine* 64 (Nov. 1918): 620–24.

"Joint Debate on the Covenant of Paris." (With A. Lawrence Lowell.) World Peace Foundation, *League of Nations* (Boston, 1919), II, pp. 49–97.

"Our Foreign Policy." *The Forum* 68 (Sept. 1922): 725–30.

"Francis Parkman." *Proceedings of the Massachusetts Historical Society* 56 (June 1923): 319–35.

"One Hundred Years of the Monroe Doctrine." *Scribner's Magazine* 74 (Oct. 1923): 413–23.

"Foreign Relations of the United States, 1921–1924." *Foreign Affairs* 2 (June 15, 1924): 525–39.

D. OTHER ARTICLES

Aaron, Daniel. "The Unusable Man: An Essay on the Mind of Brooks Adams" *New England Quarterly* 21 (March 1948): 3–33.

Abbott, Lawrence F. "More Rooseveltiana." *The Outlook* 139 (April 29, 1925): 645–46.

Allen, Howard W. "Republican Reformers and Foreign Policy, 1913–1917." *Mid-America* 44 (Oct. 1962): 222–29.

Bagby, Wesley M. "Woodrow Wilson, A Third Term and the Solemn Referendum." *American Historical Review* 60 (April 1955): 567–75.

Bailey, Thomas A. "The Lodge Corollary to the Monroe Doctrine." *Political Science Quarterly* 48 (June 1933): 220–39.

———. "Was the Election of 1900 a Mandate on Imperialism?" *Mississippi Valley Historical Review* 24 (March 1937): 43–52.

———. "Woodrow Wilson Wouldn't Yield." *American Heritage* 8 (June 1957): 21–25, 105–06.

Bernstein, Barton J., and Leib, Franklin A. "Progressive Republican Senators and American Imperialism, 1898–1916: A Reappraisal." *Mid-America* 50 (July 1968): 163–205.

Blake, Nelson M. "Ambassadors at the Court of Theodore Roosevelt." *Mississippi Valley Historical Review* 42 (Sept. 1955): 179–206.

———. "The Olney-Pauncefote Treaty of 1897." *American Historical Review* 50 (Jan. 1945): 228–43.

Blodgett, Geoffrey T. "The Mind of the Boston Mugwump." *Mississippi Valley Historical Review* 48 (March 1962): 614–34.

Bryce, James. "The Policy of Annexation for America." *The Forum* 24 (Dec. 1897): 385–95.

Buchanan, Russell. "Theodore Roosevelt and American Neutrality." *American Historical Review*, 43 (July 1938): 775–90.

Buehrig, Edward H. "Idealism and Statecraft." *Confluence* 5 (Autumn 1956): 252–63.

Burton, David H. "Theodore Roosevelt and His English Correspondents: A Special Relationship of Friends." *Transactions of the American Philosophical Society*, n.s., 63, Part 2, 1973.

Campbell, John P. "Taft, Roosevelt, and the Arbitration Treaties of 1911." *Journal of American History* 53 (Sept. 1966): 279–98.

Carroll, John M., "Henry Cabot Lodge's Contributions to the Shaping of Republican European Diplomacy, 1920–1924." *Capitol Studies* 3 (Fall 1975): 153–65.

Chance, Wade. "Wilson and Lodge." *The English Review* 42 (Feb. 1926): 195–202.

Chase, Philip Putnam. "A Crucial Juncture in the Political Careers of Lodge and Long." *Proceedings of the Massachusetts Historical Society* 70 (1950–53): 102–27.

Coker, William S. "The Panama Canal Tolls Controversy: A Different Perspective." *Journal of American History* 55 (Dec. 1968): 555–64.

Cooper, John Milton, Jr. "Progressivism and American Foreign Policy: A Reconsideration." *Mid-America* 51 (Oct. 1969): 260–77.

Darling, H. Maurice. "Who Kept the United States Out of the League of Nations?" *Canadian Historical Review* 10 (Sept. 1929): 196–211.

Dexter, Byron. "The Liberal Values and Collective Security." *Confluence* 5 (Autumn 1956): 307–19.

Dubin, Martin David. "Elihu Root and the Advocacy of a League of Nations, 1914–1917." *Western Political Quarterly* 19 (Sept. 1966): 439–55.

Egerton, George W. "The Lloyd George Government and the Creation of the League of Nations." *American Historical Review* 74 (April 1974): 419–37.

Esthus, Raymond A. "Isolationism and World Power." *Diplomatic History* 2 (Spring 1978): 117–29.

Ferrell, Robert. "Woodrow Wilson: Man and Statesman." *Review of Politics* 18 (April 1956): 131–45.

Finch, George A. "The Treaty of Peace with Germany in the United States Senate." *American Journal of International Law* 14 (Jan. and April 1920): 155–206.

Fuess, Claude M. "Carl Schurz, Henry Cabot Lodge and the Campaign of 1884: A Study in Temperament and Political Philosophy." *New England Quarterly* 5 (July 1932): 453–82.

Garraty, John A. "Henry Cabot Lodge and the Alaskan Boundary Tribunal." *New England Quarterly* 24 (Dec. 1951): 469–94.

————. "Spoiled Child of American Politics." *American Heritage* 6 (Aug. 1955): 55–59.

Good, Robert C. "The National Interest and Political Realism: Niebuhr's 'Debate' with Morgenthau and Kennan." *Journal of Politics* 22 (Nov. 1960): 597–619.

Grant, Robert. "Lodge." A Commemorative Tribute Prepared for the American Academy of Arts and Letters, 1926.

Grenville, John A. S. "American Naval Preparations for War with Spain, 1896–1898." *Journal of American Studies* 2 (April 1968): 33–47.

Gross, Leo. "The Charter of the United Nations and the Lodge Reservations." *American Journal of International Law* 41 (July 1947): 531–54.

Helbich, Wolfgang. "American Liberals in the League of Nations Controversy." *Public Opinion Quarterly* 31 (Winter 1967–68): 568–96.

"Henry Cabot Lodge, Senator of the United States." *The Literary Digest* 83 (Nov. 29, 1924): 36–42.

"Henry Cabot Lodge: American Statesman and Scholar." *North American Review* 220 (Dec. 1924): 195–98.

"Henry Cabot Lodge." *The Outlook* 138 (Nov. 19, 1924): 437–39.

Hewes, James E., Jr. "Henry Cabot Lodge and the League of Nations." *Proceedings of the American Philosophical Society* 114 (August 1970): 245–55.

Higham, John. "Origins of Immigration Restriction, 1882–1897: A Social Analysis." *Mississippi Valley Historical Review* 39 (June 1952): 77–88.

Hirschfeld, Charles. "Brooks Adams and American Nationalism." *American Historical Review* 69 (Jan. 1964): 371–92.

Hofstadter, Richard. "Cuba, the Philippines, and Manifest Destiny." In *Essays in American Diplomacy*, edited by Armin Rappaport. New York, 1967, pp. 150–70.

Holbo, Paul S. "Economics, Emotion, and Expansion: An Emerging Foreign Policy." In *The Gilded Age*, edited by H. Wayne Morgan. Syracuse, N.Y., 1970, pp. 199–221.

Israel, Jerry. " 'For God, for China and for Yale'—The Open Door in Action." *American Historical Review* 75 (Feb. 1970): 796–807.

James, William. "The Moral Equivalent of War." *McClure's* 35 (Aug. 1910): 463–68.

Johnson, Walter. "Senatorial Strategy, 1919–20: Will It Be Repeated." *Antioch Review* 3 (Winter 1943): 512–29.

Katz, Friedrich. "Pancho Villa and the Attack on Columbus, New Mexico." *American Historical Review* 83 (Feb. 1978): 101–30.

Kernek, Sterling J. "Distractions of Peace During War: The Lloyd George Government's Reactions to Woodrow Wilson." *Transactions of the American Philosophical Society*, n.s., 65, Part 2, 1975.

LaFeber, Walter. "A Note on the 'Mercantilistic Imperialism' of Alfred Thayer Mahan." *Mississippi Valley Historical Review* 48 (March 1962): 674–85.

Lancaster, James L. "The Protestant Churches and the Fight for Ratification of the Versailles Treaty." *Public Opinion Quarterly* 31 (Winter 1967–68): 597–619.

Langer, William L. "Woodrow Wilson: His Education in World Affairs." *Confluence* 5 (Autumn 1956): 183–94.

Leopold, Richard. "The Problem of American Intervention, 1917." *World Politics* 2 (April 1950): 405–25.

Leuchtenburg, William. "Progressivism and Imperialism: The Progressive Movement and American Foreign Policy, 1898–1916." *Mississippi Valley Historical Review* 39 (Dec. 1952): 483–504.

Livermore, Seward W. "The American Navy as a Factor in World Politics, 1903–1913." *American Historical Review* 63 (July 1958): 863–79.

Low, Arthur Fell. "Living American Statesman: Henry Cabot Lodge." *The Forum* 65 (March 1921): 267–72.

Lowell, A. Lawrence. "A League to Enforce Peace." World Peace Foundation Pamphlet Series 5 (Oct. 1915): 5–18.

Mallan, John P. "The Warrior Critique of the Business Civilization." *American Quarterly* 8 (Fall 1956): 216–30.

Maxwell, Kenneth. "Irish-Americans and the Fight for Treaty Ratification." *Public Opinion Quarterly* 31 (Winter 1967–68): 620–41.

Mervin, David. "Henry Cabot Lodge and the League of Nations." *Journal of American Studies* 4 (Feb. 1971): 201–14.

Morse, John T., Jr. "Henry Cabot Lodge." *Harvard Graduates' Magazine* 33 (March 1925): 439–55.

———. "Tribute to Henry Cabot Lodge." *Proceedings of the Massachusetts Historical Society* 58 (Nov. 1924): 99–110.

Mount, Ferdinand. "The Sense of Dispossession." *Encounter* (Dec. 1972): 9–16.

Olney, Richard. "Growth of Our Foreign Policy." *Atlantic Monthly* 85 (March 1900): 289–301.

Olson, William Clinton. "Theodore Roosevelt's Conception of an International League." *World Affairs Quarterly* 29 (Jan. 1959): 329–53.

Osgood, Robert E. "Woodrow Wilson, Collective Security, and the Lessons of History." *Confluence* 5 (Autumn 1956): 341–54.

Paulsen, George E. "Secretary Gresham, Senator Lodge, and American Good Offices in China, 1894." *Pacific Historical Review* 36 (May 1967): 123–42.

Pratt, Julius W. "Collapse of American Imperialism." *American Mercury* 31 (March 1934): 269–78.

———. "The 'Large Policy' of 1898." *Mississippi Valley Historical Review* 19 (Sept. 1932): 219–42.

Ratcliffe, S. K. "Senator Lodge." *The Living Age* 301 (May 3, 1919): 294–97.

Redmond, Kent C. "Henry L. Stimson and the Question of League Membership." *The Historian* 25 (Feb. 1963): 200–12.

"Roosevelt and Lodge." *The New Republic* 43 (June 17, 1925): 103–04.

Roosevelt, Theodore. "The Arbitration Treaty with Great Britain." *The Outlook* 98 (May 20, 1911): 97–98.

———. "The Foreign Policy of President Harrison." *The Independent* 44 (Aug. 11, 1892): 1113–15.

———. "The Foreign Policy of the United States." *The Outlook* 107 (Aug. 22, 1914): 1011–15.

———. "The League of Nations." *Metropolitan* 99 (Jan. 1919): 9 and 70.

———. "The Peace of Righteousness." *The Outlook* 99 (Sept. 9, 1911): 66–70.

———. "The Peace of Victory for Which We Strive." *Metropolitan* 46 (July 1917): 24 and 64–65.

———. "The Russian Treaty, Arbitration and Hypocrisy." *The Outlook* 99 (Dec. 30, 1911): 1045–47.

———. "Uncle Sam and the Rest of the World." *Metropolitan* 41 (March 1915): 11–12.

———. "Utopia or Hell." *The Independent* 81 (Jan. 4, 1915): 13–17.

———. "The World War: Its Tragedies and Its Lessons." *The Outlook* 108 (Sept. 23, 1914): 169–78.

Smith, Daniel M. "National Interest and American Intervention, 1917: An Historiographical Appraisal." *Journal of American History* 52 (June 1965): 5–24.

Stern, Sheldon M. "American Nationalism vs. the League of Nations: The Correspondence of Albert J. Beveridge and Louis A. Coolidge, 1918–1920." *Indiana Magazine of History* 72 (June 1976): 138–58.

———. "Henry Cabot Lodge and Louis A. Coolidge in Defense of American Sovereignty, 1898–1920." *Proceedings of the Massachusetts Historical Society*, 87 (1975): 118–34.

Sutton, Walter A. "Progressive Republican Senators and the Submarine Crisis, 1915–1916." *Mid-America* 47 (April 1965): 75–88.

Thompson, J. A. "An Imperialist and the First World War: the Case of Albert J. Beveridge." *Journal of American Studies*, 5 (1971): 133–50.

Thompson, Kenneth W. "Collective Security Re-examined." *American Political Science Review* 47 (Sept. 1953): 753–72.

Tracy, Frank Basil. "Henry Cabot Lodge." *New England Magazine* 33 (Nov. 1905): 299–306.

Trani, Eugene P. "Cautious Warrior: Theodore Roosevelt and the Diplomacy of Activism." In *Makers of American Diplomacy*, edited by Frank J. Merli and Theodore A. Wilson, New York, 1974, pp. 305–31.

Trow, Clifford W. "Woodrow Wilson and the Mexican Interventionist Movement of 1919." *Journal of American History* 58 (June 1971): 46–72.

Vevier, Charles. "Brooks Adams and the Ambivalence of American Foreign Policy." *World Affairs Quarterly* 30 (April 1959): 3–18.

Villard, Oswald Garrison. "Henry Cabot Lodge—A Scholar in Politics." *The Nation* 119 (Nov. 19, 1924): 539–41.

Washburn, Charles G. "Memoir of Henry Cabot Lodge." *Proceedings of the Massachusetts Historical Society* 58 (April 1925): 324–76.

Welch, Richard E., Jr. "Opponents and Colleagues: George Frisbie Hoar and Henry Cabot Lodge, 1898–1904." *New England Quarterly* 39 (June 1966): 182–209.

Wells, Samuel F., Jr. "New Perspectives on Wilsonian Diplomacy: The Secular Evangelism of American Political Economy." *Perspectives in American History* 6 (1972): 389–419.

Williams, William A. "Brooks Adams and American Expansion." *New England Quarterly* 25 (June 1952): 217–32.

Wimer, Kurt. "Woodrow Wilson's Plans to Enter the League of Nations Through an Executive Agreement." *Western Political Quarterly* 11 (Dec. 1958): 800–12.

Wimer, Kurt and Sarah. "The Harding Administration, the League of Nations and the Separate Peace Treaty." *Review of Politics* 29 (Jan. 1967): 13–24.

Woodward, C. Vann. "The Age of Reinterpretation." *American Historical Review* 66 (Oct. 1960): 1–19.

Wright, Quincy. "Woodrow Wilson and the League of Nations." *Social Research* 24 (Spring 1957): 65–86.

E. BOOKS BY LODGE (IN CHRONOLOGICAL ORDER)

The Life and Letters of George Cabot. Boston, 1877.

A Short History of the English Colonies in America. New York, 1881.

Alexander Hamilton. Boston, 1895 (originally published in 1882).

Daniel Webster. Boston, 1884.

Studies in History. Boston, 1884.

The Works of Alexander Hamilton. Edited by Lodge. 9 vols. New York, 1885–86.

The Federalist. Edited by Lodge. New York, 1906 (originally published in 1888).

George Washington. 2 vols. Boston, 1890.

Boston. New York, 1891.

Historical and Political Essays. Boston, 1892.

Speeches. Boston, 1892.

Hero Tales from American History. (With Theodore Roosevelt.) Philadelphia, 1903 (originally published in 1895).

Certain Accepted Heroes. New York, 1897.

The Story of the Revolution. New York, 1903 (originally published in 1898).

The War with Spain. New York, 1899.

A Fighting Frigate. New York, 1902.

Major Andre's Journal. Edited by Lodge. Tarrytown, New York, 1930 (originally published in 1903).

A Frontier Town and Other Essays. New York, 1906.

Speeches and Addresses, 1884–1909. Boston, 1909.

One Hundred Years of Peace. New York, 1913.

Early Memories. New York, 1913.

The Democracy of the Constitution and Other Addresses and Essays. New York, 1915.

Two Commencement Addresses. Cambridge, Mass., 1915.

War Addresses. Boston, 1917.

The Senate of the United States, and Other Essays and Addresses, Historical and Literary. New York, 1921.

Selections from the Correspondence of Theodore Roosevelt and Henry Cabot Lodge, 1884–1918. Edited by Lodge. 2 vols. New York, 1925.

The Senate and the League of Nations. New York, 1925.

F. OTHER BOOKS AND MONOGRAPHS

Abbott, Lawrence F., ed. *The Letters of Archie Butt.* Garden City, N.Y., 1924.

Abrams, Richard M. *Conservatism in a Progressive Era: Massachusetts Politics 1900–1912.* Cambridge, Mass., 1964.

Adams, Brooks. *America's Economic Supremacy.* New York, 1947.

Adams, Henry. *The Education of Henry Adams.* New York, 1931.

———. *History of the United States of America.* 9 vols. New York, 1889–91.

————. *The Life of George Cabot Lodge.* Boston, 1911.

[Adams, Henry, ed.] *Letters of John Hay,* 3 vols. Washington, 1908.

Adler, Selig. *The Isolationist Impulse.* New York, 1957.

Allen, Gardner W., ed. *The Papers of John Davis Long, 1897–1904.* Boston, 1939.

Alsop, Em Bowles, ed. *The Greatness of Woodrow Wilson.* New York, 1956.

Amory, Cleveland. *The Proper Bostonians.* New York, 1947.

Anderson, George L., ed. *Issues and Conflicts: Studies in Twentieth Century American Diplomacy.* Lawrence, Kansas, 1959.

Anderson, Thornton. *Brooks Adams: Constructive Conservative.* Ithaca, N.Y., 1951.

Armstrong, William. *E. L. Godkin and American Foreign Policy, 1865–1900.* New York, 1957.

Bagby, Wesley. *The Road to Normalcy: The Presidential Campaign and Election of 1920.* Baltimore, 1968.

Bailey, Thomas A. *Diplomatic History of the American People.* New York, 1944.

————. *Woodrow Wilson and the Great Betrayal.* New York, 1945.

————. *Woodrow Wilson and the Lost Peace.* New York, 1944.

Baker, Ray Stannard. *Woodrow Wilson: Life and Letters.* 8 vols. New York, 1927–39.

Baker, Ray Stannard, and Dodd, William E., eds. *The Public Papers of Woodrow Wilson,* 6 vols. New York, 1925–27.

Bartlett, Ruhl J. *The League to Enforce Peace.* Chapel Hill, 1944.

Bates, J. Leonard. *The United States, 1898–1928: Progressivism and a Society in Transition.* New York, 1976.

Beale, Howard K. *Theodore Roosevelt and the Rise of America to World Power.* Baltimore, 1956.

Beard, Charles. *The Idea of National Interest.* New York, 1934.

Beisner, Robert L. *Twelve Against Empire: The Anti-Imperialists, 1898–1900.* New York, 1968.

————. *From the Old Diplomacy to the New, 1865–1900.* New York, 1975.

Beloff, Max. *Foreign Policy and the Democratic Process.* Baltimore, 1965.

Bell, Sidney. *Righteous Conquest: Woodrow Wilson and the Evolution of the New Diplomacy.* Port Washington, N.Y., 1972.

Beringause, Arthur F. *Brooks Adams: A Biography.* New York, 1955.

Bernstorff, Count Johann. *Memoirs.* New York, 1936.

Bishop, Joseph B. *Theodore Roosevelt and His Time.* 2 vols. New York, 1920.

Blum, John Morton. *The Republican Roosevelt.* Cambridge, Mass., 1954.

————. *Woodrow Wilson and the Politics of Morality.* Boston, 1956.

Bonsal, Stephen. *Unfinished Business.* Garden City, N.Y., 1944.

Boorstin, Daniel, ed. *An American Primer.* Chicago, 1966.

Braeman, John. *Albert J. Beveridge: American Nationalist.* Chicago, 1971.

Braeman, John, et al., eds. *Change and Continuity in Twentieth-Century America.* Columbus, Ohio, 1964.

Brooks, Van Wyck. *New England: Indian Summer, 1865–1915.* New York, 1940.

Bryan, William Jennings. *Heart to Heart Appeals.* New York, 1917.

Bryce, James. *American Commonwealth.* 2 vols. London, 1889.

Buehrig, Edward H. *Woodrow Wilson and the Balance of Power.* Bloomington, 1955.

————., ed. *Wilson's Foreign Policy in Perspective.* Bloomington, 1957.

Burns, Edward. *The American Idea of Mission.* New Brunswick, N.J., 1957.

Burton, David H. *Theodore Roosevelt: Confident Imperialist.* Philadelphia, 1968.

Butler, Nicholas M. *Across the Busy Years: Recollections and Reflections.* 2 vols. New York, 1939–40.

Butt, Archie. *Taft and Roosevelt: The Intimate Letters of Archie Butt.* 2 vols. Garden City, N.Y., 1930.

Calvert, Peter. *The Mexican Revolution, 1910–1914: The Diplomacy of Anglo-American Conflict.* Cambridge, England, 1968.

Campbell, A. E. *America Comes of Age.* New York, 1971.

————. *Great Britain and the United States, 1895–1903.* London, 1960.

Campbell, Charles S., Jr. *Anglo-American Understanding, 1898–1903.* Baltimore, 1957.

————. *The Transformation of American Foreign Relations, 1865–1900.* New York, 1976.

Carr, Edward Hallett. *Nationalism and After.* New York, 1945.

————. *The Twenty Years' Crisis, 1919–1939: An Introduction to the Study of International Relations.* London, 1962.

Cater, Harold D., ed. *Henry Adams and His Friends.* Boston, 1947.

Challener, Richard D. *Admirals, Generals and American Foreign Policy, 1898–1914.* Princeton, 1973.

Chanler, Margaret. *Roman Spring.* Boston, 1934.

Claude, Inis L. *Power and International Relations.* New York, 1962.

Clendenen, Clarence C. *The United States and Pancho Villa.* Ithaca, N.Y., 1961.

Cline, Howard F. *The United States and Mexico.* Cambridge, Mass., 1953.

Cohen, Warren I. *The American Revisionists: The Lessons of Intervention in World War I.* Chicago, 1967.

Colegrove, Kenneth. *The American Senate and World Peace.* New York, 1944.

Coletta, Paolo F. *Threshold to American Internationalism.* New York, 1970.

Commager, Henry Steele. *The American Mind.* New Haven, 1950.

Coolidge, Archibald Cary. *The United States as a World Power.* New York, 1912.

Cooper, John Milton, Jr. *The Vanity of Power: American Isolationism and the First World War.* Westport, Conn., 1969.

————., ed. *Causes and Consequences of World War I.* New York, 1972.

Corwin, Edwin S. *The President: Office and Powers.* New York, 1957.

Cosmos [Nicholas Murray Butler]. *The Basis of a Durable Peace.* New York, 1917.

Cowles, Anna Roosevelt, ed. *Letters from Theodore Roosevelt to Anna Roosevelt Cowles, 1870–1918.* New York, 1924.

Cranston, Alan. *The Killing of the Peace.* New York, 1960.

Crapol, Edward P. *America for Americans: Economic Nationalism and Anglophobia in the Late Nineteenth Century.* Westport, Conn., 1973.

Craven, Avery, ed. *Essays in Honor of William E. Dodd.* Chicago, 1935.

Croly, Herbert. *The Promise of American Life.* New York, 1964.

Cronon, E. David, ed. *The Political Thought of Woodrow Wilson.* Indianapolis, 1965.

Cullom, Shelby M. *Fifty Years of Public Service.* Chicago, 1911.

Curry, Roy Watson. *Woodrow Wilson and Far Eastern Policy, 1913–1921.* New York, 1968.

Curti, Merle E. *Bryan and World Peace.* Smith College Studies in History, 17. Northampton, Mass., 1931.

—————. *Peace or War: The American Struggle, 1636–1936.* New York, 1936.

Curti, Merle, et al., eds. *American Issues: The Social Record.* 2 vols. Philadelphia, 1960.

Dangerfield, Royden J. *In Defense of the Senate.* Norman, Oklahoma, 1933.

Daniels, Josephus. *The Wilson Era.* 2 vols. Chapel Hill, 1944.

Davies, Wallace Evans. *Patriotism on Parade.* Cambridge, Mass., 1955.

Davis, Calvin A. *The United States and the First Hague Peace Conference.* Ithaca, N.Y., 1962.

—————. *The United States and the Second Hague Peace Conference: American Diplomacy and International Organization, 1899–1914.* Durham, 1975.

Davis, Cushman K. *A Treatise on International Law, Including American Diplomacy.* St. Paul, 1901.

DeConde, Alexander, ed. *Isolation and Security.* Durham, 1957.

Dennett, Tyler. *John Hay: From Poetry to Politics.* New York, 1933.

—————. *Roosevelt and the Russo-Japanese War.* Garden City, N.Y., 1925.

Develin, Patrick. *Too Proud to Fight: Woodrow Wilson's Neutrality.* New York, 1975.

Donovan, Timothy Paul. *Henry Adams and Brooks Adams: The Education of Two American Historians.* Norman, Oklahoma, 1961.

Dulles, Foster R. *The Imperial Years.* New York, 1956.

Duncan, Bingham. *Whitelaw Reid: Journalist, Politician, Diplomat.* Athens, Ga., 1975.

Dunn, Arthur Wallace. *From Harrison to Harding, 1888–1921.* 2 vols. New York, 1922.

Duggan, Stephen P., ed. *The League of Nations: The Principle and the Practice.* Boston, 1919.

Egerton, George W. *Great Britain and the Creation of the League of Nations: Strategy, Politics, and International Organization.* Chapel Hill, 1978.

Einstein, Lewis. *Roosevelt, His Mind in Action.* Boston, 1930.

Ekirch, Arthur A. *The Decline of American Liberalism.* New York, 1955.

Elletson, Daniel H. *Roosevelt and Wilson: A Comparative Study.* London, 1965.

Enforced Peace. Proceedings of the First Annual National Assemblage of the League to Enforce Peace. New York, 1916.

Esthus, Raymond A. *Theodore Roosevelt and the International Rivalries.* Waltham, Mass., 1970.

———. *Theodore Roosevelt and Japan.* Seattle, 1967.

Eubank, Keith. *Paul Cambon: Master Diplomatist.* Norman, Oklahoma, 1960.

Fausold, Martin L. *James W. Wadsworth, Jr.: The Gentleman from New York.* Syracuse, 1975.

Ferro, Marc. *The Great War, 1914–1918.* London, 1973.

Fieldhouse, D. K. *The Colonial Empires: A Comparative Survey.* London, 1966.

Finkelstein, Marina S. and Lawrence S., eds. *Collective Security.* San Francisco, 1966.

Fischer, Fritz. *Germany's War Aims in the First World War.* New York, 1967.

———. *War of Illusions.* New York, 1975.

Fleming, Denna Frank. *The United States and the League of Nations, 1918–1920.* New York, 1932.

Foraker, Joseph B. *Notes of a Busy Life.* 2 vols. Cincinnati, 1916.

Ford, Worthington C., ed. *Letters of Henry Adams.* 2 vols. Boston, 1930 and 1938.

Fosdick, Raymond B. *Letters on the League of Nations.* Princeton, 1966.

Fredrickson, George M. *The Inner Civil War: Northern Intellectuals and the Crisis of the Union.* New York, 1965.

Fuess, Claude M. *Carl Schurz, Reformer.* New York, 1932.

Gardner, Constance, ed. *Some Letters of Augustus Peabody Gardner.* Boston, 1920.

Garraty, John A. *Henry Cabot Lodge: A Biography.* New York, 1953.

George, Alexander L. and Juliette L. *Woodrow Wilson and Colonel House: A Personality Study.* New York, 1964.

Gerson, Louis L. *Woodrow Wilson and the Rebirth of Poland, 1914–1920: A Study in the Influence on American Policy of Minority Groups of Foreign Origin.* New Haven, 1953.

Ginger, Ray, ed. *William Jennings Bryan: Selections.* Indianapolis, 1967.

Glad, Betty. *Charles Evans Hughes and the Illusions of Innocence: A Study in American Diplomacy.* Urbana, 1966.

Gooch, G. P. *History and Historians in the Nineteenth Century.* London, 1913.

Graebner, Norman, ed. *Ideas and Diplomacy: Readings in the Intellectual Tradition of American Foreign Policy.* New York, 1964.

Graham, Otis L., Jr. *The Great Campaigns: Reform and War in America, 1900–1928.* Englewood Cliffs, N.J., 1971.

Grant, Robert. *Fourscore: An Autobiography.* Boston, 1934.

Graubard, Stephen R. *Kissinger: Portrait of a Mind.* New York, 1973.

Green, Martin. *The Problem of Boston.* New York, 1966.

Grenville, John A. S., and Young, George Berkeley. *Politics, Strategy and American Diplomacy.* New Haven, 1966.

Grieb, Kenneth J. *The United States and Huerta.* Lincoln, Neb., 1969.

Groves, Charles S. *Henry Cabot Lodge: The Statesman.* Boston, 1925.

Guttmann, Allen. *The Conservative Tradition in America.* New York, 1967.

Gwynn, Stephen, ed. *The Letters and Friendships of Sir Cecil Spring Rice.* 2 vols. Boston, 1929.

Haber, Samuel. *Efficiency and Uplift: Scientific Management in the Progressive Era, 1890–1920.* Chicago, 1964.

Hagan, Kenneth J. *American Gunboat Diplomacy and the Old Navy, 1877–1889.* Westport, Conn., 1973.

Hagedorn, Hermann. *The Bugle That Woke America.* New York, 1940.

————., ed. *The Americanism of Theodore Roosevelt.* Boston, 1923.

————., ed. *The Works of Theodore Roosevelt.* 24 vols. New York, 1926.

Haley, P. Edward. *Revolution and Intervention: The Diplomacy of Taft and Wilson in Mexico.* Cambridge, Mass., 1970.

Halle, Louis J. *Dream and Reality: Aspects of American Foreign Policy.* New York, 1958.

Harbaugh, William H. *Power and Responsibility: The Life and Times of Theodore Roosevelt.* New York, 1961.

————, ed. *Writings of Theodore Roosevelt.* Indianapolis, 1967.

Hartz, Louis. *The Liberal Tradition in America.* New York, 1955.

Hays, Will H. *Memoirs.* Garden City, N.Y., 1955.

Healy, David. *U.S. Expansionism: The Imperialist Urge in the 1890's.* Madison, 1970.

————. *Gunboat Diplomacy in the Wilson Era: The U.S. Navy in Haiti, 1915–1916.* Madison, 1976.

Herman, Sondra. *Eleven Against War: Studies in American Internationalist Thought, 1898–1921.* Stanford, 1969.

Hinsley, F. H. *Power and the Pursuit of Peace.* Cambridge, England, 1963.

Hixson, William B., Jr. *Moorfield Storey and the Abolitionist Tradition.* New York, 1972.

Hofstadter, Richard. *Social Darwinism in American Thought.* Philadelphia, 1944.

Holt, W. Stull. *Treaties Defeated by the Senate.* Baltimore, 1933.

Hoover, Herbert. *The Ordeal of Woodrow Wilson.* New York, 1958.

Howe, M. A. DeWolfe. *Barrett Wendell and His Letters.* Boston, 1924.

————. *James Ford Rhodes: American Historian.* New York, 1929.

————. *John Jay Chapman and His Letters.* Boston, 1937.

————. *Portrait of an Independent: Moorfield Storey.* Boston, 1932.

Howland, Charles P. *Survey of American Foreign Relations, 1928.* New Haven, 1928.

Huthmacher, J. Joseph. *Massachusetts People and Politics, 1919–1933.* Cambridge, Mass., 1959.

Huthmacher, J. Joseph, and Susman, Warren I., eds. *Wilson's Diplomacy: An International Symposium.* Cambridge, Mass., 1973.

Israel, Jerry. *Progressivism and the Open Door: America and China, 1905–1921.* Pittsburgh, 1971.

Jaher, Frederic Cople. *The Age of Industrialism in America: Essays in Social Structure and Cultural Values.* New York, 1968.

————. *Doubters and Dissenters: Cataclysmic Thought in America, 1885–1918.* New York, 1964.

James, Henry. *Richard Olney and His Public Service.* Boston, 1923.

Jessup, Philip C. *Elihu Root.* 2 vols. New York, 1938.

Johnson, Carolyn W. *Winthrop Murray Crane: A Study in Republican Leadership, 1892–1920.* Northampton, Mass., 1967.

Johnson, Willis Fletcher. *George Harvey: A Passionate Patriot.* Boston, 1929.

Josephson, Matthew. *The President Makers.* New York, 1964.

Karsten, Peter. *The Naval Aristocracy.* New York, 1972.

Kaufman, Burton I. *Efficiency and Expansion: Foreign Trade Organization in the Wilson Administration, 1913–1921.* Westport, Conn., 1974.

Kedourie, Elie. *Nationalism.* London, 1960.

Keller, Morton. *Affairs of State: Public Life in Late Nineteenth Century America.* Cambridge, Mass., 1977.

————. *In Defense of Yesterday: James M. Beck and the Politics of Conservatism, 1861–1936.* New York, 1958.

————., ed. *Theodore Roosevelt: A Profile.* New York, 1967.

Kelley, Alfred H., ed. *American Foreign Policy and American Democracy.* Detroit, 1954.

Kren, George M., and Rappaport, Leon H., eds. *Varieties of Psychohistory.* New York, 1976.

Kuehl, Warren F. *Hamilton Holt.* Gainesville, Fla., 1960.

————. *Seeking World Order: The United States and International Organization to 1920.* Nashville, 1969.

LaFeber, Walter. *The New Empire: An Interpretation of American Expansion, 1860–1898.* Ithaca, N.Y., 1963.

Lansing, Robert. *The Peace Negotiations: A Personal Narrative.* Boston, 1921.

Latane, John H., ed. *Development of the League of Nations Idea: Documents and Correspondence of Theodore Marburg.* 2 vols. New York, 1932.

Latham, Earl, ed. *The Philosophy and Politics of Woodrow Wilson.* Chicago, 1958.

Lawrence, William. *Henry Cabot Lodge: A Biographical Sketch.* Boston, 1925.

Leech, Margaret. *In the Days of McKinley.* New York, 1959.

Leopold, Richard. *Elihu Root and the Conservative Tradition.* Boston, 1954.

Levenson, J. C. *The Mind and Art of Henry Adams.* Stanford, 1968.

Levin, David. *History as Romantic Art: Bancroft, Prescott, Motley and Parkman.* New York, 1963.

Levin, N. Gordon, Jr. *Woodrow Wilson and World Politics: America's Response to War and Revolution.* New York, 1968.

Levine, Lawrence W. *Defender of the Faith: William Jennings Bryan: The Last Decade, 1915–1925.* New York, 1965.

Link, Arthur S. *The Higher Realism of Woodrow Wilson and Other Essays.* Nashville, 1971.

———. *President Wilson and His English Critics.* Oxford, 1959.

———. *Wilson: Campaigns for Progressivism and Peace, 1916–1917.* Princeton, 1965.

———. *Wilson the Diplomatist.* Chicago, 1965.

———. *Wilson: The New Freedom.* Princeton, 1956.

———. *Wilson: The Struggle for Neutrality.* Princeton, 1960.

———. *Woodrow Wilson and the Progressive Era, 1900–1917.* New York, 1954.

Lippmann, Walter. *Essays in the Public Philosophy.* Boston, 1956.

———. *The Stakes of Diplomacy.* New York, 1915.

———. *U.S. Foreign Policy: Shield of the Republic.* Boston, 1943.

———. *U.S. War Aims.* Boston, 1944.

Livermore, Seward W. *Politics Is Adjourned: Woodrow Wilson and the War Congress, 1916–1918.* Middletown, Conn., 1966.

Livezey, William E. *Mahan on Sea Power.* Norman, Oklahoma, 1947.

Loewenheim, Francis L., ed. *The Historian and the Diplomat.* New York, 1967.

Logan, Rayford W. *The Senate and the Versailles Mandate System.* Washington, D.C., 1945.

Longworth, Alice Roosevelt. *Crowded Hours.* New York, 1933.

McCormick, Thomas J. *China Market: America's Quest for Informal Empire, 1893–1901.* Chicago, 1967.

Maddox, Robert J. *William Borah and American Foreign Policy.* Baton Rouge, 1970.

Mahan, Alfred Thayer. *Armaments and Arbitration.* New York, 1912.

———. *The Interest of America in International Conditions.* Boston, 1918.

———. *The Interest of America in Sea Power.* London, 1898.

———. *The Problem of Asia.* Boston, 1900.

———. *Retrospect and Prospect.* Boston, 1902.

———. *Some Neglected Aspects of War.* London, 1907.

Mamatey, Victor S. *The United States and East Central Europe, 1914–1918: A Study in Wilsonian Diplomacy and Propaganda.* Princeton, 1957.

Marburg, Theodore, ed. *Taft Papers on the League of Nations.* New York, 1920.

Marchand, C. Roland. *The American Peace Movement and Social Reform, 1898–1918.* Princeton, 1972.

Margulies, Herbert F. *Senator Lenroot of Wisconsin: A Political Biography, 1900–1929.* Columbia, Mo., 1977.

Marquand, John P. *The Late George Apley.* Boston, 1937.

Marrin, Albert. *Nicholas Murray Butler*. Boston, 1976.

Marshall, Thomas R. *Recollections: A Hoosier Salad*. Indianapolis, 1925.

Martin, Laurence W. *Peace Without Victory: Woodrow Wilson and the British Liberals*. New Haven, 1958.

Massachusetts Executive Department. *A Memorial to Henry Cabot Lodge*. Boston, 1932.

May, Ernest. *American Imperialism: A Speculative Essay*. New York, 1968.

———. *Imperial Democracy*. New York, 1973.

———. *The World War and American Isolation*. Cambridge, Mass., 1959.

May, Henry. *The End of American Innocence*. Chicago, 1964.

Mayer, Arno. *Political Origins of the New Diplomacy, 1917–1918*. New York, 1969.

———. *Politics and Diplomacy of Peacemaking: Containment and Counter-revolution at Versailles, 1918–1919*. New York, 1967.

Mayer, George. *The Republican Party, 1854–1964*. New York, 1964.

Mencken, H. L. *The Vintage Mencken*. Edited by Alister Cooke. New York, 1961.

Merrill, Horace Samuel, and Merrill, Marion Galbraith. *The Republican Command, 1897–1913*. Lexington, Ky., 1971.

Miller, David Hunter. *The Drafting of the Covenant*. 2 vols. New York, 1928.

Miller, William J. *Henry Cabot Lodge*. New York, 1967.

Millis, Walter. *Road to War: America 1914–1917*. Boston, 1935.

———. *The Martial Spirit: A Study of Our War with Spain*. Boston, 1931.

Minger, Ralph Eldin. *William Howard Taft and United States Foreign Policy: The Apprenticeship Years, 1900–1908*. Urbana, 1975.

Morgan, H. Wayne. *From Hayes to McKinley: National Party Politics, 1877–1896*. Syracuse, 1969.

———. *William McKinley and His America*. Syracuse, 1963.

Morgenthau, Hans J. *In Defense of the National Interest*. New York, 1957.

Morison, Elting E. *Turmoil and Tradition: A Study of the Life and Times of Henry L. Stimson*. Boston, 1960.

———., ed. *The Letters of Theodore Roosevelt*. 8 vols. Cambridge, Mass., 1951–53.

Mowry, George. *Theodore Roosevelt and the Progressive Movement*. New York, 1960.

Nelson, Keith L. *Victors Divided: America and the Allies in Germany, 1918–1923*. Berkeley, 1975.

Neu, Charles E. *An Uncertain Friendship: Theodore Roosevelt and Japan, 1906–1909*. Cambridge, Mass., 1967.

Nevins, Allan. *Henry White: Thirty Years of American Diplomacy*. New York, 1930.

Nicolson, Harold. *Diplomacy*. New York, 1939.

Noggle, Burl. *Into the Twenties: The United States from Armistice to Normalcy*. Urbana, 1974.

Notter, Harley. *The Origins of the Foreign Policy of Woodrow Wilson.* New York, 1965.

Official Proceedings of the Twelfth Republican National Convention. Philadelphia, 1900.

Official Proceedings of the Seventeenth Republican National Convention. New York, 1920.

O'Grady, Joseph P., ed. *The Immigrants' Influence on Wilson's Peace Policies.* Lexington, Ky., 1967.

Osgood, Robert Endicott. *Ideals and Self-Interest in America's Foreign Relations.* Chicago, 1964.

O'Shaughnessy, Edith. *A Diplomat's Wife in Mexico.* New York, 1916.

Parkman, Aubrey. *David Jayne Hill and the Problem of World Peace.* Lewisburg, Pa., 1975.

Parrini, Carl. *Heir to Empire.* Pittsburgh, 1969.

Perkins, Bradford. *The Great Rapprochement: England and the United States, 1895–1914.* New York, 1968.

Perkins, Dexter. *Charles Evans Hughes and American Democratic Statesmanship.* Boston, 1956.

Perry, Bliss. *Life and Letters of Henry Lee Higginson.* Boston, 1921.

Persons, Stow. *The Decline of American Gentility.* New York, 1973.

Peterson, H. C. *Propaganda for War: The Campaign Against American Neutrality, 1914–1917.* Norman, Oklahoma, 1939.

Phillips, William. *Ventures in Diplomacy.* Boston, 1952.

Plesur, Milton. *America's Outward Thrust: Approaches to Foreign Affairs, 1865–1890.* DeKalb, Ill., 1971.

Porter, Kirk H., and Johnson, Donald Bruce, eds. *National Party Platforms, 1840–1964.* Urbana, 1966.

Pratt, Julius W. *Expansionists of 1898.* Baltimore, 1936.

Pringle, Henry F. *The Life and Times of William Howard Taft.* 2 vols. New York, 1939.

———. *Theodore Roosevelt: A Biography.* New York, 1956.

Puleston, Capt. W. D. *Mahan: The Life and Work of Alfred Thayer Mahan, U.S.N.* New Haven, 1939.

Pusey, Merlo. *Charles Evans Hughes.* 2 vols. New York, 1963.

Putnam, Carleton. *Theodore Roosevelt: The Formative Years, 1858–1886.* New York, 1958.

Quirk, Robert E. *An Affair of Honor: Woodrow Wilson and the Occupation of Vera Cruz.* Lexington, Ky., 1962.

———. *The Mexican Revolution, 1914–1915.* Bloomington, 1960.

Rhodes, James Ford. *The McKinley and Roosevelt Administrations.* Port Washington, N.Y., 1965.

Robinson, Corinne Roosevelt. *My Brother Theodore Roosevelt.* New York, 1921.

Roosevelt Club. *Reception and Dinner in Honor of Henry Cabot Lodge, A Great Defender of the Faith.* Boston, 1920.

Roosevelt, Theodore. *America and the World War.* New York, 1915.

———. *American Ideals and Other Essays, Social and Political.* New York, 1907.

———. *An Autobiography.* New York, 1920.

———. *Fear God and Take Your Own Part.* New York, 1916.

———. *The Great Adventure: Present-Day Studies in American National-ism.* New York, 1919.

———. *National Strength and International Duty.* Princeton, 1917.

———. *The New Nationalism.* New York, 1911.

———. *The Strenuous Life: Essays and Addresses.* Philadelphia, 1903.

Root, Elihu. *Addresses on International Subjects.* Edited by Robert Bacon and James B. Scott. New York, 1916.

———. *Men and Politics.* Edited by Robert Bacon and James B. Scott. Cambridge, Mass., 1925.

Rosecrance, Richard. *Action and Reaction in World Politics.* Boston, 1963.

Rosenau, James N., ed. *Domestic Sources of Foreign Policy.* New York, 1967.

Rossiter, Clinton. *Conservatism in America.* New York, 1956.

———., ed. *The Federalist Papers.* New York, 1961.

Rozwenc, Edwin C., and Lindfors, Kenneth, eds. *The United States and the New Imperialism, 1898–1912.* Lexington, Mass., 1968.

Samuels, Ernest. *The Young Henry Adams.* Cambridge, Mass., 1949.

Saveth, Edward N. *American Historians and European Immigrants, 1875–1925.* New York, 1965.

Scholes, Walter V. and Marie V. *The Foreign Policies of the Taft Administration.* Columbia, Mo., 1970.

Schriftgiesser, Karl. *The Gentleman from Massachusetts.* Boston, 1944.

Schumpeter, Joseph. *Imperialism and Social Classes.* New York, 1951.

Scott, James B., ed. *President Wilson's Foreign Policy.* New York, 1918.

Seager, Robert, II. *Alfred Thayer Mahan: The Man and His Letters.* Annapolis, 1977.

Seymour, Charles, ed. *The Intimate Papers of Colonel House.* 4 vols. Boston, 1926–28.

Smith, Daniel M. *The Great Departure: The United States and World War I.* New York, 1965.

Smith, Gene. *When the Cheering Stopped.* New York, 1964.

Solomon, Barbara Miller. *Ancestors and Immigrants: A Changing New England Tradition.* Cambridge, Mass., 1956.

Sparks, George F., ed. *A Many-Colored Toga: The Diary of Henry Fountain Ashurst.* Tucson, 1962.

Sproat, John G. *The Best Men: Liberal Reformers in the Gilded Age.* New York, 1968.

Sprout, Harold and Margaret. *The Rise of American Naval Power, 1776–1918.* Princeton, 1967.

Stanley, Peter W. *A Nation in the Making: The Philippines and the United States, 1899–1921.* Cambridge, Mass., 1974.

Stimson, Henry L., and Bundy, McGeorge. *On Active Service in Peace and War*. New York, 1948.

Stone, Ralph. *The Irreconcilables*. Lexington, Ky., 1970.

Stout, Ralph, ed. *Roosevelt in the Kansas City Star*. Boston, 1921.

Stromberg, Roland. *Collective Security and American Foreign Policy*. New York, 1963.

Taft, William Howard. *The United States and Peace*. New York, 1914.

Tansill, Charles Callan. *America and the Fight for Irish Freedom, 1866–1922*. New York, 1957.

———. *America Goes to War*. Boston, 1938.

Taylor, A. J. P. *The Trouble Makers: Dissent over Foreign Policy*. Bloomington, 1958.

Temperley, H. M. V., ed. *A History of the Peace Conference of Paris*. 6 vols. London, 1920–24.

Terrill, Tom E. *The Tariff, Politics and American Foreign Policy, 1874–1901*. Westport, Conn., 1973.

Thayer, William R. *The Life and Letters of John Hay*. 2 vols. Boston, 1915.

Tillman, Seth P. *Anglo-American Relations at the Paris Peace Conference of 1919*. Princeton, 1961.

Tocqueville, Alexis de. *Democracy in America*. Edited by Phillips Bradley. 2 vols. New York, 1948.

Tompkins, E. Berkeley. *Anti-Imperialism in the United States: The Great Debate, 1890–1920*. Philadelphia, 1970.

Tomsich, John. *A Genteel Endeavor: American Culture and Politics in the Gilded Age*. Stanford, 1971.

Trani, Eugene. *The Treaty of Portsmouth: An Adventure in American Diplomacy*. Lexington, Ky., 1969.

Tumulty, Joseph P. *Woodrow Wilson As I Knew Him*. Garden City, N.Y., 1921.

Tuveson, Ernest. *Redeemer Nation: The Idea of America's Millennial Role*. Chicago, 1968.

Vinson, John Chalmers. *The Parchment Peace: The United States Senate and the Washington Conference, 1921–1922*. Athens, Ga., 1955.

———. *Referendum for Isolation*. Athens, Ga., 1961.

Wall, Joseph Frazier. *Andrew Carnegie*. New York, 1970.

Waltz, Kenneth N. *Foreign Policy and Democratic Politics: The American and British Experience*. Boston, 1967.

Walworth, Arthur. *America's Moment, 1918: American Diplomacy at the End of World War I*. New York, 1977.

Watson, James E. *As I Knew Them*. Indianapolis, 1936.

Watson, Richard L., Jr. *The Development of National Power: The United States, 1900–1919*. Boston, 1976.

Weaver, Richard M. *Ideas Have Consequences*. Chicago, 1948.

Wehler, Hans-Ulrich. *Der Aufstieg des amerikanischen Imperialismus*. Goettingen, 1974.

Weilenmann, Alex. *Theodore Roosevelt und die Aussenpolitik der Vereinigten Staaten von Amerika.* Zurich, 1953.

Weiss, H. John, ed. *The Origins of Modern Consciousness.* Detroit, 1965.

Welch, Richard E., Jr. *George Frisbie Hoar and the Half-Breed Republicans.* Cambridge, Mass., 1971.

Weyl, Walter. *American World Policies.* New York, 1917.

Wiebe, Robert H. *The Search for Order, 1877–1920.* New York, 1967.

Williams, William Appleman. *The Tragedy of American Diplomacy.* New York, 1962.

Wilson, Woodrow. *State Papers and Addresses.* New York, 1918.

Winkler, Henry R. *The League of Nations Movement in Great Britain, 1914–1919.* New Brunswick, N.J., 1952.

Winsor, Justin, ed. *The Memorial History of Boston.* Vol. 3, Boston, 1881.

Wister, Owen. *Roosevelt: The Story of a Friendship, 1880–1919.* New York, 1930.

Wolfers, Arnold, and Martin, Laurence W., eds. *The Anglo-American Tradition in Foreign Affairs.* New Haven, 1956.

Woodward, Sir Llewellyn. *Great Britain and the War of 1914–1918.* Boston, 1967.

World Peace: A Written Debate Between William Howard Taft and William Jennings Bryan. New York, 1917.

Yates, Louis A. R. *The United States and French Security, 1917–1921.* New York, 1957.

Yeomans, Henry Aaron. *Abbott Lawrence Lowell, 1856–1943.* Cambridge, Mass., 1948.

Zimmern, Alfred. *The League of Nations and the Rule of Law, 1918–1935.* London, 1936.

Index

Compositor: Heritage Printers, Inc.
Printer: Heritage Printers, Inc.
Binder: The Delmar Company
Text: Linotype Palatino
Display: Hand Set Palatino
Cloth: Joanna Oxford 44600
Paper: P&S offset, 55 lb.